Shōtoku

Shōtoku

*Ethnicity, Ritual, and Violence
in the Japanese Buddhist Tradition*

MICHAEL COMO

UNIVERSITY PRESS

2008

OXFORD
UNIVERSITY PRESS

Oxford University Press, Inc., publishes works that further
Oxford University's objective of excellence
in research, scholarship, and education.

Oxford   New York
Auckland   Cape Town   Dar es Salaam   Hong Kong   Karachi
Kuala Lumpur   Madrid   Melbourne   Mexico City   Nairobi
New Delhi   Shanghai   Taipei   Toronto

With offices in
Argentina   Austria   Brazil   Chile   Czech Republic   France   Greece
Guatemala   Hungary   Italy   Japan   Poland   Portugal   Singapore
South Korea   Switzerland   Thailand   Turkey   Ukraine   Vietnam

Published by Oxford University Press, Inc.
198 Madison Avenue, New York, New York 10016

www.oup.com

Oxford is a registered trademark of Oxford University Press

Library of Congress Cataloging-in-Publication Data
Como, Michael I.
Shōtoku : ethnicity, ritual, and violence in the Japanese Buddhist tradition / Michael I. Como.
   p. cm.
Includes bibliographical references and index.
ISBN: 978-0-19-518861-5
1. Shōtoku Taishi, 574?–622?—Cult.   2. Buddhism—Japan—History—To 1185.

BQ986.O857C66 2006
294.3'095209021—dc22   2005050855

9 8 7 6 5 4 3 2 1

Printed in the United States of America
on acid-free paper

For Bethel and Ilio Como

Acknowledgments

Although the number of people who have assisted with this project has been far greater than could ever be acknowledged, I would like to offer my special thanks to Professor Carl Bielefeldt of Stanford University and Professor Bernard Faure of Columbia University. With each passing year I realize more and more that these were two of the best advisers anyone could have, because they believe in letting students choose their own paths, however obscure or foolish. I am also deeply indebted to the late Professor Jeffrey Mass at Stanford University for his demanding rigor and for the example he set as a passionate scholar. He made everyone who knew him work harder and with greater enthusiasm.

I am also deeply in the debt of Professors Nishiwaki Tsuneki and Aramaki Noritoshi, both of whom took me under their wing and rendered every possible kind of assistance during my stays at Kyoto University. I would also like to extend my very special thanks to Professor Yoshikawa Shinji of Kyoto University, whose enthusiasm, encouragement and sheer love of history have made our many hours of conversation together part of my most cherished memories.

During the course of my research, I was also fortunate to meet with a large number of wise counselors and colleagues who offered not only valuable advice but also friendship. Professor Silvio Vita and the late Professor Nino Forte of the Italian School of East Asian Studies in Kyoto, as well as Professors Hubert Durt and François Lachaud of the École Française d'Extrême-Orient, gave me the benefit of their vast experience as well as a second academic home. Special thanks also go to Katherine Ludvik of Kyoto, Chen Jinhua, now of the University of British Columbia, and Christian Wittern of Kyoto University, for their camaraderie and support. I will also always be grateful for the support and assistance of Hank Glassman of Haverford College, Max Moermann of Barnard College, Wendi Adamek, also of Barnard, and Elizabeth Morrison, of Middlebury College. My very special thanks go to Tom Conlan, of Bowdoin College, and David Lurie of Columbia University, both of whom provided insights and criticisms that have made this book far better than it otherwise would have been.

I would also like to thank Professor Marc Raphael of the College of William and Mary for his unstinting support and encouragement, and Professor Emeritus Jack Van Horn, a true bodhisattva who has metaphorically and literally given my family shelter in every storm. I also owe a special debt of gratitude to Lu Tun-ch'ang, Lu Lin Hsiu-chen and Yang Ning-yuan, all of whom rendered invaluable assistance during my periods of research in Taipei. Special thanks also go to Professor Wang Kuo-liang of the Academica Sinica for his patient tutelage over many years.

Most especially, however, I would like to thank my children, Maggie and Danny, and my wife, Hui-yu, upon whom I have relied so much for support of every kind during the past several years. Words fail.

This project was also made possible by generous financial support from the U.S.–Japan Fulbright Commission, the Japan Foundation, the Chiang Ching-kuo Foundation, and the U.S. Department of Education. To each of these institutions, I offer my sincere thanks. I would also like to thank the editors of the *Japanese Journal of Religious Studies*, who have kindly allowed me to use a revised version of an article that first appeared in the Spring, 2003 edition of their journal as the fourth chapter of this work. Finally, I would also like to express my deep appreciation to Cynthia Read and the editorial staff of Oxford University Press for all of their patience and assistance in the completion of this project.

M.I.C.

Contents

Abbreviations and Citation Methods, xi

Introduction, 3

1. Ethnicity and the Founding Legend of Japanese Buddhism, 13

2. Pure Land and the Millennium in the Early Shōtoku Cult, 33

3. Ancestors, Estates, and Angry Gods in the Early Royal Cult, 55

4. Ethnicity, Sagehood, and the Politics of Literacy in the Early Shōtoku Cult, 75

5. Violence, Vengeance, and Purification in the Early Shōtoku Cult, 93

6. Shōtoku and Gyōki, 111

7. Dōji, Saichō, and the Post–*Nihon Shoki* Shōtoku Cult, 133

Conclusion, 155

Appendix: Primary Sources for the Study of the Early Shōtoku Cult, 161

Glossary, 169

Notes, 185

Works Cited, 215

Index, 227

Abbreviations and Citation Methods

DNBZ	*Dai Nihon Bukkyō zensho*
NKBT	*Nihon koten bungaku taikei*
NSK	*Nihon shoki*
NST	*Nihon shisō taikei*
SNG	*Shoku Nihongi*
SNKBT	*Shin Nihon koten bungaku taikei*
SNKBZ	*Shinpen Nihon koten bungaku zenshū*
SSS	*Shinshū shiryō shūsei*
ST	*Shintō taikei*
STZ	*Shōtoku taishi zenshū*
SZKT	*Shintei zōhō kokushi taikei*
T	*Taishō shinshū daizōkyō*
ZGR	*Zoku gunsho ruijū*

Throughout this book references to the *Nihon shoki* (*NSK*) list the reign date followed by the volume and page number in the three-volume edition of the text in the *SNKBZ* series, which had as its chief editor Kojima Noriyuki. The *NSK* has also been translated in W. G. Aston, trans., *Nihongi: Chronicles of Japan from the Earliest Times to A.D. 697*. Although all translations from the *NSK* are my own, I have often been able to do little more than make stylistic changes to Aston's work. Each citation from the *NSK* will therefore also include a page reference from Aston's two-volume translation. For references from the *Shoku Nihongi* (*SNG*), I will also use the same reign-date format followed by a citation from the five-volume *SNKBT* series edition of the text, for which Aoki Kazuo was chief editor. For all references from the Buddhist canon I first cite the Taishō volume and page number followed by the Taishō number of the text under discussion.

Shōtoku

Introduction

This book charts epochal changes in the politics and religion of the Japanese islands through a study of the cult of Prince Shōtoku (573?–622?), the purported founder of Japanese Buddhism and one of the greatest cultural icons of pre-modern Japan. The work's principal focus is on the roughly 200 years between Shōtoku's death in about 622 and the death of the Tendai Buddhist patriarch Saichō in 822. This period saw a series of revolutionary developments in the history of Japanese religion, including the expansion of the Buddhist tradition in Japan; the corresponding development of new conceptions of the afterlife; the rapid development of court-sponsored rituals and cults related to semi-historical royal ancestors such as the Yamato ruler Ōjin and his mother Jingū; the emergence of the concept of the sage ruler, or *hijiri no kimi*; the importation of continental divinatory and astrological texts and methods; and the expanded use of rites of spirit pacification and resurrection at the intersections of strategic highways (*chimata*) surrounding the Japanese court.

These events played a major role in establishing the parameters for religious and cultural activity in Japan for centuries to come. Because each of these developments was also intimately connected with the rise of the Shōtoku cult, it is my hope that this book may help shed some light on the formation of some of the most basic building blocks of religious and cultural activity in pre-modern Japan. Toward this end, throughout the text I analyze the early Shōtoku cult in terms of the evolving notions of ethnicity, lineage, textuality and ritual that I argue formed the core of the religious and political discourse of the period. In the process, we shall see that the kinship groups at the forefront of the early Shōtoku cult to a remarkable degree influenced the construction of some of the most fundamental bulwarks of Japanese culture.

Throughout the text, I have highlighted the political and cultic activities of a cluster of kinship groups that claimed descent from ancestors from the Korean kingdom of Silla (henceforth referred to as "immigrant kinship groups").[1] I argue that these kinship groups were not only responsible for the construction of the Shōtoku cult but were also closely associated with the introduction of continental systems of writing, ritual, and governance. By reading the ancestral legends of these kinship groups against the Shōtoku legend corpus and court chronicles such as the *Nihon shoki* and *Kojiki*, I show that these kinship groups not only played a major role in the construction of the Japanese Buddhist tradition but also helped shape the paradigms in terms of which the royal cult, and, ultimately, the nation of Japan were conceptualized and created.[2] As a result, a new picture of seventh and eighth-century Japanese culture emerges that highlights the importance of ethnicity for understanding the construction of both the Japanese Buddhist tradition and the cultic identity of the *tennō*, the "heavenly sovereign" who reigned as the ultimate religious and political authority over the land. I further argue that this dynamic continued for centuries to come, thereby helping to shape early Japanese notions of sacred kingship and cultural identity.

Kamitsumiya and Shōtoku: The Man and the Legend

As is the case for many of the earliest figures in Japanese religious history, even the most basic facts related to the figure of Shōtoku are in dispute. Current scholarship on the prince has as a result become embroiled in a seemingly endless series of disputes concerning methodology, terminology, and sources. Unfortunately, these debates are by no means unique to the study of Shōtoku; rather, they are deeply implicated in a broader nationalist discourse that seeks to create icons of Japanese cultural uniqueness out of the purported founders of Japanese culture. For this reason, clarifying the ideological underpinnings behind traditional Shōtoku scholarship is an essential prerequisite for any analysis not only of the cult of the prince but also the religion of the period in general.

A good place to begin unraveling these confusions is with the terminological point that the appellation Shōtoku was almost certainly created after the prince's death. During his lifetime the prince was apparently known by the names Kamitsumiya and Umayado. Throughout this book, therefore, I refer to the "historical Shōtoku" as Prince Kamitsumiya. Only the figure of legend will be referred to as Shōtoku. This approach has been most forcefully advocated by Ōyama Seiichi, who argues that the distinction between the historical figure of Prince Kamitsumiya and the legendary figure of Prince Shōtoku must form the basis for our understanding of the development of the early Shōtoku cult. Ōyama goes on to add—correctly, in my view—that the vast majority of Japanese scholarship has failed to distinguish between the man and the legend, thereby leading to a distressing tendency to replicate early hagiography in modern academic discourse.[3]

Once we take such distinctions seriously, it is striking how the memory of Kamitsumiya was almost completely erased by the figure of Shōtoku. With regard to the prince's background, it is clear that Prince Kamitsumiya (573?–622?) lived during a period when rapid political and cultural changes were sweeping over the Japanese archipelago. These changes were stimulated in large part by successive waves of immigrants from the Korean Peninsula, who were arriving in the Japanese islands in large numbers by the mid-fifth century. These new immigrants brought with them knowledge of writing and continental technologies associated with metalworking, medicine, and governance. This in turn helped accelerate the centralization of power in the hands of the Yamato elite and a corresponding elevation of the status of the Yamato ruler.

Although all of these trends existed prior to Kamitsumiya and continued to gather force after his death, later generations nonetheless came to view the figure of Prince Shōtoku as emblematic of each of these developments. As a result, the great majority of references to Kamitsumiya/Shōtoku in the *Nihon shoki*—our best source of information concerning the prince—are clearly hagiographic in nature: Shōtoku is hailed as a sage, as a master of continental learning, and as a genius who could see into the future. His prayers are credited with bringing victory to the pro-Buddhist forces in the battle for the establishment of Buddhism in Japan. He is depicted as helping a sage beggar effect his own death and resurrection. He is said to have attained birth in a Buddhist Pure Land. Thus, even by the time the *Nihon shoki* was completed in 720, the figure of Shōtoku already overshadowed that of Kamitsumiya.

This abundance of materials related to the figure of Shōtoku is unfortunately matched by a dearth of information concerning the historical Prince Kamitsumiya. What little solid information we have concerning the historical prince relates to his parentage, his lineal affiliations with the powerful Soga kinship group, and his apparently close ties with the Hata, an immigrant kinship group from Silla. In addition, there are also strong grounds for believing that Kamitsumiya was associated with the destruction of the powerful Mononobe kinship group and with the construction of temples that later generations would know as Hōryūji and Shitennōji.[4]

Shōtoku Studies and the Japanese Nationalist Discourse

In spite of, or perhaps because of, this paucity of information concerning Kamitsumiya, the historical discourse concerned with the prince has long been intimately connected with the Japanese nationalist discourse. In view of the fact that Prince Kamitsumiya lived during a period that saw the formation of many of the basic elements of Japanese political and religious culture, this is perhaps not surprising; the founding narratives of any nation tend to focus on heroes who are thought to embody the culture and values of the nation in question. In the Japanese case, one of the first such heroes was the figure of Shōtoku. As a result, one recurring tendency within scholarship on Shōtoku has been to treat the prince not as an important symbol of cultural identity among eighth-century elites but rather as an architect of a Japanese national identity that emerged many hundreds of years later.

In this context, one of the greatest challenges facing the contemporary scholar of the period lies in avoiding capture by the nationalist discourse that exists just beneath the surface of much scholarly and popular interest in Shōtoku and his time. Unfortunately, the influence of the nationalist discourse on scholars sympathetic to the Japanese national tradition has often transformed their scholarship into little more than exercises designed to prove the historical validity of cherished legends for all to see. Almost as frequently, however, one finds iconoclastic scholars such as Ōyama who are pre-occupied with debunking ancient myths that have been pressed into the service of nationalist ends. In either case, the limitations of the nationalist discourse have obscured the essential point that cultural icons such as Shōtoku are laden with meaning and associations that can never be reduced to historical figures such as Kamitsumiya.

One of the largest consequences of this concern with national origins has been to cast research on the early Shōtoku cult almost entirely in terms of projects of retrieval. This tendency was accelerated in 1966, when Ienaga Saburō set forth a narrow range of primarily Buddhist sources that he argued should be used to uncover the "real" Shōtoku that had hitherto been obscured by legend.[5] Such prominent scholars as Inoue Mitsusada,[6] Ōno Tatsunosuke,[7] Sakamoto Tarō,[8] Kanaji Isamu,[9] and Nakamura Hajime,[10] have all followed Ienaga's lead, differing only in their estimations of the historical authenticity of the sources enumerated by Ienaga.

These projects have proven to be disappointing in at least two senses. First, with regard to the Shōtoku cult, there has been a relentless focus on technical questions concerning which calendrical systems were known to the Suiko court, when the term *tennō* first came to be used in Yamato, which calligraphic styles of script were current in Yamato during Kamitsumiya's lifetime, and so on. Although such questions do of course merit careful study, they have produced no consensus on the validity of any of the sources in question; Prince Kamitsumiya remains as much of an unknown as ever. Second, the list of scholars just mentioned reads like a *who's who* of scholars of early Japanese religion. As a result, the biases and methodologies inherent in these studies of the early Shōtoku cult are closely intertwined with those of Japanese scholarship on broader issues in early Japanese religion.

Crucially, these methodological orientations have served to reinforce several deeply held assumptions about Japanese national identity and the role of Shōtoku as a Japanese Buddhist icon. Four of the most important of these are as follows. (1) Because Kamitsumiya was a prince and later a national icon, the Shōtoku legend corpus is widely assumed to have been a product of the royal house. Because this approach shuts the door on the possibility that immigrant lineages created and promoted the Shōtoku legend corpus, the royal line is seen almost exclusively as a dynamic producer, not a consumer, of ideology. (2) The scholars listed above tend to ignore the abundance of contemporaneous non-Buddhist legend materials in their discussions of Kamitsumiya and the Shōtoku cult. This oversight is apparently derived from the firm conviction that Shōtoku was a Buddhist and must therefore be understood as having primarily Buddhist motivations and inspirations. This conviction is further reinforced by (3) a tendency to keep Buddhism, a "foreign" religion, separate from the purportedly "native" religious traditions of Yamato, and (4) a belief that immigrants played only a peripheral role in the development of the "native" religious institutions and beliefs at the heart of the royal cult. Because these assumptions have served to marginalize the role played by immigrant kinship groups in the political and religious life of the period, they have also served to obscure the means by which these groups drew upon cultic resources from the Korean Peninsula to help lay the foundations for much of the Japanese royal cult and Japanese culture.

Fortunately, beginning with the work of Tamura Enchō in the 1980s, there has been a renewed flurry of interest in Shōtoku by scholars willing to depart from the conventions of the past. Tamura forever changed the field by emphasizing the prince's connections with immigrant lineages from the Korean Peninsula. Instead of merely acknowledging such figures as having been associated with the prince, Tamura argued that such figures would have played a major role in shaping the prince's intellectual and political outlook. He further argued that the development of the Buddhist culture of the Asuka period could only be understood in the context of Yamato's place in relation to political and cultural developments on the Korean Peninsula.[11]

Further controversy within the field has also been stimulated by the tireless efforts of Ōyama Seiichi, whose *Nagayaōke mokkan to kinsekibun* was more notable for the vehemence of its rhetoric than for its restatement of classical criticisms of early Shōtoku sources. Ōyama has followed up this work with two further volumes that improbably ascribe the rise of the Shōtoku cult mainly to the activities of an extremely small circle of monks in the Nara period.[12]

Where from Here?

Perhaps Ōyama's greatest contribution, however, has been to refocus academic attention on the limitations that our sources impose upon us. Given the paucity of reliable information about Prince Kamitsumiya, it would appear impossible to recover much of value concerning his life and thought. In what follows, I have therefore adopted a twofold approach to materials related to the prince. First, these texts can at a minimum help us understand the history of the period if we treat the figure of Shōtoku as an emblem for the process of cultural transformation that occurred between 622 and 720. Kamitsumiya may not in fact have written the *Seventeen-Article Constitution* or the three sutra commentaries ascribed to him; nevertheless, these are early texts that contain valuable information about the intellectual history of the period. Similarly, although there is no way of knowing for certain whether Kamitsumiya was responsible for the composition of the first court chronicle or the institution of the first system of court ranks in Yamato, we do know that these events did occur and that they played an important role in the promotion of the continental cultural and political forms that Shōtoku came to represent.

Second, once we abandon the hermeneutic of retrieval, new avenues of inquiry emerge. For the student of Japanese religion, perhaps the most valuable textual sources are those that are legends or fabrications of later generations. Far from being dross to be discarded in favor of hard historical data, these entries are valuable precisely because they are not mere reportage but rather products of the religious imagination of the age. Throughout this book, I therefore consider the construction of the rites and legends of the Shōtoku cult as creative religious acts. The chapters that follow thus seek to uncover the processes behind the construction of the cult of Shōtoku, not to uncover the truth about Prince Kamitsumiya.

Raising the question of how it was possible to *think* the figure of Shōtoku, in turn, has immediate consequences for the sources and methodologies that drive this study. For most of this book, I focus on the activities of a cluster of kinship groups associated with Shitennōji and Kōryūji, two of the earliest temples to be associated with Shōtoku. I do not claim that these kinship groups all acted in unison, nor do I claim that they shared a common plan to promote the figure of Shōtoku. Nonetheless, there is ample evidence that by the time of the writing of the *Nihon shoki* these kinship groups often claimed common ancestry, frequently lived together, and participated jointly in cultic practices at shrines and temples associated with the early Shōtoku cult.[13]

The necessary textual background for understanding the emergence and role of the Shōtoku cult in early Yamato society thus far exceeds the sources set forth by Ienaga as most relevant to the figure of Prince Kamitsumiya. Understanding the construction of the Shōtoku legend corpus requires understanding the political and cultic activities—non-Buddhist as well as Buddhist— of these kinship groups. Thus I read the Shōtoku legend corpus not only against other materials related to Prince Kamitsumiya but also against a wide range of ancestral, temple and shrine legends found in court histories, temple records, and gazetteers. Where possible, I have also made use of sources from the Korean Peninsula.[14]

Ethnicity, Lineage, and Nation

Before proceeding further, a few statements about definitions and methods are in order. As should by now be apparent, much of this project centers on the role of immigrant kinship groups in the construction of several of the most important bulwarks of Japanese culture. In discussing immigrant lineages and their role in the political and religious discourses of the seventh and eighth centuries, I have often found it convenient to refer to the concept of "ethnicity" and ethnic affiliation. Although the concept of ethnicity has only comparatively recently attracted sustained attention from scholars—the first entry for the term in the *Oxford English Dictionary* only occurred in 1972, for instance—the concept has long been linked with issues of lineage, myth, and the formation of national traditions.[15] In the pages that follow, I shall use the definition of ethnicity first proffered by George De Vos in 1975:

> An ethnic group is a self-perceived group of people who hold in common a set of traditions not shared by others with whom they are in contact. Such traditions typically include "folk" religious beliefs and practices, language, a sense of historical continuity, and common ancestry or place of origin. The group's actual history often trails off into legend or mythology, which includes some concept of an unbroken biological-genetic generational continuity, sometimes regarded as giving special characteristics to the group.[16]

This definition, highlighting as it does the importance of ancestry, underscores the crucial importance of lineage and ancestral cults for the construction of ethnic identity. As we shall see shortly, "immigrant" kinship groups came to be defined as such not simply in terms of customs followed but rather in terms of their claims to lineal descent from ancestors from across the sea. Crucially, some of these same immigrant kinship groups also played a major role in the construction of the Shōtoku cult, an ancestor claimed by members of the newly minted royal line. Understanding the construction of the Shōtoku cult will thus require attention to two parallel tracks of investigation. On the one hand, it will require examining the cultic resources used by immigrant lineages as they created one of the most important cultural and religious bulwarks of pre-modern Japan. On the other, it will also require us to focus on the process by which these same immigrants were figured as an "other" in terms of which *tennō*-centered notions of "native" could be constructed.

In sorting through these issues, I have benefited greatly from the work of Bruce Batten, who argues that a sense of Japanese cultural identity emerged in the Japanese islands sometime around 700 C.E. Batten stresses, however, that this cultural identity was confined to the members of the central and regional elites that participated most actively in the cultural and political structures of the emerging royal state. Batten contends that although such links did not result in identification with non-elite strata of society, they did constitute a lateral *ethnie* that "evolved substantially over time, eventually forming the core of the Japanese 'nation,' which emerged at the end of the nineteenth century."[17] The immigrant lineages that played such a prominent role in the construction of the political and cultural forms of the royal state almost certainly participated in this lateral *ethnie*. In one of the many ironies of Japanese history, however, their very prominence may have helped stimulate the formation of nativist identities from which they were excluded.

One common element at the heart of each of these developments was the proliferation of literacy and the diffusion of continental texts from China and the Korean Peninsula. In this regard, three essential characteristics of this process were of central importance for the development of both the Japanese Buddhist tradition and the institution of the *tennō*. First, control of literacy and the conceptual apparatus of Chinese historical/cultic traditions was disproportionately concentrated among immigrant kinship groups. Second, the rise of literacy in very obvious ways facilitated the growth of bureaucratic structures and ideologies that sustained the *tennō*'s institutional power. Third, the narratives of the Japanese *ethnie* and kingship that emerged during this period not only focused on newly elaborated ancestral legends for the *tennō*, they were also strongly influenced by continental narratives of kingship. Thus, immigrant lineages exercised a great deal of influence over the construction of the court's mytho-historical chronicles even as they to a large degree helped construct these texts' horizon of reception. In so doing, they played a major role in shaping the vocabulary of kingship through which power was conceived and exercised throughout the period.

Themes and Things

In the pages that follow, I have therefore read these texts in light of this interplay among lineage, ethnicity, and kingship. Far from being unified narratives, texts such as the *Kojiki* and *Nihon shoki* were in many ways built upon the ancestral cults and legends of lineages from distant regions and historical contexts. As the court appropriated these narratives to produce its own narratives of lineage and hegemony, it appropriated a cultic and mythic vocabulary rooted in the conflicts, rites, and legends of distant lands with disparate histories. By the Nara period, several of the most important ancestral cults and legends of the royal cult had become intertwined with the cultic sites and deities of some of the immigrant lineages referred to earlier. In the pages that follow, I therefore read the legends of such royal ancestors as Shōtoku, Jingū, Ōjin, and others as part of an ongoing process of cultic sedimentation that defined the cultic topography of the Japanese islands. I also argue that understanding the flowering of the Shotoku cult requires understanding the ground in which it was figuratively and literally rooted.

   Once we begin to read the Shōtoku legend corpus against this wider range of myths and legends, a picture of the development of the Shōtoku cult emerges that is substantially different from anything envisaged by Ienaga and his successors. One motif that runs throughout this work is the tremendous extent to which immigrant kinship groups at the forefront of the early Shōtoku cult drew upon legends and cultic practices from their own ancestral traditions to fashion the cultic and mythic underpinnings for the early royal system and the emerging Japanese *ethnie*. How this process occurred is illustrated in chapter 1, which examines the construction and uses of the founding legend of Japanese Buddhism. In this chapter, I argue that the early Shōtoku cult was fueled to a large degree by conflict among immigrant kinship groups from the Korean kingdoms of Silla and Paekche. As each group sought to ally itself with the Yamato court, each sought to construct legends depicting the figure of Prince Shōtoku as a paradigm for the Japanese Buddhist tradition. One of the end products of this process was *Nihon shoki*'s account of the founding legend of Japanese Buddhism, which I suggest was based upon the founding legend of the head temple in the Silla state temple network.

The activities of these kinship groups, however, were in no way limited to the Yamato court. Chapter 2 discusses the development of early Japanese notions of Pure Lands in conjunction with such "native" conceptions of the afterlife as *tenjukoku* and *tokoyo*. This chapter demonstrates that these conceptions were deeply rooted in popular millennial movements focused upon the arrival of immigrant deities from across the sea. I also show that in many cases these deities were none other than the ancestors of the very same kinship groups that promoted the early Shōtoku cult. Thus even the "native" popular cults that are often posited as a reaction to the introduction of the "foreign" Buddhist tradition to Japan were in large part constructed by kinship groups whose ancestors came from across the sea. I argue that legends depicting Shōtoku as the first figure in the Japanese islands to attain rebirth in a Pure Land were literally physically built upon millennial cults associated with immigrant deities.

In chapter 3, I argue that these same immigrant kinship groups also played an equally large role in the construction of the ancestral cults and legends of the newly emerging royal house. This chapter focuses on the role of these kinship groups in the rapid development of the cults of such major royal ancestors as Ōjin and Jingū. This chapter details the extensive degree to which the ancestors of these kinship groups were feared and revered by Yamato rulers, who dreaded the vengeful wrath of immigrant deities from across the sea. It then examines the process by which these same kinship groups constructed for the royal house ancestral legends that showed royal ancestors worshiping these same immigrant deities. The picture that emerges reveals the substantial degree to which these kinship groups influenced the development not only of the Japanese Buddhist tradition but also popular religious movements and even the construction of the royal house's lineal and cultic identity.

One further motif that pervades this work is the importance of roadside rites of divination and spirit pacification for the development of early Japanese conceptions of sage kingship (*hijiri no kimi*) as well as sagehood (*hijiri*). Chapter 4 discusses the role of these kinship groups in the emergence of the conception of the sage ruler, or *hijiri no kimi*. This chapter argues that as immigrant kinship groups such as those at the forefront of the early Shōtoku cult propagated continental historical and divinatory texts, they laid the basis for new understandings of kingship that were susceptible to both critique and authentication through divinatory processes that these lineages controlled. As gatekeepers of this textual tradition these immigrant lineages therefore played a key role in the transformation of the means by which power was expressed and understood in early Japan.

Chapters 5 and 6 discuss the development of *chimata* rites of purification and resurrection in the context of an analysis of the legend of Shōtoku's encounter with a beggar on the road to Kataoka. Chapter 5 takes up the issue of the relationship between the figures of Kamitsumiya and Shōtoku as it details the means by which sagehood in early Japan came to be associated with control over the forces of life after death. In this chapter, I argue that one major reason for the later prominence of the figure of Shōtoku was Kamitsumiya's own association with violence and the subsequent need to pacify the hostile spirits of his enemies.

This theme is also continued in chapter 6, which discusses the role of adherents of the Shōtoku cult in the construction of the mass religious movement headed by the mendicant monk Gyōki. This chapter argues that one of the main stimuli for the development of the Buddhist tradition in Japan was the construction of a far-flung set of road networks that made possible mendicant movements such as that founded by Gyōki. This chapter suggests that even the earliest hagiography surrounding this monk was shaped in large degree by devotees of the Shōtoku cult. It then explores the means by which the cultic preoccupation of these followers with rites of blessing and spirit pacification came to influence the formation of the concept of begging at the core of Gyōki's movement.

In counterpoint to chapter 6, chapter 7 discusses how each of the developments just mentioned came to be incorporated into the political and religious structures of the Nara state. This chapter treats the development of the Shōtoku cult up to the early Heian period as it focuses on Shōtoku's adoption by the court as both guardian deity and cornerstone of the Japanese Buddhist tradition. In this regard, I focus on the role of monks such as Dōji, Ganjin, and Saichō in promoting visions of Shōtoku as both Dharma King and reincarnation of the Chinese T'ien-t'ai patriarch Hui-ssu. I conclude with a brief discussion of the central role of the figure of Shōtoku in the development of Tendai sectarianism and Pure Land belief in the early Heian period.

Each of these chapters, if viewed individually, treats the role of the kinship groups at the forefront of the early Shōtoku cult in one of the most important developments in the formation of early Japanese religion and the Japanese royal system. Taken together, however, these chapters point to the remarkably broad range of influence that a small cluster of immigrant kinship groups exerted over Buddhist and non-Buddhist phenomena throughout the Japanese islands. In so doing, they played an extraordinary role in fashioning the conceptual vocabulary with which the Japanese imagined themselves and their world for centuries to come.

As it details the motivations and cultic resources used by these kinship groups to construct the Shōtoku cult, the narrative that winds through the following pages thus bypasses many of the temples, scriptures, and courtiers that pervade most works on Shōtoku. Rather, it focuses on the sages, beggars, worms, ancestors, and demons that fueled the religious imagination of the age. In so doing, I hope to do justice to the forces that in all of their violence, variety, and ambivalence led to the invention of Japan's most famous prince.

I

Ethnicity and the Founding Legend of Japanese Buddhism

The many stuffs . . . that worlds are made of are made along with
the worlds. But made from what? Not from nothing, after all, but
from other worlds. Worldmaking as we know it always starts from
worlds already on hand; the making is a remaking.[1]

—Nelson Goodman

Or, l'essence d'une nation est que tous les individus aient beaucoup
de choses en commun et aussi que tous aient oublié bien de choses.[2]

—Ernest Renan

The idea of nation is inseparable from its narration: that narration
attempts, interminably, to constitute identity against difference,
inside against outside, and in the assumed superiority of inside
over outside, prepares against invasion and for "enlightened"
colonialism.[3]

—Geoffrey Bennington

Although the figure of Prince Shōtoku has long been associated
with peace, Buddhism, and elite Japanese culture, it is nonetheless
the case that the creation of this icon required a potent brew of violence, narrative, and amnesia. In the pages that follow, I will explore this process by focusing on the period following the death of
Prince Kamitsumiya in 622 up to the time of the completion of
the *Nihon shoki* in 720. During this time, new forms of ritual, architecture, medicine, and textual production poured into the Japanese
islands from the Korean Peninsula, thereby creating new sources of
political and cultural authority. For most of this period, the temples and shrines of immigrant kinship groups served as important

vehicles for the importation of these new forms of political and cultural organization. In so doing, they helped make possible the emergence of new and vastly expanded conceptions of kingship in conjunction with a dramatic shift in the culture of the elite segments of the population.

This cultural transformation resulted in a radical expansion and reformulation of royal authority. By the early eighth century, rulers reigned over an extensive array of bureaucratic institutions modeled on continental governmental structures and law codes. These political structures were both sanctified and rendered plausible by a permanent ritual and administrative center for the royal polity along with an extensive array of temples and shrines. As massive support of shrines and temples became an essential strategy for the maintenance of royal power, sovereigns throughout the Nara period and beyond accumulated authority and prestige by enacting the role of the virtuous sage monarch seeking divine blessings for the realm. Thus the ritual elaboration of the *tennō's* power came to be inseparable from its exercise.[4]

Both the political structures and the ideological underpinnings of the new system had deep roots in the political and religious discourses of the Korean Peninsula and the Chinese textual tradition. Although the political realities of kingship may have differed from those that obtained in the Chinese empire, there can be little doubt that the editors of the *Nihon shoki* and the *Kojiki* made strenuous efforts to represent the rulers of the Japanese islands in terms of the dominant tropes and narratives of the Chinese textual tradition. Thus by the time of the composition of the *Nihon shoki*, the title of "Great King" (J: *ōkimi*) had been replaced with a number of titles employed by Chinese rulers. These included not only the term *t'ien-huang* ("Heavenly Sovereign," J: *tennō*), but also the perennial *t'ien-zu* ("son of heaven," J: *tenshi*), *huang-ti* ("sovereign thearch," J: *kōtei*), *sheng-huang* ("sage thearch," J: *hijiri no mikado*), and *sheng-wang* ("sage king," J: *hijiri no kimi*).[5] The use of such titles, in turn, was part of a broader strategy of majestification that also involved the production of court chronicles and gazetteers, and the elaboration of an ancestral cult through which rulers could be connected with important mytho-historic moments and places across the Japanese islands. As we shall see repeatedly throughout this study, the early Shōtoku cult both helped shape and was shaped by this process.

The new state was thus not only a political phenomenon, but also, and perhaps even primarily, a cultural phenomenon. This dynamic of expanded royal authority accompanied by massive cultural transformation can be directly linked to successive waves of immigration to the Japanese islands from the Korean Peninsula in the fifth and sixth centuries. These immigrants were responsible for the introduction and diffusion of writing and continental technologies of governance to the Japanese archipelago. Yamato rulers and powerful kinship groups were quick to appreciate the uses of these techniques for the consolidation of power; by the middle of the sixth century, immigrant kinship groups in the service of the more powerful Yamato kinship groups were engaged in the construction and operation of canals and granaries and undertaking land surveys. In so doing, they made large-scale state formation possible for the first time in the history of the Japanese islands.[6]

Although the expansion of seventh-century Yamato power was contemporaneous with the establishment and spread of Buddhist practices and beliefs throughout the country, the spread of the Buddhist tradition was led not by Yamato rulers but rather by immigrant kinship groups from the Korean kingdoms of Silla and Paekche. Because these immigrant groups were often affiliated with more powerful native kinship groups, their influence spread rapidly throughout the Japanese islands. By the early seventh century, the more powerful kinship group blocs began to build temples and shrines for the advancement of their material and political ends. As successive rulers moved to appropriate the mantle of sponsor and protector of Buddhism throughout the country, it was therefore necessary to appropriate a measure of control over kinship group temples and their legends as well. The resulting royal ideology was thus a multi-valent, negotiated phenomenon, as rulers and immigrant kinship groups transformed local cultic narratives into narratives of a new religious and cultural identity for the elite elements of the emerging *tennō*-centered state.

The new religious and cultural forms promoted by these immigrants, in particular continental notions of writing and kingship, were thus essential elements in the seventh-century formulation of royal authority. Indeed, they were so essential that the royal line, far from being the main engine that drove these changes, is probably best described as one product of the cultural transformation that swept over the archipelago. One of the best examples of this process can be seen in the construction of the figure of Prince Shōtoku as a paradigm of continental culture and learning for the newly emerging polity of Nara Japan.[7]

Problematizing early Japan in this way opens two related fields of inquiry for the scholar of early Japanese religion. Once we ask the question "How was it possible to *think* Japan?" we are forced to ask how the Buddhist and non-Buddhist religious traditions promoted by immigrants in the Japanese archipelago made such cultural imagining possible. Second, focusing on the role of immigrant lineages at the earliest temples and shrines on the Japanese islands enables us to locate the development of royal ideology and the cultural identities with which it was associated within a broader cultural/ideological context. Ironically, the narratives, temples, and shrines of immigrant lineages were important vehicles by which both ethnic and "native" identities were constructed during the period.

Section One: Textuality, Lineage, and the Birth of a Tradition

Perhaps the best indication that we have of the importance of such issues within contemporaneous discourse can be found in the *Shinsen shōjiroku* (*Newly Compiled Records of Kinship Groups*), a genealogical compendium that was composed sometime around 815 and details the ancestry of the roughly 1,180 lineages that vied for the attention of the court. The preface of this text states that among the most important reasons for its composition was the following:

During the [Tempyō] Shōhō era [749–756] there were from time to time edicts permitting the several immigrants to be granted [surnames] in accordance with their wishes. And so it came about that the characters for the older [Japanese] surnames and the newer surnames [granted to the immigrants] became thus alike; whether a family was immigrant or Japanese became doubtful; lowly families everywhere numbered themselves among the offshoots of the nobles; and foreign residents from Korea claimed descent from the gods of Japan.[8]

This concern on the part of the text's editors to clarify genealogical claims was rooted in a desire to maintain barriers and distinctions between immigrant kinship groups and those who claimed descent from the "native" gods of the Japanese islands. As everyone at court was keenly aware, genealogies were the foundation upon which social relations, rank, and status were built and sustained. Assuring the integrity of lineal claims was thus essential for maintaining the stability of the system and the position of the handful of lineages that dominated the upper strata of the court hierarchy.

The alarm felt by the text's authors that many immigrant kinship groups were "passing" as native suggests that by the early Heian period such kinship groups had penetrated even the upper levels of court life. In response to this, the text's editors sought to justify social barriers with lineal classifications that were defined in terms of the water barrier that separated the Japanese islands from the Korean Peninsula. Henceforth, in spite of—or perhaps even because of—their success within the Japanese *ethnie*, members of immigrant lineages were to be viewed as originally from outside the Japanese islands and therefore relegated to the social periphery.

Although the authors of the *Shinsen shōjiroku* may not have realized it, this project of erasure led not to the return of some timeless *status quo ante*, but rather to the emergence of a new political ideal of kingship. By emphasizing the distinction between descendents of "native" gods and descendents of ancestors from across the sea, the *Shinsen shōjiroku* aided the formation of notions of "native" cultural and political identities that were defined in terms of the lineages and ancestors of the major figures at court and for what later came to be known as the "royal house."

Ironically, the "native" identities and prerogatives that the editors of the *Shinsen shōjiroku* wished to protect had themselves been shaped and codified in court-sponsored texts such as the *Nihon shoki* and *Kojiki* roughly 100 years earlier. Given the importance of lineage for legitimizing and sustaining power, it is hardly surprising that these texts constructed an elaborate narrative of native cultural identity built upon genealogical tropes. Because control of literacy was disproportionately concentrated among immigrant kinship groups during this period, however, immigrant lineages exerted a disproportionate influence over the production of these and other texts. As a result, although the narratives of the court chronicles were heavily oriented toward the ancestors of the ruling line, they were also strongly influenced by the cults and legends of immigrant lineages.

Within the *Nihon shoki*, the power of the native genealogical trope can be seen in two types of legends of foundation. The first of these consisted of legends of royal ancestors that connected Yamato rulers to the gods that were credited with the creation and pacification of the Japanese islands. This link with antiquity helped associate the *tennō's* rule with a wide variety of non-Buddhist cultic practices and legends even as it masked the very newness of the emerging royal order.[9] The second legend of foundation presented Prince Shōtoku as the fountainhead of both the Japanese Buddhist tradition and the cultural institutions that formed much of the core of the royal tradition of the Japanese islands. In so doing, the *Nihon shoki* portrayed the royal house as the source and center of the cultural transformation that swept over the Japanese islands in the sixth and seventh centuries.[10]

The emergence of the royal system was thus accompanied by the development of the cult of Prince Shōtoku, who came to be worshiped as one of the paramount religious and cultural heroes of Japan.[11] The *Nihon shoki* states that Shōtoku wrote the first political treatise in the Japanese islands, produced the first historical chronicle in the Japanese islands, initiated the first system of court ranks and was responsible for the establishment of diplomatic and cultural contacts with the Chinese empire. Shōtoku was most remembered, however, for his role as the founder of the Japanese Buddhist tradition. The *Nihon shoki* states that Shōtoku built some of the oldest and most important temples in the Japanese islands, that he was the first Japanese to lecture on the Buddhist sutras, that he had acquired supernatural powers of perception, and that his fame as a sage had spread to foreign lands.

This image of the prince as both religious and cultural hero also served to redefine the Japanese Buddhist tradition in royal terms. For centuries to come, virtually every new sect to arise in the Japanese islands claimed a connection with the prince. As a result, the list of Shōtoku devotees includes many of the most eminent Japanese monks from the Nara period and beyond. Dōji, the most prominent scholar-monk of the Nara period, led members of the court in services asking for the protection afforded by Shōtoku's august spirit. The Chinese monk Chien-chen (J: Ganjin) claimed that it was because of Shōtoku that he had struggled to bring the Buddhist precepts from China to the Japanese islands. Saichō, the founder of the Tendai sect, referred to Shōtoku as his spiritual grandfather. During the Kamakura period, the figure of Shōtoku played a pivotal role in the vocations of such prominent monks as Shinran, Nichiren, Ippen, Eison and Myōe.[12]

In what follows, I propose to focus on the role of an influential cluster of immigrant kinship groups in the construction of perhaps the best-known narrative of the Shōtoku cult—the *Nihon shoki* narrative concerning the founding of Japanese Buddhism. By centering my discussion on the role of immigrant kinship groups, I hope to highlight the role of ethnicity and local legends in the construction of royal ideology and the early Japanese myth of native

identity. Once the *Nihon shoki's* account of the founding of Japanese Buddhism is read in this light, it becomes possible to say how, by whom and for
whom it was created. It also becomes possible to elaborate a new paradigm
that details how immigrant lineages helped construct what would later be understood as one of the most enduring symbols of the Japanese nation and the
Japanese Buddhist tradition.

The Nihon shoki *Narrative*

The founding narrative of Japanese Buddhism as found in the *Nihon shoki*
begins in the year 552, when the king of Paekche is said to have sent a Buddhist statue to the Yamato court.[13] The narrative may be divided into two
parts, the first of which centers around the statue's reception at court and its
eventual worship by Soga no Iname, the head of the powerful Soga kinship
group. Because the Soga rose to prominence in the sixth century through
close association with Paekche immigrant groups settled in the Yamato plain,
they are widely believed to have themselves been Paekche immigrants.[14] Regardless of whether they were "really" from Paekche, however, the Soga's
close links to Paekche culture and Paekche immigrants resulted in their will-
ingness to push early and hard for Paekche-style Buddhist worship in the
Japanese islands.

The arrival of the statue from Paekche is said to have caused a rift at the
Yamato court. The *Nihon shoki* states that Kimmei, the ruler of Yamato, vac-
illated on the issue of whether to worship the statue because of opposition
from powerful conservative kinship groups such as the Mononobe and Nakatomi. The text also states that these groups, which appear to have been
closely connected with ritual affairs at court, were worried that the gods of the
Japanese islands would be angry if they started to worship a foreign god.[15]

Early records from the Soga kinship group temple of Asukadera (later
renamed Gangōji), however, state that the main opposition to the worship of
Buddhist images came not from the Mononobe but from Kimmei and his
successor, Bidatsu.[16] This has led Japanese scholars such as Sonoda Kōyū to
conclude that because these rulers derived much of their authority from claims
to descent from Yamato deities they were therefore reluctant to embrace the
new religion.[17] Regardless of whether or not this was actually the case, however, there is widespread agreement that during this interval, the leadership of
the Buddhist community in the Japanese islands lay firmly in the hands of the
Soga and their affiliated Paekche immigrant kinship groups.

The second part of the *Nihon shoki* narrative introduces the figure of
Shōtoku as a counterpoint to the Soga leadership. This section begins with an
account of the military conflict between the Soga and the Mononobe, which
came to a head in the summer of 587. As the Soga and their allies battled with
the forces of the Mononobe and Nakatomi, the *Nihon shoki* states that Prince
Shōtoku, though only a boy, fought on the pro-Buddhist side. During the battle, he is said to have sought divine assistance for the Buddhist cause:

At this time, Prince Umayado [Shōtoku] assessed [the situation] and said "Will we not be beaten? Without a vow, we cannot succeed." So he cut [branches] from a *nuride* tree and quickly made images of the Four Heavenly Kings. Placing them in his top-knot he made a vow, saying "If victory over our enemies is now granted to us, I will without fail make offerings to the Four Kings who defend the world, and I will build [for them] a temple with a pagoda..."[18]

After the uprising had been quieted, the Temple of the Four Heavenly Kings (Shitennōji) was built in Settsu Province.[19]

By assigning credit for the victory of the pro-Buddhist forces not to the Soga leadership but rather to the prince, the editors of the *Nihon shoki* thus helped construct an image of Shōtoku as both savior and patriarch of the Japanese Buddhist tradition. In so doing, they also helped the royal house bind itself to the emerging religion and redefine itself in Buddhist terms.

This definition of royal authority was manifested within the text in subtler ways as well. Japanese scholars have identified several passages throughout the *Nihon shoki*, for instance, that use language explicitly drawn from the *Golden Light Sutra* (Ch: *Chin-kuang-ming ching*, J: *Konkōmyōkyō*) and its re-translation, the *Golden Light Excellent King Sutra* (Ch: *Chin-kuang-ming tsui-sheng-wang ching*, J: *Konkōmyō saishōōkyō*). Such insertions are particularly prominent in the founding narrative of Japanese Buddhism, including the description of Buddhism attributed to the king of Paekche, and Shōtoku's vow at the climactic moment of the narrative.[20]

The *Golden Light Excellent King Sutra*, which was first brought to the Japanese islands by the monk Dōji in 718, was chanted daily at state monasteries in the eighth century and was a favorite scripture of the Nara court. The reason for the court's interest in this text almost certainly lay in the sutra's explicit statements regarding the benefits that would accrue to a ruler who sponsored Buddhist institutions and worshiped the Four Heavenly Kings. The sutra's sixth chapter states:

The Four Deva Kings, the Guardians of the World, promise with all their numberless followers (demons and spirits) to protect the kings (together with their families and countries), who attentively listen to this sutra and respectfully make offerings, receiving and keeping this holy text.[21]

All of this is of immediate note because it suggests that the editors of the *Nihon shoki* were consciously seeking to present Shōtoku as a paradigmatic figure who worshiped the same Buddhist deities as the Nara court and dedicated a temple to these same Four Heavenly Kings.[22] Equally importantly, the use of the *Golden Light Excellent King Sutra* in passages related to Shōtoku has also helped scholars better understand the process by which the *Nihon shoki* was edited. Since this text was brought to the Japanese islands by the monk Dōji in 718, we can be sure that passages containing quotes from the sutra were being edited less than two years before the text's completion in 720.[23]

Sources of the Legend

The fact that the *Nihon shoki* narrative concludes with the founding of Shitennōji—Four Heavenly Kings Temple—provides us with other important clues for understanding the legend's formation. Assuming that the lineages with the greatest interest in Shitennōji were most likely to furnish sources for the legend, the most likely candidates would be kinship groups from Naniwa, the site of Shitennōji, that were directly involved in the composition of the text. Fortunately, entries in the *Nihon shoki* from the reigns of Temmu (reigned 673–686), and his successor, Jitō (reigned 690–697), that detail which lineages submitted records for the chronicle make it relatively easy to isolate the most likely sources of the legend.[24]

Listed among these lineages are the Abe, one of the most prominent kinship groups of the late seventh and eighth centuries, and the Kishi, an immigrant kinship group from the Korean kingdom of Silla.[25] The Abe were among the pre-eminent kinship groups in Naniwa, and the Kishi functioned as their close retainers.[26] Relations between the Abe and the Kishi appear to have been so close in fact that they claimed descent from a common ancestor.[27] As we shall see shortly, both of these groups also figure prominently in the history of the Shitennōji.

One further kinship group, the Hata, also appears to have been intimately connected with the construction of the legend. Although the Hata are not explicitly mentioned as providing sources for the writing of the *Nihon shoki*, they appear frequently in the *Nihon shoki* passages related to Shōtoku. The Hata are also known to have had close relations with the other Naniwa kinship groups, and later versions of the founding legend of Japanese Buddhism tend to highlight the Hata's close connections with Shōtoku and with Shitennōji. The Hata, based in Yamashiro Province, were also an immigrant kinship group of Silla descent.[28]

The *Shoku nihongi*, an eighth-century court chronicle, apparently refers to the continuation of Temmu's historical project during the reign of Temmu's daughter-in-law Gemmei (reigned 707–715). The *Shoku nihongi* states that in the second month of 714 Gemmei asked Ki no Asomi Kiyohito and Miyake no Omi Fujimaro to compile an historical chronicle for the court.[29] The Miyake were yet another Silla immigrant kinship group from Naniwa who claimed common ancestry with the Abe and the Kishi.[30] Miura notes that the Miyake and Kishi enjoyed such close relations that a sub-group of both lineages, known as the Miyake-Kishi, also emerged during this period.[31]

The close links among these kinship groups were reflected in close co-operation at rites held at Shitennōji. The *Shoku nihongi* notes the performance of the "Kishi dance" at Shitennōji, for instance, some fourteen years after the completion of the *Nihon shoki*.[32] This dance was performed in concert by members of the Abe, Kishi, Miyake, and Kusakabe for generations thereafter as part of the *tennō*'s accession rites.[33] In view of the close genealogical and cultic links between the Abe, Kishi, Miyake and Kusakabe, Gemmei's choice of a Miyake editor takes on added significance; not only was Gemmei herself Prince Kusakabe's consort, she is also cited in the *Nihon shoki* as "the Princess Abe" before her accession to the throne.[34]

The presence of a Miyake editor at the head of Gemmei's project of 714, coming just six years before the completion of the *Nihon shoki* in 720, could not but have given the Naniwa kinship groups a large influence upon the final shaping of the *Nihon shoki*. The final years of this project saw extensive rewriting of the *Nihon shoki* in general and the Shitennōji narrative in particular. At this crucial juncture, the picture that emerges is of the former "Princess Abe" asking a member of the Miyake to edit an historical project using Kishi, Hata, and Abe sources.

This configuration of kinship groups appears to have markedly influenced those sections of the *Nihon shoki* that relate to Shitennōji and to Prince Shōtoku. Kishi, Hata, and Abe figures are featured prominently in these sections, so much so that Sakamoto speculates that the *Nihon shoki* sections dealing with the period covering Shōtoku's lifetime must have relied heavily upon sources from the Kishi kinship group.[35] Most likely as a result of such influence, the Naniwa kinship groups appear to have left a strong imprint upon the subject matter of the Shōtoku legends included in the *Nihon shoki*. Thus, whereas the founding of Shitennōji is presented in the text as the culmination of the battle to establish Buddhism in Yamato, the *Nihon shoki* is notoriously terse in its accounts of the founding, burning, and rebuilding of Hōryūji.[36] In a similar vein, the shrines and legends of the ancestral deities of Silla immigrant kinship groups associated with Shitennōji are also ubiquitous throughout the text. One looks in vain, however, for references to the shrines of the ancestral deities of Paekche immigrant kinship groups associated with the Soga, Hōryūji and Asukadera. Thus it seems fair to speculate that at an early point there was a bifurcation in the Shōtoku cult, with one strand centered on the Silla immigrant groups associated with Shitennōji and the other centered on the Paekche immigrant kinship groups affiliated with Hōryūji and Asukadera. It also appears that the kinship groups affiliated with Shitennōji managed to shut out Paekche immigrant kinship group sources from this and other sections of the *Nihon shoki*.

All of this suggests that the figure of Shōtoku was a disputed cultural symbol at the time of the writing of the *Nihon shoki*. This dispute highlights the importance of Shōtoku as a source of political and religious authority even as it indicates a lack of consensus in just these areas. The fact that this dispute centered on three of the oldest and largest temples in the Japanese islands underscores the depth of this division. The need on the part of the Naniwa kinship groups and the royal house to suppress a rival legend cycle similarly testifies to the strength of the resistance that they encountered. The Shōtoku legends included in the *Nihon shoki* thus appear to have been produced both in response to this conflict of authority and by the desire for its erasure.

Perhaps the most surprising aspect of this conflict, however, is that the fault lines did not fall upon a Japan-Korea axis; instead, the dispute over the figure of Shōtoku suggests deeper inter-ethnic conflicts between Silla and Paekche immigrants. The fact that this conclusion is surprising should alert us to a methodological anachronism that has up until now dominated much scholarship on the period. This anachronism, stated baldly, occurs when the actors of the period are portrayed as either "Japanese" or "Koreans." This framework has obscured the fact that notions of "Japanese" or "Korean" identity were only beginning to emerge during this period, and that it took several centuries for them to emerge fully.[37] Thus, although there is evidence of a great deal of cooperation among Paekche and Silla kinship groups—they all promoted Buddhist culture, for example—this should not blind us to several crucial differences that separated them. Silla and Paekche immigrant groups appear to have promoted divergent types of Buddhism, their native countries were frequently at war, and they were as often as not allied with rival regional factions. Taking these differences seriously will mean focusing on areas of conflict and resistance among the royal house, the Silla immigrant groups from Naniwa, and the Paekche immigrant groups from the Yamato plain.

Inter-ethnic Conflict and the Shōtoku Cult

Ironically, one of the main sources of tension between Paekche and Silla immigrant lineages appears to have been the very battle that led to the establishment of Shitennōji in 587. Following their victory over the Mononobe, the Soga, at the head of a powerful network of Paekche immigrant kinship groups, dominated life at court and the royal house. The Soga kinship temple, Asukadera, similarly assumed a paramount position among Buddhist temples affiliated with the court. As the Soga and their affiliated Paekche immigrant kinship groups sent students, nuns, and monks to Paekche for training and ordination, they also encouraged Paekche monks, artisans, and carpenters to come to the Japanese islands to build and staff Buddhist temples.[38] As a result, the vast majority of Buddhist temples from the early seventh century reflect the influence of Paekche Buddhism. Similarly, of the nearly fifty monks that the *Nihon shoki* records as coming to the Japanese islands from the Asian continent during the Soga ascendancy, virtually all were from Paekche.[39]

Hōryūji, Kamitsumiya's kinship group temple, appears to have been closely affiliated with the Paekche-oriented Buddhism of the Soga. Architecturally and iconographically, the temple was profoundly influenced by developments in Paekche. Hōryūji also appears to have been staffed by monks from Paekche and the Korean kingdom of Koguryô. The *Jōgū Shōtoku taishiden hoketsuki (Supplemental Record to the Biography of Crown Prince Shōtoku of the Upper Palace)*, an early to mid-Heian period text, states that after Shōtoku's lineage was destroyed in 643, several monks from Hōryūji left to found temples in immigrant centers in Ōmi and Kawachi provinces. Because the *Hoketsuki* explicitly states that virtually all of these monks were from Paekche, their decision to relocate in these areas may have been motivated by regional and ethnic considerations.[40]

In contrast with this trend toward Paekche Buddhism, a *Nihon shoki* entry for the year 623 states that Buddhist ritual implements and flags from the Silla court were installed at Shitennōji and that a Buddhist statue from Silla was installed at the temple of Kōryūji in the Kadono district of Yamashiro Province.[41] Because Kōryūji was the kinship group temple of the Hata, the installation of Silla statuary and ritual implements in these temples would at the very least suggest that these immigrant groups were aware of developments at Buddhist institutions in Silla. Because the timing of these gifts corresponds closely with the death of Prince Shōtoku, Tamura Enchō has suggested that the editors of the *Nihon shoki* meant to imply that these offerings were meant for Shōtoku's departed spirit. If this was the case, it would be the earliest evidence outside of the temple's founding legend that Shōtoku was associated with Shitennōji.[42] Although, given the paucity of sources, we can only speculate on the historical situation following the prince's death, such entries do suggest that by the early Nara period Kōryūji and Shitennōji were associated with a Silla-oriented wing of the Shōtoku cult.

All of this suggests that the Shōtoku cult may have bifurcated almost from its inception along ethnic lines, as networks of Paekche and Silla immigrant kinship groups alike utilized Buddhist temples to construct and maintain cultural identities in the face of inter-ethnic conflict. Indeed, the earliness of this split forces us to consider whether the Shōtoku cult was at least in part created and sustained by the inter-regional and inter-ethnic conflicts that convulsed Yamato in the middle years of the seventh century.

A second major catalyst for inter-ethnic disputes appears to have been the issue of Yamato policy toward the kingdoms of Paekche and Silla. The early seventh century saw virtually continuous warfare between Paekche and Silla, and inter-ethnic tensions in Yamato appear to have worsened correspondingly. Within the *Nihon shoki* we find that one of the most prominent of the pro-Silla faction at court were the Kishi, one of the Silla immigrant kinship groups from Naniwa that were most closely associated with Shitennōji. The text particularly highlights Kishi involvement in diplomatic affairs during Shōtoku's lifetime. During this period, the *Nihon shoki* reports that the Kishi undertook for the Yamato court three missions to territories on the Korean Peninsula that were claimed by Yamato (in 575, 591, and 600), one to the Sui court (in 608), and four to Silla (in 584, 591, 597, and 600).

In the picture presented by the *Nihon shoki*, tensions at the Yamato court over international policy issues came to a head shortly after Shōtoku's death, when a group of pro-Paekche kinship groups purportedly launched an abortive attack upon Silla. Regardless of whether such an attack actually happened as described, the text's startlingly blunt level of anti-Paekche invective conveys a palpable sense of animosity: "Paekche is a country full of deception. They even lie about the distances between roads. Nothing they say can be trusted."[43]

Within the *Nihon shoki*, these inter-ethnic conflicts are depicted with increasing intensity as a series of violent succession disputes polarized the

Yamato court for much of the seventh century. If the text may be believed, a central element in these disputes was the growing power of the Soga kinship group network at the expense of other kinship groups with claims upon the throne. These tensions are readily apparent in the text's account of a succession dispute that broke out upon the death of the Yamato ruler Jomei in 641. Resistance to the Soga is said to have centered on Kamitsumiya's son, Prince Yamashiro no Ōe, who was purportedly put forward as a candidate for the throne. Although the *Nihon shoki* is clearly sympathetic to the cause of Prince Yamashiro, the Soga are portrayed as usurpers who block Yamashiro's accession. Soon thereafter, Yamashiro and his kinsmen are said to have been attacked at the behest of Soga no Emishi, the Soga leader. After a brief flight into the mountains, Yamashiro and his supporters apparently died en masse at Hōryūji, thus bringing Shōtoku's line to an end.[44]

Within early Shōtoku hagiography there are some indications that the destruction of Kamitsumiya's line had a further polarizing effect among the Silla immigrant kinship groups associated with Shōtoku. Shitennōji-related legend sources such as the *Hoketsuki*, for instance, stress the military connection between the Hata and Shōtoku, while *Nihon shoki* suggests that the Hata helped raise Yamashiro no Ōe and that they were poised to fight for him at the time of his death.[45] In a similar vein, although the Abe are shown in the *Nihon shoki* as cooperating with the Soga during the early part of the century, after the destruction of Kamitsumiya's lineage, the Abe are said to have switched sides. They are depicted as allies of Prince Naka no Ōe (later the ruler Tenji) and Fujiwara no Kamatari, who are said to have plotted to bring down the main Soga line and institute a broad, continental-style revision of government in which the position of the ruler would be strengthened and the power of rival kinship groups kept in check. These efforts are said to have resulted in a palace coup in 645 that involved the assassination of Soga no Emishi and the elimination of the dominant branch of the Soga kinship group. Thus once again, the text presents Silla and Paekche immigrant lineages on opposite sides of a bloody political dispute.

Immigrant Rivalry from Kōtoku to Temmu

Although no one today would take the events as described during this period at face value, it would appear that one side-effect of these conflicts was a change in the balance of power among Paekche and Silla immigrant groups.[46] The *Nihon shoki* informs us that immediately after the coup the capital was moved from Yamato, the stronghold of the Soga, to Naniwa, the stronghold of the Abe. We are further told that the ruler Kōgyoku abdicated the throne and was succeeded by Abe no Uchimaro's son-in-law, who is known to later generations as the ruler Kōtoku. As Kōtoku's father-in-law and as the maternal grandfather of the heir apparent, Abe no Uchimaro was named Minister of the Left, the highest post in the land.

In the decades that followed, as leaders at court sought to transform the relationship between the ruler and court *vis-à-vis* provincial kinship groups, they also moved to transform their relationship with the Buddhist institutions that were affiliated with these kinship groups. Whereas previously the Soga had been the largest sponsor of Buddhist institutions at court, by the end of the seventh century, rulers such as Tenji and Temmu had in large part assumed the mantle of both patron and regulator of Buddhist institutions in the Japanese islands.

The shift of the court to Naniwa during Abe no Uchimaro's tenure as Minister of the Left also appears to have had a direct effect upon the relationship between rulers and Buddhist institutions near the court. With its close connections with the minister of the Left, its location in the capital, and a historical connection with Shōtoku that rivaled that of Asukadera and Hōryūji, Shitennōji soon began to receive support from the highest echelons of the Yamato court.[47] Within decades, the temple was a major cultic center for the worship of Shōtoku and the Four Heavenly Kings—deities upon whom rulers came to rely increasingly for protection in the years ahead.

Shitennōji's new connection with the court in turn apparently led to a reinvention of the temple's identity. According to the *Nihon shoki*, in 648 Abe no Uchimaro led a ceremony at the temple where four Buddhist images—presumably images of the Four Heavenly Kings—were installed. Although Hirano speculates that the Silla-oriented Buddhism of Shitennōji could emerge only after the Paekche-oriented Buddhism of the Soga had been suppressed, many Japanese scholars have concluded from the installation of Buddhist images that the temple was not completed until 648.[48] It is possible that the temple's name as well as its connection with the Four Heavenly Kings developed not during Kamitsumiya's lifetime but only after Yamato rulers had come to play a role as the temple's sponsor.

The ascendance of Shitennōji, however, was to prove short-lived. Although Abe no Uchimaro's power continued unabated until his death in 649, Uchimaro's grandson and heir apparent, Prince Arima, was unable to maintain his position without Uchimaro's support. Just nine years later, the Soga apparently engineered Prince Arima's downfall by goading him into plotting a rebellion, which they immediately reported to Prince Naka no Ōe (later the ruler Tenji), the power behind the throne.[49] When Tenji subsequently assumed the throne, he increasingly relied upon Soga support, filling fully half of his council of state with members of the Soga kinship group and their allies. In the aftermath of the Arima incident, relations between the Abe and Tenji remained distant throughout Tenji's reign.

Tenji's reign was dominated by events on the Korean Peninsula. In 660, Silla and T'ang China united to crush the kingdoms of Paekche and Koguryô. By 663, Paekche had fallen, but the Yamato court sent a large force to assist Paekche resistance. The Yamato forces were soon routed at the battle of Paekchon River, however, leaving them with no choice but to withdraw from the Peninsula. In 668, Koguryô fell and was incorporated into the T'ang empire. As a result, the Korean Peninsula was no longer divided, and a newly resurgent T'ang empire, allied with Silla, was expanding its influence across its eastern borders. Thus, in the space of just a few years, the Yamato court found itself dangerously weakened and isolated in the face of the resurgent Silla and T'ang.[50]

The Yamato court's immediate reaction to their defeat was to institute a policy of isolation. Although the debacle on the continent was followed by the arrival of five separate missions from the T'ang in the next eight years, these missions seem to have had the effect of intimidating the Yamato court even further. Fearing an invasion, the court refused to meet the first of these missions and allowed the rest to advance only as far as Kyūshū. The Yamato court itself did not send another mission until 703, fully forty years after their defeat.

Bruce Batten has argued that the sense of crisis that gripped the Yamato court following their defeat on the mainland helped spur a series of reforms aimed at creating a stronger, more centralized state. This project was aided by the large number of refugees from Paekche that flooded into Yamato following the destruction of their country. Throughout his reign, Tenji appears to have favored both recent and more established Paekche immigrant kinship groups, putting their superior technical skills to use in fortifying the country.[51] Paekche refugees were charged with building at least seven fortresses along the coast of the Japan Sea and Kyūshū. At the same time, Tenji moved the capital to the area of Ōtsu in Ōmi Province. Ōmi, as we noted earlier, was a center for long-established Paekche immigrants as well as for the newly arrived refugees. It would appear likely that one side effect of the rise of these new immigrants was that the influence of Silla immigrant groups diminished accordingly.

Shortly after Tenji's death in 671, regional and ethnic tensions erupted into a full-scale civil war that profoundly altered the political and religious institutions of Yamato.[52] The Jinshin War, as it is known, originated as a succession dispute between Prince Ōtomo, Tenji's son and apparent favorite, and Tenji's brother Prince Ōama (known to later generations as Temmu tennō).[53] The great majority of high ranking kinship groups, including the Soga and the Paekche immigrant kinship groups at the capital, supported Prince Ōtomo. The influence of the Paekche immigrant kinship groups at the capital was therefore dealt a heavy blow with Ōama's victory in the seventh month of 672. Prince Ōama was supported not by the traditional power centers, however, but rather by lower-ranking or disaffected kinship groups such as the Kishi and the Abe. As a result, Ōama's victory owed very little to the influential kinship groups of the capital and a great deal to the support of the Abe and other provincial kinship groups. Freed from dependence upon traditional power centers, Temmu set about in earnest building many of the foundations of the new, tennō-centered state.[54] At this crucial juncture in Japanese history, the Naniwa kinship groups found themselves well-placed to influence policy in the Temmu era and beyond.

As Temmu moved to augment the sacral authority of the ruler, the immigrant lineages at the forefront of the early Shōtoku cult to a surprising degree helped shape the ideological underpinnings for the emerging new polity. At the heart of Temmu's program lay a redefinition of the sacral authority of the ruler both in terms of being a living god and in the vocabulary of Buddhist kingship. Thus, during Temmu's reign, the "foreign religion" purportedly feared by predecessors such as Kimmei became a core element in the definition of Yamato kingship.[55]

Temmu's redefinition of the sacral authority of the royal house was also manifested institutionally through the construction of a series of temples and shrines. This process continued for decades, culminating in the establishment of a network of temples for the protection of the state in 741.[56] These temple and shrine complexes in effect situated local and regional deities in a trans-local and a trans-regional context. The result was the creation of a set of native symbols centering upon the royal house.

One of the main pillars of this symbolic framework was the figure of Prince Shōtoku, who became emblematic of the new polity. One indication of the degree to which Shōtoku was identified with the new state's emerging sense of self-identity can best be seen from in scriptural commentaries attributed to Shōtoku that were on a number of occasions sent with missions to T'ang China.[57] The inscription at the top of one such commentary states that "This was composed by Prince Kamitsumiya [Shōtoku] of the country of Yamato. It is not a foreign work."[58] Shōtoku was thus a cultural icon for the emerging Japanese state as it represented itself to the T'ang and Silla in terms of its most recent cultural borrowings.

An odd sort of cultural inversion thus seems to have taken place with the creation of the *tennō*-centered state. To a substantial degree, the sources for the core of the new state's cultural identity lay not with the nobility in the capital but with immigrant kinship groups on the social periphery. As a result, the court came to define itself in terms of the visions and narratives of these immigrant kinship groups. This process was far from simple; Shōtoku was transformed into a state deity only after the Paekche and Silla immigrants had recreated him in their own images of sacred kingship.

Immigrant Images of Shōtoku

Several hints as to how this process may have unfolded can be seen in the visions of Shōtoku produced by Hōryūji, Asukadera, and Shitennōji. Although difficult to reconstruct, these temples appear to have represented the prince in terms that broadly reflected the contemporary trends of Paekche and Silla Buddhism. Hōryūji and Asukadera, for example, promoted an image of Shōtoku as a Priest-King. Temple records submitted to the court in 747 emphasize Shōtoku's prowess as an exegete, his relationship with his Paekche and Koguryŏ teachers, and his devotion to the *Lotus Sutra*.[59] Other texts such as the *Jōgū Shōtoku hōō teisetsu* (*Record of the Dharma Ruler Shōtoku of the Upper Palace*) supplemented this view of Shōtoku as high priest with a vision of Shōtoku as sage ruler and Dharma King (*hōō*).[60] This term had specific connotations of divine rulership relating to Asoka, the much-emulated Indian Buddhist monarch, as well as the historical Buddha Shakyamuni himself. Shōtoku's identification with Shakyamuni was made even more explicit in Hōryūji's statuary; the inscription on the reverse of the temple's main image both refers to the prince as a Dharma ruler and, even more remarkably, states that the statue was built according to the proportions of the prince.[61]

In contrast with this image of Shōtoku as priest-king, the Naniwa kinship groups depicted Shōtoku as a warrior-king capable of offering security and prosperity to the imperiled court. Narratives stressing Shōtoku's military prowess and connection with the Four Heavenly Kings, for example, can be found not only in the *Nihon shoki* but also in subsequent Shitennōji-affiliated texts such as the *Hoketsuki*, the *Shōtoku Taishi denryaku* (*Chronological Biography of Crown Prince Shōtoku*) and the *Shitennōji goshuin engi* (*Account of the Origins of Shitennōji, with the Regental Handprint*) from Shitennōji.[62] Further evidence of Shōtoku's apotheosis as a guardian avatar for the new state can also be found in the iconography of a cluster of seven temples that claimed to have been founded by the prince.[63] Tamura Enchō has shown that the main image at almost all of the seven Shōtoku temples was a seated *hanka shii*-style statue of the bodhisattva Maitreya.[64] Tamura has further demonstrated that these images were worshiped not simply as representations of Maitreya but rather as representations of Shōtoku himself.[65] Shōtoku's association with Maitreya was doubtless facilitated by the fact that several Buddhist scriptures predicted that Maitreya would appear in the form of a prince who as a youth would turn the wheel of the Buddhist Law.[66] Thus did the Japanese Buddhist tradition come to represent itself as springing fully formed from royal roots in Japanese soil.[67]

Shōtoku's identification with Maitreya also served to connect him with a broader East Asian tradition of Maitreyan messianism. Although the Buddhist scriptures stated that Maitreya would not appear for over 5.6 billion years, millennarian cults centering upon the advent of Maitreya spread throughout East Asia in the sixth and seventh centuries.[68] These movements often assumed that Maitreya would come to Earth in the form of a prince to rid the world of its wrongs and usher in a new golden age. Because such movements had obvious revolutionary potential, they were frequently proscribed by governments throughout East Asia.

One exception to this trend was the Korean kingdom of Silla, where Maitreya worship was closely connected with rites of worship for the Silla state. State worship of Maitreya made frequent use of *hanka shii*-type images of Maitreya that were of the same type as those found in the Shōtoku temples. In light of the fact that at least two of the images at Shōtoku temples—those at Shitennōji and Kōryūji—are thought to have been made in Silla, the prince's association with Maitreya may thus have reflected the influence of Silla upon the early Shōtoku cult.

Hanka shii images were also prominent in the cultic activities of the *hwarang*, a Silla cult of noble youths that were organized into small fraternities for the pursuit of cultural and military activities.[69] The *hwarang* are said to have been instrumental in fighting for Silla in the mid-seventh century and appear to have used *hanka shii* representations of Maitreya as their main images of worship.[70] Thus, during the reign of Temmu *tennō*, the ascendant wing of the Shōtoku cult seems to have been dominated by Silla immigrant kinship groups using Silla statuary intimately connected with a state-sponsored Silla messianic cult.

The Nihon shoki Narrative and the Silla State

Our founding narrative has thus taken us not to the emerging state's center but rather to its borders and beyond. These borders, as we noted earlier, were redrawn with the unification of the Korean Peninsula in the mid-seventh century. Almost immediately after the subjugation of Paekche and Koguryô had been completed, however, fighting erupted between the T'ang and Silla for control of the Peninsula. In 676, the T'ang withdrew, leaving Silla with uncontested mastery of most of the Peninsula.

Temmu's response to these events was to seek to improve relations with Silla while severing all ties with the T'ang. Whereas only one mission was sent to the T'ang in the next thirty years, Temmu in less than 13 years upon the throne received eight missions from Silla and sent another four in return. These missions brought student priests to Silla for study in Silla state temples. Many, upon returning home, assumed prominent positions in the State ecclesial hierarchy. As a result, during the time of the construction of the *tennō*-centered state, Japanese contacts with the T'ang were minimal, whereas contacts with Silla were at their peak. All of this suggests that to a surprising degree the Yamato court may have looked to Silla rather than the T'ang for a model for their new state.

One of the most important areas of Silla influence on the Japanese royal system can be seen in the construction of a state network of temples focused on the worship of the Four Heavenly Kings. At the center of the Silla temple network was a temple named Sach'ŏnwangsa (Four Heavenly Kings Temple), that was credited with allowing Silla to defeat the T'ang empire. Although we have no way of knowing how the Yamato court first learned of Sach'ŏnwangsa, during a mission to Silla in 675, an embassy from the Yamato court that was co-led by an envoy named Miyake-Kishi Irishi would almost surely have learned of the temple, which was being constructed in part to commemorate Silla's victory over the T'ang.[71] Sach'ŏnwangsa appears to have made a tremendous impression upon the Yamato court; so much so that the architectural pattern for officially sponsored temples in Yamato subsequently mirrored the layout of the Silla temple. Thus, whereas Sach'ŏnwangsa, which was one of the first temples in Silla to use a double pagoda structure, was completed sometime before 679, Yakushiji, the largest temple in the Japanese islands at the time of its completion in 691, became one of the first temples in the Japanese islands to use the double pagoda structure. The double pagoda structure subsequently became a model for all later state temples.[72]

How Sach'ŏnwangsa related specifically to the Shōtoku cult and the *Nihon shoki* legend is suggested by the temple's founding legend in the *Samguk yusa* (*Memorabilia from the Three Kingdoms*), a thirteenth-century history of Korean Buddhism. The legend is set in the year 674, when the T'ang army fought with Silla for control of the Korean Peninsula. The legend reports that the

T'ang sent a vast armada to attack Silla. At a loss, the king of Silla summoned the priest Myŏngnang and asked him what should be done:

> The monk advised the King, saying: "To the south of Wolf Moun-
> tain is a sacred grove. If you build a temple to the Four Heavenly
> Kings on this spot then all will be well." At that time an envoy from
> Chŏngju arrived and reported: "A T'ang army of innumerable (sol-
> diers) has reached our borders, marauding on the sea." The King
> called Myŏngnang and said "The situation is already urgent in the
> extreme. What should we do?" Myŏngnang said: "Build a tempo-
> rary [temple] with colored cloth." Accordingly they built a temple with
> colored cloth and constructed from grass sacred images for the five
> directions. Then twelve accomplished esoteric monks led by
> Myŏngnang performed an esoteric rite. Then, before the T'ang and
> Silla armies had engaged, there arose raging wind and waves and
> the T'ang ships all sank into the water.
>   Afterwards they rebuilt the temple and named it "Four Heavenly
> Kings Temple" (K: Sach'ŏnwangsa, J: Shitennōji).[73]

Given the similarities between this legend and the *Nihon shoki* account of the founding legend of Japanese Buddhism, there can be little doubt that Sa-chonwangsa influenced not only Japanese temple architecture, but also the ideological foundations of the court as well. In both the *Nihon shoki* legend of the establishment of Japanese Buddhism and in the founding legend of Sa-chonwangsa, a sagelike figure creates images of the Four Heavenly Kings out of grass or branches and promises to build a temple should the Four Heavenly Kings grant victory in battle. After victory is achieved through divine interven-tion, a temple named "Four Heavenly Kings Temple" is then built. Although we can only speculate on the exact chain of events leading to the Yamato court's appropriation of the Sachonwangsa legend for its own uses, we can state with a fair degree of confidence that a Miyake-Kishi emissary to Silla would have learned of the temple in 675 and that the Miyake-Kishi were also intimately connected with Shitennōji and the early Shōtoku cult. We can also be certain that by 691 the court was building state temples using the double-pagoda architectural layout used at Sachonwangsa. Finally, we also know that the *Nihon shoki* founding legend of Japanese Buddhism was edited between 718 and 720 in order to incorporate terminology from the *Golden Light Ex-cellent King Sutra*, a main scriptural source for the worship of the Four Heav-enly Kings. In light of this, it would thus appear extremely likely that the founding legend of Japanese Buddhism was to a large degree based upon the founding legend of the largest temple in the Silla state.

Conclusion

To paraphrase the quotation from Nelson Goodman at the beginning of this chapter, much of the world of Nara Japan was created by immigrants from other worlds. These immigrant groups created an ideological basis for the emerging royal system by utilizing new conceptions of writing and kingship. Only after the conceptual horizons of the court and the immigrants had been fundamentally altered was it possible to conceive of the new, *tennō*-centered polity of the Nara period.

These new conceptions of kingship found expression in the Shōtoku cult and in the narrative of the founding of Japanese Buddhism. Almost from its inception, however, the Shōtoku cult also served as a focal point for the construction and expression of ethnic ideals and identity. The development of the cult soon became intertwined with the chronic, often violent inter-ethnic conflicts that raged in the Japanese islands throughout the seventh century. As each group sought to supersede its ethnic rivals through alliances at court, Shōtoku narratives came to depict the royal house as the source of the cultural transformation that swept over the Japanese islands in the sixth and seventh centuries. Ironically, these immigrant lineages eventually succeeded so thoroughly in this task that their role in constructing the new state was all but erased.

Inter-ethnic conflict thus served as a catalyst both for the construction of ethnic identities and for the creation of a Japanese cultural identity. As the culturally and militarily insecure Yamato court sought a religious and military hero whose works were not "foreign," Shōtoku the Naniwa deity was transformed into Shōtoku the guardian and benefactor of royal Japan. In the process, the Buddhist religion that Yamato rulers had resisted scarcely 100 years earlier became a central element in the definition of Japanese kingship.

These motifs of resistance and erasure were in turn linked to a larger set of power relations that existed among Yamato, Silla, and the T'ang. There can be little doubt that the foreign crisis facing Yamato at the end of the seventh century was a major stimulus for the creation of royal ideology and the *tennō*-centered state. Keenly aware of their own military and cultural weaknesses, the Yamato court could not help but be impressed by the evident success of Silla in unifying the Korean Peninsula and defeating the T'ang. The Silla state's military strength, the high degree of cultural contact between the two states, and the influence of Silla immigrant kinship groups in Yamato all contributed to Silla's influence over the creation of royal ideology and institutions in the Japanese islands.

In light of recent history, there is certainly more than a little irony in the degree of cultural borrowing that went into the construction of the emerging state's symbols of identity. The figure of Shōtoku as culture giver, guardian deity, and priest-king became part of the basic vocabulary with which the Nara court represented itself to itself and to its neighbors. In many ways, this vocabulary still resonates in Japan today. To the degree that this vocabulary was effective, we may say that the Japanese turned to their rivals across the sea for their very means of self-understanding.

2

Pure Land and the Millennium in the Early Shōtoku Cult

Although today the figure of Shōtoku is remembered most prominently for his role in the founding legend of Japanese Buddhism,
much of the success of the early Shōtoku cult can be traced to two
other factors: Shōtoku's association with early Pure Land belief, and
the ability of the early Shōtoku devotees to absorb popular cultic
movements within the emerging Japanese Buddhist tradition. Thus,
although historians may debate the degree to which the historical
Prince Kamitsumiya helped reshape the political and cultural terrain of his era, there is little doubt that the figure of Shōtoku served
for centuries as a catalyst for the development of new conceptions
of the afterlife across the Japanese islands.

One of the most important popular movements in this regard
occurred in 644, when a millennial cult with a wide following among
the populace burst into prominence in the capital and countryside.
As one Ōfube no Ōshi[1] urged his followers to prepare for the advent
of the *tokoyo no kami*, large numbers of believers began worshiping
a god that Ōfube described as a worm that could be found on the
tachibana, or Japanese orange tree. Believing the *tokoyo* divinity would
come and bestow riches and immortality upon the faithful, Ōfube's
followers engaged in ecstatic singing and dancing as they disposed
of all of their possessions upon the roadsides. The cult proved to be
short-lived, however, as Hata no Kawakatsu, probably the most powerful figure in Yamashiro and a central figure in the early Shōtoku
cult, killed Ōfube as disorder spread.[2]

Ōfube's movement has attracted the interest of scholars of early
Japanese religion because it is the sole reference in the *Nihon shoki*
to a non-elite religious movement. Several have seen the cult as a

means of understanding popular religiosity. Others have seen it as an early
political movement that expressed widespread hostility to the introduction of
continental forms of governance. Folklorists have also studied the cult in the
hopes of better understanding "native" religiosity and the popular conception
of *tokoyo no kuni*, a term that is generally glossed as the land of ancestors,
gods, or life after death.[3]

Unfortunately, these efforts at understanding Ōfube's movement have
been hampered by the lingering influence of pre-war Japanese scholarship
that treated Buddhism as a "foreign" religion in opposition to the "native" cultic practices of early "Shintō."[4] Because supposedly "native" cults such as
Ōfube's have been studied with little regard to the contemporaneous introduction of Buddhist ideas and ritual, both the origins of the movement and its
relationship to the Shōtoku cult have been obscured. Thus, even as the importance of immigrant lineages for the transmission of Buddhism to Japan is
taken for granted by contemporary scholars, there has been considerably less
interest in examining the role of such groups in the formation of royal ritual
and myth. Such oversights are particularly unfortunate in this instance because
the ancestral cults of immigrant lineages such as the Hata and the Miyake
played a major role in shaping popular religious movements across the Japanese islands.

This process was amply illustrated in the decades following the death of
Prince Kamitsumiya. Tradition has it that roughly twenty years prior to the
emergence of Ōfube's millennial cult, Inabe Tachibana no Iratsume, the
fourth wife of Prince Kamitsumiya, commissioned a member of the Hata kinship group to oversee the production of a tapestry in honor of her deceased
husband.[5] The tapestry depicts Shōtoku's ascent to *tenjukoku* ("heavenly land
of long life") in what many Japanese scholars believe to be the first reference
in the Japanese islands to rebirth in a Pure Land:

> At that time Tachibana no Ōiratsume grieved and sighed. She went
> before [Suiko] *tennō* and reverently said: "...My lord must surely
> have been born into *tenjukoku*. However, the shape of that land can-
> not be seen with the eye. I wish to have a likeness made so that I can
> have an image of the land into which my lord has been born."[6]

Because the term *tenjukoku* is not found in any Buddhist scriptures, there is as
yet no consensus as to which, if any, Pure Land is depicted by the tapestry. The
tapestry's potential importance for the understanding of early conceptions of
the afterlife in the Japanese islands, however, has spurred a host of art historians to try to match the scenes depicted on the tapestry with representations of
any number of Pure Lands. To date, however, no convincing explanation has
been found.[7]

Both the *tenjukoku* tapestry and the Ōfube no Ōshi's millennial cult raise
several important questions about how our understanding of what was native
to the Japanese islands has influenced our understanding of the religion of
the period. Ōfube's millennial cult, for example, has often been depicted by
Japanese scholars as a reaction to the influx of the "foreign" religious and

political structures advocated by the Soga kinship group.[8] One by-product of this approach has been that almost no work has been done on how this and other *tokoyo* cults of the period were influenced or stimulated by the introduction of Buddhist concepts of other worlds. Conversely, study of the *tenjukoku* tapestry has been fundamentally hampered by the widespread presumption that a funerary tapestry for a paradigmatic Buddhist figure such as Shōtoku *must* have depicted a view of the afterlife that was fundamentally Buddhist.

Once we juxtapose the *tenjukoku* tapestry of the Suiko court with Ōfube's mass millennial cult, however, a surprisingly deep and broad set of connections emerges. If our sources may be believed, one could hardly hope for greater geographic and chronological proximity. Thematically, both cult and tapestry also highlight the symbol of the *tachibana*, and both indicate a focus on the world of life beyond death. Finally—and perhaps most important of all—both the millennial cult and tapestry inscription are explicitly connected with the Hata kinship group and Yamashiro Province, an early center of Shōtoku worship.

In what follows, I therefore propose to examine these connections through a survey of a broad range of immigrant deities and ancestors of the Shōtoku cult's earliest adherents. These figures provide essential clues for understanding both the development of early Pure Land belief in the Japanese islands and the contemporaneous rise of millennial movements centered on the *tokoyo* deity. By providing a way out of the Buddhist/native dichotomy that continues to plague much scholarship on the period, they illustrate the degree to which the very same groups that associated Shōtoku with early Pure Land belief were also involved with the supposedly "nativist" millennial movements that centered on *tokoyo*. Even more spectacularly, they also suggest that a rich panoply of continental rites associated with weaving, sericulture, and immortality exerted a powerful influence upon the religious imagination of the Asuka and Nara periods.

Pure Land Belief and the Early Shōtoku Cult

An understanding of the linkages among the notions of *tokoyo*, *tenjukoku*, and the Pure Land is essential for our purposes because the association of Shōtoku with Pure Land belief in Japan was undoubtedly one of the main reasons for the Shōtoku cult's success. By the time of the writing of the *Nihon shoki* or shortly thereafter, Shōtoku had become an object of veneration among Pure Land believers. In addition to the tapestry and the *Nihon shoki* legend corpus, there is also evidence for this in statuary housed in Hōryūji, where an image of Kuse Kannon was built "to the prince's size."[9]

Several indications concerning the origins of Shōtoku's association with Pure Land belief can be found in the *Nihon shoki*, which asserts that Shōtoku was the first figure in the Japanese islands to attain birth in a Buddhist Pure Land:

At this time the Koguryô monk Hyeja heard of the death of the crown prince Kamitsumiya and he grieved greatly. He therefore held a feast for Buddhist monks in honor of the prince. On the day when he personally expounded the scriptures, he made a vow, saying: "In the land of Yamato there was a sage known as Prince Kamitsumiya no Toyotomimi. Born in the land of Yamato, he was truly blessed by Heaven with the virtues of a sage. Having penetrated the depths of the three sage founders he continued the plans of the former sages. He reverenced the Three Treasures and saved the people from distress. He was truly a great sage. Now the prince has died. I, although from a different land, was in my heart closely bound to him. Now that I am alone, what benefit is there in living? [Therefore] next year, on the fifth day of the second month, I will certainly die. In this way we shall meet in the Pure Land [*jōdo*] and together work for the salvation of all sentient beings." Now on the [foretold] day Hyeja died. At this people said to one another "Prince Kamitsumiya was not the only sage. Hyeja was also a sage."[10]

Among the most intriguing aspects of this legend is the connection it draws between Shōtoku's birth in the Pure Land and the theme of the foreign sage acknowledging the sagehood of the Yamato prince who "saved the people from distress."[11] These motifs are further highlighted by the text's setting in Koguryô and by the declaration of the Koguryô monk Hyeja that "although from a different land" he was nonetheless "closely bound" to the Yamato prince. All of this highlights the undoubtedly major role played by immigrant priests and lineages in the formation of early Pure Land belief in the Japanese islands. Perhaps even more importantly, it also suggests that such beliefs may have been particularly prominent in areas heavily influenced by immigrant cults and monks from Koguryô.

Koguryô, Koshi, and Kamitsumiya

The prominence of Koguryô in the first Japanese Pure Land narrative most likely reflects the widespread impact of Koguryô on the development of early Japanese Buddhism. Influence from Koguryô can be seen in the Soga kinship group temple Asukadera, which was built on a distinctive Koguryô-style layout and which, according to the *Nihon shoki*, also housed a large Buddha that had been made from metal provided by Koguryô.[12] Koguryô is also known to have sent several missionary priests to Yamato to propagate the Buddhist religion, where they were accorded top ranks. Among these, apparently, was Hyeja, the purportedly sage monk who is said to have declared that Shōtoku had been reborn in the Pure Land.

Koguryô's role in fostering the Buddhist tradition in Yamato appears to have been directly related to the geopolitical realities of the age. Within the *Nihon shoki*, frequent contacts between Koguryô and Yamato can be traced back to the reigns of the rulers Kimmei (539–571) and Bidatsu (572–585) in the late sixth century, when a number of diplomatic missions from Koguryô are said to have arrived at the northeastern port of Tsunuga in Koshi on the coast of the Japan/Eastern Sea.[13] Koguryô's interest in Yamato is generally thought to have been related to the reunification of the Chinese Empire in 589 and subsequent belligerence toward Koguryô on the part of the Sui dynasty. The opening of relations between Yamato and the Sui court in 600 is also generally seen in this framework. This diplomatic activity brought with it increased cultural contacts across Asia, as both the Sui and Koguryô courted Yamato as a potential ally.[14] Thus, although the resumption of contacts between Yamato and the Chinese Empire is often heralded as a watershed moment in Japanese history, the cultural impact of Koguryô may have been greater in the early seventh century.

Such geopolitical considerations also affected regional developments within the Japanese islands in a variety of ways; increased contacts with Koguryô appear to have sparked the Yamato court's interest in the region of Koshi in general and the port of Tsunuga in particular.[15] As a result, from an early date extensive cultural contacts appear to have developed between Koshi and southern Yamashiro, which was easily reached by waterway from the Japan/Eastern Sea. The *Nihon shoki* states that guest houses for foreign embassies landing in Koshi were built in Tsunuga and southern Yamashiro and that immigrants from Koguryô were settled in the area beginning in the sixth century.[16] In addition to such textual sources, archeological evidence of contacts between Koshi and Koguryô can be found in metal implements from gravesites in Koshi that date back at least as far as the mid-fifth century.[17] All of this suggests that the development of links between Koshi and Yamashiro may have made possible the penetration of immigrant cults from the Japan Sea into southern Yamashiro and beyond. As Yamato's "back door" to the continent increased in importance in the international and domestic politics of the period, immigrant cults associated with this area appear to have gradually assumed an important role in the construction of royal myth and conceptions of the afterlife.[18]

One example of how links between Koguryô and southern Yamashiro affected developments within the Kinai region can be seen in the Manta district of Kawachi Province immediately adjacent to southern Yamashiro. Because the Manta region housed a canal that linked Yamashiro with the port of Naniwa and the Inland Sea, its political and economic value was considerable. As an important node in the region's transportation network, the Manta Canal also allowed cultic practices originating on the coast of the Japan/Eastern Sea to spread from Yamashiro across the Kinai region. Beyond this, the Manta area is also of interest to us because the waterway is said to have been built by the Hata, the same immigrant kinship group that was responsible for the creation of the *tenjukoku* tapestry and the suppression of the millennial *tokoyo* cult.[19]

In addition to all this, the Manta area also appears to have had a special connection with Prince Kamitsumiya during his lifetime. Kamitsumiya's main heir, Yamashiro no Ōe, for instance, was apparently raised by the Hata in this region.[20] Kamitsumiya's daughter (and Yamashiro no Ōe's main consort),

Tsukishine no Hime, also appears to have been raised by a kinship group centered at the Manta royal estate, and Kamitsumiya's uncle also bore the name of Manta.[21] It thus seems fair to speculate that Kamitsumiya and his successor, Yamashiro no Ōe, cultivated a special relationship with kinship groups from this region. Such efforts most likely reflected the importance of the royal estate at Manta both as a source of revenue and as a connecting link between Naniwa and the resources of the northeast.

Because Silla immigrant groups such as the Miyake and the Hata appear to have been at the forefront of metalworking, canal building, and estate administration here as elsewhere, these links in turn help to explain the prominent role played by these groups in the formation of the early Shōtoku cult. They also suggest that these and other such immigrant kinship groups would have been well-placed to incorporate within the early Shōtoku cult elements from cultic centers in Koshi or even Koguryô.[22]

Shōtoku Devotees and the Advent of Immigrant Deities

Kamitsumiya's lineage was not the only one, however, to form links with this region; as Koshi increased in importance, other lineages also sought to establish political and cultic footholds in the area. Among the most prominent kinship groups to establish links with the Koshi region were the Soga and the Abe. As we saw in chapter 1, the Abe were closely connected with Shitennōji and the early Shōtoku cult. By the early seventh century the Abe appear to have formed alliances with several kinship groups from Koshi and other regions and cemented these ties through creative use of ancestral genealogies. Thus, by the time of the composition of the *Nihon shoki*, one of the main branches of the Abe—the Hiketa Abe—were claiming to be directly related to lineages from the Hiketa district of Koshi.[23]

These lineal and cultic ties almost certainly helped the Abe expand their influence in northeastern Japan. With the fall of the main line of the Soga in 645, the Abe apparently emerged as the leading Yamato kinship group with ties to the region. Throughout the rest of the century, the Hiketa Abe in particular are depicted within the *Nihon shoki* as having led military campaigns in Koshi as the Yamato court sought to strengthen its grip over the region. These campaigns often included extensive naval activity along the coast of the Japan/Eastern Sea as the Abe made use of their contacts in the region.[24]

The absorption of immigrant deities from Koshi into the ancestral cult of powerful lineages such as the Abe also reflects a broader truth about the influence of Koguryô on Yamato religion; cultic influences from the continent extended far beyond the sphere of Buddhism. Such linkages with Koguryô culture were regularly reinforced by immigration from Koguryô and Silla to the area from the fifth century onward. The impact of such immigrants on local cultic practices throughout the region can be seen in shrine centers bearing such names as Shiragi Jinja (Silla shrine) and cults to immigrant deities such as Tsunuga Arashito.[25] Because several such immigrant deities were also ancestral deities of early devotees of the Shōtoku cult, they played a key role in the development of both royal ritual and early Pure Land belief. How this process unfolded can be seen in the career of Tsunuga Arashito and a host of other immigrant deities whose influence extended from the coast of the Japan/Eastern Sea across the Japanese islands.

Tsunuga Arashito and the Kehi Shrine

Tsunuga Arashito is presented in the *Nihon shoki* and *Kojiki* as an immigrant deity housed in the largest cultic center in Tsunuga, a major port of entry for immigrants from Silla and Koguryô.[26] Tsunuga Arashito's presence in Yamato is explained in the *Nihon shoki* with two distinct narratives. The first account of Tsunuga Arashito's arrival in the Japanese islands, much like the legend of the sage monk Hyeja's declaration of Shōtoku's rebirth in the Pure Land, features the motif of a sage who crosses the sea in search of the sage ruler of Yamato. Here Arashito describes himself as a prince from a confederacy of small states on the Korean Peninsula:

> In one writing it is said that in the reign of Mimaki *tennō* there was a man with a horn (*tsuno*) on his forehead who came by boat and stopped in the Bay of Kehi in the land of Koshi. . . . They asked him what land he was from and he replied "I am a son of the King of Great Kara. My name is Tsunuga Arashito, [though] I am also known as "Ushiki Arishichi Kanki." He told them that, having heard that in the land of Japan there is a sage king, he had come to offer his allegiance."[27]

The second account of Tsunuga Arashito's arrival, however, is far more elaborate and makes no mention of the Yamato ruler:

> In one writing it is said that in the beginning, when Tsunuga Arashito was in his native land, he went into the countryside with a yellow ox bearing farming implements. The ox suddenly disappeared. He therefore went in search of its footprints, which stopped in the middle of a district office. At this an old man said to him, "The ox you are looking for entered this district office. But the village chieftains said 'Judging from the implements that the ox was carrying, [the owner] was planning on killing the ox. If its owner comes looking for [the ox], we will compensate him.' They then killed and ate it. If they ask you what you wish in compensation, do not ask for any treasure. Just say 'I wish for the god that is worshipped in this district.'" Shortly thereafter the village chiefs came to [Arashito] and asked him what he wished in compensation for the ox and he answered as the old man had instructed. Now the god that they worshipped was a white stone. Therefore they gave him the white stone as compensation for the ox.

So he took the stone with him and [that night] placed it in his bedroom, whereupon the stone was transformed into a beautiful young woman. Arashito was delighted and wished to be joined with her. However, when Arashito went elsewhere, the young girl suddenly disappeared. Arashito was greatly surprised and asked his wife "Where has that young girl gone?" He was told she had headed towards the east. He therefore went after her, finally floating across the sea and arriving in the land of Japan. The young girl that he sought after came to Naniwa, where she became the deity of the Himegoso shrine. Going to the Kunisaki district of Toyokuni, she also became the deity of the Himegoso shrine there. She is worshipped in both places.[28]

Taken together, these two legends offer a series of contrasts. In the second account, we find no mention of a desire to serve the sage Yamato ruler. Instead we have a deity associated with prosperity/cows and with the worship of divine stones, all common motifs among immigrant cults on the Japan/Eastern Sea. Thus the *Nihon shoki* appears to have preserved two separate layers of legend—one local, the other with a royal overlay.

The development of such legends relating Tsunuga Arashito to the royal house was almost certainly related to the growing geopolitical importance of the port of Tsunuga. Elsewhere in the *Nihon shoki* and *Kojiki* the Kehi shrine is portrayed as a central element in the rapidly developing royal cult. No longer simply a regional divinity, the Kehi deity is portrayed as having a special ritual relationship with the ancestors of the royal house. In the following passage from the *Kojiki*, for instance, the royal ancestor Ōjin seeks and receives a special blessing from the god prior to his accession to the throne:[29]

Thus Takeuchi no Sukune no Mikoto took the crown prince [Ōjin] to perform a rite of purification. When they had passed through Ōmi and Wakasa provinces to Tsunuga at the mouth of the Koshi Road, they built a temporary palace where [Ōjin] resided. Then the god of that area, the great god Izasa Wake, appeared to [Ōjin] in a dream and said "I wish to exchange my name with that of the prince." At this the prince made a vow (*kotohoki*) and said to [the god] "How terrifying! But they shall be exchanged in accordance with your command." Then the god directed him, saying "Tomorrow morning, go to the beach and I will make an offering [to acknowledge our] exchanging names." Thus on the next morning when they went to the beach, the whole bay was filled with broken nosed dolphins. At this the prince said to the god "You have given to me food consecrated to you!" Then they praised [the god] hailing him as the "Great Consecrated Food Deity (Miketsu Daijin)." Thus he is now called "Kehi Daijin."[30]

This legend is noteworthy not simply for the intimate connection forged between Ōjin and the Kehi deity but also for the nature of that relationship.

Scholars such as Tsukaguchi Yoshinobu have argued that the rite that Ōjin is depicted as performing here was meant to mark Ōjin's accession to adulthood. He cites numerous ethnographic accounts of such ceremonies across the Japanese islands, wherein the young initiate would take on the name of a god with whom the initiate had a special ritual bond.[31] The fact that Ōjin was portrayed in the chronicles as performing such a rite at the shrine of Tsunuga Arashito (referred to here as "Izasa Wake") thus underlines the importance of Tsunuga Arashito for the royal house in a particularly emphatic manner.[32]

Tsunuga Arashito and the Ame no Hiboko Cult

The close identification of Tsunuga Arashito and Ōjin is of note because the figure of Tsunuga Arashito also appears to have been merged from an early date with that of Ame no Hiboko, yet another immigrant deity with a strong cultic base on the coast of the Japan/Eastern Sea. Crucially, for our purposes, Ame no Hiboko was also the founding ancestor of the Miyake Muraji, a Silla immigrant lineage that, as we have already seen, was at the forefront of the early Shōtoku cult. As in the case of Tsunuga Arashito, the *Nihon shoki* and *Kojiki* present multiple accounts of Ame no Hiboko's arrival from across the sea. As was the case with Tsunuga Arashito, the first such account in the *Nihon shoki* establishes a clear link between Ame no Hiboko and the royal house:

> In the beginning, Ame no Hiboko rode on a ship and stopped in the village of Shisawa in Harima Province. The *tennō* then sent Ōtomonushi, an ancestor of the Miwa no Kimi, and Ogaochi, an ancestor of the Yamato no Atahi, to Harima [to meet him]. They asked him "Who are you, and what land are you from?" Ame no Hiboko answered, saying "I am a son of the ruler of Silla. However, I have heard that there is a sage king in the land of Japan. Therefore, I have left my land to my younger brother Chiko and I have come to offer my allegiance."[33]

As in the cases of Tsunuga Arashito and the Koguryô monk Hyeja, this legend highlights the now familiar motif of a sage-like figure who crosses the sea in search of the sage Yamato ruler. Yet another account of Ame no Hiboko's arrival in the *Kojiki* closely mirrors the Tsunuga Arashito legend cycle, even to the point of including such common elements as concern for cows, the search for a stone god, and marriage to the female deity of the Himegoso shrine.[34]

Further clues as to the nature of the Ame no Hiboko cult can be seen from the type of regalia associated with the deity. The list of these items provided by the *Nihon shoki*, for instance, is dominated by magical stones, metal objects, and military implements such as the "Isasa Short Sword," which is said to have been one of eight regalia housed in the Izushi shrine in Tajima Province.[35] In the *Kojiki* account, however, the list of Ame no Hiboko regalia in the *Kojiki* suggests that the deity was also closely associated with woven items:

> The things that Ame no Hiboko brought over, which were known as the "precious treasures," were: two strings of pearls, a wave-raising scarf, a wave-cutting scarf, a wind raising scarf, a wind cutting scarf, a mirror of the fords and a mirror of the shore. Altogether there were eight kinds. (These are the Eight Great Deities of Izushi).[36]

These treasures, which apparently were worshiped as the embodiment of the deity (*shintai*), underscore the deity's connection not only with the sea but also with woven amulets for the preservation of life.[37] This discrepancy between the *Kojiki* and *Nihon shoki* accounts most likely reflects the *Kojiki*'s emphasis upon Ame no Hiboko's connection with the Izushi shrine. Izushi was not only a major center of Ame no Hiboko worship but also an important point of entry for weaving and sericulture technologies during the period.[38] Located in Tajima Province, Izushi was also yet another port on the Japan/Eastern Sea with a large immigrant population. Crucially for our purposes, among the most prominent lineages in the region were the Kusakabe and the Hata, two lineages that were at the forefront of the early Shōtoku cult. Because Ame no Hiboko, the main deity of the Izushi shrine, was also the founding ancestor of the Miyake, it would appear that several of the lineages at the forefront of the early Shōtoku were directly connected not only with sericulture and weaving but also with Ame no Hiboko and the Izushi shrine.[39]

Tajima Mori and Tokoyo

Further glimpses of the cultic significance of weaving and woven implements for the Miyake Muraji can be found in the legend cycle of another Miyake ancestor, Tajima Mori. In both the *Nihon shoki* and the *Kojiki* accounts of the Tajima Mori legend cycle, Tajima Mori is ordered to travel across the sea to *tokoyo* in order to find and bring back the fruit of immortality for the dying ruler Suinin. This, we are told, Tajima Mori is able to do. To his great distress, however, he is too late to save Suinin, who has already been entombed in the area of Tsutsuki in Yamashiro Province. Overwhelmed by grief, Tajima Mori lays his load of *tachibana* (oranges) before Suinin's tomb and then immediately expires:

> 90th year, Spring, 2nd month, 1st day. The *tennō* commanded Tajima Mori to go to *tokoyo* to search for the fruit that is everlastingly fragrant. This is now called the *tachibana*.[40]

> 100th year, Spring, the 3rd month.
> Thereupon Tajima Mori returned from *tokoyo* bearing the fruit that is everlastingly fragrant.

> Tajima Mori was filled with grief and wept, saying, "Having received an order from the Heavenly court, I have gone to a distant

land, crossing over ten thousand leagues (*ri*) of waves and the distant weak waters. This land of *tokoyo* is where the immortals conceal themselves, and no common man can go there. Thus in the course of this voyage ten years passed. How could I have thought that all alone I could withstand the high waves and return to my native land? Yet depending on the spirits of the sage kings, I have barely managed to return. [But] now the *tennō* is already dead and I cannot make my report. Although I remain alive, what would it profit me? He then went and wailed before the *tennō*'s tomb and then himself died. When the ministers and people heard of this, they were all moved to tears.[41]

Among the most remarkable aspects of this legend are the many ways in which it mirrors themes from Ōfube's millennial cult, the *tenjukoku* tapestry, and the *Nihon shoki* account of the monk Hyeja's vow to join Shōtoku in the Pure Land. Here we have several notable thematic convergences, including a sage-like figure hailing a Yamato ruler as a sage; an immigrant sage who follows a member of the royal line into death; an explicit identification of the fruit of immortality as the *tachibana*; and a close connection drawn between *tokoyo no kuni*, a cultic center on the coast of the Japan/ Eastern Sea, and southern Yamashiro, the site of Suinin's tomb and the main base of the Hata kinship group.[42]

Most crucially, however, this text also suggests that the Miyake Muraji were involved with a broad range of cultic practices concerned with weaving and the quest for immortality. Here the text more or less explicitly asserts that Tajima Mori is an immortal ("no common man") who can travel beyond the "weak waters" to the land where the fruit of immortality grows.[43] Because both the motif of the fruit of immortality and the distinctive phrase "weak waters" were closely associated with the domain of the Queen Mother of the West on Mount K'unlun in China, it would appear that the Miyake Muraji incorporated elements from one of the most ancient and widespread cults in Chinese religion within their own ancestral legend cycle.[44]

For our purposes, the appearance of elements from the cult of the Queen Mother of the West is of immediate note because the Queen Mother was thought to govern the spirits of the dead as well as a realm for immortals. Here we find that *tokoyo* has been more or less explicitly identified with the Queen Mother's domain on Mount K'unlun, while the peaches of immortality normally associated with the Queen Mother in Chinese sources are explicitly conflated with the symbol of the *tachibana*. The incorporation of the cult of the Queen Mother into the ancestral legends of the Miyake thus suggests that the symbols and rites associated with the Queen Mother may have played an important role in shaping conceptions of the afterlife among adherents of the early Shōtoku cult.

Further evidence suggesting that cults related to the Queen Mother may have played an important role in the formation of the conceptions of *tokoyo* and *tenjukoku* may be found once we consider the Queen Mother's close associations with sericulture and the *tanabata* cult of the Weaver Maiden and the Cowherd. The importance of sericulture and weaving for the cult of the Queen Mother can be seen both in her role as the mother or grandmother of the Weaver Maiden and in her most distinctive iconographic trait, which was a weaving implement known as a *sheng* that formed an essential part of her headdress.[45]

The Queen Mother's close association with weaving cults in turn helps explain several elements in the cults of the other immigrant deities that we have seen thus far. Recall, for instance, the legend cycles of Ame no Hiboko and Tsunuga Arashito, both of whom are depicted in the role of cowherds prior to their advent to the Japanese islands. In light of the fact that Akaru Hime, the purported wife of these deities, was herself a weaving deity who received weaving implements as offerings, it would appear that weaving cults and deities played a large role in the legend cycles of a number of immigrant deities at cultic centers along the coast of the Japan/Eastern Sea.[46]

Tokoyo, Tenjukoku, and Sukuna Bikona no Mikoto

The Tsunuga Arashito, Ame no Hiboko and Tajima Mori legend cycles also shared close geographic and thematic affinities with the legend cycle of Sukuna Bikona no Mikoto, yet another immigrant deity that is explicitly associated with *tokoyo* in the *Nihon shoki* and the *Kojiki*. Several such connections are suggested in the *Nihon shoki* description of Sukuna Bikona no Mikoto's advent to the Japanese islands:

> In the beginning, when Ōnamuchi no Kami was pacifying the land, he came to Obama in Isasa in Izumo Province. He was about to have some food and drink when suddenly there was a human voice [coming] from the surface of the sea. He was surprised by this and sought for [the source] but he could see nothing. After a while a single small boy appeared riding on a boat made of *kagami* rind and wearing a garment made of wren feathers.... This was Sukuna Bikona no Mikoto.[47]

Here we have yet another deity arriving at a port on the coast of the Japan/ Eastern Sea. The name of this port, Isasa, provides strong evidence that the cult of Sukuna Bikona no Mikoto had put down roots in soil very similar to the cults of Ame no Hiboko and Tsunuga Arashito. Recall, for instance, that in the *Nihon shoki* account of the advent of Ame no Hiboko to the Japanese islands, Ame no Hiboko is said to have offered the Short Sword of Isasa to the sage ruler of Yamato. Because the regalia offered by Ame no Hiboko are also referred to in the *Nihon shoki* as "the eight deities of Izushi," it would appear that the Isasa sword was itself one of the main objects of worship of the Ame no Hiboko cult. In a similar vein, we also find the deity Tsunuga Arashito identified with Isasa during Ōjin's encounter with the god at the Kehi shrine. In this account, recall, Ōjin agrees to exchange names with the god after he identifies himself by the name of "The Great Deity Izasa Wake." Thus the *Nihon shoki* account of the arrival of Sukuna Bikona no Mikoto to the Japanese islands serves to underscore the fact that the port of Isasa appears at the very least to have served as a point of common mythic focus for the cults of each of these immigrant deities.

How the figure of Sukuna Bikona no Mikoto in turn related to the *tokoyo* cult can be seen in both the *Nihon shoki* and the *Kojiki*, where he is presented as a co-creator of Japan along with the main deity of Izumo, Ōnamuchi no Mikoto:

> Now Ōnamuchi no Mikoto and Sukuna Bikona no Mikoto joined their strength and with one heart created the world. Then for the people and animals of the visible world they determined the methods for healing diseases. Also, in order to do away with disasters brought on by birds, beasts and insects, they also established the [ritual] means for their control. The populace down to today enjoys these blessings everywhere.
>
> Long before, Ōnamuchi had said to Sukuna Bikona no Mikoto "Can we not say that the land that we have made was well made?" Sukuna Bikona no Mikoto answered "Some places are complete, but others are not yet complete." These words must have a deep, mysterious meaning. After this, Sukuna Bikona no Mikoto went to the cape at Kumano and eventually proceeded to *tokoyo*.[48]

While this passage again highlights the themes of creative plenitude, healing, and *tokoyo*, what is most striking about the text is Sukuna Bikona no Mikoto's assertion that his work is incomplete. As we shall see shortly, because the expectation that Sukuna Bikona no Mikoto would return to make the world complete persisted for centuries among the populace, this deity appears to have played an important role not only in the royal cult but also in the popular religious imagination of the age.

Several hints concerning the forms of worship most common to the Sukuna Bikona no Mikoto cult can be found in the *Kojiki* and *Nihon shoki* in a set of banquet toasts exchanged between Jingū and her counselor Takeuchi no Sukune. The *Kojiki* account is as follows:

> 13th year, 2nd month, 8th day. Takeuchi no Sukune was commanded to go with the crown prince and worship the Great God of Kehi in Tsunuga.
>
> 17th day. The crown prince returned from Tsunuga. On this day the Queen Consort [Jingū] gave a banquet for the crown prince in the Great Hall. The Queen Consort raised her cup to offer a toast wishing long life [*sakahokai*] for the crown prince—. She thus made a song saying:

This fine liquor
Is not my fine liquor.
The potion-master
Who dwells in Everworld [*tokoyo*]
The rock-standing
Deity Sukuna
With godly blessing,
Blessing in frenzy,
With abundant blessing
Blessing around and around
Came and offered
This fine liquor:
Drink unsparingly
Sa! Sa!

Thereupon Takeuchi no Sukune no Mikoto replied on behalf of the prince:

He who brewed
This fine liquor—was it because
He took his drum
And standing it up like a mortar,
Singing while he brewed
Did the brewing of the beer
Dancing while he brewed
Did the brewing of the beer,
That this fine liquor,
Fine liquor,
Makes me feel so extra good?
Sa! Sa![49]

Although these songs were undoubtedly created in a context different from that presented in the *Nihon shoki* and *Kojiki,* by the late seventh century the tradition of linking the Kehi deity and Sukuna Bikona no Mikoto with Ōjin and Jingū had become authoritative. Hints as to how and why these linkages were established may be seen in Jingū's toast; just as the Kehi deity is said to have offered food to Ōjin, so here liquor, normally offered by humans to gods, is said to have been offered by the god Sukuna Bikona no Mikoto to the prince. It would thus appear that in the *Nihon shoki* pre-existing mythic traditions that depicted Tsunuga Arashito and Sukuna Bikona no Mikoto as bringers of plenitude were transformed into narratives that showed these deities making special offerings to royal ancestors.

Within the preceding songs, however, tensions between these two layers of narrative can also be seen; both center upon the deity Sukuna Bikona no Mikoto, whom they associate with *tokoyo*, blessings, and long life. Both songs also reveal a *tokoyo* cult involving drinking, singing, dancing, and "frenzy."

Thus, behind the stately world of banquet toasts depicted in the *Nihon shoki* we can perhaps glimpse more communal, bacchanalian forms of worship in the Kehi and Sukuna Bikona no Mikoto cults.

A close reading of the two songs reveals further continuities with cultic practices associated with other immigrant deities as well. The reference in the second song to "rock-standing" Sukuna Bikona no Mikoto for example, is apparently related to worship of Sukuna Bikona no Mikoto and Ōnamuchi no Mikoto in the form of sacred stones; in Noto Province, for instance, the two gods were installed in shrines that specifically named them as stone deities.[50] This in turn suggests further affinities with the Ame no Hiboko and Tsunuga Arashito legend cycles as well—recall, for instance, that both Ame no Hiboko and Tsunuga Arashito come to Yamato in search of Akaru Hime, a deity they first obtained in the shape of a stone.

The association of Sukuna Bikona no Mikoto and Ōnamuchi no Mikoto with sacred stones can also be seen in an entry for the twelfth month of the third year of Saikō (857) in the *Nihon Montoku tennō jitsuroku*, (*Veritable Records of Montoku Tennō*) a tenth-century court history:

> (857) Hitachi kuni reported that *kami* had descended to earth in Kajima district, Ōaraiisosaki. At first the local people who boil sea [water for] salt from the sea saw bright lights as if it were day over the sea in the evening. When daylight came they found two coal rocks that were aflame. They were each about one *shaku* high. Their bodies appear to have been divinely made—they were not made by humans. The old salt gatherers wondered at this and fled. A day later there were over twenty small rocks which faced the [original] rocks as if they were waiting in attendance. Their color was extraordinary. Some resembled monks except for the fact that they had neither ears nor eyes. When the gods possessed someone, they said; "We are Ōnamuchi and Sukuna Bikona no Mikoto. Of old when we created this land, we left for the Eastern Sea. Now we have returned to save the people."[51]

Although this text was composed considerably later than the *Nihon shoki* and *Kojiki*, this passage exhibits several points of continuity with the banquet songs quoted previously. Here again we very clearly have motifs of deities arriving from the sea in order to bring plenty to the people. This is consistent with the references to Sukuna Bikona no Mikoto as a source of "abundant blessing/ Blessing around and around" in Jingū's toast. Once again, the deities are associated with healing and long life; later entries in the *Montoku jitsuroku* indicate that they were so closely associated with the Medicine Buddha Yakushi that they were installed in a shrine known as "Yakushi Bosatsu Jinja."[52] Jingū's reference to "rock-standing" Sukuna Bikona no Mikoto is also once again here echoed in the arrival of the deities in the form of sacred stones. All of this thus suggests a strong popular basis for the Sukuna Bikona no Mikoto cult that was accurately reflected in the banquet songs in the *Nihon shoki*.

The *Montoku jitsuroku* also contains one important note of discontinuity with the banquet passages from the *Nihon shoki* and *Kojiki*. As we have already seen, the banquet songs in the court chronicles depict Sukuna Bikona no Mikoto as making offerings to Ōjin. As with the cases of Tsunuga Arashito, Ame no Hiboko, and Tajima Mori, the god is presented as acknowledging the exalted status of a royal ancestor. In the passage from the *Montoku jitsuroku*, however, Sukuna Bikona no Mikoto and Ōnamuchi no Mikoto do not come from across the sea in order to pledge their allegiance to the sage ruler in Yamato. Instead they declare that they have returned in order to "save the people." Thus there is at least the suggestion of a millennial note here, wherein the age-old yearning for the world creator to return as world savior is once again given expression.[53]

Thus the cult of Sukuna Bikona no Mikoto appears to have developed in two divergent directions—one leading to the exaltation of the royal line, the other pointing toward festival and the hope for earthly abundance and corporate salvation. These tendencies, I would suggest, were in large part responsible for the creation of the concept of *tenjukoku* as well as Ōfube no Ōshi's millennial movement. I will discuss the role of the Sukuna Bikona Mikoto cult in the formation of each movement in turn.

Sukuna Bikona and the Tenjukoku Tapestry

One further piece of evidence suggesting that immigrant kinship groups from the Koshi area played a major role in the formation of the concept of *tenjukoku* and early Pure Land worship can be found in the background of Prince Kamitsumiya's putative fourth wife, Inabe Tachibana no Iratsume, who is said to have been the originator of the tapestry project. As Hirano Kunio has noted, the name "Inabe" most likely reflects a special relationship with the Inabe kinship group, most likely as the group that supported her during childhood. Hirano also argues that the Inabe were Silla immigrants who were closely related to the Hata. In support of this, he quotes two passages from the *Nihon shoki* that link the two kinship groups and notes three separate Hata family registers from Koshi that show members of the Hata and Inabe living together.[54] Lady Tachibana's connection with the Inabe, coupled with the fact that a member of the Hata kinship group was put in charge of making the *Tenjukoku* tapestry, thus again suggests that Silla immigrants involved with the cults of deities such as Sukuna Biko no Mikoto, Tsunuga Arashito, and Ame no Hiboko were closely involved in the formation of both the tapestry and the concept of *tenjukoku*.[55]

Fortunately, this hypothesis can be checked against a reference to "*jukoku*" (*kotobuki no kuni*) in Nara period literature.[56] This term appears in a remnant of the *Iyo kuni fudoki* (*Records of the Customs and Lands of Iyo*), one of the provincial gazetteers ordered composed by the court in 713. Within the remnant, the term appears in a transcription of a stele purporting to commemorate Shōtoku's visit to a hot spring in the Isaniwa shrine in Iyo Province in Shikoku.[57] In this text, known as the Dōgo inscription, we again find

Shōtoku associated with a Pure Land that also features his teacher, the Ko-guryô monk Hyeja:

> The Dharma King and Great King [Shōtoku] came to this village in Iyo with Master of the Law Hyeja and the Kazaraki no Omi. See-ing the sacred well they sighed at such a wondrous sign. Wishing to express their feelings, they composed a small stele inscription: "Now the sun and moon in the heavens shine above without [thoughts of] self, and [the water from] the sacred well beneath the ground comes forth without reserve. When the land is governed virtuously, there is a miraculous response and the people are at ease. As the [sun and water] pour down without discrimination, it is truly not different from *kotobuki no kuni* [the Land of Long Life].[58]

This passage in many ways closely tracks the *Nihon shoki* account of Shōtoku's attainment of the Pure Land. Whereas in the *Nihon shoki* Hyeja and Shōtoku are shown as sages that are to meet in the Pure Land, here we find Shōtoku and Hyeja together in a land "not different from *kotobuki no kuni*." Yet this account depicts Shōtoku and Hyeja in circumstances that differ markedly from the Buddhist environment portrayed in the *Nihon shoki*: here we find almost no Buddhist vocabulary and no references to Buddhist scriptures or Buddhist feasts.

This absence of Buddhist vocabulary, combined with widespread doubts about the historicity of the prince's visit to Iyo, has led many Japanese schol-ars to abandon efforts to use the text as a resource for understanding the meaning of *tenjukoku* and the Shōtoku cult.[59] Further complicating matters have been questions concerning the date of the text's composition: because the *Iyo kuni fudoki* is no longer extant, we only know of the inscription from a quotation in the *Shaku nihongi*, a medieval text composed in the thirteenth century. As a result, an extensive literature has emerged centering on the twin issues of whether the Dōgo inscription quoted within the *Iyo kuni fudoki* is genuine and whether the *Iyo kuni fudoki* itself should be treated as a Nara period text.[60]

While it is highly unlikely that a prince from the Suiko court would have traveled to Iyo Province on the island of Shikoku, I would argue that there are several compelling reasons to accept the *Iyo kuni fudoki* remnant as a Nara period text. One important clue in this regard is the lack of Buddhist vocab-ulary within the account, which suggests that the text was composed before Buddhist thought and terminology had penetrated the culture of the local elites in Iyo. Had the text been composed during the medieval period, when the figure of Shōtoku was closely identified with Pure Land belief, one would expect far more Buddhist vocabulary. More concretely, several important clues as to the provenance of the text can be found in archeological and textual sources related to the area around the shrine and hot spring that serve as the setting for the inscription. Of particular note in this regard is the fact that the Isaniwa shrine was immediately adjacent to a village known as "Tachibana Sato." Because the *Hōryūji garan engi*, a text that is known to have been composed in 747, lists among its holdings lands from Tachibana Sato, we can be confident that by the early Nara period the area around Tachibana sato had at the very least come into contact with an important institution of the early Shōtoku cult.[61]

Although we can only speculate as to which kinship group donated land from Tachibana Sato to Hōryūji, wooden documents known as *mokkan* and extant village registers indicate that Tachibana Sato was headed by members of the Hata kinship group. As we have repeatedly seen, the Hata were closely connected both with the early Shōtoku cult as well as the cults of immigrant deities such as Tsunuga Arashito and Ame no Hiboko.[62] Because these local Hata are also known to have claimed close genealogical relations with other lineages at the forefront of the early Shōtoku cult it appears highly likely that the local Hata would have been connected in some way with the donation of lands in Tachibana Sato to Hōryūji.[63] All of this thus suggests that although the historical Prince Kamitsumiya may never have arrived in Iyo Province, by the early Nara period the cult of Prince Shōtoku probably had.

One further reason for ascribing an early Nara period date for the text can also be found in the thematic content of the inscription. Within the text we find a cluster of symbols common not only to the very early Shōtoku legend corpus, but also to legends of immigrant deities such as Sukuna Bikona no Mikoto and Tajima Mori that appear most prominently in Nara period literature. Here again Shōtoku appears in tandem with the Koguryô monk Hyeja in an area associated with the Hata, the *tachibana*, and the land of long life. The simplest explanation for this overlap would appear to be that the same lineages that produced the legends for deities such as Tajima Mori and Sukuna Bikona no Mikoto also produced the inscription in which Shōtoku is said to have hailed the area around Tachibana Sato as "not different from *kotobuki no kuni*."

I would therefore suggest that although the text almost certainly cannot help us to reconstruct the life or thought of Prince Kamitsumiya, it nonetheless remains an invaluable document for understanding the beliefs and aspirations of the Shōtoku cult's devotees. Indeed, the constructed nature of the legend is precisely what allows us to observe an important moment in the development of the Shōtoku cult and the concept of *tenjukoku*. Once we read the gazetteer in this light, the importance of immigrant deities such as Sukuna Bikona no Mikoto for the development of both the early Shōtoku cult and the concept of the "Land of Long Life" becomes obvious. Consider the gazetteer's account of the shrine's origins:

> Yu District—Ōnamuchi no Mikoto looked and was filled with regret and shame and wished to bring Sukuna Bikona no Mikoto back to life. So he brought water underground from the spring at Hayami in Ōkita [to this place], and bathed Sukuna Bikona no Mikoto [with it]. After a while Sukuna Bikona no Mikoto then came back to life and awoke, and languorously said "I must have slept for a little bit."

The footprint from where he bounded up can be seen in a stone that is in the middle of the spring.

The marvelous healing power of this water did not exist only in the age of the gods. Even today it is an elixir which washes away the illnesses of all who are stained with disease.[64]

This text, when read in conjunction with the Dōgo inscription, amply illustrates the intimate connections between the cults of immigrant deities such as Sukuna Bikona no Mikoto and the early Shōtoku cult. Indeed, these connections are so close that here the Shōtoku cult appears as a virtual overlay on the cult of Sukuna Bikona no Mikoto, the deity from *tokoyo*. Here we are told that the spring that Shōtoku purportedly visited in Iyo was a healing spring used by Ōnamuchi no Mikoto to bring Sukuna Bikona no Mikoto from death back to life. We are further told that the water that Shōtoku purportedly hailed as coming "from the sacred well beneath the ground . . . without reserve" is none other than "an elixir which washes away the illnesses of all who are stained with disease." The healing spring that is both site and cause of Sukuna Bikona no Mikoto's resurrection is thus the very site that the Shōtoku account states "is truly no different from *kotobuki no kuni*."[65] All of this thus suggests that the early Shōtoku cult built both figuratively and literally upon the cults of immigrant deities such as Sukuna Bikona no Mikoto as it created the first Pure Land narratives in Yamato. As the figure of Shōtoku came to be ensconced in local cultic centers associated with healing and the conquest of death, only a short transition was required before Shōtoku could emerge as an object of devotional worship to whom those who wished for rebirth in *tenju-koku* could pray for assistance. Thus was the Japanese Pure Land tradition rooted firmly in conception and in actual fact in ground first hallowed by deities from across the sea.

Ōfube no Ōshi and the Tokoyo Kami

And yet the very pervasiveness and powerful appeal that made the Sukuna Bikona no Mikoto cult an asset to the development of royal mythology may also have made it a danger that needed to be suppressed. Thus in spite of his importance as a co-creator of the world, Sukuna Bikona no Mikoto seldom appears in the narratives of the *Nihon shoki* and the *Kojiki*. As a divinity who was believed capable of arriving suddenly for the material salvation of the populace, Sukuna Bikona no Mikoto proved to be difficult for the court to control. The millennial tendencies inherent in the cult had obvious revolutionary potential and at the very least could be a source of disorder. According to the *Nihon shoki*, scarcely twenty years after Shōtoku 's death, and during the very period when the royal mythology was undergoing rapid development, this is apparently what happened:

A man from the eastern lands in the area of the Fuji river named Ōfube no Ōshi encouraged the people in the villages to worship an insect, saying "This is the god of the everlasting world [*tokoyo no kami*]. If you worship this god, it will bring you wealth and long life." Shamans pretended to receive oracles saying "If [they] worship the *tokoyo no kami*, the poor will become wealthy and the old will return to youth." They thus increasingly encouraged the people to throw away their household valuables, and line up *sake*, vegetables and the six domestic animals by the roadsides. They also had them cry out "The new wealth is coming!" People in the capital and the countryside took the *tokoyo* insect and installed it on sanctified platforms. They sang and danced for wealth and threw away their treasures without obtaining any benefit. The loss and waste were extreme.

At this Hata no Miyatsuko no Kawakatsu from Kadono, hating to see the people so deluded, killed Ōfube no Ōshi. The shamans were frightened by this and ceased encouraging the cult. The people of the time thus made a song, singing:

> "It's a god, a god!"
> So came its fame resounding
> But Uzumasa
> Has struck down and punished it
> That god of the Everworld [*tokoyo*].

This insect usually breeds on the *tachibana* (Japanese orange) or *hosoki* trees. It is over four inches in length and its thickness is about that of a thumb. It is green colored with black spots and in every way resembles a silkworm.[66]

As I noted at the beginning of this chapter, this is the only passage in the *Nihon shoki* that characterizes a mass religious movement. Japanese scholars such as Shimode Sekiyo and Hino Akira have tended to see the movement as a nativist response to economic hardship and cultural/political upheaval. Both Shimode and Hino also see Hata no Kawakatsu's suppression of the cult as evidence of conflict between the continental, Buddhist culture represented by the Hata and a nativist culture represented by Ōfube no Ōshi.[67] This view has also been adopted by Robert Ellwood, who has argued persuasively that Ōfube's movement is an example of an early cargo cult.[68]

In opposition to this mainstream position, Hirano Kunio in 1961 set out the radical view that the Ōfube were actually Silla immigrants who were allied with the Hata.[69] In Hirano's scenario, Hata no Kawakatsu's suppression stemmed not so much from a desire to support Buddhism in opposition to native cultic beliefs but simply from a desire to keep order in the face of spreading chaos. Katō Kenkichi has since revived and extended Hirano's hypothesis. Starting from the premise that the Hata raised Kamitsumiya's son Yamashiro no Ōe in Yamashiro, he cites instances where the term *mibu*, which was generally used to refer to laborers and service groups dedicated to members of the court, was written with the characters in the name "Ōfube." Katō concludes that the Ōfube/Mibu were laborers under the jurisdiction of the Hata who were dedicated to the service of Kamitsumiya's lineage.[70]

All of these scholars, with the possible exception of Hirano, have tended to view Ōfube's cult as an isolated phenomenon separate from the other cultic practices represented in the *Nihon shoki* and the *Kojiki*. Yet once we look at Ōfube's cult in relation to the Ame no Hiboko and Sukuna Bikona no Mikoto cults, the continuities among immigrant *tokoyo* movements become obvious. The association of *tokoyo* and the *tachibana*, the role of *sake* and food offerings, the anticipation of the arrival of a god from *tokoyo* who will bring prosperity to the populace, and even the ecstatic singing and dancing all appear to have been basic elements of each of the cults we have examined so far.

This impression of continuity is further strengthened once we examine the areas where the Ōfube are known to have lived; in almost every case, these areas can be correlated with other Silla immigrant groups and *tokoyo* cultic centers.[71] Perhaps the most startling example of overlap between the Ōfube and other immigrant cults can be found in the port of Izushi in Tajima Province; not only do family registers demonstrate that members of the Ōfube and Hata lived together in the area, but the Ōfube also maintained the Ōikube Heinushi Jinja only a few kilometers away from the main cultic centers of Ame no Hiboko and Tajima Mori.[72] In other words, Ōfube no Ōshi's worship of the *tokoyo no kami* as a worm on the *tachibana* tree was rooted in the same soil as that of the Miyake ancestor Tajima mori, who was said to have brought *tachibana* from *tokoyo* to the Japanese islands.

Such roots mattered. Izushi, like many immigrant centers along the coast of the Japan/Eastern Sea, was an important point of entry not only for continental cults but also for material culture related to weaving and sericulture. Perhaps the strongest evidence suggesting that Ōfube no Ōshi's millennial movement was related to the cults of immigrant deities such as Tajima Mori and Ame no Hiboko can be found once we recall that both of these deities were closely associated with weaving cults and the Queen Mother of the West. In light of the fact that the *Nihon shoki* described the *tokoyo* deity that appeared on the *tachibana* tree as an insect that "in appearance entirely resembles the silkworm," it would appear likely that these cults drew upon the same cultic resources and beliefs that lay at the base of the cults of immigrant deities such as Tajima Mori, Sukuna Biko no Mikoto, and Tsunuga Arashito.

All of this brings us back to the issues of nativism and resistance that we raised at the beginning of this chapter. It is now clear that the followers of Ōfube's *tachibana* worm cult drew upon a reservoir of symbols associated with immigrant deities from Silla as well as weaving cults and goddesses originally rooted in western China. The fact that they did so does not preclude the possibility that this was indeed a nativist movement—yet it does show the extraordinary depth to which such symbols from across the sea had penetrated into the religious consciousness of the populace.

They were not alone in this. Indeed, these symbols were used in equal degree by the architects of the emerging royal cult as they effected a reinvention of the *tennō*'s ancestral line. In chapter 3, we will see how the very

completeness of the triumph of these symbols led to an equally thorough erasure of their origins, as royal ancestors such as Jingū, Chūai, and Ōjin displaced Silla deities from their cultic centers in Koshi, Kyūshū, and Naniwa.

In a final irony, these same cults and symbols also played a major role in
the conceptualization and creation of Pure Land devotion in Japan. By the time
of the composition of the *Nihon shoki*, Shōtoku was already being hailed as
the first figure in the Japanese islands to attain birth in a Buddhist Pure Land.
Only a few decades later he was being venerated as an incarnation of Kuse
Kannon—"Kannon the World Saver" by those who sought his assistance in
bringing them to a land of bliss. Thus did the "foreign" tradition purportedly
resisted by Ōfube no Ōshi draw its inspiration from the same impulses and
deities that grounded the millennial cult itself.

3

Ancestors, Estates, and Angry Gods in the Early Royal Cult

While immigrant deities such as Sukuna Bikona no Mikoto played a major role in the popular religious movements of the Asuka period, they also played an essential role in one the most important political/religious projects of the age: the construction of the broad array of ancestors and deities that formed the core of the emerging royal cult. The rapid development of royal ancestral legend cycles during the period was fueled both by the centralization of power in the hands of Yamato rulers and by the extension of Yamato power to such distant regions as Chikuzen in what is now Northern Kyūshū. Because the figure of Shōtoku can hardly be understood outside of the context of the developing royal cult, understanding the cultic and political activities of the immigrant lineages that were at the center of each of these developments is essential for understanding the early Shōtoku cult.

The subject matter of this chapter will therefore not be the legends and institutions of the Shōtoku cult *per se*; rather I will focus on the role of the Silla immigrants at the center of the early Shōtoku cult in shaping the cultic and geopolitical realities of the age. In so doing I hope to achieve three goals: (1) to make clear the connections between the early Shōtoku cult and other major contemporaneous developments in Asuka and Nara religion; (2) to clarify how and why mid-ranking immigrant kinship groups could exert such a tremendous influence on the formation of royal ideology; and (3) to demonstrate that the cultic influence of immigrant kinship groups such as the Miyake and Hata was not limited to the introduction of Buddhism, but rather pervaded a broad range of religious life across the Japanese islands.

One of the clearest examples of each of these processes can be found in the development of the cults of the royal ancestors Jingū and Ōjin during this period. Because the levels of support and attention that the court lavished on the cults of these two figures were matched only by the cult of the sun goddess Amaterasu, the construction of these figures as royal ancestors was a major event in the formation of the cultic identity of Japanese rulers for centuries to come. Ironically, however, as Yamato rulers sought to impose their political and religious authority upon the hostile terrain of regions such as Northern Kyūshū, they increasingly drew upon the cultic resources afforded by immigrant deities affiliated with the Hata and other lineages at the forefront of the early Shōtoku cult. As a result, the figures of Ōjin and Jingū, no less than Prince Shōtoku, came to be physically and mythically rooted in ground prepared by immigrant kinship groups from across the sea. As the Hata, Miyake and others remade the cults of these figures in the image of Kyūshū deities and Silla kings, they thus played a major role in the construction of non-Buddhist conceptions of royal authority and of the royal heritage itself. In the process, they also helped establish the parameters for Buddhist and non-Buddhist discourse in the Japanese islands for centuries to come.

Vengeful Gods and Terrified Rulers

One of the most important stimuli to the development of legends of royal ancestors such as Shōtoku, Jingū and Ōjin lay in the often tempestuous relationship between the Yamato court and local deities from Northern Kyūshū. Although the Yamato court dramatically expanded its control over this region during the latter half of the seventh century, the projection of Yamato power into the region did not automatically yield a corresponding position of hegemony for cults. Rather, it appears to have stimulated resistance from powerful local cultic centers. Thus throughout the *Nihon shoki* and the *Kojiki* there are indications that Yamato rulers were frequently over-awed if not terrified by local divinities from the region. Consider the following three legends of rulers and angry gods:

(1) The *Nihon shoki* states that in the summer of 661 the Yamato ruler Saimei (reigned 642–645 and 655–661) died at the palace of Asakura in Chikuzen Province, in what is now Northern Kyūshū.[1] Saimei had gone there in order to oversee preparations for a military campaign against the combined forces of the T'ang empire and Silla on the Korean Peninsula. Although the circumstances surrounding Saimei's death have seldom been discussed by scholars of Japanese religion, they are extremely important for understanding the role of local cults and legends in the formation of the royal cult.[2] The *Nihon shoki* account is as follows:

> 5th month, 9th day. The *tennō* moved her residence to the Palace of Asakura no Tachibana no Hironiwa.

At this time trees belonging to the Asakura shrine were cut down and cleared away in order to build this palace. The god there was thus very angry and demolished the building. Within the palace there were also mysterious fires. Because of this the Grand Treasurer and many of those in waiting took ill and died.

6th Month. Prince Ise died.

Autumn, 7th month, 24th day. The *tennō* died in the palace of Asakura.

8th month, 1st day. The crown prince, waiting in attendance with the *tennō*'s remains, went back to the Palace of Iwase. That evening, on the top of Mount Asakura, there was a demon wearing a great hat who looked down on the funeral ceremonies. The people all uttered exclamations of astonishment.[3]

Thus the *Nihon shoki* records that when Saimei and her court ran afoul of local deities from Chikuzen, the consequences were severe: not only does the *Nihon shoki* record that several ministers died, there is also a clear suggestion that Saimei herself was struck down as well.

This suggestion of royal vulnerability to the wrath of local deities is echoed in the *Nihon shoki* account of the final days of the life of Saimei's son, Temmu *tennō*; the text states that it was determined by divination that Temmu's final illness was caused by the sword of the Atsuta shrine in Owari Province.[4] Thus in the space of twenty-five years the court was twice rocked by the death of a sovereign thought to have been cut down by an angry deity. This suggests that the elaboration of legends of vengeful deities in the court chronicles was rooted at least in part in the court's perceptions of actual historical events. It also suggests that even as Yamato rulers were tightening their hold over such distant regions as Chikuzen they remained fearful of powerful local divinities over whom they had little control.

(2) The *Nihon shoki* and *Kojiki* record one other instance where a ruler was felled by an angry local deity. Both texts state that the Yamato ruler Chūai also died in Northern Kyūshū at a site extremely close to the Asakura Palace.[5] In the *Kojiki* account of the legend we are told that Chūai angered the Sumiyoshi deities by disobeying the gods' instructions to cross the sea to attack Silla.[6] Doubting the existence of such a land, Chūai accuses the gods of deception:

At this the Queen Consort [Jingū] was possessed by gods who revealed to them the following command: "In the west there is a land of many rare and dazzling treasures beginning with gold and silver. I will now bestow it upon you." Then the *tennō* [Chūai] replied, saying: "When I climb up to a high place and look westward, I see no land, but only the great sea." Then, saying "They are lying deities," he pushed away his zither [*koto*], ceased playing it, and sat silently. At this the gods were very angry and said: "You should not rule this land! Go to the one road!"[7] . . . Then [Chūai] slowly took back his zither and played on it listlessly. Almost immediately the sound of the zither became inaudible. When they then held up a light and looked, he was already dead.[8]

The legend continues after Chūai's death with his pregnant wife, Queen Consort Jingū, crossing the sea and conquering Silla as the gods have commanded. Immediately upon her return to Chikuzen she gives birth to her son, the future ruler Ōjin, who inherits dominion over the Korean kingdoms as promised by the Sumiyoshi deities.

Because this legend asserts that Jingū conquered Silla and that Yamato rulers had divine sanction for their attempts to control the Korean Peninsula, it was a key element in pre-war imperialist assertions of divine sanction for the Yamato court's ambitions on the Korean Peninsula. Chūai's death at the hands of the Sumiyoshi deities, however, points to another, darker, side to the legend; the power of the Sumiyoshi deities both to destroy Yamato rulers and to grant favors to those rulers with whom they were pleased.

The vulnerability of Yamato rulers to the wrath of the Sumiyoshi deities is all the more significant in light of the fact that these gods were closely associated with the Korean Peninsula. The identification of the Sumiyoshi deities with the kingdom of Silla is hinted at in the gods' elegaic description of Silla. This is true both for the *Kojiki* text quoted above and in the *Nihon shoki*, where the deities describe Silla as "a land of treasure, like a beautiful woman . . . full of gold, silver and colored treasures dazzling to the eyes."[9] Shrine records from the period also state that the daughter of the Sumiyoshi deities was Akaru Hime, yet another immigrant deity from Silla with shrine centers in both Chikuzen and Naniwa.[10] All of this is consistent with a broader pattern of events suggesting that the Yamato court felt that reaching an accommodation with Silla-affiliated deities from Chikuzen was literally a matter of life-or-death urgency.

(3) Lest the reader come to feel à la Lady Bracknell that losing two rulers in Chikuzen smacks of carelessness, the *Nihon shoki* and *Kojiki* also record a legend showing how several generations earlier the Yamato ruler Suinin had exercised the better part of valor when dealing with the immigrant deity Ame no Hiboko. Because, as we saw in chapter 2, Ame no Hiboko was none other than the founding ancestor of the Miyake kinship group and the husband of Akaru Hime, the ability of his descendants to intimidate a ruler such as Suinin is particularly noteworthy:

[Suinin] addressed his ministers saying, "I have heard that when the Silla Prince Ame no Hiboko first came [to the Japanese islands] he brought with him treasures that are now in Tajima. From the beginning the people of that country have reverenced them as divine treasures. I therefore wish to see them." That day an envoy was dispatched to Ame no Hiboko's great grandson Kiyohiko, ordering him to offer them up [to Suinin]. Kiyohiko, upon receiving the order, himself immediately brought the treasures as offerings.... However, there was one short sword that was called "Izushi" that Kiyohiko suddenly decided not to present [to Suinin]. He therefore hid it within his own garment and wore it as his own. The *tennō*, not knowing that Kiyohiko wanted to conceal the short sword, wished to treat him with favor and ordered that *sake* be brought to him. At that moment, the short sword stuck out from Kiyohiko's garment and was visible. When Suinin saw it, he himself asked Kiyohiko about it, saying "What is that short sword that you are wearing?" At this Kiyohiko realized that there was no way to conceal the short sword, so he reverently said, "This is one of the sacred treasures that I wish to present." Suinin then said to Kiyohiko, "How could you hope to keep this apart from the other offerings?" So Kiyohiko took it out and offered it [to Suinin].

All of the [sacred treasures] were stored in the sacred treasure house. However, later, when they opened the treasure house and looked, the short sword had disappeared of its own accord. They therefore asked Kiyohiko about this, saying, "The short sword that you offered has suddenly disappeared. Has it returned to you?" Kiyohiko replied "Last evening the short sword by its own power returned to my residence, but in the morning it disappeared." The *tennō* was thus awestruck and did not look for it further. After this the Izushi short sword went of its own accord to Awaji island. The people of the island believed it to be a god and built for it a shrine, where it is worshipped today.[11]

Although this legend does not take place in Chikuzen, there are several reasons to believe that it is related to the development of the Jingū/Ōjin cult in Chikuzen. The Miyake were a prominent kinship group in the Chikuzen region and the cults of Ame no Hiboko and his wife Akaru Hime were also extremely powerful throughout Kyūshū. In addition, and most spectacularly, the *Kojiki* account also states that the Silla Prince Ame no Hiboko was the founding ancestor of Queen Consort Jingū's distaff lineage and that Kiyohiko was none other than her great-grandfather.[12]

When examined together these passages thus yield a cluster of issues concerning the circumstances and impetus for the development of the Jingū/Ōjin legend cycle. Each of the above entries highlights an undercurrent of profound insecurity on the part of the Yamato rulers vis-a-vis local deities, particularly those from Northern Kyūshū. Each deals with the issue of the hostile relations between Yamato and Silla. Finally, each deals with the importance of Kyūshū for the Yamato court and the need for the court to find a means of accommodation with such volatile deities from the Chikuzen area as the Sumiyoshi Daijin, their daughter Akaru Hime and her husband, Ame no Hiboko.[13]

Immigrant Kinship Groups and the Expansion of Yamato Authority in Northern Kyūshū

Because each of the above items are related to issues of political control and resistance, I would suggest that the first key for understanding the means by which the cults of royal ancestors such as Jingū and Ōjin were introduced into Chikuzen lies in understanding the mechanisms by which the Yamato court extended its control over Chikuzen during this period. Major developments in this regard were (1) the prominent role of immigrant kinship groups in the development of royal estates in the region (2) the elaboration of royal genealogies linking royal ancestors to the cults of local deities and (3) the use of immigrant kinship groups in the construction and maintenance of canals and waterways linking Northern Kyūshū with Naniwa and Yamashiro.

According to the *Nihon shoki*, the first impetus for the formation of such estates in the Chikuzen region came in 530, when a powerful local leader named Tsukushi no Kuni no Miyatsuko Iwai sought to break out of the Yamato orbit through an alliance with Silla. Because access to the Korean Peninsula, on which the Yamato court was dependent for metal and other technologies, was possible only through Chikuzen, such an alliance would have posed an immediate and powerful threat to Yamato's interests. The *Nihon shoki* tells us that after a period of military conflict, the Yamato court asserted more thorough control over the area.[14]

Following Iwai's uprising, the court appears to have moved to establish a series of royal estates throughout the area at sites that would at once enhance the court's coffers and serve as outposts for supervising the region.[15] According to Naoki Kōjirō, these estates were of at least two different types. In many cases the court would simply lay claim to the land of a local paramount and then appoint him as its administrator. In areas of extreme strategic importance, however, the court appears to have appointed its own administrators. Naoki Kōjirō has argued that these estates most likely carried special administrative functions for the court in addition to the simple extraction of local resources.[16] It is widely believed that among the kinship groups chosen to serve as estate administrators were immigrant kinship groups such as the Hata, Miyake and Kishi.[17]

Although the establishment and administration of royal estates was a phenomenon of obvious importance for the economic and institutional history of the Japanese islands, I would suggest that such estates also exerted a tremendous influence on the development of both local legends and rituals. Because strategic areas of economic development and transport were often occupied by powerful local kinship groups, royal estates located in these areas were frequently situated in close proximity to major cultic centers sponsored by regional elites. In Kyūshū, for example, the Yamato governor's administrative headquarters (and Saimei's Asakura palace) were located next to the Natsu royal estate. This estate was in turn located in extremely close proximity to the Sumiyoshi shrine.[18] It is likely, therefore, that royal estates served as conduits facilitating interactions between the royal cult and local cultic practices. Thus estate representatives such as the Miyake and the Hata were uniquely well placed both to extend Yamato influence in the region and to absorb forms of myth and ritual emanating from the cultic centers of powerful local deities.

These cultic interactions did not always go smoothly; as the examples of angry deities cited at the beginning of this chapter make eminently clear, the spread of the royal cult into Northern Kyūshū carried with it risks as well as rewards for the Yamato court. Even as the court solidified its control over the area, it was exposed to a set of gods that were closely connected to Silla and largely beyond the control of Yamato rulers. Thus although it is commonly assumed that cultic developments served to mirror power relations within Yamato society as a whole, this was clearly not the case for Kyūshū; almost 150 years after the purported suppression of Iwai's rebellion, Yamato rulers still felt vulnerable to the wrath of deities such as the Sumiyoshi Daijin, Ame no Hiboko and Akaru Hime.

Genealogies and the Construction of Authority

A second important mechanism for the expansion of Yamato authority into the Chikuzen region was the elaboration of ancestral legends linking the newly minted royal lineage with the ancestors of local elites. Throughout the premodern period one's place in society and one's religious affiliations were to a large degree determined by the identity of one's ancestors. The difference between immigrant lineages and those claiming descent from Yamato deities or nobility, for instance, hinged on the distinction between those who claimed descent from people and gods from across the sea and those who did not. Recall, for instance, the preface to the *Shinsen shōjiroku*, the earliest extant genealogical compendium in the Japanese islands, which, as we saw in chapter 1, explicitly states that it was compiled in part because members of some immigrant kinship groups were claiming descent from Yamato deities.

The worry of the compendium's editors that people were fudging their genealogies highlights an essential point: in early Yamato the definition and characterization of ancestry were central tools in the contestation of power. The explosive proliferation of ancestral tombs, shrines and legends during the period can only be accounted for if we consider their value as vehicles for "majestification" of lineage and the projection of power.[19] This was clearly understood by successive Yamato rulers who sought to control the elaboration of ancestral claims by institutionalizing them in a hierarchy of court ranks and codifying them in official texts such as the *Kojiki* and the *Nihon shoki*. In theory, the court's permission was also required before a group's name could be altered or a new lineage or sub-lineage created. As the concerns of the editors of the *Shinsen shōjiroku* made abundantly clear, however, throughout the period genealogies proved to be at once authoritative and flexible as they were adapted to fit the needs of the moment. Over time a group's genealogy could go through dramatic changes as ancestors were either added or forgotten and as ancestral legends were elaborated.

Yet even as Yamato rulers were seeking to control the development of ancestral legends and cults of important kinship groups, they were also eagerly amplifying the ancestral cults particular to their own specific sublineages. Here again, the Yamato court seems to have turned to immigrant kinship groups such as the Miyake and Hata for assistance in the literary/ historical task of constructing ancestral legends and lineages. These kinship groups, in turn, utilized resources from their own cultic traditions to augment the status of their own ancestors even as they helped construct the royal lineage.

One of the best examples of this process can be found in the development of the Jingū/Ōjin legend cycle. Although little is known about the origins of the Jingū legend, she is commonly referred to in the literature of the period as Okinaga Tarashihime, a name that indicates a clear connection with the Okinaga kinship group. The Okinaga, based in Ōmi Province and south-western Yamashiro, appear to have been closely connected with the Koshi region and with the spread of metal technology in Yamato.[20] If the court chronicles may be believed, during the late fifth and early sixth centuries they provided consorts to several rulers, including Ōjin.[21]

Okinaga Tarashihime also appears to have been associated from an early date with the figure of the Silla prince Ame no Hiboko. As we saw in chapter 2, Ame no Hiboko was the founding ancestor of the Miyake Muraji, an immi-grant kinship group from Silla that was at the forefront of the early Shōtoku cult. Okinaga Tarashihime's connection with Ame no Hiboko was expressed genealogically in the *Kojiki* by his position as the founding distaff ancestor for Okinaga Tarashihime.[22] Given the prominent role of affinal relations in early Yamato, this was a position of tremendous importance.

Okinaga Tarashihime's association with Ame no Hiboko was most likely influenced by the deity's status as a metal deity and Okinaga involvement in metalworking. Genealogical and geographic overlap between the Okinaga and the Miyake Muraji, who also claimed descent from Ame no Hiboko, also undoubtedly facilitated such connections. The importance of such local cultic connections was greatly amplified by the construction of a series of canals and waterways that facilitated transport both within Yamato and between Yamato and such distant regions as Chikuzen. Thus the *Nihon shoki* states that Ame no Hiboko traveled by waterway through Yamashiro and Ōmi provinces in areas known to have been inhabited by the Okinaga. Jingū's tomb and main cultic centers, similarly, were all in areas known to have been populated by the Miyake Muraji.[23]

Although, as in the case of royal estates, the study of the impact of the construction of canals on early Yamato would appear to be the domain of economic and institutional historians, the construction of such links between regions was, if I may use such a phrase, a watershed moment in the devel-opment of Japanese popular religion. Because such waterways allowed for a wider diffusion of people and gods, they facilitated interactions between previously separate local deities. Thus although it is extremely doubtful that a Silla prince ever traveled from Northern Kyūshū to Naniwa and Yamashiro by waterway, for instance, it is highly probable that the cult of such a prince did. Legends depicting Ame no Hiboko traveling by waterway across the Japanese islands thus highlight the importance of water links and the construction of canals for the movement of cults and deities across large distances. As a result of this process, ancestral deities such as Okinaga Tarashihime could travel from Yamashiro to Northern Kyūshū even as immigrant deities such as Ame no Hiboko and his wife Akaru Hime could travel the same route in the opposite direction. Seen in this context, it is thus hardly surprising that several of the deities and ancestors of the lineages that constructed and administered these waterways burst into prominence during this period.

Among the most prominent kinship groups in this process were immigrant lineages such as the Hata and the Miyake Muraji. The *Kojiki* states that Jingū's grandson Nintoku ordered the Hata to construct the Naniwa canal, an important waterway extending from the port of Naniwa to Yamashiro and the Manta region of Kawachi Province.[24] Naoki Kōjirō has argued that control over this canal and the Manta estate allowed the Hata to expand their influence beyond Yamashiro into Naniwa, where members of the Miyake, Kishi and Kusakabe kinship groups occupied the highest administrative posts for much of the eighth century.[25] The resulting political and geographic linkages between the Miyake and Hata in turn help explain the close connections that existed between the cults of Queen Consort Jingū, Akaru Hime and the Sumiyoshi deities. By the middle of the eighth century these connections were institutionalized as Akaru Hime was worshipped as a daughter of the Sumiyoshi deities even as Jingū was installed as one of the Sumiyoshi shrine's main deities.[26]

One important by-product of this process was the prominence of Silla in the myths and cultic practices related to the Sumiyoshi Daijin and Akaru Hime. Shrine centers to these gods in both Northern Kyūshū and Naniwa were located in close proximity to the main reception centers for Silla envoys traveling to the Yamato court, and rituals of state associated with the arrival of envoys from Silla were regularly performed at the Sumiyoshi shrine in Naniwa.[27] These connections with Silla were made even more apparent with the transformation of the Sumiyoshi shrine in Naniwa into a temple-shrine multiplex at the end of the eighth century: the new institution was subsequently known as "Shiragi-dera (Silla temple).[28] Thus the very same deities who were said to have granted Yamato rulers dominion over Silla were closely associated with Silla immigrant groups, Silla immigrant deities and rituals of State associated with the arrival of envoys from Silla. One further corollary of this process was that as the figures of Jingū and Ōjin became associated with these cults, resonances from Silla mythology and conceptions of sacred kingship became central elements in the royal house's understanding of its own ancestral heritage.

Okinaga Tarashihime and the Jomei/Saimei Line

Even as immigrant kinship groups such as the Hata and Miyake were ex-panding the network of canals and estates in seventh century Yamato, the legend cycle involving Jingū, her husband Chūai and her son Ōjin underwent a period of equally rapid development. Scholars such as Naoki Kōjirō have ar-gued that this expansion was closely connected with the rise of the line stemming from the ruler Jomei (reigned 629–641) and his wife and successor Saimei, in the mid-seventh century.[29]

The reasons for this consensus are not difficult to understand; both Jomei and Saimei were of Okinaga descent. Jomei's posthumous name "Okinaga Tarashi Hihironuka Hiko" was strikingly similar to Jingū's "Okinaga Tara-shihime."[30] This link between Okinaga Tarashihime (Jingū) and Okinaga Tarashi Hihironuka Hiko (Jomei) provides important information about the legend's political uses. Jomei came to the throne following the death of the Yamato ruler Suiko in 628 with the strong support of the Abe, whose center in Sakurai was also Jomei's home base. Exalting ancestors of the current sover-eign as sage rulers would have been an appealing strategy for bolstering the authority of Jomei, Saimei and their descendents.[31]

The connection of the Jingū/Ōjin legend cycle with the rise of Jomei and Saimei was a pivotal moment in the construction of genealogies and authority in the late seventh century. Because Jomei and Saimei both claimed descent from the Okinaga, the elevation of Okinaga ancestors provided an ideal plat-form upon which to justify the continuation of their line.[32] As Tsukaguchi has pointed out, the legend also served to distinguish them from the previous several Yamato rulers, none of whom could claim such close connections with the Okinaga.[33]

Jomei's need to bolster his genealogical standing once again illustrates the importance of lineage for the contestation of power during the period. Because patrilineal succession had not yet been established, Jomei and his descendants had to contend with a multiplicity of lineages that could provide heirs to the throne. Neither Jomei nor Saimei were the child of a Yamato ruler; Jomei's claim rested on his being the grandson of the Yamato ruler Bidatsu, while Saimei was Bidatsu's great granddaughter. This comparatively weak genealog-ical standing is reflected in the Nihon shoki's account of the period prior to Jomei's accession, in which the court's lack of consensus over Jomei's candi-dacy is made abundantly clear. Exalting Jomei's ancestor Okinaga Tarashihime would have been one way for Jomei and his descendants to boost the prestige of his line. Because Jomei's line has continued down to the present, Okinaga Tarashihime's role as a guardian royal ancestor continued to expand for cen-turies.

Okinaga Tarashihime and the Conquest of Silla

The Jingū/Ōjin legend cycle appears to have gone through a third phase of development following Saimei's death in Chikuzen in 661. Several of the most important events in the Jingū chapter appear to have been constructed in order to provide precedents for events that occurred during Saimei's reign. Both the Jingū and Saimei chapters of the *Nihon shoki* include such important motifs as (1) a female ruler of Yamato succeeding her husband to the throne (2) the sudden death of a Yamato ruler in Chikuzen, and (3) a female monarch at the head of an army preparing to attack Silla. If we accept that such basic elements of the Jingū/Ōjin legend cycle were developed only after Saimei's reign, then it is highly likely that the Jingū/Ōjin legend cycle became associated with Northern Kyūshū and Silla in the latter half of the seventh century—a period which also saw the rapid development of the Shōtoku cult and the formation of a new, *tennō*-centered polity.

Hirano Kunio has also pointed out that what the *Nihon shoki* and *Kojiki* do not say is also powerful evidence for this dating of the legend. Hirano argues that had the conquest of Silla been a part of the pre-Saimei version of the Okinaga Tarashihime legend cycle, there would almost certainly been references within the legend to the Korean kingdom of Koguryô, Yamato's powerful and longtime adversary. The fact that the legend only mentions Silla suggests that it was composed after Silla's unification of the peninsula and that the legend was addressing the concerns of the post-Saimei court.[34] Thus this portion of the legend cycle can be read as an idealized version of what the court wished had happened during Saimei's reign: unlike Saimei, Okinaga Tarashihime is portrayed as defeating Silla.

Jingū and Ōjin as Guardians of the Nation

One indicator of the degree to which the Nara court came to depend upon Jingū and Ōjin for protection from Silla can be seen in an incident that occurred during the Tempyō era, some seventy years after the death of Saimei. The *Shoki nihongi* records that in the ninth year of Tempyō (737) relations with Silla once again reached a crisis point.[35] At a military disadvantage, the Nara court could not afford an outbreak of hostilities. Instead the court responded by making offerings to a small group of shrines including the Kehi shrine in Tsunuga, the Sumiyoshi shrine in Chikuzen, the Kashi shrine in Chikuzen and two Hachiman shrines in Buzen.[36]

Crucially, all of these shrines were major institutional centers of the Jingū/Ōjin cult. It would thus appear that the importance of these shrines and the Jingū/Ōjin legend cycle for the Yamato court was enormous. Throughout the Nara period these shrines, which were accorded the highest rank and patronage by the Nara court, were the main cultic centers to which the court turned in times of crisis. They were also the shrines at which Jingū is said to have made offerings before her successful invasion of Silla. All of this suggests that in the seventy years between Saimei's death and the Tempyō crisis with Silla, the Jingū/Ōjin cult came to assume a pre-eminent role among the ancestral legends of the royal house. Jingū and Ōjin had assumed the role of guardian deities that would protect the interests of their descendants both at home and abroad.

Ironically, the area where the legends of the Jingū/Ōjin legend cycle were given ritual and institutional expression was the very area where local deities had taken their vengeance on the court of Saimei. With the exception of the Kehi shrine in Tsunuga, all of the Jingū/Ōjin cultic centers to which the court turned were located in Northern Kyūshū, not far from the site of Saimei's Asakura palace.[37] Yet because these ancestors were by no means the first deities to arrive in Northern Kyūshū, the development of their legend cycles almost certainly required accommodation with the cults of local deities and ancestors that already inhabited the region. All of this thus suggests that by the time of the writing of the *Nihon shoki* the Yamato court was convinced that the support of these deities was essential if it were to succeed in resisting the growing power of Silla. It also suggests that the introduction of the royal cult into Northern Kyūshū was inextricably linked with an accommodation between the cults of Kyūshū deities and the Yamato court.

Marriage, Adoption, and the Introduction of Regional Gods in Yamato

One byproduct of the heightened tensions between Yamato and Silla was a determination on the part of the Yamato court to strengthen its control over Northern Kyūshū in preparation for a possible invasion from the mainland. Following the defeat of Yamato forces at Paekchon in 663 the Yamato court began building a series of forts in the area in order to strengthen its first line of defense against naval assault. During this period royal governors also arrived from Yamato and the court system of ranks and administration was extended to include figures from prominent local lineages. As communication between center and periphery increased, people and goods moved between Yamato and Northern Kyūshū with increasing frequency. In the process local kinship groups were drawn more deeply into the sphere of politics of the Yamato court.[38]

The Yamato court also pursued two further strategies of control that involved creating kinship ties with regional elites; Yamato princes often took consorts from distant regions, and regional kinship groups were encouraged to figuratively adopt the children of high-ranking families. In this way, in return for providing support for the upbringing of a prince or princess, local lineages could hope to have a future patron at court as the child reached maturity. In such cases the child in question would often take the name of the adoptive kinship group, and it appears that the children of such adoptions were also expected to participate in the ancestral cults of their adoptive families.

How such familial politics influenced the construction of the royal line can be seen in the case of the Munakata, a kinship group from the Chikuzen area that provided a consort for one Prince Ōama sometime during the reign of Kōtoku. Prince Ōama is generally thought to have taken his name from the kinship group of that name that was based in the Ama district in Owari Province and that appears to have helped raise him.[39] The selection of the prince's consort and adoptive family appear to have been closely related; the Ōama and Munakata claimed common ancestry, and the two groups lived together in several areas in Kyūshū.[40]

There are numerous reasons for believing that the Munakata helped spur the Yamato court's interest in several of the most important shrines in Northern Kyūshū; they were, for instance, officiants not only at the Munakata shrine in Chikuzen Province, but also at numerous shrines across Kyūshū and along the Inland Sea as well.[41] For our purposes it is also highly significant that the Munakata also appear to have had extremely close relations with the Hata: family registers from 702 in the area of the Hachiman shrine, for instance, show that members of the Hata and Munakata lived together.[42] The close relations between the Munakata and the Hata were also manifested cultically in 701 when the Munakata deity was moved to the Matsuno'o shrine, a Hata cultic center in Yamashiro Province.

The Munakata's connection with Prince Ōama proved to be of tremendous importance for the shaping of the royal cult, for Prince Ōama later assumed the throne and was known to subsequent generations as Temmu *tennō* (reigned 673–686). One hint of Temmu's personal involvement with the Munakata cult can be found in his posthumous name, which incorporated characters from the names of the Munakata shrines.[43] Temmu's son by his Munakata consort, Prince Takechi also enjoyed widespread popularity at court and was regarded as a hero in the civil war that brought Temmu to the throne. As a result, the Munakata enjoyed the support of both the *tennō* and an important prince precisely at the time when the *Nihon shoki* and *Kojiki* were being written.[44] All of this suggests that the very same mechanisms that allowed for the introduction of the royal cult into Northern Kyūshū may also have allowed for the penetration of cults from Chikuzen into the Yamato area.

The Munakata Cult and Prince Kusakabe

The rise of the Munakata during Temmu's reign had far-reaching consequences for the orientation of the royal cult. Most notably, there are strong reasons for suspecting that Temmu's involvement with the Munakata deities helped bring Silla cults and deities into the heart of the emerging cultic tradition. Certainly links between the Munakata cult and Silla appear to have been strong: archeological evidence indicates that Munakata shrines and tombs in Northern Kyūshū and the island of Oki no Shima are virtual treasure troves of ritual implements from the Korean Peninsula and T'ang China.[45] The Munakata deities are also listed in the *Nihon shoki* as children of Susanoo no Mikoto, yet another deity who is said to have descended from heaven to Silla before crossing over to Yamato.[46]

Such connections with Silla can also be glimpsed in the Yūryaku chapter of the *Nihon shoki*, which states that the Munakata deities warned Yūryaku not to lead an attack on Silla. When Yūryaku nonetheless ordered such an attack with other generals in charge, the text states the Yamato forces were badly defeated. Although most Japanese scholars have interpreted this as indicating that the Munakata deities had assumed the role of guardians of the royal house from an early date, I am inclined to follow Taketani Hisao's suggestion that the text is implying that the defeat was the work of the Munakata deities.[47]

This vengeful aspect of the Munakata cult can also be seen in a legend from the Richū chapter of the *Nihon shoki* that shows that Munakata deities from Chikuzen could bully rulers more directly if they so chose. Here the immediate victim, however, is not the ruler but his consort:

> 5th year, Spring, 3rd month, 1st day. The three deities who dwell in Tsukushi appeared within the palace and said, "Why were our people taken from us? We will now disgrace you." At this [Richū] prayed, but made no offerings.

> 9th month, 19th day. There was a sound like a blast of wind calling out in the sky, saying "Prince of the Sword!" It also said "The daughter of the bird-fluttering Hata has been buried in Hasa!" And again it said "Sanakita Komotsu no Mikoto has been buried in Hasa!" Suddenly a minister came and said "The royal consort is dead." The *tennō* was greatly shocked, and immediately returned in his carriage.

> Winter, 10th month, 11th day. The royal consort was buried. After this the *tennō*, regretting that he had not pacified the gods' wrath and had thus caused the death of his consort, again sought after the offense [that caused the gods' anger].

> 6th year, Spring, 1st month, 6th day. Princess Kusaka Hatabi was named as Queen Consort.[48]

This legend is significant not only as yet another example of a Silla-affiliated deity from Chikuzen intimidating a Yamato ruler, but also because the legend concludes with with the accession of Princess Kusaka to the position of Queen Consort. The Kusakabe, in addition to being at the forefront of the early Shōtoku cult, were one of the most prominent kinship groups in Northern Kyūshū.[49] Because Prince Kusakabe, Temmu's son and heir apparent, was raised with the support of the Kusakabe Kishi, the text's conclusion with the elevation of the Princess Kusaka would thus suggest that this legend was most likely actively promoted during or after Temmu's reign, when the crown prince was a participant in the cults associated with the Kusakabe.[50]

Further evidence for post-Temmu development of the legend can be found in the text's reference to the ruler of Yamato as the "Prince of the Sword." I take this to be a reference to one of the royal regalia, the Kusanagi sword from the Atsuta shrine in Owari Province.[51] As we have already seen, this sword was believed to have caused the illness and death of Kusakabe's father Temmu, who had kept the sword close to him at all times. Yokota Ken'ichi, noting that Temmu was raised by the Ōama from Owari Province, has suggested that Temmu may have felt that his own well-being was directly related to the influence of the sword.[52] Ueda Masaaki notes that the Owari shrine is located in extremely close proximity to the Ōama's main base in the Ama district of Owari Province. He also notes that the Owari shrine was the kinship group shrine of the Owari Muraji, who in turn claimed common descent with the Ōama.[53] All of this thus suggests that the above legend was created in the post-Temmu era even as the Jingū/Ōjin legend cycle and the Shōtoku cult were also undergoing rapid development.

Because Prince Kusakabe and Prince Takechi were the two highest-ranking ministers in the government of Jitō *tennō* (reigned 690–697), sponsorship of the Munakata deities and other local cults from the Chikuzen area appears to have been a high priority for two major sub-lineages at the Yamato court. Although neither of these two princes assumed the throne, the influence of their lineages continued well beyond the writing of the *Nihon shoki*. Prince Kusakabe's descendants included several rulers, including his son, Mommu *tennō* (reigned 697–707), his daughter, Gemmei *tennō* (reigned 707–715), his grandson Shōmu *tennō* (reigned 724–749) and his great-granddaughter Kōken *tennō* (reigned 749–758 and 764–770).[54] Prince Takechi's son, Prince Nagaya, was a contender for the throne until his fall from power and subsequent suicide in 729.[55] Thus throughout the Nara period the Yamato court was dominated by lineages that both claimed Jingū as an ancestor and had a strong interest in promoting cultic centers in the Chikuzen area.[56] This suggests that the key to understanding the basis for the court's newly ascendant ancestral cult lies in the mythic roots of the Chikuzen cults themselves.

Ame no Hiboko, Akaru Hime, and Ōjin

As the Jingū/Ōjin cult was introduced to Northern Kyūshū it acquired a new set of resonances based upon local legends and even legends of sacred kingship with roots in the Korean Peninsula. One hint as to the means by which immigrant lineages and their ancestral cults may have influenced this process can be seen in an account from the *Chikuzen fudoki* (*Records of the Customs and Lands of Chikuzen*) that depicts the local paramount of the Ito district of Chikuzen welcoming the ruler Chūai to the region. Because of Ito's location on the coast of the Eastern/Japan Sea in close proximity to the Korean Peninsula, it was for centuries an important site of cultural interchange between Yamato and the Korean kingdoms. While few people today would accept the text's account of the penetration of Yamato political influence in this region, the legend nonetheless sheds important light on the process by which the royal cult reached an accommodation with local paramounts and their ancestors:

> Ito district. Of old, when Itote, the ancestor of the Ito Agatanushi,
> heard that the *tennō* who ruled from the palace at Toyoura in Anato
> [Chūai] had come to attack the *kumaso* in Tsukushi, he sailed out
> to greet the *tennō* in a boat with a multi-branched *sakaki* tree. . . .
> When he was asked who he was he replied: "I am a descendant of
> Hiboko, who descended from heaven to the top of Mount Oro in
> the land of Koguryô."[57]

In addition to illustrating the prominence of immigrant lineages in this part of Chikuzen, this legend also appears to have been designed at least in part as a result of cultic and social disruptions resulting from the extension of Yamato control over the region: here, a local paramount is shown explicitly affirming the legitimacy of the Yamato ruler's claims over the region even as he cites his own ancestral pedigree from across the sea. Thus, this legend appears to have been cast in much the same mold as other legends that we have already seen that feature immigrant ancestors arriving in the Japanese islands and hailing the Yamato ruler as a sage.[58]

Perhaps most crucially for our purposes, however, this legend also suggests that the figure of Ame no Hiboko was an important element in this process of cultural negotiation. Ame no Hiboko, as we have already noted, was none other than the founding ancestor of Jingū's distaff lineage. Here, his descendant is shown pledging his loyalty to Jingū's husband and Ōjin's father Chūai. Thus we have not simply a descendant of an immigrant ancestor hailing a Yamato ruler, but rather an explicit, and extensive, genealogical linkage between the Yamato ruler and the local paramount.

The *Kojiki* account of why Ame no Hiboko decided to come to Yamato in turn provides further clues for understanding how the cults of Jingū and Ōjin put down roots amidst local deities from Northern Kyūshū and Silla:

> In the land of Silla there was a pond called "Agunuma." On the bank of the pond there was a poor young girl who was napping. As she was doing so the sun sparkled like a rainbow and penetrated her private parts. There was also a poor man there who thought this strange and so constantly observed her actions. Now, from the time of her nap the girl became pregnant, and she gave birth to a red jewel. At this, the poor man who had been observing her begged her for the jewel, which he thereafter he always kept tied around his waist.
>
> This man had a rice field in a valley. When he loaded food and drink for the field workers upon an ox and brought it into the valley, he met Ame no Hiboko, the son of the ruler of the country. [Ame no Hiboko] then asked the man "Why are you bringing this ox loaded with food and drink into the valley? You will surely kill the ox and eat it." He then seized the man and was going to put him in prison, when the man answered, saying "I wasn't going to kill the ox. I was just bringing food for the laborers in the field." However, [Ame no Hiboko] would still not release him. Therefore the man undid the jewel that was tied around his waist and offered it to the prince, who then released the man.
>
> [Ame no Hiboko] then took the jewel [home]. When he placed it beside his bed it turned into a beautiful young woman. He immediately married her and she became his chief wife. Now, the young woman would constantly make all sorts of delicacies that she would feed to her husband. When the prince therefore grew arrogant and

scolded his wife, she said "I am not a woman who should be wife to you. I will go to the land of my ancestors." She then secretly got into a small boat and fled [to the Japanese islands], where she stopped in Naniwa. *This is the deity called Akaru Hime, who resides in the Himegoso shrine in Naniwa.*[59]

This legend is of immediate note for several reasons. Most obviously, it further highlights the penetration of local immigrant deities within the royal cult by establishing Akaru Hime as both the wife of Ame no Hiboko and as the deity of the Himegoso shrine in Naniwa. As the daughter of the Sumiyoshi deities that gave Ōjin dominion over the Korean Peninsula, Akaru Hime thus represents another important link between immigrant deities such as Ame no Hiboko, on the one hand, and the royal line on the other.

Equally importantly, however, the legend of Akaru Hime's advent to the Japanese islands is also an excellent illustration of the extensive geographic overlap that existed between the figures of Akaru Hime and Ame no Hiboko on the one hand and Jingū and Ōjin on the other. As Jingū came to be worshipped within the precincts of the Sumiyoshi shrine in Naniwa, for instance, the Jingū/Ōjin cult perforce came into close proximity with the Himegoso shrine and the immigrant lineages that sustained the cults of Akaru Hime and Ame no Hiboko. This pattern was repeated in Kyūshū, where Ōjin took up residence in the Hachiman shrine in Chikuzen Province in the midst of several cultic centers dedicated to the worship of Akaru Hime. Crucially, each of these areas was populated by immigrant lineages from the Korean Peninsula.[60] It thus seems fair to speculate that, even if such linkages were not done by design, the close geographic proximity of these cults would have facilitated interactions between the cults of immigrant deities and royal ancestors such as Jingū and Ōjin.

The potential significance of such interactions becomes apparent once we recall that Ame no Hiboko himself is said to have been a Silla prince and, therefore, a member of the royal lineage of Silla. To see how that heritage might have influenced the Ame no Hiboko and Ōjin legend cycles, consider the following extremely suggestive legend of T'arhae, the fourth king of Silla. The legend as it is recounted in the *Samguk sagi* (*Historical Records of the Three Kingdoms*), the oldest historical chronicle of the Korean kingdoms, is as follows:

T'arhae was born in the country of Tap'ana. That country is one thousand *ri* northeast of Yamato. Of old, the king of that country married the queen of a country of women. She became pregnant for seven years, and gave birth to a large egg, at which time the King said:

"A human being born from an egg is an inauspicious omen. Throw it away." But the queen could not bear to simply throw it away, and so she wrapped the egg in a silk cloth and placed it along with some treasures in a box and set it floating upon the sea, where she lost sight of it. . . . It thereupon floated to the coast of Ajinp'o . . . where an old woman picked it up. When she opened the box, there was a small boy inside.[61]

Mishina Shōei and others have demonstrated that this legend illustrates a common motif of the nation-founding legends of the Korean kingdoms wherein a child of the sun who is "hatched" from an egg is sent floating on the sea until he reaches a kingdom that has been promised to him. In the Ame no Hiboko/Akaru Hime legend cycle we find at least part of this motif repeated as Akaru Hime, apparently the daughter of the sun god, crosses over to Yamato from Silla after "hatching" from a stone that Ame no Hiboko has metaphorically incubated for an evening.[62]

Perhaps even more importantly, for our purposes, the Ame no Hiboko and T'arhae legend cycles, when read together, shed important light on the means by which the Jingū/Ōjin legend corpus took root in Northern Kyūshū and was thereby transformed. One example of this can be seen in the following legend from the *Chikuzen fudoki* detailing the circumstances and location of Ōjin's birth:

> Ito-ken, Kou no hara. There are two stones . . . white, hard and round as if they had been worn smooth. The people of the area say that when Okinaga Tarashihime [Jingū] wished to lead her army to attack Silla, as she was reviewing the troops, the child in her womb began to move. At that time, she took the two stones, put them in her loins beneath her skirt and proceeded to go and attack Silla. On the day of her victorious return she arrived in Umino and gave birth to the prince. Because of this, this place is called "Umino ["Birth Field]."[63]

One clue as to the sources of this legend can be found in the cultic geography of the text; here we are told that Ōjin's mother Jingū gave birth to the prince at the very site where Chūai was said to have been hailed by Ame no Hiboko's descendant upon the Yamato ruler's entry into the region. It would thus appear that the text is explicitly concerned to inscribe the figure of Ōjin into a cultic setting already occupied by the cult of Ame no Hiboko. As we have already seen, such geographic overlap appears to have typified the relations between the cults of Jingū and Ōjin on the one hand and immigrant deities such as Akaru Hime and Ame no Hiboko on the other. Just as cultic centers for both Ōjin and Ame no Hiboko put down roots in the very same village in the Ito district of Chikuzen Province, so too did the figure of Jingū come to be worshipped alongside the purported parents of Akaru Hime in the Sumiyoshi shrines in Kyūshū and Naniwa. Indeed, by the early Heian period even Ōjin's ill-fated father Chūai eventually took up residence as a deity at the Kehi Shrine in Tsunuga, the very shrine that housed Akaru Hime's other purported husband, the immigrant deity Tsunuga Arashito.[64]

Such geographic overlap appears to have in turn helped stimulate thematic overlap within the respective legend cycles of these deities. In the *Chikuzen fudoki* narrative we find such motifs as the worship of sacred stones, the miraculous birth of a prince, a journey across the sea, and the arrival in a kingdom that the child is destined to inherit. All of these motifs are entirely consistent with both the legend of T'arhae's birth as well as the legends of immigrant deities such as Ame no Hiboko, Tsunuga Arashito, Akaru Hime and Sukuna Bikona no Mikoto. Just as Akaru Hime is said to have crossed over the sea from Silla after Ame no Hiboko metaphorically incubated her for an evening as a stone, here we are told that Ōjin was miraculously born after his mother removed two "white, hard and round" stones from her loins immediately after Jingū has crossed over the sea from Silla.[65]

Conclusion: Ancestors, Violence and the Politics of Erasure

All of this thus suggests that the cults of such deities as Ame no Hiboko, Akaru Hime, Tsunuga Arashito, T'arhae and others were important sources for the basic structure of the Jingū/Ōjin legend cycle. In addition to substantial geographic and thematic overlap, by the time of the composition of the *Nihon shoki* these cults exhibited extensive connections in a number of registers. Genealogically, the court chronicles state that Ame no Hiboko was the founding ancestor of Jingū's distaff lineage while his wife Akaru Hime was worshipped as the daughter of the same Sumiyoshi deities that granted Ōjin dominion over Silla. Politically, Ame no Hiboko's descendent, the local Chikuzen paramount Ito Agatanushi, was represented as acknowledging the authority of Jingū's husband, the Yamato ruler Chūai. Perhaps most dramatically, as we saw in chapter 2, Ōjin's relations with Akaru Hime's husband Tsunuga Arashito were said to be so close that the Ōjin even adopted the name of the deity during the prince's coming of age ceremony. Such varied and extensive links all suggest that to a remarkable degree these cults both literally and metaphorically occupied the same cultic terrain. It would thus appear that the very same kinship groups that were at the forefront of the early Shōtoku cult also played a major role in the formation of yet another major bulwark of the royal cult. Once again the result seems to have been that an insecure Yamato court defined itself in terms of the myths and cults associated with immigrant gods and kings from across the sea.

It is tempting to simply conclude from all of this that kinship groups such as the Miyake and Hata exerted extensive influence over the development of the royal cult. Yet the points of overlap between the cults of Shōtoku, Akaru Hime, Sukuna Bikona no Mikoto, Ame no Hiboko, Jingū and Ōjin suggest something even more astonishing; that a small cluster of immigrant kinship groups exerted a remarkable degree of influence across a wide spectrum of religious activity in Asuka and Nara Japan.

The cultic influence of these groups, in turn, highlights a broader point concerning the mechanics of myth and power in pre-modern Japan. As we have seen repeatedly in the previous pages, the construction of each of these legends was closely bound up with issues of social control and resistance. We have also repeatedly seen that the process of constructing lineage, cult or legend in early Japan was inextricably linked with a process of erasure predicated upon the use of violence or other mechanisms of social control.

It thus seems likely that the success of kinship groups such as the Hata and Miyake in the cultic arena may have been due at least in part to their central role in estate administration, canal and roadway construction and textual production—all key elements in the exercise of power. Through their prominence in the formation and administration of royal estates and waterways these groups were able to transmit the royal cult to regions such as Northern Kyūshū, thereby aiding the royal house in obtaining the support of once hostile deities and lineages. At the same time they also played a major role in the construction of the royal lineage and the ancestral legends upon which so much of the royal cult was based. As they helped define the character and cultic expression of the *tennō*'s ancestors, they also played a major role in shaping royal house's heritage and thus authority.

Yet kinship groups such as the Miyake and Hata did not stand apart from this process of appropriation and erasure. In the end, the lack of an independent power base on the part of these kinship groups led to the erasure of their contributions to the mythic and ritual heritage of Japan. By the end of the Nara period, the main deity at the Usa Hachiman shrine in Buzen Province was no longer thought of as an immigrant deity, but rather as the spirit of Ōjin. Similarly, the Sumiyoshi shrine in Naniwa soon housed the spirit of Jingū, while Chūai took up residence at the Kehi shrine in Tsunuga. Thus father, mother and son came to dominate the main ports of entry into the Japanese islands, gatekeepers for an increasingly defensive and inward-looking court and nation in the throes of self-invention.

Seen against this background the cult of Shōtoku thus appears to have been one of a number of royal ancestral cults that were propagated by immigrant kinship groups such as the Miyake and the Hata. As we have seen in this and previous chapters, these kinship groups played a major role in transforming conceptions of nation, kingship, millennialism, afterlife and ancestry both for the Yamato court and for the broader populace across the Japanese islands. In the following chapters I will examine how some of the most pressing concerns of these kinship groups—conceptions of sagehood, death rituals, rites of purification and the resurrection of the dead—helped shape the parameters of not only the Shōtoku cult, but also a much wider range of religious discourse for centuries to come.

4

Ethnicity, Sagehood, and the Politics of Literacy in the Early Shōtoku Cult

According to the *Nihon shoki*, in 513, three scholars from the Korean kingdom of Paekche arrived in the Japanese islands for the purpose of promoting literacy and knowledge of the Chinese classics.[1] Although this event has been given surprisingly little notice in histories of early Japanese thought and religion, the transmission of the Chinese textual tradition to Yamato was in many ways of far greater importance than the transmission of Buddhist icons and scriptures that purportedly commenced shortly thereafter. While nobody would take the *Nihon shoki*'s chronology at face value, from at least Kamitsumiya's lifetime down to the writing of the *Nihon shoki*, teachers of the Chinese classics and Buddhist monks from the three Korean kingdoms were a continuous presence in Yamato; as a result, the narrative structures and tropes of Chinese historical and divinatory texts soon became central elements in the political discourse of the Yamato court elite.[2]

Within the *Nihon shoki*, the figure most closely associated with the advent of the Chinese textual tradition was Prince Shōtoku. Virtually alone among figures for this period he is singled out as having studied under tutors from the Korean Peninsula.[3] Shōtoku's biography in the text states that he was well versed in both Buddhist scriptures and in the Chinese classics; sage wisdom was matched by mastery of the textual tradition inspired by Chinese sage kings:

> He was able to speak from birth and he had the wisdom of a sage. When he grew up he could hear the suits of ten people at once and evaluate them without error. He was able to know the future in advance. Further, he learned the inner [Buddhist] teachings from the Koguryô monk Hyeja and the

outer classics from the learned scholar Kakka. In both areas he attained equal mastery.[4]

This connection between sagehood and Chinese learning is reiterated elsewhere in the *Nihon shoki*. Recall the text's account of Shōtoku's death, where Shōtoku is again presented as a paragon of continental learning:

At this time the Koguryô monk Hyeja heard of the death of the Crown Prince Kamitsumiya and he grieved greatly. He therefore held a feast for Buddhist monks in honor of the prince. On the day when he personally expounded upon the scriptures, he made a vow, saying: "In the land of Yamato there was a sage known as the Prince Kamitsumiya no Toyotomimi. Born in the land of Yamato, he was truly blessed by heaven with the virtues of a sage. Having penetrated the depths of the three sage founders he continued the plans of the former sages. He reverenced the Three Treasures and saved the people from distress. He was truly a great sage. Now the prince has died. I, although from a different land, was in my heart closely bound to him. Now that I am alone, what benefit is there in living? [Therefore] next year, on the fifth day of the second month, I will certainly die. In this way we shall meet in the Pure Land and together work for the salvation of all sentient beings." Now on the [foretold] day Hyeja died. At this people said to one another "Prince Kamitsumiya was not the only sage. Hyeja was also a sage."[5]

Although Shōtoku is thought of today primarily in the context of the development of the Japanese Buddhist tradition, these passages suggest that an eclectic mix of Buddhist and Confucian models of sagehood was used to construct the figure of the paradigmatic sage prince. Here the Buddhist monk Hyeja lauds Shōtoku for continuing the work of Chinese sage kings even as he declares that Shōtoku has been reborn in the Pure Land. Perhaps even more striking, however, is the emphasis each passage places upon divination and the ability to foretell the future. Virtue, wisdom, and divine favor in early Yamato were all manifested and confirmed through supernatural omens. For that reason, all would-be sages and sage kings in early Yamato paid close attention to the arts of divination.

One further, equally striking aspect of these passages is their emphasis on Shōtoku's close relationship with his teacher, the sage counselor Hyeja. Both do far more than simply present Shōtoku as a sage possessed of superhuman abilities of perception, intellect, and cultural/religious acumen. Rather, each text seems specifically designed to highlight Shōtoku's spiritual connection with the Koguryô monk. In both texts, the sagehood of the Yamato prince is inextricably bound up with the status of his teacher from across the sea; indeed, the ties that bind them are shown to be stronger than even death itself.

This chapter will explore the role of ethnicity and hermeneutic authority in the formation of the conceptions of the sage king (*hijiri no kimi*) and the sage counselor (*sakashihito*) in seventh-century Yamato. I will focus on the role of a cluster of immigrant kinship groups associated with the early Shōtoku cult in the dissemination of Chinese historical and divinatory texts over which they claimed unrivalled mastery. Underlying this project will be two premises concerning the conception and exercise of power. The first of these is derived from Foucault's dictum that embedded within every system of power is a system of knowledge that both organizes and makes meaningful the formation and use of that power.[6] In what follows, I propose to examine how the introduction of a system of knowledge—in this case Chinese historical and divinatory classics—produced a host of unforeseen cultic and political consequences at the Yamato court. We shall see that in the process the immigrant kinship groups at the heart of the early Shōtoku cult helped initiate new understandings of the ruler's identity that facilitated the emergence of new conceptions of political and religious authority. In this regard it is highly significant that sovereigns of the period adopted for themselves the title of *tennō*, which was firmly rooted in ancient conceptions of the pole star within the Chinese astrological tradition.

The second premise underlying this project stems from the assumption that the primary significance of the introduction of the Chinese textual tradition was not necessarily located within the texts themselves. In what follows, I will focus instead on the power relations engendered by the dependence of the Yamato court elite upon immigrant kinship groups with vastly superior levels of control over and access to the Chinese textual tradition. Once we adopt this focus, it becomes possible to see how issues of textual and political authority in the period were entangled with issues of ethnicity, as immigrant kinship groups served as gatekeepers and custodians of the continental textual tradition and the political/cultural manifestations that it engendered.

Governance and the Diffusion of Textuality

One of the most compelling illustrations of the process just discussed can be seen in the composition of the *Nihon shoki* itself. As we noted in chapter 1, the prominence of immigrant lineages from the early Shōtoku cult in the composition and editing of the *Nihon shoki* reflected a long-standing dominance by immigrant kinship groups in virtually all matters related to literacy and the continental textual tradition. This linkage between ethnic affiliation and literacy was even more pronounced during Kamitsumiya's lifetime, when Buddhist priests from Paekche served as tutors and counselors for students who were drawn in large part from a pool of immigrant kinship group families. The effects of this process, however, soon transformed the mechanics of governance in early Yamato; by the time Temmu assumed the throne in 673, a functioning bureaucratic structure was possible in which officials from regions throughout the Japanese islands could communicate in writing and routinely record administrative tasks and expenditures.[7]

The influence of immigrant kinship groups did not stop, however, with the simple mechanics of administration; they also changed the fundamental premises by which the exercise of political power was made possible and in terms of which it was understood. One of the most important ways in which they did so was through the introduction of continental forms of ritual and divination. These are attributed in the *Nihon shoki* to the Paekche monk Kwallǔk, who was noted mainly for having introduced to the court continental techniques of astrology and magic:

> Suiko 10.10. The Paekche monk Kwallǔk arrived and presented [as tribute] books on calendar-making, astronomy and geography as well as books on invisibility and other divinatory arts. At this time three or four students were chosen to study with Kwallǔk... All studied until they had attained proficiency.[8]

This interest in continental divinatory texts and techniques continued throughout the pre-modern period. If the *Nihon shoki* may be believed, even during the Suiko court these techniques appear to have occupied a position of paramount importance within the Buddhist clergy; Kwallǔk, for example, is said to have later been named as the first head of the Buddhist clergy of Yamato.[9]

The Yamato court's interest in continental techniques of calendar making and astronomy was doubtless also fueled by conceptions of kingship in Yamato that existed prior to the widespread diffusion of the Chinese textual tradition. During Kamitsumiya's lifetime, Yamato rulers appear to have derived much of their authority from claims to a special relationship with the sun. This can be seen, ironically, from accounts in Chinese court histories that record sporadic contacts between the Chinese and Yamato. The *Sui shu* (*The Sui History*), a Chinese court history that summarizes accounts of diplomatic missions between the Yamato court and the Sui dynasty during the reign of the Yamato ruler Suiko, offers particularly valuable insights into the Yamato court as it existed during Kamitsumiya's lifetime. The text's account of the first Yamato mission to the Sui reports:

> The envoy reported thus: "The King of Wa [Yamato] deems heaven to be his elder brother and the sun, his younger. Before the break of dawn he attends the court, and, sitting cross-legged, listens to appeals. Just as soon as the sun rises, he ceases these duties, saying that he hands them over to his brother.[10]

This connection between Yamato rulers and the sun appears to have translated etymologically into the reading that the Japanese gave to the Chinese character for sage: *hijiri*. The earliest verifiable use of the term uses the characters for "sun" (*hi*) and "to know," (*shiru*). This second character, in addition to the sense of "to know" also carried the meaning of "to master" or "to govern."[11] Thus, from a very early date, kingship and sage wisdom in Yamato appear to have been linked with the sun.

Set against this horizon of reception, the introduction of Chinese astronomical and calendar making techniques was important for two reasons: first, it helped produce a revolution in the cosmological and political beliefs prevalent in Yamato. Perhaps even more importantly, it also led to the creation of a restricted group of practitioners with competence in these techniques. This in turn helped create a class of intellectuals with unchallenged control over a body of knowledge that was believed to be crucial for the exercise of power.

For Yamato rulers seeking to expand the range of their authority, the conceptions of sage kingship and divination found in the Chinese textual tradition also offered two important advantages. The cosmological and divinatory techniques entering Yamato at this time presumed a highly centralized governmental structure centered on the person of the Son of Heaven. The conceptual framework of the sage king thus facilitated the creation of political ties between ruler and minister based upon conceptions of loyalty and deference that transcended kinship and regional limitations. Second, continental divination techniques promised not only accurate prediction of future events but also served as a vehicle for proclaiming Heaven's favor with rulers of great virtue.[12] In effect, the Chinese textual tradition allowed Yamato rulers to lay claim to a new type of cosmic sanction that could be verified for all to see.

There was along with this, however, one significant danger for any Yamato ruler claiming the status of sage ruler—by relying upon propitious omens and placing the virtue of the ruler at the center of political discourse, Yamato rulers also opened themselves up to potential critique. The concept of the sage king rested on the belief that Heaven would favor a ruler of great virtue and wisdom. This differed in a fundamental way from later claims of royal divinity; Heaven's favor could be lost if the ruler failed to attend to the duties of state. In China, such critiques served as one of the main checks on the Son of Heaven's power; indeed, the authority to make such critiques was the *quid pro quo* extracted by Chinese intellectuals for supporting would-be rulers. With the adoption of this intellectual framework in Yamato, the hermeneutics of divination soon became an important arena for the contestation of power. No faction that aimed to seize power could ignore the political uses of omens and divination, nor could they neglect the textual tradition and intellectuals with whom authority for interpreting omens rested.[13]

Divination and the Hermeneutics of Power

Just how important omens and divination could be for political discourse is made abundantly clear in the *Nihon shoki* account of the period following Kwallŭk's purported arrival at the Yamato court. In this section of the text we find an explosion of entries in the *Nihon shoki* that record omens portending political disaster.[14] Tamura, noting that the text also states that Kwallŭk took up residence in the Soga kinship group temple Asukadera, has therefore suggested that the Soga used Kwallŭk's divinatory knowledge as a political tool with which to criticize the ruler Suiko.[15]

Tamura further argues that Suiko's successor, Jomei, eventually broke the Soga monopoly on divination by turning to the monk Min for assistance in recording and interpreting omens. Min, a member of an immigrant kinship group that claimed Chinese descent, had been sent by Jomei to T'ang China for study as a scholar-monk. Upon his return, he was accorded enormous deference by Jomei and his successors, whom Min rewarded with favorable interpretations of omens. The prominence of figures such as Kwallŭk and Min thus suggests the rise of a new type of intellectual in Yamato with the hermeneutic authority not only to interpret omens but also, in effect, to pass judgment on the ruler himself.[16]

Throughout the rest of the century and beyond, Yamato rulers took a keen interest in the discovery and interpretation of omens—over fifty such omens are listed in the *Nihon shoki* alone for the period dating to the reign of Jitō *tennō* [reigned 690–697].[17] We shall see shortly that several of these entries are intimately connected with the Silla immigrant kinship groups that helped create the early Shōtoku cult.

In fashioning a new role for themselves as keepers of the Chinese textual tradition, immigrant kinship groups also built upon pre-existing models that were rooted in Chinese political and hermeneutical traditions. From at least the Han dynasty onward the "discovery" of omens portending the waxing or waning of dynastic lineages was an essential element in the authentication of any ruler. Howard Wechsler notes:

> By Han times there arose a belief that Heaven not only could grant or revoke a Mandate to rule, but also constantly supervised a ruler's administration by means of its power to reveal auspicious or calamitous omens. Heaven-sent anomalies of nature—comets, eclipses, droughts, floods, earthquakes, and the like—were especially intended to warn the ruler that he was in danger of losing the Mandate. . . According to the doctrines of *t'ien-ming* and of Heaven-sent portents, there was a mutual interaction between Heaven and man, especially between Heaven and ruler. Such doctrines gave rise, during Han times and afterward, to incessant and vocal warnings by counselors that rulers had to practice virtue and avoid idleness . . . all would-be dynastic founders and insecure rulers searched hungrily for any phenomena that could be interpreted as signs that they indeed were the rightful occupiers of the throne.[18]

The importance of divination in the Chinese political process if anything intensified during the centuries following the Han as the Buddhist ideal of the Dharma King augmented Confucian notions of the sage king, who rules with the mandate of Heaven. Propitious omens were used to demonstrate not only the virtue of the Son of Heaven but also the vast karmic merit accumulated by the ruler both during his reign and in former lives. By the Sui dynasty, rulers were no longer content to simply wait for the appearance of auspicious omens. Sui Yang-ti, for instance, had himself proclaimed a "Bodhisattva of Absolute Control," while his father, Sui Wen-ti organized a nationwide search for stupas and relics from the Buddhist Dharma King Asoka.[19] Omens continued to play an important role in the contestation of power throughout the period;

Wechsler notes that the end of the Sui dynasty and subsequent rise of the T'ang was marked by multiple claims of auspicious omens on the part of both the Sui and T'ang.[20]

Because envoys and exchange students from Yamato visited the Sui court at this time, it is highly likely that the Yamato court was aware of Sui Yang-ti's program. Evidence for this can be seen from the fact that the letter sent by the Yamato court along with the first Yamato mission to Sui China addressed Sui Yang-ti as "Bodhisattva Son of Heaven."[21] Soon thereafter, Yamato rulers apparently began to adopt similar strategies for augmenting their political and religious authority; within the *Nihon shoki* we find numerous entries from roughly this period stating that omens of sage rulership were offered to Yamato rulers from far-flung reaches of the realm. How such omens functioned in the religious and political theater of the court becomes clear once we ask who within the text offers such omens and who interprets them.

The Hakuji *and the Early Shōtoku Cult*

One of the most dramatic illustrations of the importance of the role of omens in court politics can be found in a *Nihon shoki* account for the year 650, less than thirty years after the death of Prince Kamitsumiya and barely twenty years after the establishment of the T'ang dynasty. In the second month of that year, we are told, a white pheasant, or *hakuji*, was presented to the court of the Yamato ruler Kōtoku by Kusakabe Muraji Shikibu, an official in Anato in western Honshū.[22]

The text's assertion that this bird was offered to the court by a member of the Kusakabe kinship group is of immediate note because it suggests that kinship groups associated with the early Shōtoku cult were involved in constructing this new ideological pillar for Yamato rulers. As we have already seen, the Kusakabe were a prominent kinship group based in Naniwa with close affiliations with Shitennōji and with such kinship groups as the Abe, Hata, Kishi, and Miyake. Such affiliations are crucial for understanding the politics of the omen because Kōtoku's reign was also an early peak in the power of the Abe and these same immigrant kinship groups; Kōtoku's Minister of the Left—the highest post in the land—was Abe no Uchimaro. Uchimaro was also the father of Kōtoku's chief consort and the maternal grandfather of the crown prince. If the *Nihon shoki* may be believed, it would appear that these connections between Kōtoku and the Naniwa kinship groups were bolstered by Kusakabe Muraji Shikibu's presentation of the *hakuji*; the following year, Kōtoku moved his capital to Naniwa, where Uchimaro had already led a ceremony installing a set of Buddhist images at Shitennōji.[23] Thus the presentation of omens of sage rulership may have emerged at the heart of political discourse just as the Abe and their affiliated immigrant kinship groups hit their first peak of power.[24]

How the presentation of omens such as the *hakuji* could affect the political and religious discourses of the day can be seen from the text's account of the omen's reception and interpretation. Confronted with the anomalous omen, the court is said to have asked the opinion of dignitaries from Paekche, members of the ecclesial bureaucracy, other foreign dignitaries, and the priest Min for help in interpreting its meaning. After each of these groups refer to historical precedents for the appearance of such an omen in the dynastic records of Koguryô and China, the final word is given to the monk Min, who is unequivocal about the omen's true meaning:

> This is termed an auspicious omen and there is sufficient [justification] to treat it as a rare object. I have heard that when a ruler's influence flows throughout the four quarters, then white pheasants will be seen. . . . When a ruler is a humane sage, then they will also appear. During the time of Chou Cheng-wang, a family from Yüeh-shang offered a white pheasant as tribute. . . . Also, in the first year of the Hsien-ning era during the reign of Chin Wu-ti, one was seen in Sung-tzu. Thus this is an auspicious omen. A general amnesty should be granted.[25]

According to the text, in order to mark this great event, the name of the reign year was then changed to *Hakuji* and a rite proclaiming the divine sanction for the sage ruler of Yamato was performed in the capital. After the entire court turned out for a procession of senior ministers and princes bearing a palanquin carrying the bird to the Vermilion Gate at the palace, a senior minister is said to have offered the following congratulatory address:

> Because Your Majesty governs the realm with pure and serene virtue, a white pheasant has come out of the West. This is a sign that Your Majesty will continue for a thousand autumns and ten thousand years to peacefully govern the Great Land of Eight Islands of the four quarters. It is the wish of your Ministers, officials and the people that they may serve [you] with the utmost zeal and loyalty.[26]

Lest anyone fail to get the point of the ceremony, the *Nihon shoki* recounts a speech purportedly given by Kōtoku summing up the significance of the event:

> When a sage ruler appears in the world and rules the Empire, Heaven is responsive to him, and manifests favorable omens. In ancient times, during the reign of Ch'eng-wang of the Chou dynasty, a ruler of the Western land, and again in the time of Ming-ti of the Han Dynasty, white pheasants were seen. In this our land of Japan, during the reign of Homuda *tennō*, a white crow made its nest in the Palace. In the time of the Ōsazaki *tennō*, a Dragon horse appeared in the West. This shows that from ancient times until now, there have been many cases of auspicious omens appearing in response to virtuous rulers.[27]

This event highlights several salient features concerning the role of omens in the political discourse of the period. If the *Nihon shoki* may be believed, by 650 the Yamato court had apparently adopted the Confucian language of sage kingship as a means of expressing and defining its authority. This would have in effect placed the figure of the ruler within the context of continental narratives recording the activities of ancient Chinese sage kings. This in turn would have profoundly altered the political context in which literacy and textual interpretation were situated; by claiming a status equivalent to that of sage rulers from the Chinese past, Yamato rulers would also have ensured a place within political discourse for the study and interpretation of (continental) historical texts in which those sage rulers were represented. This would thus suggest that by 650 the use of omens as a source of political authority and political critique had become a basic element in the contestation of power.

If we assume that the text cannot be read as a straightforward account of events in the seventh century, however, then the text would underscore the degree to which at the time of the composition of the *Nihon shoki* omens were used by several factions at court, including the Silla immigrant kinship groups at the center of the early Shōtoku cult. Indeed, if the editors of the *Nihon shoki* fabricated or embroidered an elaborate account of the presentation of an auspicious omen to Kōtoku, that in itself would strongly suggest that the significance of such auspicious omens was widely accepted at court. The fact that the text's editors chose to highlight the role of one of the lineages at the forefront of the early Shōtoku cult would also suggest that these lineages were considered highly plausible candidates for such activities.

Seen in this light, the *Nihon shoki* account of the presentation of the *hakuji* is perhaps most notable for its representation of the near-complete dependence of the court upon immigrant intellectuals for interpretations of omens indicating Heaven's favor or displeasure. Within the narrative members of immigrant kinship groups who are most familiar with continental historical texts and interpretive methodologies are in effect responsible for interpreting the will of Heaven and assessing the virtue of the Yamato monarch. We shall see shortly that such interpretation was a creative process through which new and distinctive conceptions of sage kingship and sagehood were fashioned.

Sage Kings, Counselors, and the Chinese Canon

The Chinese textual tradition promulgated by immigrant kinship groups in Yamato was itself the product of an intellectual class that saw itself as indispensable servants of Chinese rulers even as they served as a check on the power of those rulers.[28] The early Chinese philosophical tradition thus focused in large part on issues concerning the proper relations between the ruler and his ministers drawn from the intellectual class. These same intellectuals, in turn, were represented as the guardians of the textual tradition which constrained would-be despots in two ways: first, it offered normative guidelines for rulership; and second, this same tradition would pass judgment upon each ruler for the edification of future generations. It is instructive in this regard that Ch'in Shih-huang-ti, the first and last emperor to attempt to turn against the textual tradition itself, has been condemned for millennia as a despot.

After Ch'in Shih-huang-ti, Chinese rulers sought not to eliminate the Chinese textual heritage but rather to standardize and regulate it; henceforth sage rulers were depicted as guardians and regulators of the Chinese literary tradition. Thereafter, standardization and regulation became two of the most basic functions of rulership in China and Yamato. These functions played a central role even in Chinese conceptions of Buddhist kingship. From the fourth century onward, rulers frequently portrayed themselves as Dharma Kings who could regulate the Buddhist clergy and guard the orthodoxy of the Chinese Buddhist tradition.[29]

One result of these conceptions of sage rulership was the creation of a canon of authoritative texts that served as the basis for political and philo-sophical discourse. This in turn stimulated the rise of commentarial traditions based upon that canon. As the authority of the textual tradition became clearly demarcated, so, too, did mastery of the canon provide a mechanism for ap-propriating at least some of the canon's authority for the critique of past and contemporary events.

This dynamic of focused authority within the canon also invaded the texts that comprised the canon; just as certain texts were considered authoritative, so, too, did the words and actions of authoritative figures within these texts come to be considered without fault. These figures—sage kings and sage counselors—provided a starting point for post-Han commentators wishing to discuss the perennial issue of the proper standards for rulers and intel-lectuals.[30]

The Classification of Sages

The concept of the sage king (Ch: *sheng-wang*, *sheng-huang*, or *sheng-ti*; J: *hijiri no kimi*) appears to have originated in Han dynasty texts stressing the ap-pearance of omens reflecting Heaven's approval of legendary sage kings from the distant past. Divination and the conception of the sage king thus appear to have been linked from the beginning. For heuristic purposes, four types of sage ruler can be distinguished in the Chinese context. First are the "Three Sovereigns" (*san-huang*), three sage rulers who play an important role in the creation legends found in the *Shih-chi* (*Records of the Historian*), one of the most authoritative texts in the Chinese canon.[31] The text discusses the formation of Heaven and Earth and then immediately proceeds to describe the emergence of sage rulers for Heaven (*t'ien-huang*), Earth (*ti-huang*) and human society (*jen-huang*). Because the *Shih-chi* was one of the Five Classics that were taught by the Confucian scholars from Paekche, it is highly likely that the conceptions of sage kingship represented by these figures would have been among the first to disseminate in Yamato among those familiar with continental learning.[32]

The *Shih-chi* also details the activities of five sage rulers who played the role of culture-givers for humanity, teaching the uses of fire, agriculture, writing, and so on. These five were grouped together under the term "Five Thearchs" (*wu-ti*).[33] The currency and importance of *san-huang* and *wu-ti* are attested by the title assumed by the first Ch'in emperor, who called himself *huang-ti*. Rulers of China assumed this title thereafter.

The conceptual underpinnings for the language of sage kingship in ancient China lay primarily in classical Chinese texts that celebrated the virtue and wisdom of these legendary rulers. During the Six Dynasties period, the *san-huang wu-ti* were a basic element of political discourse. Taoists depicted them as sages possessing the secrets of divine rule and immortality. Confucians viewed them as models of benevolence and propriety who served to mediate the workings of Heaven and Earth. All agreed that as the sage ruler worked together with Heaven to bring order to human society, his actions resonated both with Heaven and the innate goodness at the core of each of his subjects.[34] A third group of seven sage rulers consisted of the founders and prominent rulers of three ancient dynasties. These rulers featured prominently in the thinking of Confucius and his successors, who sought the essence of sage kingship through the study and emulation of these rulers.

Finally, the founders of dynasties that post-dated Confucius also served as important models for the Yamato court. These rulers were never referred to as sage kings and were depicted in official histories of Chinese dynasties in terms that are more human than mythic. Nonetheless, the founders of the Ch'in and Han dynasties in particular appear to have enjoyed special status in the eyes of later generations not only in China but in seventh century Yamato as well. In this regard, it is noteworthy that the Yamato no Aya, the most powerful cluster of Paekche immigrant groups in seventh-century Yamato, claimed descent from the founder of the Han dynasty, and the Hata claimed descent from Ch'in Shih-huang-ti, the founder of the Ch'in dynasty.

Although classed well below the ancient sage kings, virtually all dynastic founders are also depicted in the Chinese histories as having access to supernatural support either through the favor of Heaven or the support of powerful deities. In addition, several are depicted as enjoying the support of sage ministers (*sheng-ch'en*), sage counselors (*hsien-hsiang*), or simply Wise Men (Ch: *hsien-jen*; J: *sakashihito*) who possessed extraordinary powers of magic and divination. Among the most famous such Wise Men were Chang Liang, a counselor to the first Han emperor, who was later depicted as a Taoist immortal, Chiang T'ai-kung, the famed counselor of the sage king Chou Wen-wang, and Kuan-tzu, the counselor of Ch'i Huan-kung.[35]

By the early Han dynasty, the conceptions of sage ruler (*sheng-huang*) and sage counselor had taken on a symbiotic role in which the sage counselor guaranteed the legitimacy of the ruler's Heavenly mandate through the bestowal of tokens of authority that had been manifested by Heaven.[36] Throughout the Six Dynasties period, rulers had themselves declared Buddhas, bodhisattvas, and Taoist sages by assorted clerics and would-be spiritual rulers of China. The importance of these titles is attested by the fact that they were known throughout East Asia. Recall, for instance, that when relations between Yamato and the Sui resumed during the period of Shōtoku's regency, the Yamato court addressed the Sui monarch as the "Bodhisattva Son of Heaven"—apparently in reference to the title "Bodhisattva of Absolute Control" that was conferred upon Sui Yang-ti by the T'ien-t'ai patriarch Chih-i.

By the time of the composition of the *Nihon shoki* in 720, these conceptions of sage kingship had gained widespread currency at the Nara court. Perhaps the most extended statement of such views can be found in the Seventeen-Article Constitution[37] attributed to Shōtoku. This text, which is filled with quotations and allusions from classical Chinese sources, represents the best statement on the concept of the sage ruler in early Yamato literature. The importance attached to this document by the time of the writing of the *Nihon shoki* can be seen from the inclusion of the entire text within the *Nihon shoki*. Although the *Nihon shoki* attributes authorship of the text to Shōtoku, it is far more prudent to treat it as reflecting the views of the immigrant kinship groups associated with the early Shōtoku cult. Even if we do accept the *Nihon shoki*'s rather dubious assertion that Kamitsumiya was the author of the text, the prince's approach to the Chinese textual tradition would doubtless have been greatly shaped by his immigrant teachers.

Ōno Tatsunosuke has analyzed the Constitution from the standpoint of its Chinese conceptual background. He concludes that, in addition to Buddhist influences, the text closely resembles the *Kuan-tzu*, an important apocryphal compilation from the fourth century that purports to record the teachings of the sage counselor Kuan-tzu.[38] This affinity with a text that claims to be the work of a Chinese sage counselor reflects the Constitution's pre-occupation with delineating the role of the counselors and ministers of Yamato rulers. The text contains five direct references to the concept of the sage ruler, virtually all of which emphasize the importance of the *sakashihito*:

> Regardless of their degree of urgency, if you meet a wise man, matters will by themselves become settled. For this reason the state will last throughout the ages and society will never be endangered. For this reason the sage kings of the past sought men to fill [ministerial] positions, and did not seek [ministerial] positions for men.[39]

The Constitution also highlights the role of the *sakashihito* as an indispensable element in rulership: "If the sage does not meet a sage counselor (*sakashihito*), then how shall he rule?"[40] Indeed, within the text, the *sakashihito* takes on a supernatural aura of only a slightly lower order than the sage king: "The chance to meet a man of wisdom [*sakashihito*] comes only once in five hundred years and it is difficult to meet one sage in a thousand years."[41]

Counselors of the Yamato Sage

This belief in the importance of the role of the *sakashihito* is also apparent in several accounts of events leading to the accession of Yamato rulers. The ruler Kimmei, for instance, is spoken of in the *Nihon shoki* in terms from the *Shih-chi*'s account of King Wen of Chou—thus Kimmei is judged to be worthy of the throne because he "treats the wise (*sakashihito*) with courtesy, and all day long neglects his food while he waits on others."[42] Although no one takes such passages to be literally true, they are nonetheless vital for our purposes because they suggest that by the time of the writing of the *Nihon shoki*, such sentiments were a basic part of the rhetoric of Yamato kingship.

The role of immigrant kinship groups in promoting this conception of the *sakashihito* as an indispensable element of rule can be clearly seen once we ask who were the "wise people" that Kimmei is said to have treated with such courtesy. This is also spelled out in the text:

When the *tennō* was young he had a dream in which someone said to him "If you favor a man called Hata no Ōtsuchi, then when you come of age you will surely possess the realm." When he woke up, he sent emissaries to search everywhere [for Hata no Ōtsuchi], and in Fukakusa Township in the Kii District of Yamashiro Province, they found him.[43]

Kimmei's dream appears to be based upon a similar legend in the *Shih-chi* in which the sage king Chou Wen-wang is told by a divination expert prior to a hunting trip that his catch for the day will be a (sage) counselor who will bring him the empire.[44] This supposition is supported by the fact that the *Nihon shoki* continues to refer to Kimmei in terms originally used in the *Shih-chi* that highlight Chou Wen-wang's respect for sages.[45] Thus the *Nihon shoki* appears to have modeled Kimmei more or less explicitly upon the sage king Chou Wen-wang, while the Hata ancestor Ōtsuchi plays a role akin to that of the sage counselor Chi'ang T'ai-kung, making possible Kimmei's accession.[46]

A closer look at the legend also reveals how immigrant kinship groups such as the Hata used the ideal of the *sakashihito* to weave their own ancestral cults into the basic fabric of Yamato kingship. The text continues:

When [Kimmei] awoke, he sent messengers out to search everywhere. In Fukakusa township in the Kii district of Yamashiro Province they found a man whose surname and name were the same as that of the dream. At this [Kimmei] was delighted through and through and he exclaimed "There has never been such a dream!" He then asked [Ōtsuchi] if anything [unusual] had happened to him. He answered "Nothing. However, when your servant was returning from a trading expedition to Ise I encountered two wolves on a mountain that were fighting and soiled with blood. I then dismounted from my horse, rinsed my mouth and hands and prayed to them, saying: "You are august deities but you delight in violence. If you should meet with a hunter, you would very quickly be captured." At this I stopped them from fighting and wiped and cleaned the blood from their fur. I then released them, having saved both of their lives." The *tennō* said "This must be your reward." Thereafter he kept [Ōtsuchi] close by his side and favored him anew each day, so that he eventually accumulated great wealth. When Kimmei ascended the throne, he appointed him to the Treasury.[47]

This legend highlights two important points regarding the role of the Hata in the construction of the conception of the Yamato sage king. First, it shows how the Hata and other such immigrant kinship groups used the conception of the sage ruler to promote local cults and heroes with whom they were closely affiliated. The notion of the *sakashihito* proved to be a boon, not a challenge, to pre-existing local cults; in this case, the legend appears to be related to be closely related to the Fushimi Inari shrine, a Hata cultic center in Fukukusa.[48] Second, unlike Chinese sage counselors such as Chiang T'ai-kung, Hata no Ōtsuchi's abilities are mainly sacerdotal; his good fortune is "undoubtedly a reward" for his propitiation of two "august deities." We shall see shortly that the ancestral deities of Silla immigrant kinship groups frequently doubled in the *Nihon shoki* as *sakashihito* for the sage rulers of ancient Yamato.

The preceding legend, with its suggestion of the importance of the *sakashihito* as kingmaker, appears to be closely related to the hermeneutic authority of the immigrant kinship groups that declared Yamato rulers to be sage kings. A close reading of other legends that depict Yamato rulers as sage kings suggests that such rulers were almost always paired with a second sage to hail the ruler's virtue. This pairing of sages was in keeping with Chinese conceptions of sage rulership; it was not enough for a ruler to be deemed a sage by an ordinary mortal: confirmation could only come from another figure in possession of sagelike wisdom. Thus the *Wei shu* (*History of Wei*) notes: "Only a wise man (J: *sakashihito*) knows a wise man. Only a sage knows a sage."[49] This belief appears to have been particularly prominent in the early Shōtoku legend corpus. In addition to the legend of the death of the monk Hyeja, it is explicitly stated at the end of another legend recounting Shōtoku's encounter with a sage beggar on the road to Kataoka, which concludes by saying: "At the time the people all marveled at this and said 'It is true that a sage knows a sage!' and they were more and more in awe of him."[50]

The strong ethnic coloration of this motif of pairing sages can be seen from table 4.1, which chronicles every use of the term "sage king" in the *Nihon shoki* in terms of speaker, referent, and ethnic affiliation. Perhaps more importantly, table 4.1 provides several clues for understanding conceptions of sage kingship in Yamato. Most obviously, the sheer volume of references to sage kings indicates that the concept of the sage ruler was a central element in the construction of royal authority by the time of the writing of the *Nihon shoki*.[51] More important than the frequency of the term's use, however, are the twin issues of who had the authority to use the term and whom the term designated. Once we distinguish between cases where the term is used by Yamato rulers and those cases where it is used in reference to Yamato rulers, the degree to which immigrant kinship groups at the forefront of the early Shōtoku cult shaped the discourse on sage kingship during the period becomes apparent.

TABLE 4.1. References to Sage Kings in the *Nihon shoki*

Chapter	Speaker	Referent	Speaker's Ancestral Nation
1. Suinin	Ame no Hiboko	Suinin	Silla
2. Suinin	Tsunuga Arashito	Suinin	Mimana
3. Suinin	Tajima Mori	Suinin	Silla
4. Chūai	"people"	Jingū	?
5. Jingū	Silla king	Jingū	Silla
6. Jingū	Paekche king	Jingū	Paekche
7. Jingū	Paekche envoy	Jingū	Paekche
8. Nintoku	Prince Uji	Nintoku	Yamato
9. Nintoku	Nintoku	Ancient Kings	Yamato
10. Nintoku	Nintoku	Ancient Kings	Yamato
11. Nintoku	editor	Nintoku	—
12. Yōmei	editor	Shōtoku	—
13. Suiko	(Shōtoku)	Ancient Kings	Yamato
14. Suiko	Hyeja	Shōtoku	Koguryč
15. Suiko	Monk Tohon	Suiko	Paekche
16. Jomei	Yamashiro Ōe	Shōtoku[52]	Yamato
17. Kōtoku	Kōtoku	Ancient Kings	Yamato
18. Kōtoku	Kōtoku	Ancient Kings	Yamato
19. Kōtoku	Kōtoku	Ancient Kings	Yamato

Use of the Term "Sage King" by Yamato Rulers

As table 4.1 makes clear, in each instance where the term "sage king" or its equivalent is used by a Yamato ruler, the referent is always either a royal ancestor or the ancient sage kings of China. This suggests that by the time of the writing of the *Nihon shoki* the ancient sage kings from China were normative models of kingship for Yamato rulers. The adoption of Chinese rulers as models also entailed adoption of a particular historical perspective in which the will of Heaven was manifested periodically within history through the appearance of omens. In proclaiming their desire to follow in the tradition of the ancient Chinese sage kings, Yamato rulers thus also presented themselves as working in a continuously unfolding historical narrative; in the monk Hyeja's words, they "continued the great plans" of the ancient Chinese sage kings. This rhetoric is particularly pronounced for texts purportedly written during and just after Shōtoku's lifetime; Shōtoku's constitution and Kōtoku's proclamations contain over fifteen direct and indirect references to ancient Chinese sages.

The above chart also shows that, along with the Yamato ruler Jingū, the Yamato figure most frequently associated with the concept of the sage king was Shōtoku. He is referred to as such by Yamashiro no Ōe, by Hyeja, and by the editors of the *Nihon shoki*.[53] Jingū's association with the concept most likely reflects the fact that, as we saw in chapter 3, the Jingū legend cycle, as well as the concept of the sage king, was undergoing extensive development during the period of the composition of the *Nihon shoki*.[54]

Shōtoku's association with the concept, on the other hand, may have been a result of the frequent use of such language in the Seventeen-Article Constitution, which was attributed to him. As we have already seen, this text features several references to continental conceptions of sage kings and counselors. All of this thus suggests that kinship groups affiliated with the cults of Jingū and Shōtoku played a major role in the formation of the concept of the Yamato sage king.

Uses of the Term "Sage King" by Non-royal Speakers

Perhaps the most striking aspect of table 4.1, however, is that, excluding attributions from editors and "the people," in virtually every instance where Yamato rulers are referred to as sage kings, the speaker either comes from one of the Korean kingdoms or is from an immigrant kinship group that traces its ancestry back to the Korean kingdoms. Simply put, in the *Nihon shoki*, it is foreign envoys, immigrant gods, and immigrant monks that declare Yamato rulers to be sages.

Furthermore, and crucially, a closer look at the list of people who declare Yamato rulers to be sage kings also indicates that in the majority of cases these *sakashihito* were ancestors of the immigrant kinship groups at the forefront of the early Shōtoku cult. Thus the first three figures on the list—Ame no Hiboko, Tsunuga no Arashito, and Tajima Mori—are not only heralded in the *Nihon shoki* as gods or sages, but are also identified as ancestral deities of immigrant kinship groups such as the Miyake. In addition, a fourth figure—the Koguryô monk Hyeja—plays the role of Shōtoku's *sakashihito*.

This pattern is also repeated in the apparently unrelated case of the Paekche monk Tohon, who makes his declaration to one Naniwa Kishi Muraji no Tokumaro, ancestor of one of the most prominent kinship groups in the early Shōtoku cult.[55] Even the instance of the "people" hailing Jingū as a sage ruler at the Bay of Nuta in Wakasa Province may reflect the influence of the kinship groups at the forefront of the early Shōtoku cult; wooden documents known as *mokkan* from the area suggest that it was populated by both the Miyake and the Hata.[56] Add to this the cases directly involving Shōtoku and it becomes apparent that the majority of references in the *Nihon shoki* to Yamato rulers as sage kings are closely related to the immigrant kinship groups that helped create the early Shōtoku cult. These kinship groups created the legends that hailed ancient Yamato rulers as sage kings. These kinship groups claimed to have discovered omens such as the *hakuji* that established living Yamato rulers as sages. These kinship groups established Shōtoku as the paradigmatic sage of Yamato. Finally, these kinship groups also established their own ancestors as the wise counselors who served to authenticate the sage wisdom and virtue of the rulers of Yamato.

Conclusion

The introduction of Chinese historical and divinatory texts into Yamato from Paekche in the sixth century led to a reformulation of royal authority based upon Chinese conceptions of sage kingship. In adopting this framework, Yamato rulers needed to construct a fairly elaborate conceptual and social apparatus based upon a textual corpus controlled mainly by immigrant kinship groups from the Korean Peninsula. Among the most important aspects of this new framework was the propagation of Chinese historical texts in which the actions of previous sages were recounted and in terms of which the actions of Yamato rulers could be explained. These texts also expounded on the nature of sage kingship, methods of divination, and the interpretation of omens. The introduction and adoption of these texts was accompanied by the formation of a class of intellectuals with mastery of this corpus and authority to interpret signs of Heaven's favor or displeasure with the ruler.

Because immigrant kinship groups served as the interpreters and gate-keepers of this textual corpus, they were in a uniquely privileged position from which to transform continental models of kingship within the framework of early Yamato society. Kinship groups affiliated with the early Shōtoku cult used this position both to construct an image of Shōtoku as the paramount sage of Yamato and to ensure that their ancestors were portrayed as *sakashihito*, or wise men, paired with Yamato sage kings. In so doing, they helped redefine the basis for the exercise of power in early Yamato.

By establishing their own ancestral legends as the basis of the court's understanding of sage kingship, these kinship groups also ensured that the cultic centers and practices associated with their ancestral cults became basic elements in royal myth and ritual. Thus did the close correlation between literacy and ethnicity in seventh-century Japan help lead, ironically, to the construction of a new identity for royal ancestors and a new cultic identity for rulers thereafter.

5

Violence, Vengeance, and Purification in the Early Shōtoku Cult

Although Shōtoku is lauded today as a progressive visionary, the reinvention of the historical Prince Kamitsumiya as a Buddhist sage may well have been due to his association with political violence. Just as the notion of the Yamato sage king was deeply implicated in the chronically violent contestation for power that characterized pre-Nara Japan, so, too, did the linkage between learning and violence lay close to the heart of the early Shōtoku cult. Prince Kamitsumiya, after all, rose to prominence only after the destruction of the main lineage of the Mononobe kinship group and the appropriation of Mononobe lands and slaves. Thus, the most widely hailed sage of the realm came to power only after shedding copious amounts of the blood of his enemies.

Such bloodshed mattered because violence—especially violence directed against entire lineages—had important cultic consequences in Asuka and Nara Japan. As we saw in chapter 3, violence produced angry spirits and deities that could be ignored only at great peril. This logic of violence and propitiation was not simply defensive, however, but also and inevitably productive. In the case of the Shōtoku cult, it is thus likely that this dynamic was an integral part of the process by which the figure of Kamitsumiya was transformed into Shōtoku. Perhaps even more importantly, however, the logic of violence and propitiation also led to the production of a new ideal religious type—referred to in the *Nihon shoki* primarily as *hijiri*—that closely correlated sagehood with the ability to control the processes of death and resurrection.

In order to understand how the figure of Shōtoku was created as a sage, it will therefore be necessary to further probe the relationship between violence and spirit propitiation during the period. Indeed,

TABLE 5.I. Sages in the *Nihon shoki*

Term	Speaker	Referent	Occasion
1. immortal	editor	Uranoshimako	journey to *tokoyo*
2. no common man	Tajima Mori	Tajima Mori	journey to *tokoyo*
3. sage	Prince Uji	Nintoku	resurrection
4. sage	Hyeja	Shōtoku	rebirth in Pure Land
5. sage	"people"	Hyeja	rebirth in Pure Land
6. sage	"people"	Shōtoku	meets beggar/sage
7. sage	Shōtoku	beggar	resurrection

once we place the figure of Shōtoku within the context of contemporaneous legends of resurrection and sagehood, this logic of violence and spirit quelling emerges as one of the most powerful forces driving the construction of Shō-toku as the paramount sage of the Japanese islands. It also helps clarify the relationship between the ideals of the sage king (*hijiri no kimi*) that were discussed in chapter 4, and the ideal of the sage (*hijiri*).

To see just how closely the early Shōtoku cult was identified with early conceptions of sagehood, one need only focus on instances where the term "sage" (*hijiri*) or an equivalent is used in the *Nihon shoki* without reference to kingship. Consider table 5.I, which lists all figures in the *Nihon shoki* who are declared to be such sages.[1]

A brief glance at table 5.I confirms two points. First, each of these legends contains the motif of a sage who attains some form of life after death or who effects his own resurrection. Second, the concept of *hijiri* correlated extremely closely with the figure of Shōtoku and with the lineages at the forefront of the early Shōtoku cult. This is true not only for figures 4–7 but also for the Miyake ancestor Tajima Mori, a figure whom we have seen repeatedly in previous chapters in connection with the development of the early Shōtoku legend corpus. To find out why this might have been the case, however, we will need to focus on the figures in table 5.I that were not obviously connected with the Shōtoku cult. Only after we understand how Uranoshimako, Prince Uji, and the Kataoka beggar came to be considered as *hijiri* will we be able to determine the role of the Shōtoku cult in the formation of the concept.

Sages, Immortality, and Ancestors

One of the most important sources of information we have concerning early conceptions of sagehood and immortality can be found in the legend cycle of Uranoshimako, the first figure in table 5.I. His journey to the land of the immortals is detailed in the following brief passage from the *Nihon shoki*:

> A man named Mizunoe no Uranoshimako, from Tsutsukawa in the Yoza district of Tamba Province, went fishing in a boat and eventu-ally caught a large turtle. This immediately turned into a beautiful

woman with whom Uranoshimako fell in love and married. Together
they went into the sea until they came to Mount Hōrai (*tokoyo*),
where they saw many immortals (*hijiri*). The story may be found in
another writing.[2]

Because this legend also appears in two longer versions in the *Manyōshū*
(*Anthology of Ten Thousand Leaves*) and the *Tango kuni fudoki* (*Records of the
Customs and Land of Tango*), it would appear that the legend had achieved
considerable currency by the time of the writing of the *Nihon shoki*. The popularity of Uranoshimako's cult is also well-attested by the existence of numerous shrines to Uranoshimako along the coast of the Japan/Eastern Sea.[3]

The *Manyōshū* and *Tango fudoki* versions of the legend also shed important
light on the development of the cult of Uranoshimako in early Yamato; in the
Tango fudoki account, for instance, Uranoshimako is said to be the ancestor of
the Kusakabe Obito in Tamba.[4] This is of course of immediate note because, as
we saw in chapter 4, a member of the Kusakabe kinship group was said to have
discovered the *hakuji* that was hailed as a sign of Heaven's pleasure with the
sage ruler Kōtoku. This is the first of several indications we shall see that
suggest that lineages such as the Kusakabe were active in the development of
the twin ideals of the sage and sage king.

Several further hints about the mythic and ritual sources for these legends
of sagehood and resurrection can be found in the various genealogies associated with the Kusakabe in early Yamato literature. The *Shinsen shōjiroku* states
that the founding ancestor of the Kusakabe kinship group was one Hiko no
Imasu Mikoto, who was in turn descended from the fire god Ama no Ho no
Akari no Mikoto.[5] The *Nihon shoki* in turn states that Hiko no Imasu Mikoto's
mother was from the Wani, yet another lineage that claimed ultimate descent
from the fire god Ama no Ho no Akari no Mikoto.[6] Because the ancestral legend cycles of both these kinship groups centered upon the fire cult and death
rituals, they make an ideal point of departure for inquiry concerning the emergence of the conception of *hijiri* in early Japan.

One of the most important legends that details the role of the Kusakabe in
the formation of death rituals in early Yamato can be found in the *Nihon shoki*
and *Kojiki*, both of which state that the Yamato ruler Suinin took as consorts
several granddaughters of the founding Kusakabe ancestor Hiko no Imasu
Mikoto.[7] The eldest of these women (and Suinin's main consort) was one Hibasu Hime, a figure whose death is depicted in both texts as a pivotal moment
in the development of Japanese funerary customs. According to these texts,
Hibasu Hime's death led to the creation of several funerary service groups, and
her funeral is also said to have been the first in which *haniwa*, or ritual figurines, were buried with the dead:

32nd year, 7th month, 6th day.
The Queen Consort Hibasu Hime no Mikoto died. After some days of
temporary interment had passed, the *tennō* commanded his ministers, saying, "We already know that the practice of following the

deceased into death should not be observed. How should we now perform this burial?" At this Nomi no Sukune came forward and said "The practice of burying living people in the tombs of lords and nobles is not a good one. Why should we transmit this custom to later generations? I ask [to be allowed to] determine and submit a suitable [method]." He then sent a messenger to Hanibe no Momohito in Izumo and ordered him to personally oversee the Hanibe in making clay figurines of people, horses and various other shapes. He then submitted these to the *tennō*, saying, "Henceforth, let it be the law for future generations to take such clay implements and substitute them for living humans around tombs." ... The *tennō* greatly rewarded Nomi no Sukune for his service.... His original title was changed to "Haji no Omi." This is why the Haji no Muraji are charged with the burials of rulers. Nomi no Sukune was thus the founding ancestor of the Haji no Muraji.[8]

This legend has been analyzed closely by Hirabayashi Akihito, who argues that in addition to its obvious role as the founding legend of burial service groups such as the Haji no Muraji, the legend also sets out several hitherto overlooked features of Yamato funerary rites. He notes that elsewhere within the *Nihon shoki* Nomi Sukune is said to have engaged in a *sumō* match on the seventh month of the seventh day of the seventh year of Suinin's reign at the Tagima crossroads, or *chimata*.[9] The fact that Hibasu Hime is said to have died on the sixth day of the seventh month, combined with the discovery at various tomb sites of clay figurines modeled in *sumō* postures, leads Hirabayashi to conclude that the performance of *sumō* at *chimata* was somehow connected with rites of spirit quelling for the dead.[10]

Hibasu Hime also appears in yet another *Kojiki* legend involving *tokoyo* and sages, this one involving the Miyake ancestor Tajima Mori, the second figure on our list of sages in table 5.1. In this legend, Tajima Mori is sent to *tokoyo* to recover a *tachibana*, or fruit of immortality, for the ruler Suinin:

> The *tennō* also sent an ancestor of the Miyake Muraji named Tajima Mori to *tokoyo* to seek the fruit of the tree that is everlastingly fragrant. Tajima Mori finally reached that land and picked the fruit, bringing back eight fruits speared on branches and eight fruits speared on sticks. While he was bringing them back [however] the *tennō* died. So Tajima Mori divided [the fruits] into two sets with [each having] four fruits speared on branches and four fruits speared on sticks. He offered four fruits on branches and four fruits on sticks to the Queen Consort [Hibasu Hime] and then placed the four fruits on branches and the four fruits on sticks in offering at the entrance to the *tennō*'s tomb.[11]

This legend is notable not only for its reference to the fruit of immortality but also for its depiction of the surprisingly close connections between the Miyake ancestor Tajima Mori and the Kusakabe ancestor Hibasu Hime. Remarkably, out of the over 1,180 lineages known to have existed in early Yamato, the Kusakabe and Miyake are virtually the only two kinship groups to claim descent from male immortals.[12] Even more remarkably, here the Miyake ancestor Tajima Mori leaves the fruit of immortality as an offering at the tomb of the Kusakabe ancestor Hibasu Hime.

Prince Uji and the Wani

The same cluster of motifs centering around sagehood, resurrection, and Kusakabe/Wani ancestors also informs the legend of the death and resurrection of Prince Uji, yet another figure from table 5.1. Prince Uji is particularly noteworthy because, like Shōtoku, he is depicted within the *Nihon shoki* as a *taishi*, or crown prince, who is a master of continental culture.[13] Within the *Nihon shoki*, Prince Uji, like Shōtoku at Kataoka, is featured in a meeting between two superhuman figures, one of whom dies, is mourned, and is resurrected:

> Three days had already passed since the death of the crown prince [Uji]. Prince Ōsazaki [Nintoku] beat his breast and wailed with tears as if he knew not what to do. He loosened his hair and lay across the corpse and cried out three times "My younger brother the Prince!" At this he [Prince Uji] suddenly came back to life and sat up. Then Ōsazaki said to the crown prince "How sad, how awful! Why did you die of your own will? If the dead have knowledge, what would the previous sovereign [our father] say of me?" At this the crown prince said to his older brother "It is the command of Heaven. Who could stop it? If I go to where the *tennō* is, I will tell him of all my older brother's sage [nature], and my ceding [the throne]. However, the sage king [Nintoku] has traveled so far and so fast upon news of my death, you must be exhausted." He then offered [Nintoku] Yata no Himeko, his sister by the same mother. . . . Then he lay down in his coffin and died. Prince Ōsazaki then put on funerary garments and was filled with grief as he wailed and lamented. They then buried [Prince Uji] at the top of Mount Uji.[14]

Although it is tempting to dismiss this legend as a crude attempt to depict members of the ruling line as paragons of selfless virtue, a closer reading suggests that the text was rooted at least in part in local legends and conflicts. One clue concerning the background for the legend's construction can be seen in the location of Prince Uji's palace and tomb on Mount Nara in the Uji district of Yamashiro Province. This region, which was important not only for the Prince but also for his lineage, the Wani kinship group, features prominently in several Wani legends concerning death rituals and rites of spirit propitiation. One example of particular note, for our purposes, is the following legend, in which the Abe ancestor Ōhiko, after receiving a mandate from the Yamato ruler Sujin to kill the rebel Haniyasu Biko, goes to a slope of the very mountain where Prince Uji was purportedly entombed. There, with the aid of the Wani ancestor Hiko Kunibuku no Mikoto, they engage in roadside rites of spirit pacification before attacking the ruler's purported enemy:

> Ōhiko and Hiko Kunibuku, the distant ancestor of the Wani no Omi, went out towards Yamashiro to attack Haniyasu Biko. At this they took sacred jars [iwahibe] and installed them at the top of the Taka-suki slope in Wani.... Hiko Kunibuku shot [an arrow] at Haniyasu Biko. The arrow hit him in the breast and killed him.[15]

In many ways the most important information in this account lies not in its content, but in the characters that it brings together and the site at which they are said to meet. This legend is notable not only for its depiction of a Wani ancestor using clay ritual vessels but also for its depiction of the close relationship between Wani and Abe ancestors. This characterization most likely reflects the fact that the Wani appear to have been drawn into the Abe orbit in the post-Taika era, when the Abe first came to prominence. As the Wani came under the political influence of the Abe, the Shōtoku cult was thus able to absorb and transform the mythic and ritual resources of Wani ancestral cults for its own purposes. How such mythic resources might have been utilized by the early Shōtoku cult can be seen once we begin reading the Wani legend corpus.

The Wani and Tokoyo

One of the most important sources of information concerning the Wani ancestral legend cycle can be found in the poetry of Kakinomoto no Hitomaro. Hitomaro, the most famous poet of the period, was a semi-official voice of the Temmu court, and his use of mythic themes is credited with helping establish the basis for the tennō's claim of divinity.[16] In this regard, Yoshimura Teiji has noted that Hitomaro's kinship group, the Kakinomoto, were one of a cluster of lineages that claimed descent from the Wani, and that much of Hitomaro's poetry was composed at places related to Wani ancestral legends.[17] One of Hitomaro's most famous poems deals with his journey to the Karu crossroads, where he is said to have composed a song in memory of his deceased wife. Consider the following excerpt:

> Soaring through the sky!
> On the Karu Road
> is your village, my love;
> although I desired to meet you intimately,
> if I went there too much
> the eyes of others would cluster
> around us ...

Then came the messenger...
to tell me,
in a voice
like the sound
of a catalpa bow....
that you my love
who had swayed to me in sleep
like seaweed of the offing,
were gone
like the coursing sun
gliding in the dusk....

I stood at the Karu market
where often you, my love, had gone,
and listened,
but could not hear
the voices of the birds
that cry on Unebi Mountain....
I could do nothing
but call your name....
and wave my sleeves.[18]

This poem is of particular interest for our discussion for two reasons. First, the poem is set at the Karu crossroads, or *chimata*, where rituals of spirit quelling appear to have been regularly performed.[19] Second, Hitomaro represents himself in the poem as waiving an article of his deceased wife's clothing while calling out to her spirit—both standard elements in funerary rites designed to encourage the spirit to return to the land of the living. These images, coupled with the fact that the Wani were known to have performed rites of spirit quelling at other crossroads, have led Maeda and others to conclude that Hitomaro's disappointment at not seeing his wife was more than simple poetic conceit.[20] Whether or not this was in fact the case, it is clear that the poet was consciously invoking these associations in order to heighten the poem's emotional and dramatic effect.

Hitomaro's poetry thus serves to highlight some of the most salient funerary images that appear in the legends of other Wani ancestors who achieve entry into *tokoyo*. The following legend, for instance, again features the symbol of the scarf as a funerary talisman as it relates the circumstances surrounding the death and burial of Inami no Waki no Iratsume, a Wani ancestor and the mother of the legendary Prince Yamato Takeru:

After some years, Waki no Iratsume died at this palace. They thus built a tomb at Hioka to bury her. As they transported her corpse down the Inami River, a whirlwind blew from under the river and the corpse was submerged in the middle of the river. Though they looked [for her remains] they could find nothing but her comb box and

scarf. So they buried these two items in the tomb, which is called
hire haka [scarf tomb].[21]

This account of the origins of the "Scarf Tomb" again illustrates the role of
woven items such as scarves as ritual implements that could be used to locate
and engage the spirits of the dead. Further clues as to the fate of Waki no
Iratsume's spirit can also be seen in the importance attached in the text to her
comb box. Because the ritual waving of scarves was a common method of
summoning spirits of the dead, while the word for comb, *kushi*, is homophonous with the term for medicine (and by extension, immortality) Yoshimura
argues that the motifs of the discovered scarf and comb were meant to suggest
that Waki no Iratsume, like her kinsman Uranoshimako, had successfully jour-
neyed to *tokoyo* beneath the sea.[22]

For our purposes, this latter motif is particularly noteworthy because a
similar motif also figures in the *Tango fudoki* account of the Uranoshimako
legend. In the *Tango fudoki* account, Uranoshimako decides to leave *tokoyo*
beneath the sea in order to see once more his native village. Before he leaves,
Uranoshimako's wife gives him a comb box (*tama kushige*) with a warning not
to open it until he has returned to *tokoyo*. When Uranoshimako nevertheless
opens the box, the box flies away, leaving Uranoshimako to regret breaking his
promise and with no way to return to *tokoyo*.[23]

The motif of the *kushi* from *tokoyo* can also be found in the following
legend of Yamato Takeru's wife, Oto Tachibana Hime.[24] In this legend from
the Keikō chapter of the *Kojiki*, Oto Tachibana Hime plunges into the sea in
order to appease the local sea god, who in anger at Yamato Takeru has pre-
vented his ship from advancing:

> When he went in from there and was crossing a place where the sea
> flowed in a swift current, the god of the crossing raised waves and
> spun the boat around so that it was unable to proceed. Thereupon
> his consort, whose name was Oto Tachibana Hime no Mikoto,
> spoke and said, "I shall take the place of the Prince and go into the
> sea. Let the Prince fulfill his charge of government and return to
> make his report." And when she was about to go into the sea, they
> spread eight thicknesses of sedge mats, eight thicknesses of skin
> mat, and eight thicknesses of silk mats on the waves, and she went
> down and sat upon them. At this the rough waves calmed of them-
> selves, and the boat was able to proceed. And so his consort sang:
>
> > You who asked of me
> > As you stood amid the flames
> > Of the burning fire
> > On the moor of Sagamu
> > Of the thrusting peaks—you, lord.

Now, after seven days his consort's comb washed ashore. And they
took her comb and made a grave and placed it in the mound.[25]

Because this legend again highlights the role of a comb as a symbol for a female Wani ancestor who has plunged into the sea, it would appear that this symbol was commonly used in Wani depictions of death and resurrection. Note that, as if to emphasize the special religious significance of the *kushi*, the text actually states that the comb was enshrined in a tomb. This assertion appears to have been rooted in contemporaneous cultic realities, as several shrines dedicated to Oto Tachibana Hime bear names such as "Kushitama Jinja" (Comb Spirit shrine).[26]

Yamato Takeru

The fact that Yamato Takeru's wife and mother were both said to have left behind personal belongings before going to *tokoyo* beneath the sea in turn sheds light upon Yamato Takeru's own remarkable death narrative. In the *Nihon shoki* account he is said to have left behind his court cap when his spirit bursts out of his tomb (*misasagi*) in the form of a bird:

> At this time Yamato Takeru no Mikoto was transformed into a white bird, whereupon he left his tomb (*misasagi*), and flew off in the direction of Yamato. When the ministers thus opened the coffin and looked [within], all that was left was his empty funerary clothing without the corpse. Messengers were then sent to follow the bird.... However, in the end it flew high up to Heaven and only his clothing and his court cap were buried.[27]

Although this legend has generally been read in the light of legends involving the "liberation from the corpse" by Chinese immortals, it also underscores the degree to which such motifs were characteristic of Wani ancestral legends.[28] Recall that Yamato Takeru was not only the husband of a Wani consort but also the son of a Wani mother. Further evidence for the prominence of the Wani in such legends can be seen in table 5.2, which is composed of figures from pre-Heian sources that leave behind personal effects before attaining life after death.

As table 5.2 makes clear, the death narrative of Yamato Takeru suggests strong connections not only with other Wani ancestral legends but also with the legend of Shōtoku and the beggar at Kataoka. Indeed, the closeness of the

TABLE 5.2. Personal Effects and the Attainment of Life Beyond Death

Name	Items Left Behind	Type of Life After Death
Yamato Takeru	clothes/cap	liberation from corpse (transformation into white bird)
Oto Tachibana Hime	comb	*tokoyo*
Wake no Iratsume	comb, scarf	*tokoyo*
Uranoshimako	comb box	*tokoyo*
Kataoka beggar	robe	liberation from corpse

fit between the Wani legend corpus and the legend of Shōtoku and the Kataoka beggar strongly suggests that the Kataoka legend was at least partially rooted in the myths and rites associated with the Wani ancestral cult. Understanding how and why those connections developed would thus appear to be key to understanding the formation of the concept of *hijiri*.

Fire, Resurrection, and the Kataoka *Chimata*

Several clues concerning how and to what degree the early Shōtoku cult was influenced by the Wani legend corpus can be found in the text of the *Nihon shoki* account of Shōtoku's encounter with a beggar/sage on the road to Kataoka:

> 21st year, 12th month, 1st day.
> The crown prince made a journey to Kataoka. At that time there was a starving man who was lying at the side of the road. He asked for [the beggar's] name, but he said nothing. The crown prince, seeing this, gave him food and drink. He then took off his cloak and covered the beggar with it, saying "lie there in peace." He then made a song.
>
> 12th month, second day.
> The crown prince sent a messenger to see the starving man. The messenger returned and said "The starving man is already dead." The crown prince was greatly saddened by this and he therefore had them bury the man at that spot in a tomb that was firmly shut. Several days later the crown prince called one of his personal attendants and said to him "The starving man we saw laying by the road several days ago was no ordinary man. He must certainly have been an immortal (*hijiri*). So he sent [another] messenger to look [at the tomb]. The messenger returned and said "When I arrived at the tomb, [the earth] was firm and had not moved. [Yet] when I opened it and looked inside the corpse had already disappeared. There was only the clothing folded above the casket."
>
>   At this the crown prince once again sent the messenger back to retrieve the clothing. He then wore it as he always had done. The people then all marveled at this and said "It is true that a sage knows a sage!" and they were more and more in awe of him.[29]

This legend in many ways closely parallels other legends from the Shōtoku legend corpus and the lineages at the forefront of the early Shōtoku cult. Shōtoku's declaration that the beggar was "no ordinary man" appears to be closely correlated with both the Seventeen-Article Constitution and the legend of Tajima Mori's visit to a land that "no common man" can attain.[30] The motif of the "people" declaring Shōtoku and the beggar as sages likewise closely correlates with the death narratives of Hyeja and Shōtoku, where, as we have already seen, "the people" again declare both principals as sages.[31] Thus, the legend of the beggar at Kataoka displays deep resonances with other legends from the Shōtoku legend corpus even as it utilizes motifs from the legends of Wani ancestors such as Prince Uji and Prince Yamato Takeru.

When considered within the framework of the logic of violence and propitiation that pervaded so many legends of the period, however, the commonalities among the legends of Prince Uji, Yamato Takeru and Shōtoku take on even greater significance. One such common element is the fact that all of these legends eulogize princes who never attained the throne. Yamato Takeru and Prince Uji are even presented as paragons of virtue who die violent deaths in the service of the realm. This suggests the intriguing possibility that the legend cycles of these princes were at least in part designed to mask succession disputes in which they—and their lineages—were the losers. Seen from this perspective, the Kataoka legend thus presents us with an important puzzle, as it is the one legend considered in this chapter in which the figure who achieves resurrection is depicted without reference to lineage.

Fire Gods and Resurrection

Although we cannot be certain which lineage, if any, was most closely associated with the figure of the Kataoka beggar, the extremely close fit between the Kataoka legend and the Wani ancestral legend corpus suggests that the Wani ancestor Ama no Ho no Akari no Mikoto may hold important clues concerning the Kataoka legend's formation. In addition to his position as ancestor of the Wani and Kusakabe, Ama no Ho no Akari no Mikoto also played a prominent role in the legend of Yamato Takeru's death and resurrection. Both the *Nihon shoki* and *Kojiki* state that Yamato Takeru was killed by the god of Mount Ibuki, a deity closely related to, if not one and the same as, Ama no Ho no Akari no Mikoto.[32] The *Nihon shoki* also states that the prince's sword came to be worshiped as a deity at the Atsuta Jinja, the family shrine of the Owari Muraji, yet another kinship group descended from Ama no Hoake no Mikoto.[33]

The importance of this fire deity is also highlighted by one further distinctive feature of the legend cycles of Prince Uji and Yamato Takeru; both of these princes are said to first achieve resurrection (i.e. they return from death to life in this world) before they depart for the afterworld. Throughout the literature of the period, there is a strong correlation between fire deities and legends of resurrection. Just how strong this correlation was can be seen in table 5.3, which lists all figures who are said to achieve resurrection in the *Nihon shoki*.

As table 5.3 makes clear, every legend of resurrection in the *Nihon shoki*, with the exception of the legend of Shōtoku's encounter with the beggar at Kataoka, involves a figure connected in some way with a fire cult. In the case of

TABLE 5.3. Figures Who Achieve Resurrection in the *Nihon shoki*

Name	Cause of Death	Connection to Fire God
Izanami	fire	son
Ōnamuchi no Mikoto	fire	son
Yamato Takeru	fire god	ancestor (Wani)
Prince Uji	suicide	ancestor (Wani)
Nichira	assassination	ancestor (Hi no Kimi)
Kataoka beggar	starvation	?

deities such as Izanami[34] and Ōnamuchi no Mikoto, this means death from fire gods who are their children.[35] In the case of humans such as Yamato Takeru, Prince Uji, and Nichira, this means descent from a fire deity.

One clue as to how fire cults might have been related to cults of resurrection can be found in the legend cycle of Izanami no Mikoto, the first figure in table 5.3:

> When it was time for the fire god Kagutsuchi to be born, his mother Izanami was burned and died. Izanagi no Mikoto said bitterly: "[I have] exchanged my dearest love for just one child!" He then crawled about at her head and feet, wailing and crying teardrops.... Finally he drew his ten-span sword from his belt and cut Kagutsuchi into three pieces, each of which changed into a god. Also, the blood that dripped from the sword became the many rocks in the bed of the Yasukawa River in Heaven. This was also the father of the god Futsunushi no Kami.[36]

This legend is of particular interest not only for its account of the death of Izanami, but also for its account of the birth of Futsunushi no Mikoto, an ancestor of the Mononobe kinship group.[37] Futsunushi no Mikoto is portrayed in the *Nihon shoki* as a spirit-quelling deity who is allied with the *chimata* deity Kunado no Kami. This pairing almost certainly reflects the fact that Futsunushi no Mikoto was the chief deity of the Isonokami shrine, a Mononobe cultic center located near the Isonokami *chimata* along the northern Great Lateral Highway. This location is of particular note because, in addition to connecting the court with the port of Naniwa, the northern Great Lateral Highway also passed through Kataoka, the site of Shōtoku's encounter with the beggar as well as the area of Takasuki, which, as we have already seen, was a main base of the Wani. During the Mononobe's ascendancy in the sixth century, much of this road—along with several of the lineages based near it—appears to have been firmly under the control of the Mononobe.[38] All of this thus suggests that the Wani ancestral legend cycle itself may have been influenced by the rites and practices of the Mononobe. If this was in fact the case, then it is entirely possible that the figure of the Kataoka beggar may have been created not by the kinship groups of the early Shōtoku cult but rather by the Mononobe and/or the Wani.

Several clues as to how the legend of the death and resurrection of the beggar at Kataoka may have been influenced by the Mononobe can be seen in the *Sendai kuji hongi* (*Records of Old Matters from Previous Ages*), a ninth-century liturgical/historical text that refers to *chimata* rites performed at the Isonokami shrine. In one such passage, the Mononobe ancestor Umashimaji no Mikoto is credited with instructing the Yamato ruler Jimmu in the performance of the Spirit Pacification Ceremony (*Chinkonsai, Mitama shizume matsuri*), a major rite of spirit pacification performed by the court during the New Year. After performing a rite of blessing and pacification, Umashimaji no Mikoto relates a Mononobe spell of resurrection and states that Mononobe resurrection rites were the basis for the *Mitama shizume matsuri*, one of the most important rites in the court's liturgical calendar.[39]

Although few contemporary scholars would accept the assertion that Mononobe rites were the historical basis for the *Mitama shizume matsuri*, the *Sendai kuji hongi* at the very least establishes Mononobe involvement in rites of spirit pacification and even resurrection during the early Heian period. The fact that these assertions could be plausibly made early in the ninth century also illustrates the tremendous degree to which Mononobe rites and legends came to be intertwined with the royal cult. Matsumae Takeshi has noted in this regard that references to the Mononobe's Isonokami shrine continued in the court's rites even in much later periods.[40] Finally, and perhaps most importantly, the fact that the Mononobe were the very kinship group that was said to have been destroyed by Shōtoku in the fight to establish Buddhism in Japan also suggests that the logic of violence and propitiation may have helped drive the creation of the legend of the beggar at Kataoka.

Chimata *Rites, the Fire Cult, and Kamu Yaimimi no Mikoto*

Further evidence suggesting that fire cults and rites such as the *Mitama shizume matsuri* helped shape the horizon of reception for the Kataoka legend can be found in the Ata district of Hyūga Province in Kyūshū. This district, in addition to being the birthplace of Ama no Ho no Akari no Mikoto, was also home to several kinship groups associated with the performance of *chimata* rites of spirit quelling and purification. These groups, several of which claimed descent from the royal ancestor Kamu Yaimimi no Mikoto, provide the final pieces to the puzzle of the construction of the legend of Shōtoku and the beggar at Kataoka.

Among the most prominent kinship groups from Ata that claimed descent from Kamu Yaimimi no Mikoto were the Sakaibe and the Chisakobe, two lineages that were closely associated with *chimata* spirit-quelling rites and rituals for quelling lightning deities. The Chisakobe are especially noteworthy for our purposes because they are also credited in the *Shinsen shōjiroku* with helping constitute the Hata kinship group.[41] Scholars such as Katō Kenkichi have argued that the *Shinsen shōjiroku* account reflects close contacts between these two groups. In support of this view, Katō notes that the Hata and Chisakobe lived together in Yamato and that the two kinship groups cooperated ritually.[42]

Perhaps the most important evidence of links between the kinship groups
that claimed descent from Kamu Yaimimi no Mikoto and the early Shōtoku
cult can be found in the legend of the death and resurrection of Nichira, the
second-to-last figure in table 5.3:

> Nichira moved from the village of Kuwaichi to the guest residence in
> Naniwa. [The Paekche envoy] Togi and others plotted day and night
> as to how to kill him. At that time Nichira's body was radiant like
> a flame. Because of this, Togi and the others were afraid and did not
> kill him. Finally on the final night of the twelfth month [when there
> was no moon] they saw that his radiance disappeared and they killed
> him. [But] Nichira came back to life and said "This was done by
> my servants. It was not done by Silla." After saying this, he died.[43]

As is so often the case, Nichira's lineal affiliations provide several highly
suggestive clues concerning the nature of his cult. According to the *Nihon
shoki*, Nichira's father was named Hi no Ashikita no Kuni no Miyatsuko
Arashito.[44] The Hi no Ashikita no Kuni no Miyatsuko were apparently a sub-
branch of the Hi no Kimi, yet another kinship group that, like the Chisakobe,
was originally based in southern Kyūshū and claimed descent from Kamu
Yaimimi no Mikoto. The Hi no Kimi also appear to have been associated with
fire cults and rites of resurrection. Evidence for this can be seen in the
preceding legend's remarkable assertion that the Paekche envoys feared the
flames that radiated from Nichira's body, as well as in the name "Hi no Kimi"
(literally, "Fire Lord"). In addition, at least one further reference in the literature of the period depicts a member of the Hi no Kimi performing a rite of
resurrection and spirit pacification.[45] All of this thus suggests that the legend
of Nichira's death and resurrection may have been related to the beliefs and
practices of lineages such as the Hi no Kimi and Chisakobe.

As was the case with the Wani, however, there is also good evidence within
the *Nihon shoki* that suggests that the Hi no Kimi and the cult of Nichira had by
the end of the seventh century come under the sway of the Abe. Nichira's tomb
in Naniwa, for instance, was located on the small islet of Himejima by the
Himegoso shrine. This area was also the home of the sub-lineage of the Abe
kinship group known as the Himegoso Abe.[46] The location of Nichira's tomb is
thus of immediate interest for our purposes for two reasons. First, the deity of
the Himegoso shrine was none other than Akaru Hime, the wife of the Silla
prince Ame no Hiboko. Second, the fact that Nichira's tomb was said to be
located in a base of an Abe sub-lineage suggests that by the end of the seventh
century the Abe were already in the process of appropriating control of important cultic centers of the Hi no Kimi.[47] This process appears to have been
ongoing: by the time of the completion of the *Nihon shoki* in 720, the Hi no
Kimi and Abe claimed common ancestry and jointly participated in rites such
as the Kishi Dance at Shitennōji. Such cultic interactions between the Abe and
the Hi no Kimi are of particular interest in light of the fact that this same
period witnessed the formation of the nascent Shōtoku cult.

One clue as to how these interactions may have helped shape early conceptions of Shōtoku and the legend of the Kataoka beggar can be seen in the timing of Nichira's death and resurrection. Because the last evening of the lunar year was one of the most important moments in the ancient ritual calendar, this account of Nichira's death and resurrection appears to have been designed to track closely with the court's ritual cycle. On this day, several rites took place at important *chimata* in and near the capital in order to purify the court and to ensure that no malevolent spirits approached the court during the New Year. Two of the most important of these rites were the Ceremony of Roadside Offerings (*Michiae no matsuri*) and the Fire Pacification Ceremony (*Hoshizume no matsuri*).[48]

The New Year's rites of fire pacification and purification were carried out in conjunction with a further set of rites at court that, as we have already seen, were extensively influenced by Mononobe rites and legends. At the heart of the New Year's rites were the *Mitama shizume no matsuri* and the *Yasojima no matsuri* (Ceremony of the Eight Islands), wherein the ruler's body was purified through the removal of his clothes and the collection of his breath in special clay vessels.[49] These were then taken to *chimata* outside of the capital, where they were sent by waterway to the depths of the netherworld (*ne no kuni*). Because these rites involved the use of ritual dolls (*hitogata*), or substitute bodies, that were sent, along with the ruler's clothes, to *Ne no kuni*, they resonate closely with Shōtoku's offering of his clothes to the beggar at the Kataoka *chimata* shortly before the beggar's death, resurrection, and departure from this world.[50]

Shōtoku's Kataoka and the Return of the Repressed

To see how and why such rites may have played a role in the formation of a legend of resurrection near Kataoka, one need only consider the cultic and physical topography of the region. Although the Kataoka area of Yamato was not heavily populated in the seventh century, Kataoka was nonetheless situated on the northern Great Lateral Highway just before the Heguri mountain range. Foreign embassies traveling to Asuka from the port of Naniwa are thought to have taken the Tatsuta Highway to Kataoka, where they would either continue along the northern Great Lateral Highway to the Wani center by the Isonokami *chimata* or they would travel down the Taishi Michi to the Karu *chimata*, where Chisakobe ancestors are said to have tamed thunder deities and Hitomaro sought to meet his deceased wife.[51] The strategic importance of the Kataoka area was manifested ritually in its selection as the only inland site where *chimata* purification rites for the arrival of embassies from Silla were performed.[52] Not surprisingly, following the demise of the Mononobe, the Soga moved to assert control over the northern Great Lateral Highway.[53]

Crucially, for our purposes, the importance of Kataoka as a *chimata* ritual center is highlighted in the legend cycle of Kamu Yaimimi no Mikoto, the founding ancestor of *chimata* ritualists such as the Hi no Kimi, Chisakobe, and

Sakaibe. Specifically, within the *Nihon shoki* it is at Kataoka that Kamu Yai-mimi no Mikoto, a prince, relinquishes his claim to the throne and instead assumes for himself and his descendants the role of liturgist for the royal line. The text begins with an account of how Kamu Yaimimi no Mikoto loses his nerve when he and his brother, Kamu Nunakawa Mimi no Mikoto plot to kill a would-be usurper of the throne named Tagishi mimi no Mikoto:[54]

> When the bows and arrows were all prepared, Kamu Nunakawa Mimi no Mikoto wished to use them to kill Tagishi Mimi no Mikoto. Just at that time Tagishi Mimi no Mikoto was in a great enclosure in Kataoka.... Now Kamu Yaimimi no Mikoto was greatly troubled and he submitted himself to his brother, yielding [his claim to the throne], saying "Though I am the older brother, I am timid and weak ... it is right that you should illuminate the heavenly rank and inherit the work of the royal ancestors. I shall serve you by attending to the worship of the gods of Heaven and Earth."[55]

Given Kataoka's position as a *chimata* ritual center where rites of purification were regularly performed for the court, this legend's depiction of the founding ancestor of the Hi no Kimi and Chisakobe assuming liturgical responsibility for the royal line at Kataoka strongly suggests that these lineages were ritually connected with this area. Because these rites were originally centered upon a fire god and were designed to purify the land by sending evil spirits to *Ne no kuni*, Kataoka represents an important ritual nexus of the fire cult, *chimata* rites, and lineages claiming descent from Kamu Yaimimi no Mikoto.

Conclusion

All of this suggests that the legend of Shōtoku's encounter with the beggar at Kataoka was based on local cults of resurrection and roadside rites of spirit quelling associated with a cluster of kinship groups that claimed descent from the fire god Ama no Ho no Akari no Mikoto. Located at a crucial intersection along the northern Great Lateral Highway, a road dominated first by the Mononobe and later by the Soga and Abe, Kataoka was a site where *chimata* rituals of spirit quelling were regularly undertaken by the Yamato court.

The ritual importance of this area was reflected in legend by its designation as the site where Kamu Yaimimi no Mikoto, the ancestor of several kinship groups that specialized in performing *chimata* rites of spirit pacification and resurrection, assumed control of ritual matters for the court. Several of the most important themes found in the rites and legends associated with the area—including such motifs as leaving behind an article of clothing before resurrection, the use of substitute bodies, and the entry into a world beyond death at a *chimata*—were directly manifested in the *Nihon shoki*'s account of Shōtoku's encounter with the beggar on the road to Kataoka. To these motifs were then added the motif of the sage who knows a sage.

Although we can only speculate on the motivations for the creation of this legend, the setting of the legend along the northern Great Lateral Highway at an important *chimata* center strongly suggests that the answer to this riddle lies in the history of this road. As I noted earlier, the northern Great Lateral Highway stretched from Naniwa by the sea all the way to the Isonokami crossroads. This highway was dominated for most of the sixth century by the Mononobe kinship group until their demise at the hands of the Soga. After the fall of the Mononobe, major intersections along the highway came to be dominated by the Soga and their allies.

One of the most prominent members of the Soga kinship group was none other than Prince Kamitsumiya himself. Kamitsumiya's establishment of his residence along the Great Lateral Highway near Kataoka was almost certainly made with an eye toward controlling one of the most strategic transport centers in Yamato. Such a move had important cultic consequences. The *Nihon shoki* states that after the defeat of the Mononobe, half of their lands and slaves were given over to Kamitsumiya, who used them to build, among other things, a temple in Naniwa that later came to be known as Shitennōji.[56] Shōtoku's ascendancy, as well as the cult that was created in his name, were thus deeply rooted in violence and bloodshed.

By moving to Kataoka, Kamitsumiya thus established himself in the domain of former adversaries that he himself had helped vanquish. These adversaries, who had been among the pre-eminent ritualists of their day, had been closely involved with the fire cult and with *chimata* rites of purification and resurrection. These rites and legends over time would have been deeply inscribed in the religious topography of the region. Thus it would appear that construction of the legend of Shōtoku and the beggar on the road to Kataoka was an attempt to come to terms with the cultic practices and deities of Shōtoku's defeated enemies.

One of the many ironies of Japanese scholarship on the Shōtoku cult is that scholars such as Umehara Takeshi have speculated that one of the main motivations for the formation of the Shōtoku cult was a sense of guilt or fear of divine vengeance on the part of those who destroyed Kamitsumiya's lineage.[57] Umehara and those who follow this line, however, have forgotten that Kamitsumiya was not only a victim but also, perhaps primarily even, an executioner. Just as royal ancestors such as Ōjin and Jingū eventually took up residence alongside the hostile deities of Chikuzen, so, too, did the logic of cult and violence result in a legend in which the figure of Shōtoku is hailed at Kataoka by the ghost of the region's vanquished.

6

Shōtoku and Gyōki

In 608, the advent of a mission from Sui China to the court of the
Yamato ruler Suiko helped spur a rapid acceleration in the dissemination of continental culture in the Japanese archipelago. The resulting influx of continental conceptions of rulership accelerated the
centralization of power in the hands of Yamato rulers. Expanded
central authority, in turn, resulted in intensified efforts to build roadways, canals, and estates to connect the court's rapidly expanding
domain of influence. A second by-product of the closer contacts with
the Chinese was the rapid diffusion of Buddhist institutions; within
decades, Buddhist temples, images, and ideas had become integral
parts of the physical and mental landscape surrounding the Yamato
court.

Yet the influx of continental culture also served to stimulate the
use of roadside rites of purification and spirit propitiation across
the Japanese archipelago.[1] As the construction and expansion of
highways and waterways across Yamato gathered speed, so, too, did
the need for protection from once-distant deities and spirits that were
believed to travel along the roadsides of Japan. Ironically, among
those most in need of such rites were the itinerant monks and nuns
who spread the Buddhist teaching to the farthest reaches of the
Japanese countryside.

This chapter will build upon chapter 5 by examining the role
played by roadside rites of begging, blessing (hokai) and spirit propitiation in shaping interactions between the Shōtoku cult and popular religious movements of the Nara and early Heian periods.
Specifically, I will focus on interactions between the cults of Shōtoku
and Gyōki (668?–749), a mendicant monk whose thousands of
itinerant followers organized lay believers across the Japanese islands

into communities united for the purpose of performing meritorious works. Gyōki is of direct relevance to these issues not only because of his role in disseminating the Buddhist tradition in the Japanese islands, but also because his followers expended huge amounts of labor constructing and repairing the roads and waterways of early Yamato. Because these roads and waterways became important sites for local cults and rites of blessing and spirit pacification, they also played a major role in the emergence of Shotoku and Gyōki as two of the most important cultic icons of the age.

Historical Background and Legacy

The importance of Gyōki's movement in Japanese religious and social history is well-attested in court records such as the *Shoku nihongi* as well as later hagiographical works such as the *Gyōki nenpu* (*Gyōki Chronology*), the *Gyōki bosatsuden* (*Biography of the Bodhisattva Gyōki*), and the *Nihon ryōiki*.[2] These sources, combined with a small amount of epigraphical evidence, have formed the basis for most research on the figure of Gyōki. Scholars such as Inoue Mitsusada, Yoshida Yasuo, Nakai Shinkō, and Nemoto Seiji have analyzed these texts in detail in order to reconstruct the trajectory of Gyōki's career through the course of his building activities and temple affiliations. These scholars are in general agreement that Gyōki was ordained as a monk in a state-regulated monastery, that he studied doctrine at Gangōji, and that he left the temple in defiance of recently formulated statutes that prohibited preaching to the populace at large. The movement that he led is thought to have emphasized the acquisition of merit through the performance of good works. There is also general agreement that toward this end, Gyōki and his disciples organized lay believers into sodalities for the purpose of performing such meritorious tasks as building bridges, canals, and temples.[3]

As Gyōki and his followers traveled across the country organizing communities and their many endeavors, it would also appear that itinerancy and begging became central elements in their religious practice. Far from being unique in this regard, however, Gyōki's movement is probably best understood as being emblematic of a broader cultic trend. The common use of the term *ubasoku*, which was derived from the Sanskrit term for early Indian Buddhist mendicants (*upasaka*), as a general term for such (male) lay believers highlights the degree to which begging and itinerancy were practiced during the period.[4]

For all of these reasons, Gyōki has been a figure of considerable interest to scholars of Japanese religion. His movement is often seen as a direct challenge to the court's attempts to control the process of ordination and assert its authority over the Buddhist clergy, or *sangha*. Gyōki's ability to resist the wishes of the court testifies to the enormous popular support his movement attracted beyond court circles. As such, he is seen as representative of an alternative form of Buddhism in which the definition of the clergy and its relationship to the lay community were understood in terms radically different from those propagated by the Nara court. Scholars such as Nakai Shinkō have even argued that Gyōki's emphasis on begging as a religious practice, coupled with his success in organizing vast numbers of believers into communities outside of regulated state structures, helped lay the groundwork for popular Buddhist movements of the Heian and even Kamakura periods.[5]

Followers and History

Although the picture just described of Gyōki and his movement is coherent and often compelling, before accepting these characterizations, a few methodological points are in order. With regard to sources, although a brief biography as well as scattered references concerning the historical figure of Gyōki can be found in entries from the *Shoku nihongi*, a court chronicle completed in 797, it is virtually impossible from such limited references to reconstruct much of the nature of Gyōki's career. These references are also supplemented by contemporaneous references to Gyōki in sutra inscriptions written by his followers, as well as Gyōki's epitaph as recorded in the *Daisōjō sharibyōki* (*Gravestone Memorial of the Senior Primary Prelate*), which provides us with limited information concerning Gyōki's career and his family background.[6]

Unfortunately, the great majority of characterizations regarding Gyōki's career in the work of the aforementioned scholars are therefore based upon hagiographical accounts found in the *Nihon ryōiki*, a Buddhist tale collection completed sometime around 822, as well as the *Gyōki bosatsuden* and the *Gyōki nenpu*, two late Heian texts thought to have been created in the eleventh and twelfth centuries, respectively. These texts provide ample information concerning not only the nature but also the locations of Gyōki's activities. Because the *Gyōki bosatsuden* and *Gyōki nenpu* are widely accepted in Japanese academic circles as reliable accounts of Gyōki's life and work, scholars such as Yoshida and others have relied heavily on these two texts for their understanding of both the man and his movement. In light of the fact that so much information concerning Gyōki first appears in sources composed some four hundred years after his death, however, the need for extreme caution in accepting these accounts is obvious. Given the paucity and nature of the sources that are at hand, this chapter will thus assume that many of even the most basic questions concerning the historical Gyōki are beyond the reach of historical investigation.[7]

Beyond the methodological difficulties involved in the sources that Yoshida and others have used to construct their image of Gyōki, however, lies a second set of issues concerning the focus and nature of their inquiry. Simply put, this picture may leave out much of what was most important for the movement that Gyōki founded and that continued after his death. Perhaps most crucially, in spite of the tremendous amount of scholarship that has been lavished upon Gyōki the leader, comparatively little work has been done on the beliefs and concerns of Gyōki's followers. Even during his lifetime, however, Gyōki was apparently venerated as a bodhisattva and sage with superhuman powers of perception and insight. Evidence for the cult of Gyōki can be found not only in tale collections such as the *Nihon ryōiki* but even in official court histories such as the *Shoku nihongi*.[8] How the historical Gyōki is related to the superhuman figure created by Gyōki's lay following, however, is a question that remains largely unexplored.

This blurring of myth and history, coupled with an awareness of Gyōki's undoubted influence upon Japanese Buddhist history, has in turn reinforced two further biases in contemporary scholarship. The first of these concerns the almost relentless focus within Japanese scholarship on issues concerning Gyōki's relationship to the court. Because Gyōki apparently violated the court's regulations regarding the activities of monks and nuns, he makes for an invaluable case study for a raft of important issues concerning the means by which the court enforced its own statutes, the court's policies toward the Buddhist clergy, and so on. These proclivities are further reinforced by the fact that references to Gyōki in the "hard" historical entries contained in the *Shoku nihongi* also naturally focus on the issue of Gyōki's relationship to the court. Yet neither the biases of court records nor the interests of contemporary scholars should lead us to assume that devotees of Gyōki's movement shared this agenda.[9] Although Gyōki's followers may have been deeply concerned with whether the court supported or proscribed their activities, there is no reason to believe that issues such as the nature of ordination or the role of the precepts were their central concern.

A second and more fundamental bias within the work of the scholars cited earlier consists of the fact that, to date, Gyōki has been viewed almost exclusively as a Buddhist figure. This in turn has led to a general reluctance to deal with cultic elements in Gyōki's movement that cannot be derived from Buddhist scriptures or institutions. Thus, even though it is generally acknowledged that Gyōki's followers may have engaged in forms of divination and healing, there has been virtually no research into the specific gods and cultic practices in which Gyōki and his followers engaged. There is no reason to believe, however, that these practices were peripheral or degenerate aspects of Gyōki's message. On the contrary, there is good reason to believe that they were actually core elements in the formation both of Gyōki's movement and the figure of legend to which that movement looked for inspiration.

This chapter will therefore examine the practices of Gyōki's movement within the context of the broad range of religious activities of Gyōki's followers. By focusing on where, and with whom, the constructed figure of Gyōki was associated in texts such as the *Nihon ryōiki* and the *Gyōki nenpu*, I propose to read the development of the cult of Gyōki—as opposed to the historical Gyōki—against the background of the local rites and legends of these areas and the various kinship groups that inhabited them.

Given the fragmentary and limited nature of sources at hand, such a project presents considerable challenges. Enough evidence is available, however, to suggest that such local rites were not specifically Buddhist in nature; indeed, I will argue that roadside rites involving blessing and spirit pacification also formed the basis of much of the royal cult. The major goal of this endeavor will thus not be to recover the lost figure of the historical Gyōki but rather to envision in greater breadth the social and religious terrain in which Gyōki's movement took shape and to which it responded.

This terrain was shaped to a surprisingly large degree by devotees of the early Shōtoku cult. As we have already seen, these kinship groups had an abiding interest in roadside rites of purification, spirit pacification, and resurrection. Much of the hagiography related to Gyōki suggests that the bulk of Gyōki's career was spent in areas populated by kinship groups at the center of the early Shōtoku cult. The frequency and depth of Gyōki's associations with these kinship groups suggest two possible conclusions: if we accept as historically accurate the information provided in such sources as the *Gyōki bosatsuden* and the *Gyōki nenpu*, then it would appear that Gyōki himself was a devotee of the Shōtoku cult and that he relied upon other Shōtoku devotees to help sustain his movement. If we do not accept the assertions made in these texts, however, then it would appear that the linkages between the cults of Gyōki and Shōtoku were strong enough to endure for several hundred years and that such linkages played a major role in the development of the hagiography of one of the most famous monks in Japanese history.

The rest of this chapter will therefore be divided into two parts. The first, which examines the trajectory of Gyōki's career in such texts as the *Shoku nihongi, Gyōki nenpu*, and the *Gyōki bosatsuden*, highlights the close correlation between the areas where Gyōki was purportedly active with specific kinship groups associated with the Shōtoku cult. The second part focuses primarily on the *Nihon ryōiki* in order to examine a series of legends associated with these groups that feature a cluster of motifs related to rites of blessing, begging, and spirit pacification. These legends highlight the prominent role of such rites across a broad spectrum of religious activity in the Nara and early Heian periods. They also help clarify the means by which the agenda and horizon of reception for the cults of both Shōtoku and Gyōki were shaped by the perceived need to propitiate the spirits of near and distant dead across the roadways of the Japanese islands.

Gyōki and the Shōtoku Cult

Scholars such as Yoshida Yasuo have long noted that, according to the *Daisōjō sharibyōki*, Gyōki was born in the Ōtori district of Izumi Province to a minor branch of the Kawachi no Aya, a kinship group that claimed as its founding ancestor a scholar from the Korean kingdom of Paekche named Wani.[10] Sakuma Ryū attached great importance to such lineal affiliations, as they indicate that one of Gyōki's predecessors and kinsmen was the monk Dōshō, one of the most famous monks of the pre-Nara period.[11] As Sakuma and others have pointed out, Dōshō's biography in the *Shoku nihongi* in many ways mirrors that of Gyōki as it is presented in the *Gyōki bosatsuden* and the *Gyōki nenpu*.[12] Like Gyōki, Dōshō is said to have studied at Gangōji only to leave the confines of the temple in order to lead an itinerant life of preaching among the populace. Both Gyōki and Dōshō are also said to have built temples, roads, and bridges across the country. Sakuma has thus even gone so far as to suggest that Gyōki could have been Dōshō's disciple at Gangōji.[13] Although we can only speculate about Gyōki's personal relationship with Dōshō, Gyōki's genealogical links to the Kawachi no Aya are significant in one other way as well: Gyōki was born less than twelve kilometers away from Yachūji, Dōshō's kinship group temple and an early center of the Shōtoku cult.[14] It is thus entirely plausible that Gyōki's kinship affiliations as well as the geographical location of his childhood home would have brought him into contact with the Shōtoku cult from an early age.

Gyōki and Takamiyadera

Yoshida, Nemoto, and others have sought further clues concerning the formation of Gyōki's religious thought by examining the doctrines and practices of the temples with which he was first associated.[15] Yoshida notes, for instance, that the *Gyōki bosatsuden* states that Gyōki was ordained at Takamiyadera, an early center of the Shōtoku cult.[16] In light of the fact that both Gyōki and Shōtoku were associated with this temple, the following legend from the *Nihon ryōiki* is especially intriguing:

> The Venerable Ensei, a disciple of Dharma Master Shaku, was a national preceptor of Paekche. He lived in the Takamiyadera at Kazuraki in Yamato Province in Japan. In the north chamber of that temple, there once lived a monk whose name was Gangaku, who used to go out to the village at dawn and come back at dusk. When a lay brother, a disciple of the Venerable Ensei, told his master about Gangaku, the master said "Don't say a word about him." The lay brother secretly bored a hole in the wall of Gangaku's chamber to spy on him and found the chamber full of light.... Before long it happened that Gangaku suddenly passed away. Ensei told the lay brother to cremate him and bury the ashes, and this was done. Later the lay brother came to live in Ōmi. Once he heard someone say, "Here lives the Venerable Gangaku." At once he paid a visit, finding Gangaku exactly as he had been. Gangaku said to the lay brother, "It is a long time since I last saw you, but I have been thinking of you all the time. How have you been getting along?"[17]

This text is striking in two ways: first, it specifically depicts the monk Gangaku, like Gyōki, as regularly going to the nearby village to mix with the populace from dawn until dusk. Presumably this would have involved both preaching and begging.[18] Second, the legend suggests that by the time of the completion of the *Nihon ryōiki* sometime around 822. Takamiyadera was associated not only with the Shōtoku cult but also with legends of monks who both mix with the populace and are able to effect their own resurrection.

The connections between Takamiyadera and the early Shōtoku cult also appear to have been prominent in the mind of Kyōkai, the editor of the *Nihon ryōiki*. As Iida Mizuho has pointed out, Kyōkai departed from his usual practice by presenting this legend in conjunction with another legend; apparently Kyōkai felt the relationship between the two was so close as to warrant their inclusion under the same number and heading.[19] The legend to which the Takamiyadera tale was joined was none other than an account of Shōtoku's encounter with the beggar at the crossroads (chimata) near Kataoka.

Geography of a Movement

Although both the Gyōki bosatsuden and the Gyōki nenpu state that Gyōki spent a period of time studying Hossō doctrine at Gangōji, next to nothing is known of Gyōki's activities prior to 717. An edict from that year as recorded in the Shoku nihongi criticizes the "small monk" Gyōki and his followers for gathering at the roadsides of the capital, promoting criminal activities, performing acts of self-immolation, and deceiving the populace.[20] Although rivers of ink have been spilled concerning the question of why the court was so alarmed by Gyōki's movement, it is difficult to be certain how much of the text reflects the practices of Gyōki's movement and how much of the text is simply a formulaic condemnation of the movement in general. Repeated injunctions in the Shoku nihongi against monks and nuns casting spells and/or engaging in itinerant preaching strongly suggest that Gyōki and his followers represented but one of many such volatile religious movements in early Japan.[21]

One example of the persistence of such movements over time has been discussed by Yoshida Yasuo, who notes that in 794 the court found it necessary to order the removal of an icon of Yakushi Buddha that had been made at the Otokuni shrine in Yamashiro. The court's decision to remove the image was apparently prompted by the spontaneous appearance of huge crowds at the shrine seeking miraculous cures for disease. Shortly thereafter, the court then exiled two figures, one claiming to be a divinity and the other styling herself "Koshi no Ubai," (the Koshi mendicant) for performing divinations at the crossroads and bewitching the populace.[22] Such events illustrate both the volatility of such movements and the ease with which popular religious leaders could appropriate the Buddhist vocabulary of movements such as Gyōki's.

The events at the Otokuni shrine also provide an important glimpse into the cultic geography in which the cults of Gyōki and Shōtoku developed. Although there is no evidence that the Koshi no Ubai claimed to be a devotee of Gyōki's, the connections of Gyōki's movement with this area were extremely strong; less than thirty years after this incident, legends depicting Gyōki at this very spot were already being recorded in the Nihon ryōiki. Equally importantly, this legend also demonstrates how easily local cults and rites performed at chimata intermingled with Buddhist practices and institutions associated with the early Shōtoku cult; Katō Kenkichi has demonstrated not only that the Otokuni shrine was administered by the Hata but also that the icon of Yakushi Buddha was later transferred to Kōryūji, the Hata kinship group temple and one of the earliest centers of the Shōtoku cult.[23]

Such geographic overlap between Gyōki's movement and devotees of the Shōtoku cult is a recurrent theme in hagiographic accounts of Gyōki's career.

At some point after the edict of 717, Gyōki appears to have shifted his activities from the area of the capital to his birthplace in Izumi Province. Here Gyōki was apparently able to forge a religious movement predicated not upon the support of high-ranking nobility of the capital but rather from middle-ranking local gentry and prominent local families. According to the *Gyōki nenpu*, Gyōki and his followers built no less than six temples in the Ōtori district of Izumi between 724 and 727. Further evidence of Gyōki's activities in Izumi can be found in a sutra inscription written during a massive sutra copying campaign carried out by over 700 devotees in the Ōtori district of Izumi in 730.[24] The inscription states that the campaign was led by the district chieftain, one Kusakabe no Obito Maro. Since, as we have repeatedly seen, the Kusakabe were one of the kinship groups most closely associated with Shitennōji and the early Shōtoku cult, this inscription is an invaluable piece of evidence from the Nara period that suggests that lineages affiliated with the early Shōtoku cult may have played an active role in Gyōki's movement. Indeed, Inoue Kaoru has argued that the support of the local Kusakabe must have been a crucial element in Gyōki's organizing efforts in the region. In support of this, he notes that the *Gyōki nenpu* lists no fewer than two temples, a training hall, a nunnery and an irrigation ditch that were purportedly built by Gyōki in the Ōtori district in or around the Kusakabe base of Kusakabe sato.[25] Thus, even if we do not accept the *Gyōki nenpu* account at face value, it nonetheless appears that Gyōki's movement in Izumi put down deep roots in territory under the control of an important lineage of the early Shōtoku cult, and that it relied upon local gentry such as the Kusakabe for support.

According to the *Gyōki nenpu*, by 730 Gyōki had expanded his sphere of activities, moving from Izumi into the area of Naniwa in adjacent Settsu Province, where he is said to have built seven training halls for members of his movement. Yoshida speculates that Gyōki's building efforts would not only have required the tacit consent of court-appointed officials but may also have involved the mobilization of corvée labor supplied by the court. More solid evidence of a gradual rapprochement with the court can be found in an edict from 731 in the *Shoku nihongi* in which the court referred to Gyōki as a "master of the law" (*hōshi*) and declared that it would allow male devotees of Gyōki's movement over the age of 61 and female devotees over the age of 55 to be ordained.[26]

A closer look at the kinship groups inhabiting the regions in Settsu where Gyōki was active suggests further links between Gyōki's movement and the early Shōtoku cult. Yoshida has noted, for instance, that most of the building activities attributed to Gyōki in Settsu took place along the waterway in the Ina district.[27] This area was home to the Inabe, yet another immigrant kinship group that was closely involved with the early Shōtoku cult and with the Hata. One indication of the strength of such links can be found in the figure of Inabe Tachibana no Iratsume, Shōtoku's fourth wife and the purported originator of the famed Tenjukoku tapestry that depicted Shōtoku's attainment of life after death.[28]

Gyōki's association with the Ina waterway highlights a broader pattern in the *Gyōki nenpu* and *Gyōki bosatsuden*; in both of these texts, Gyōki is frequently shown working in areas near major waterways and canals. Thus most of the projects attributed to Gyōki in Kawachi Province, for instance, are located in areas close to the Manta Canal, which the *Kojiki* states was built by the Hata.[29] Regardless of whether Gyōki (or, for that matter, the Hata) ever actually worked on the Manta waterway, for our purposes what is most important is that this area was heavily populated by members of the Hata kinship group and that hagiographical texts such as the *Gyōki bosatsuden* associated Gyōki with the area.

By 731, Gyōki is depicted in the *Gyōki nenpu* as having brought his movement to Yamashiro Province in the heart of Hata territory. During this period, Gyōki is said to have built temples at important Shōtoku centers such as Kadano, the site of the Hata kinship group temple Kōryūji; Fukakusa, the Hata center where Shōtoku's son Yamashiro no Ōe was raised; and Otokuni. These and other projects—if they did in fact occur—would have had to have been undertaken with the close cooperation of the Hata and their leader, Hata no Shimamaro.[30]

Here again there is some evidence from Nara period sources to suggest that hagiography associating Gyōki with Hata centers in Yamashiro may have reflected actual cooperation in building projects undertaken by Gyōki. In 741, when the court was threatened by a revolt in Kyūshū, a panicked Shōmu *tennō* turned to Hata no Shimamaro for help in both financing and constructing a new capital in the Kuni district of Yamashiro Province. This Shimamaro did, with the result that administrative centers around the new palace were completed by 742. Gyōki apparently worked with Shimamaro on this project; the *Shoku nihongi* states that some 750 *ubasoku* completed at least one major bridge at Kuni.[31] These activities were quickly reflected in Gyōki hagiography; as we shall see shortly, legends placing Gyōki in Yamashiro were well developed by the time of the completion of the *Nihon ryōiki* sometime around 822. By the time of the composition of the *Gyōki nenpu* and the *Gyōki bosatsuden*, Gyōki was said to have built during the course of his career no fewer than eleven temples and nunneries in Yamashiro Province.[32]

Evidence of Followership

Although the above evidence concerning the historical Gyōki's relationship to the kinship groups at the forefront of the early Shōtoku cult is far from conclusive, the overall picture suggests considerable overlap between Gyōki's followers and the early Shōtoku cult. To summarize the most important evidence for this from Nara period sources: (1) Gyōki was born in or near Kusakabe sato in the Ōtori district of Izumi. Members of the Kusakabe, one of the foremost kinship groups of the early Shōtoku cult, also appear as leaders of sutra copying activities led by Gyōki. (2) Gyōki himself was from a sub-lineage of the Kawachi no Aya, yet another kinship group with close ties to the early Shōtoku cult. Less than twelve kilometers from Gyōki's birthplace was Yachūji, the kinship group temple of one of the main branches of the Kawachi no Aya and an early center of the Shōtoku cult. (3) Gyōki is also known to have been active in Yamashiro Province during the period when the Kuni capital was being constructed there. This area was the main base of the Hata, yet another immigrant kinship group at the forefront of the early Shōtoku cult. Gyōki's participation in this project would almost certainly have brought him into contact with Hata no Shimamaro, the figure in charge of construction of the project. (4) Members of both the Kusakabe and the Hata also feature prominently among the known followers of Gyōki.

Further linkages that are suggested by hagiographical texts such as the *Gyōki bosatsuden* and the *Gyōki nenpu*, include the *Gyōki bosatsuden*'s assertion that Gyōki trained at Takamiyadera, a center of the early Shōtoku cult. The *Gyōki nenpu* also details Gyōki's activities in the Ina district of Settsu Province as well as his activities along the Manta waterway in Kawachi Province. These areas were inhabited by kinship groups such as the Inabe, Hata and Kawachi no Aya that were also at the forefront of the early Shōtoku cult. Finally, the *Gyōki nenpu* also states that Gyōki built several temples in Yamashiro Province at sites closely associated with both Shōtoku and the Hata.

Taken together, these texts thus suggest that later hagiography closely correlated Gyōki's activities with areas inhabited by devotees of the early Shōtoku cult. There are several possible reasons for this. Among the most plausible would be that Gyōki's own kinship affiliations, as well as the site of his birth, meant that virtually any account of his life would have lent itself to linkages with the early Shōtoku cult. Alternatively, such correlations might reflect the fact that devotees of the early Shōtoku cult were in many cases immigrant kinship groups that were also involved in the construction of temples, roadways and waterways across the Japanese islands. These groups would therefore have been natural allies for Gyōki and his movement. If we accept that Gyōki did actually engage in several projects at important waterways, this by itself would have made it likely that he and his followers would come in contact with kinship groups such as the Hata and the Inabe. Perhaps the best evidence that members of these lineages may have directly helped shape the received image of Gyōki for later generations, however, comes from statements in both the *Gyōki bosatsuden* and the *Gyōki nenpu* that they had relied upon an early account of Gyōki's activities that was purportedly composed by one Hata Horikawa no Kimitari in 742.[33] Although we of course cannot be certain that such a text really did exist in the Nara period, it is clear that by the time of the composition of later hagiographical texts such as the *Nenpu* and the *Bosatsuden*, material attributed to the Hata was already influential in shaping popular understandings of Gyōki and his movement.

Thus even if we do not assert that there was a grand design to link Gyōki one by one to centers of the early Shōtoku cult, the likelihood that large numbers of Shōtoku devotees were also part of Gyōki's movement suggests that they would have played an influential role in constructing the Gyōki legend corpus. This has two consequences. First, this suggests that the rites and legends associated with kinship groups such as the Hata, Kusakabe and Inabe may also have played an important role in shaping both the received image of Gyōki and the movement that was inspired by the man and legend. Second, and more broadly, the fact that devotees of both Gyōki's movement and the cult of Shōtoku were closely linked with the construction of waterways, bridges, canals and roadways highlights a crucial connection between changes in the political and physical landscapes on the one hand, and the transformation of the cultic landscape on the other. This suggests the intriguing possibility that the centralization of political power that accompanied the importation of continental systems of technology and governance did more than aid in the transmission of the Buddhist tradition to Japan. Ironically, this same process may also have stimulated the development and diffusion of local cults and roadside rites of spirit pacification across the Japanese islands.

Gyōki, Shōtoku, and Rites of Spirit Pacification

Several clues concerning how this process might have influenced Gyōki's movement can be found in the *Nihon ryōiki*'s account of the death and resurrection of Ōtomo no Yasunoko, one of Shōtoku's purported retainers. The text states that shortly before his return from the land of the dead, Ōtomo encountered both Shōtoku and Gyōki. The legend, and Kyōkai's gloss, are as follows:

> Lord Ōtomo no Yasunoko no muraji of the Great Flower rank was an ancestor of the Ōtomo no muraji in Uji, Nagusa district, Kii Province....
>
> On the eighth day of the twelfth month of the thirty-third year, Yasunoko died suddenly at Naniwa. His corpse was unusually fragrant, and the empress declared seven days' mourning in honor of his loyalty. He returned to life in three days, however, and told his family the following tale:
>
>> "There were five-colored clouds like a rainbow stretching to the north. I was walking along that roadway of clouds, and it smelled fragrant, as if valuable incense was being mixed. At the end of the way there appeared a golden mountain which dazzled my eyes as I approached it. There the late Prince Regent Shōtoku was waiting for me and we climbed to the summit together. A full-fledged monk was standing on the top of the golden mountain. Bowing to the prince, he said, 'I have come from the Palace of the East. In eight days you will fall into danger. I beseech you to take this elixir of life.' Then he gave one bead of his bracelet to be swallowed, and, with the penetrating eye, he had the prince recite three times, 'Homage to the Bodhisattva of Miraculous Power' and retired. I came back along the way I had taken before, and all of a sudden I was brought back to life."

"Bodhisattva of Miraculous Power" corresponds to Bodhisattva Manjuśri, the "one bead" which was swallowed is a pill to escape danger. The Most Venerable Gyōki, a contemporary of Shōmu *tennō*, is an incarnation of Bodhisattva Manjuśri. This is a miraculous story.[34]

This legend and its interpretation suggest several avenues of inquiry. Most obviously, it demonstrates that by the time of the completion of the *Nihon ryōiki* the figures of Gyōki and Shōtoku were being connected in popular Buddhist legends. Even more importantly, the legend also suggests that both figures were being associated not only with each other, but also with motifs of resurrection and the afterlife. These associations continued for centuries as the two figures appeared in numerous tale collections such as the *Nihon ōjō gokurakuki* (*Japanese Records of Birth in the Pure Land*), the *Sanbōe kotoba* (*Illustrated Words on the Three Jewels*), and the *Dainihonkoku hokekyōkenki* (*Miraculous Tales of the Lotus Sutra in the Great Land of Japan*).[35]

One possible source of such associations might be found in the intermingling of the two movements in regions where the figures of both Shōtoku and Gyōki were reverenced. As we saw above, Gyōki's connections with the Hata and Yamashiro are suggested both in the *Shoku nihongi* and in sutra inscriptions. As Gyōki's followers put down roots in the midst of the Hata and other Shōtoku devotees in Yamashiro, simple geographic proximity appears to have facilitated the seepage of Hata cults and legends into the fabric of the emerging Gyōki cult. One example of the intermingling of Gyōki's followers with the Shōtoku cult in Yamashiro can be seen at Otokuni shrine, the site of the mass movement to which I referred above. This shrine was in turn situated in extremely close proximity to a temple known as "Kanimanji," where the *Nihon ryōiki* suggests Gyōki had a strong following.[36] Several clues as to how such local cults in Yamashiro helped shape Gyōki's movement can be seen in *Nihon ryōiki* account of the founding legend of Kanimanji. This text, which centers upon one of Gyōki's devotees in Yamashiro, highlights several cultic motifs associated with the Hata:

In Kii district, Yamashiro Province, there lived a woman whose name is unknown. In the reign of Shōmu *tennō*, young cowherds in her village caught eight crabs in a mountain brook and were about to roast and eat them. She saw this and begged them, "Will you please be good enough to give them to me?" They would not listen to her, but said, "We will roast and eat them." Repeating her wholehearted entreaty, she removed her robe to pay for the crabs. Eventually they gave the crabs to her. She invited a *dhyana* master to give a blessing in releasing them.

Afterward she was in the mountain and saw a large snake swallowing a big toad. She implored the large snake, "Please set this frog free for my sake, and I will give you many offerings." The snake did not respond. Then, she collected more offerings and prayed, saying, "I will consecrate you as a kami. Please give it to me." Still without answering, the snake continued to swallow the toad. Again she pleaded, "I will become your wife in exchange for this toad. I implore you to release it to me." Raising its head high, the snake listened and stared at her face, then disgorged the toad. The woman made a promise to the snake, saying, "Come to me in seven days."

At that time the Most Venerable Gyōki was staying at Fukaosa-dera in Kii district. She went and told him what had happened. When he heard her story, he said, "What an unfathomable story! Just keep a steadfast faith in the Three Treasures." With these instructions she went home, and, on the evening of the appointed day, she tightly closed the house, prepared herself for the ordeal, and made various vows with renewed faith in the Three Treasures. The snake came, crawled round and round the house, knocked on the walls with its tail, climbed onto the top of the roof, tore a hole in the thatch of the roof with its fangs, and dropped in front of her. She merely heard the noise of scuffling, as if there was jumping and biting. The next morning she found the eight crabs assembled and the snake cut to shreds by them. She then learned that the released crabs had come to repay her kindness to them.

From this time on, people in Yamashiro Province have honored big crabs in the mountain streams and, if they were caught, set them free in order to do good.[37]

Because this legend depicts Gyōki at early Shōtoku cultic centers such as Otokuni and Fukaosa/Fukakusa, it appears that geographic linkages and overlap among followers between Gyōki's movement and the Shōtoku cult may have already begun to influence Gyōki hagiography by the completion of the *Nihon ryōiki* sometime around 822.[38] Seen in this light, it would also appear that the assertions in the *Gyōki nenpu* and elsewhere that Gyōki built temples at this site were rooted in beliefs that may have already developed by the early Heian period. If this is in fact the case, then it would appear that by the early ninth century Gyōki's movement was increasingly rooted both figuratively and literally in ground prepared by the cult of Prince Shōtoku.

The Kanimanji legend is especially noteworthy, however, because of the pervasiveness of non-Buddhist cultic elements within the legend. Although the text has clearly been given a Buddhist gloss, at its crux it is a tale of a young woman's struggle to propitiate a cruel spirit. Central to this struggle are such common cultic motifs as the maiden's offer to consecrate the snake as a god, her presentation of her robe to the deity and her offer to serve as a bride/shamaness for the god.

Several further clues within the text also suggest that the horizon of reception for the legend was shaped by local Hata cults and legends. Crucially, several Hata cultic centers in the region were also closely associated with both spirit pacification and sericulture deities linked to the cult of the Weaver Maiden and the Cowherd; the Konoshima shrine in Uzumasa, for instance, housed a sub-shrine known as the Kaiko Jinja (Silkworm Breeding shrine).

Elsewhere in the Japanese islands, as we saw in chapters 2 and 3, the Hata were also active in the cults of such cowherd deities as Ame no Hiboko and Tsunuga Arashito.

One hint of the possible influence of such cults in the Kanimanji legend can be seen in the central role given to crabs in the story; the Japanese term for crab—"kani"—is homophonous with woven items (kani, kanihata) associated with female shamans (miko) and spirit propitiation in early Yamato.[39] One further indication suggesting that this legend was related to the cult of the Weaver Maiden and the Cowherd can be seen from the text's representation of the boys in the legend as cowherds. All of this, coupled with the fact that the temple known as "Kanimanji" is situated in close proximity to a silkworm shrine known as "Kaiko Jinja," strongly suggests that by the time of the composition of the Nihon ryōiki the figure of Gyōki had been reshaped as it was inscribed in territory long associated with weaving cults and rites of spirit pacification in Yamashiro Province.

One further hint as to the nature of such cults can be seen in the text's reference to a "hokai," which Nakamura understands to be a prayer. Katata has argued that this term is best understood as an utterance which carries with it a spiritual force sufficient to bring about that which is wished for.[40] Because hokai were frequently used in the form of toasts, blessings and rites of spirit pacification, they appear sporadically throughout the Nihon shoki and the Kojiki. One further intriguing attribute of these passages is that in several cases hokai are used in reference to begging, blessing and, occasionally, crabs.[41]

One of the clearest examples of how looms and hokai came to be associated with roadside rites of spirit pacification during the period can be seen in the following legend from the Hizen fudoki (Records of the Customs and Land of Hizen):

> Himegoso township. Of old, to the west of the river here there was a wild god that would kill travelers on the roadsides. Half [of those who passed by] would die, half would be allowed to escape. A divination was done to determine why the god was wreaking its vengeance (tatari) thus, and they were told "In the Munakata district of Chikuzen, have a man named Azeko build a shrine and worship me. If you do as I request, I will no longer have a violent heart." At this they found the man named Azeko. When they instructed him to build a shrine and worship the god, Azeko took a banner (hata) and raised it in his hands, praying "If my worship is truly needed, may this banner fly on the wind and fall at the place where the god who seeks me resides." At this the banner was suddenly taken up by the wind and flew away. It flew to the Mihara district and fell to the ground at the Himegoso shrine. It then once again flew up into the air and returned, falling to the earth in the fields near a small village by a small mountain river. Azeko thus knew where the wild deity resided, and at night he had a dream in which a loom and a reel (tatari) came dancing before Azeko, pushing him. At this he knew that the wild god was a

female deity and immediately built a shrine and worshiped her. After that travelers were no longer killed on the roadsides. For this reason, the shrine was called "Himegoso" (the Princess' shrine) and today, the village takes its name from the shrine.[42]

This legend not only suggests the remarkable degree to which looms and weaving implements were identified with female deities during the period, it also illustrates the close association between roadways, *hokai* and spirit pacification in the Japanese islands; indeed, the trope of the vengeful spirit that vents its wrath upon travelers along the roadsides is a commonplace in early Japanese literature.[43] For our purposes, however, this legend is of immediate interest in light of the fact that, as we saw in chapter 3, the deity of the Himegoso shrine was none other than Akaru Hime.[44] Because this deity was said to be the wife of Hata cowherd deities at the Kehi and Izushi shrines, the legend also amply illustrates the degree to which weaving implements and *hokai* pervaded Hata shrines across the Japanese islands.

Hokai *and Court Liturgies*

The use of *hokai* and motifs from weaving cults, however, was by no means limited to the shrines of immigrant lineages such as the Hata. Indeed, *chimata* rites involving *hokai* appear to have pervaded much of the court ritual from the period. Several reasons for why these elements were clustered together can be found in the Ōdono no hokai (*Blessing of the Great Palace*), a rite of purification and spirit pacification that was performed at regular intervals throughout the year in conjunction with the most important events in the court ritual calendar. The liturgy of this rite again highlights the intimate connection between blessing and spirit pacification in early Yamato:

> The Sovereign Ancestral Gods and Goddesses,
> Who divinely remain in the High Heavenly Plain,
> Commanded the Sovereign Grandchild to occupy the heavenly high seat,
> And presenting unto him the mirror and sword, the heavenly signs [of royal succession],
> Said in blessing:
> 'Our sovereign noble child, oh Sovereign Grandchild,
> Occupying this heavenly high seat,
> [Retain] the heavenly sun-lineage for myriads of thousands of long autumns,
> And rule tranquilly the Great Eight-Island Land of the Plentiful Reed Plains and of the Fresh Ears of Grain as a peaceful land.'
> Thus entrusting the land to him,
> By means of a heavenly council,
> They silenced to the last leaf
> The rocks and the stumps of the trees,

Which had been able to speak,
And [caused him to] descend from the heavens
To reign over this kingdom . . .

To you, Ya-bune no mikoto, [do I address] marvelous heavenly words
    of blessing,
And bless and pacify, humbly speaking:

In the location of the great palace where he holds sway,
To the farthest extent of the bed-rock beneath,
May there be no woes from the roots of vines and creeping insects;
May there be no woes from blood dripping [from the heavens] and
    from flying birds . . .
I speak the names of the deities who thus tranquilly and peacefully
    give their protection . . .

Therefore on the long strings of myriad *mi-fuki* noble beads,
Which have been purified and sanctified by the sacred bead-makers,
Have been attached colored cloth, radiant cloth;
And I, Imibe-no sukune So-and-so, hanging a thick sash over my
    weak shoulders,
Bless and pacify.[45]

Several elements from this liturgy demonstrate the ease with which *hokai* (blessings) could be used for different purposes within early Yamato ritual. At the beginning of the text, the command of the gods and goddesses of the high heavenly plain ordering the heavenly grandchild to descend to Yamato takes the form of a blessing. Yet the act of blessing does far more than simply express good wishes; rather it serves a means of effecting change in the world. Such blessings are also inextricably linked within the liturgy with a project of purification and spirit pacification; the attainment of a long, prosperous reign is contingent upon the conquest of the spirits of the land in which the Heavenly grandchild resides. Thus at the crucial moment in the liturgy the pacification of evil spirits and the dispersal of spiritual pollutants is effected with the formula "[I] bless and pacify."

This linkage between blessing and spirit propitiation pervaded other forms of court ritual as well; just as blessings and petitions for good fortune came to be linked with rites of spirit pacification, so too did exorcisms and rites of pacification come to function as rites of blessing. In the annual rite of spirit-pacification performed for the *tennō* (Chinkonsai, *Mitama shizume no matsuri*), for instance, the liturgy concludes as follows:

Bless the court of the *tennō* as eternal and unmoving,
Prosper it as an abundant reign,
And grant that [his spirit] may abide tranquilly here in its abode
From this twelfth month
Until the twelfth month to come.

With this prayer, on the such-and-such day of the twelfth month of
    this year,
I bless and pacify [his spirit]. Thus I humbly speak.[46]

This formula of simultaneous blessing and spirit pacification was not confined, however, to rites in court-sponsored shrines; blessing and spirits pacification were also central elements in the roadside rites that were performed at
chimata across Yamato. Within the liturgy of the *Michiae no matsuri* (*Ceremony
of Roadside Offerings*), a rite of offerings to the *chimata* deities charged with
pacifying roadside demons, one again finds the linkage of blessing and spirit
pacification:

I humbly speak your names:
    Ya -chimata-hiko,
    Ya-chimata-hime,
    Kunato,
And fulfill your praises

[with the prayer] that you will not be bewitched and will not speak
    consent
    To the unfriendly and unruly spirits
    Who come from the land of Hades, the underworld;

If they go below, you will guard below,
    If they go above, you will guard above,
    And will guard in the guarding by night and the guarding by day,
    And will bless . . .

Bless the Sovereign Grandchild eternal and unmoving,
And prosper him as an abundant reign. Thus I humbly speak.

Further, [with the prayer] that you may bless tranquilly
    The princes of the blood, the princes, the courtiers,
    the many officials,
As well as even the common people of the kingdom,
I, as priest, fulfill your praises
    By the heavenly ritual, the solemn ritual words.
        Thus I humbly speak.[47]

Liturgies such as this not only suggest that *chimata* deities were propitiated by
the court, they also suggest that the court, no less than the populace, employed ritual means to bless and pacify the living and dead on the roads of
Yamato. Perhaps even more importantly, by highlighting the need for protection from the "unfriendly and unruly spirits" on the roads of early Yamato,
this liturgy also suggests an important reason why such rites would have been
of interest to the *ubasoku* that traveled in droves along the highways of early
Yamato.

Beggars and Hokai *in Shōtoku Hagiography*

Such cultic concerns also appear to have played an important role in shaping the early Shōtoku cult. Most dramatically, the importance of roadside rites involving *hokai*, begging and blessing appear to have played a large role in shaping the legend of Shōtoku's encounter with a beggar on the road to Kataoka. As I've already noted, this legend was paired in the *Nihon ryōiki* with the legend of the monk Gangaku's resurrection at Takamiyadera. Within the *Nihon shoki* account of the Kataoka legend, Shōtoku composes the following song expressing sorrow for the plight of the beggar:

> On slope-shining
> Kataoka Mountain
>   Starved for rice,
>   He lies fallen—
> Alas, that poor traveler!
>   Without a parent
> Were you born into this world?
>   Have you no master
> Flourishing as young bamboo?
>   Starved for rice,
>   He lies fallen—
> Alas, that poor traveler![48]

The tone of Shōtoku's ode is reminiscent of a poem from the *Manyōshū* in which a beggar composes the following song for a dead crab:

> In far-shining
> Naniwa there built a hut
> In a little creek
> Where it lived all out of sight
> A reed-crab,
> And the great lord summoned him:
>
> Now why can it be
> That you summon me, my lord?
> I know the reason—
> Its as clear as it can be.
> Is it as a singer
> That you summon me, my lord?
> Is it as a piper
> That you summon me, my lord?
> Is it as a strummer
> That you summon me, my lord?[49]

The similarities between Shōtoku's ode to the beggar at Kataoka and the beggar's ode to the *kani* are surprisingly deep; in both cases the poet offers a song for a deceased or dying figure that the poet has encountered while traveling. Both songs serve to give voice to the grief of the fallen, presumably in order to console and thereby pacify the spirit. As in the case of the court liturgies that we discussed above, both songs also make reference to the "lord" governing the land and express bewilderment at the plight of the deceased. Perhaps most importantly, these poems also highlight the frequency with which beggars and travelers must have encountered death and corpses—whether of humans or animals—on the roadsides of Nara Japan.

Nishimura Sey has argued on linguistic grounds that the song attributed to Shōtoku must have been from a pre-existing oral tradition of Japanese origin. He speculates that the song may have been a common requiem for the pacification of the spirits of travelers who had died along the roadsides of early Yamato.[50] The prominence of invocations of blessing and spirit pacification in these legends may thus have been motivated by fears that roadsides in early Yamato were filled with corpses, robbers and wandering spirits. In such circumstances the need for rites of spirit pacification and purification would have been most acutely felt by such figures as beggars, mendicants and travelers.

By the time of the completion of the *Nihon ryōiki* at the start of the Heian period, the linkages between begging, blessing and spirit pacification were taken for granted by the text's author, Kyōkai. Thus in the *Nihon ryōiki* account of the legend of Shōtoku and the Kataoka beggar it is the beggar who is given the final word:

> Once, when the prince regent lived at the Palace of Okamoto in Ikaruga, he happened to go to Kataoka and, on the way, he found a sick beggar lying by the side of the road. Alighting from his palanquin, the prince talked with the beggar, took off his cloak to cover him, and went on his way. On his return he did not see the beggar, but only his cloak hanging on the branch of a tree. The prince put it on again. One of his ministers said to him, "Are you so poor that you must wear the soiled garment once worn by a beggar?" "It's all right, you wouldn't understand," was his reply. Meanwhile, the beggar died in another place. The prince sent a messenger to have him buried temporarily while a tomb was built for him at Moribeyama in the northeast corner of Hōrinji in the village of Okamoto. A messenger sent to visit the tomb found it too tightly closed to allow anybody to enter. Only a poem was found at the door, and it read:
>
> > The name of my Lord
> > Would be forgotten,
> > Should the stream of Tomi of Ikaruga
> > Cease to flow.[51]

For our purposes one of the most important elements of the *Nihon ryōiki* presentation of the legend is the focus given to the beggar's parting words for Shōtoku. Whereas in the *Nihon shoki* account of the legend it is Shōtoku who composes a poem of consolation for the beggar, in the *Nihon ryōiki* account it is the beggar who composes an ode for Shōtoku. Further, in the *Nihon ryōiki* account, of the legend the beggar is explicitly shown bestowing his blessing upon Shōtoku from beyond the grave.

All of this suggests that by the time of the composition of the *Nihon ryōiki* at the latest rites of begging and blessing in Nara Japan had been incorporated into the Shōtoku cult. Within the text itself the central importance of *hokai* and spirit pacification for the construction of the beggar's identity is not left open to doubt; the reading supplied by the oldest commentaries for the characters that Nakamura renders as "beggar" is none other than *hokaihito*.[52]

Cultic Topography and Sedimentation

How the fear of spirits and disease helped shape the cultic agenda of Gyōki's movement as well as that of the Shōtoku cult can best be seen in the context of two political developments from the Nara period that dramatically altered the political balance at court and, as a consequence, the court's religious outlook. The first event was the downfall of one Prince Nagaya, the main center of opposition to the Fujiwara in the early part of the eighth century. In 729, Nagaya was accused of attempting to use black magic to destroy his enemies and was forced to commit suicide.[53]

Nagaya's downfall left the way open for the Fujiwara to install a Fujiwara woman, Kōmyō, as Shōmu *tennō*'s chief consort. Yet Nagaya's death was also followed by a series of earthquakes, famines and other natural disasters. By 737 the heads of all four of Fujiwara Fuhito's sons had been killed by a deadly plague, leaving Kōmyō virtually alone as standard bearer for the Fujiwara.

As a result of these and other disasters the court in general and the Fujiwara in particular became preoccupied with finding the means to placate angry spirits. Following the death of her mother in 733, an apparently terrified Kōmyō turned to the spirit of Shōtoku for protection. In 737 the Fujiwara began reconstruction of the famed Yumedono at Shōtoku's family temple of Hōryūji. This structure housed an image of the Kuse Kannon, "built to the Prince's size" and served for later generations as a cultic center where Kōmyō and her heirs could pray to the prince for protection."[54]

Yoshikawa Shinji has recently suggested that it was at this moment, as Shōmu and Kōmyō desperately sought the means to pacify the spirits believed to be threatening Fujiwara and the nation, that the court embraced Gyōki's movement. According to the *Gyōki nenpu*, that year Gyōki built a series of small practice halls in Yamato along the northern Great Lateral Highway. Yoshikawa has noted that the *Gyōki nenpu* account corresponds well with an entry in the *Shoku nihongi* that refers to six such small halls built by Gyōki in Yamato Province.[55] He has further suggested that these halls served as way stations for laborers brought in to the Ikaruga area of Yamato in order to complete work on the Yumedono and other buildings at Hōryūji. If this is in fact did happen, then it would appear that Gyōki himself helped literally construct one of the most important institutional and cultic manifestations of the Shōtoku cult.

Yoshikawa also believes that he has discovered the remains of one of these practice halls. Remarkably, the location of this hall is also in the exact area where the *Nihon ryōiki* states that Shōtoku met the beggar on the road to Kataoka. What is most striking about this discovery, however, is the name of the temple as it is listed in the *Gyōki nenpu*: "Zudain," which can be roughly translated as "Beggar's Hall."[56]

The existence of a temple at this particular site does not, of course, prove that it was built by Gyōki. It is eminently possible that the later tradition ascribed the temple's origins to Gyōki. What is so striking about this find, however, is that such connections appear to have already been in the mind of Kyōkai prior to his completion of the *Nihon ryōiki* sometime around 822. Thus even if we do not, with Yoshikawa, assume that Gyōki actually built the Beggar's Hall on the site of Shōtoku's supposed encounter with the Kataoka beggar, it is nonetheless the case that a no less remarkable construction of linkages between the figures of Gyōki and Shōtoku, rooted in their common associations with roadside rites involving begging and *hokai*, had already occurred less than eighty years after Gyōki's death.

Conclusion

It would appear that by the time of the completion of the *Nihon ryōiki* the figure of Gyōki was already closely associated with Shōtoku devotees such as the Hata as well as a series of Shōtoku cultic centers in Yamashiro Province. Not only were Gyōki and Shōtoku paired in legends of otherworld journeys, Gyōki was depicted as visiting, and building upon, prominent centers of Shōtoku worship associated with the Hata. The Hata, however, were involved in a broad range of non-Buddhist cultic practices related to sericulture and spirit pacification. Thus within the *Nihon ryōiki* Gyōki himself appears in a legend involving a (weaving) maiden, cowherds and crabs (*kani*). This and other legends involving crabs and begging also highlight the importance of *hokai*, or rites of blessing and pacifying in Nara cultic life. Such rites are also found in a broad range of court rituals from the period. The degree to which such roadside rituals of blessing and pacifying shaped the horizon of reception for the cults of both Shōtoku and Gyōki can also be seen in the legend of Shōtoku's encounter with the beggar at Kataoka. Here the centrality of *hokai* to the practice of begging can be found in the text's use of "*hokaihito*" as an appellation for the beggar.

The fact that later hagiography then asserted that Gyōki had built a practice hall (*in*) at that very spot known as "Beggar's Hall" further suggests the remarkable degree to which the figure of Gyōki was rooted both physically and metaphorically in ground prepared by the early Shōtoku cult. This process was apparently already well under way by 822, when the monk Kyōkai recorded legends depicting Gyōki at Shōtoku centers in Fukakusa, Otokuni and, finally, on the road to Kataoka. By the time of the completion of the *Gyōki nenpu*, Gyōki was depicted as building practice halls and bridges in Izumi, Settsu, Kawachi,

Yamato and Yamashiro provinces at sites heavily populated by Shōtoku devotees. In the process, the movement that centered upon the legendary Gyōki
drew upon the complex of legends and cultic practices associated with the early
centers of the Shōtoku cult even as it expanded and amplified them.

All of this thus suggests that the horizon of reception for both the Shōtoku cult and Gyōki's movement were shaped to a surprisingly large degree by
rites and legends that are in no sense distinctively Buddhist. On the contrary,
Shōtoku's encounter with the beggar on the road to Kataoka can only be understood within the context of rites of propitiation and resurrection at *chimata*.
Indeed, by 739 the figure of Shōtoku was being enlisted by the court as an aid
in the pacification of evil spirits with unprecedented power.[57]

More broadly, it would also appear that a complicated symbiosis characterized relationships between local cults and the early Japanese Buddhist tradition. As continental influences spurred the development of roadways and
waterways across the Japanese islands, these new networks of travel and communication allowed for the increasingly rapid and deep penetration of religious
conceptions and practices associated with the Buddhist tradition. Devotees of
both Gyōki and Shōtoku were deeply involved in this process, both as builders
of roads and as builders of cults.

Yet the proliferation of roadways and waterways also set in motion the cults
of local gods and spirits across the land. As spirits of the dead and vengeful
deities were thought to wreak havoc and death on the roads of the living, rites of
spirit propitiation and pacification came to be woven ever deeper into the fabric
of religious life across the islands. Eventually such practices came to be the
foundation of such court rites as the *Ōdono no hokai*, the *Michiae no matsuri* and
the *Mitama shizume no matsuri*. Thus did the *hokaihito* of early Japan help
establish the parameters of religious discourse for both Buddhist and royal
cults for centuries to come, as the ever-increasing need to control both the
living and the dead occupied the minds of rulers and beggars alike.

7

Dōji, Saichō, and the Post–
Nihon Shoki Shōtoku Cult

Following the completion of the *Nihon shoki* in 720, the figure
of Shōtoku became a key reference point in several religious debates
that occupied the attention of the Nara court. Among the most
pressing of these were questions concerning the definition and status
of monks, the proper relationship between Buddhism and the state,
and the place of Japanese Buddhism within Buddhist history.
Throughout the Nara period, however, each of these issues developed
against a backdrop of increasing concern over vengeful spirits, disease, and spirit pacification. As a result, the figure of Shōtoku increasingly came to be seen as both Dharma King and protective
deity by a court riven with often-deadly divisions. In this role, the
figure of Shōtoku exerted a profound influence over the development
of state-sponsored Buddhist institutions as well as sectarian Buddhist movements of the Heian period and beyond.

One figure at the center of this unfolding dialectic was the monk
Dōji, one of the pre-eminent intellectuals of his day and quite possibly an editor of the *Nihon shoki*. In addition to being one of the chief
architects of Buddhist-state relations of the Nara period, Dōji also
played a central role in the reconstruction of Hōryūji and the establishment of Shōtoku as Dharma King and guardian deity of the
court. Spurred in part by Dōji's emphasis upon Chinese models of
Buddhist kingship, the Shōtoku legend corpus continued to grow
throughout the Nara period as the pre-eminent sage of the Japanese
islands was identified as an incarnation of the Chinese T'ien-t'ai
patriarch Hui-ssu. Because the legend of Hui-ssu's incarnation as
Shōtoku facilitated the absorption of Buddhist influences from China
and the Korean Peninsula, it would later play a pivotal role in the
development of a series of Buddhist movements within the Japanese

islands. By the beginning of the Heian period, this process was in full swing as Shōtoku *cum* Hui-ssu was enshrined as a core element in the emerging Tendai tradition's self-definition and as a cornerstone of early Heian conceptions of the broader Buddhist tradition.

Dōji, Prince Nagaya, and the Rebuilding of Hōryūji

Among the most important developments for the Shōtoku cult following the completion of the *Nihon shoki* was the court's increased patronage of Kamitsumiya's kinship group temple Hōryūji during the reign of Shōmu *tennō*. Temple records indicate modest royal patronage for Hōryūji prior to Shōmu's reign.[1] This lack of support from the court is reflected in the paucity of references to the temple in the *Nihon shoki* and *Shoku nihongi*. Although the *Nihon shoki* tersely states that the temple was completely burned in 670, for instance, it fails to record the circumstances surrounding the disaster and its aftermath.[2] This paucity of written records has led to a long-lived debate in Japanese scholarship concerning the issue of whether the current temple is in fact the original temple built by Prince Kamitsumiya or a later reconstruction.[3]

The ferocity of this debate, however, has in some ways obscured other, more pressing issues concerning the role of the temple in the development of the Shōtoku cult and later Japanese religion. For our purposes, the most important issue is not whether the current temple was "really" built by Kamitsumiya. Of far greater significance is the fact that much of the temple was apparently not rebuilt immediately after its destruction; construction of major buildings such as the famed Yumedono, for instance, was not begun until almost seventy years after the fire recorded in the *Nihon shoki*.[4] It is therefore doubtful that the temple could have been a major driving force for the early Shōtoku cult. Rather, the circumstances surrounding the reconstruction of the Yumedono in the 730s suggest that Hōryūji was not so much a source as a product of the Shōtoku cult's early success.

Hōryūji and Daianji

Probably the best place to begin unraveling the puzzle of how and why Hōryūji's restoration occurred is with the founding legend of Dōji's temple Daianji, another state temple with less obvious though important links to the early Shōtoku cult. These links can be seen in the *Daianji garan engi narabi ni ruki shizaichō* (*Historical Account and Inventory of Holdings of Daianji*), which was submitted to the court in 747. The account begins as follows:

> When the *tennō* [who reigned] at the Okamoto palace [Jomei] had not yet ascended to the throne, he was called Prince Tamura. At that time the Exalted *tennō* [who reigned] at the palace at Owarida [Suiko] summoned Prince Tamura and sent him to the Ashigaki palace at Akunami to inquire about the illness of Prince Umayado [Shōtoku].

She also ordered him to ask about his condition, if there was anything she could do for him or anything that he wished for. [Tamura]
reported [that Shōtoku had replied], "Having received the *tennō*'s
benefactions, there is nothing more [worldly] in which I could
take delight. But I [your servant] have begun a Buddhist hall at the
village of Kumakori. I hope to offer it for the benefit of successive
generations of sovereigns from the distant past and on into the
future. I wish this hall to become a great temple. This is my only
wish. I ask fearfully that the court grant it." The Exalted *tennō* agreed
to the request.

After three days the Prince [Tamura] went on his own to Akunami
to ask after [Umayado's] sickness. At this Prince Kamitsumiya said to
Prince Tamura "Such delight! How wonderful that you, my nephew,
should yourself come to inquire about my illness! This makes me
wish to offer you some treasure. Yet treasures are easily lost and
cannot be guarded forever. Only the Three Treasures of the Law can be
eternally transmitted without cease. Therefore I will offer you Kumakori temple, as you are one well suited to eternally transmit the
Three Treasures of the Law. Prince Tamura was delighted and again
made obeisance, saying "I will in accordance with your instructions accept [this temple] and offer it [for the benefit of] past sovereigns
and princes. Successive generations of *tennō* and their descendants
will ceaselessly preserve and transmit this temple [forever].[5]

As Mizuno Ryūtarō has noted, this text is somewhat unusual because it in
effect invokes both Kamitsumiya and Jomei as founders of Daianji, and thereby
provides the temple with two sources of authority.[6] In view of the fact that
Jomei's line defeated Kamitsumiya's in their struggle for the throne, it would
thus appear that by the time of the composition of this record Jomei's descendents had laid claim to the charisma of the very line that they themselves had
displaced.

There is some suggestion within the *Daianji engi* that there was resistance
to this move. The text states, for instance, that after the temple was moved from
Kumakori village, its pagoda was destroyed by the angry deity of the Chisakobe
shrine:

Now in the second month of the eleventh year after the *tennō* [Jomei]
assumed the throne, they cut down [wood belonging] to the Chisakobe shrine by the Kudara river and built a temple with a nine story
pagoda. They also endowed [the temple] with 300 households
[for its support], and they named it Great Kudara Temple. At this
time the god of the shrine was angry and caused a fire which
destroyed the nine story pagoda.[7]

Much as rulers such as Temmu and Saimei had been intimidated by vengeful
deities during in the latter half of the seventh century, there is ample reason to

believe that the creation of this legend was fueled in large part by the logic of violence and propitiation that underlay so many of the legends in the Shōtoku corpus. The founding ancestor of the Chisakobe (and presumably the god of their ancestral shrine) was none other than Kamu Yaimimi no Mikoto, whom, as we saw in chapter 5, was closely connected with Kataoka and with *chimata* rites of spirit pacification. Because the Chisakobe and several other lineages descending from Kamu Yaimimi no Mikoto were closely allied with the early Shōtoku cult, this account of Kamu Yaimimi no Mikoto striking the temple may suggest not hostility to the Buddhist tradition per se but rather hostility brought about by the attempt by Jomei's line to appropriate the charisma of Shōtoku for their own. As we shall see shortly, this logic of violence and pro- pitiation, which loomed so large throughout the Nara period, contributed di- rectly to the rebuilding of Hōryūji.

A second clue for understanding the founding legend of Daianji lies with the siting of the temple in Nukata sato in the Akunami district of Yamato. Nukata sato is generally believed to have been the home of the Nukatabe kinship group.[8] Because Dōji was both the head of Daianji and a member of the Nukatabe, Mizuno has argued that Dōji must have fabricated this part of the legend in order to associate both Shōtoku and the temple with his ancestral home.[9] If this is in fact the case, then the temple's claim to affiliation with Shōtoku illustrates the degree to which Shōtoku had become a pre-eminent source of authority in Buddhist circles by 747.[10]

Dōji's attempt to highlight the Nukatabe's connection to Shōtoku also illustrates the more general point that kinship group affiliations directly in- fluenced the activities and beliefs of Buddhist monks in pre-modern Japan. Throughout the Nara period and beyond, renunciation of lay life apparently did not entail renouncing one's ancestors or their cults. As a result, during the period issues of ethnicity, kinship, and regional affiliation played a major, often dominant, role in the development of Buddhist institutions across the Japanese islands. Dōji's career illustrates this point extremely well; the ancestral and cultic affiliations of the Nukatabe and related kinship groups appear to have directly influenced not only Dōji's actions but also the general development of Daianji, Hōryūji, and the early Shōtoku cult.

One example of how kinship group affiliations affected the development of temples such as Hōryūji can be found in the *Harima kuni fudoki*, which records legends of members of the Nukatabe performing rites of spirit paci- fication at the village of Sasayama in the Iibo district of Harima.[11] This area is notable not only for the presence of large numbers of Silla immigrant kinship groups associated with the early Shōtoku cult, but also for recent archeological discoveries of the remains of temples built with the same lay- out as Hōryūji.[12] Even more to the point, Sasayama is listed in the *Hōryūji garan engi narabi ni ruki shizaichō* (*Historical Account and Inventory of Hold- ings of Hōryūji*) as the site of one of several estates in Harima belonging to Hōryūji.[13]

The economic importance for Hōryūji of these estates is underlined in the following legend from the *Nihon shoki*:

Autumn, 7th month. [Suiko] *tennō* ordered the crown prince to
lecture on the *Shōmangyō*. He finished his lectures in three
days.

In this year the crown prince also lectured on the *Lotus Sutra* in
the palace at Okamoto. The *tennō* was greatly pleased and gave the
crown prince 100 *chō* of irrigated land in Harima Province. They
were therefore dedicated to Ikaruga temple.[14]

Although it is an open question whether Prince Kamitsumiya ever expounded
upon Buddhist scriptures, it is probably safe to accept the text's suggestion
that Hōryūji's estates in Harima served as an important part of the temple's
main economic base. Although the text states that these lands were a gift of
Suiko, the amount of lands from this area listed among the temple's holdings
in 747 far exceeds the amount stated in the *Nihon shoki*, suggesting that kinship groups from this area had been major contributors to the temple.[15] Seen
in this light, the presence of the Nukatabe at the precise location of this estate
thus raises the possibility that the Nukatabe may have been early sponsors of
the temple.[16] In addition to the Nukatabe, other kinship groups from the early
Shōtoku cult such as the Miyake, the Kusakabe, the Hi no Kimi, and the Hata
are also prominent in the *Harima kuni fudoki* account of the Iibo district.[17]

Dōji and Prince Nagaya's Vow

Although little is known of Dōji's career prior to his journey to China, he seems
to have obtained the patronage of the Fujiwara after establishing a reputation
as a promising scholar-monk.[18] Dōji was sent to China for further study in 703,
most likely with Fujiwara support.[19] During his stay, Dōji was exposed to the
most current trends in Chinese state Buddhism. His long period of residence
at Hsi-ming ssu, a major temple in the Western capital Ch'ang-an, would have
exposed him to the work of Yi-ching, a major intellectual figure who completed a new translation of the *Golden Light Excellent King Sutra* there in 703.
This text would later play a major role in Dōji's formulation of the Japanese
state Buddhist tradition. Dōji's prolonged stay at Hsi-ming ssu must also have
given him prolonged exposure to the works of Tao-hsüan, an exegete famous
for his study of the Buddhist precepts (*vinaya*) who served as the temple's first
abbot. This background appears to have strongly influenced Dōji's later career
as precepts master (*risshi*) for the Nara state.[20] Upon his return to the Japanese islands in 718, Dōji was regarded as one of the pre-eminent scholar/
intellectuals in the Japanese islands. This gave him entry into the inner circles
of such powerful figures as Fujiwara no Fuhito, the head of the Fujiwara
kinship group, and Prince Nagaya, the foremost opponent of the Fujiwara and
a sponsor of many of the leading intellectuals of the day.

The rivalry between these two factions cast a shadow over political and
religious events throughout the Nara period. Because Dōji was on friendly
terms with both factions, he was uniquely well-placed to put his personal
stamp on the development of the court religion of the period. This he did,

promoting both Chinese models of sacred kingship and the figure of Shōtoku as cornerstones of the emerging state Buddhist tradition. One major part of this effort was the restoration of Hōryūji as a shrine for the worship of Shōtoku in the guise of guardian deity for the Japanese state, the Fujiwara, and the throne.

These events unfolded, however, against a background of increasingly deadly political tensions at court. The end game did not begin, however, until 727, when Shōmu *tennō's* Fujiwara consort Kōmyō gave birth to a son.[21] The child was named crown prince after only three months, giving disparate Fujiwara factions a reason to unite. In 728, however, the child died and a non-Fujiwara consort produced a son and possible replacement candidate for the throne. The Fujiwara response was to press for the elevation of Kōmyō—a non-royal—to the position of Queen Consort. Prince Nagaya, who seems to have served as a spokesman for royal privilege, stood in the way of such a plan. In the second month of 729, the Fujiwara struck; Nagaya was accused by a Fujiwara ally of using black magic. Nagaya was forced to commit suicide days later, and within six months Kōmyō was named Queen Consort.[22]

Shortly before his death, Prince Nagaya appears to have been aware that his position at court had become untenable. In what is generally thought to have been one last attempt to profess his loyalty to Shōmu, Nagaya copied the *Greater Sutra on the Perfection of Wisdom* (Ch: *Ta po-jo po-luo mi-tuo ching*; J: *Dai hannya haramita kyō*) and dedicated the merit deriving from this act to the royal line.[23] The vow dedicating this merit was apparently composed by Dōji, whose name appears at the head of a list of several figures on Nagaya's staff. Shinkawa Tokio has analyzed the language of the text and concluded that its somewhat unusual terminology is consistent with that used in the *Nihon shoki* accounts of Tajima Mori and Yamato Takeru—two figures that, as we saw in chapter 5, were also depicted in terms drawn from Chinese tropes of immortality and resurrection.[24] Shinkawa also notes strong similarities between this vow and contemporaneous epigraphy from Silla.[25]

Although most scholars simply dismiss the charge of black magic out of hand as a fabrication on the part of the Fujiwara, a close look at Nagaya's cultic and social affiliations helps explain why such a charge would have been plausible in the highly charged political and religious atmosphere of the time. Perhaps even more importantly, it again illustrates the degree to which concerns over spirit pacification affected the development of the Buddhist tradition in the Japanese islands.

As I noted earlier, several members of Prince Nagaya's staff were from Silla immigrant kinship groups associated with *chimata* rites of purification and spirit pacification. These rites often involved the use of *hitogata*, or substitute bodies, which were thought to be capable of carrying impurities to the underworld. Discoveries at several sites of caches of such bodies inscribed with curses have also established that during this period substitute bodies were also used on occasion in order to curse or harm others.[26]

Nagaya's lineal affiliations suggest a close connection with such rites. His father, Prince Takechi was the son of Temmu *tennō* and a consort from the

Munakata kinship group.[27] Prince Nagaya's own affiliation with the Munakata cult appears to have been extremely deep; after Nagaya's death, his surviving son served as an officiant at the Munakata shrine in Yamato Province.[28] As we saw in chapter 3, the Munakata shrine off the coast of Kyūshū was a virtual treasure trove of artifacts from Silla as well as ritual implements such as *hito-gata*.[29] Because the Munakata deities were portrayed in the *Nihon shoki* as vengeful gods that struck down members of the court, Nagaya's association with the cult of these vengeful deities helps explain both the plausibility of the Fujiwara charge of black magic and the later belief that Nagaya himself had become a vengeful spirit who sought to destroy the Fujiwara.[30] It was in this environment of fear that Dōji was able to promote both the establishment of Chinese Buddhist paradigms for Buddhist-state relations on the one hand and a new image of Shōtoku as a guardian deity for the court on the other.

Shōtoku Worship and the Rise of Dōji

As the leading authority on T'ang culture and Buddhism of the day, Dōji was in a position to exercise enormous influence over the formation of Nara Buddhism and the Shōtoku cult. In the same year that Nagaya met his end, Dōji was named *risshi*, or *vinaya* master, by the court.[31] This position placed him in charge of enforcing monastic discipline for the officially sanctioned Buddhist clergy. Dōji was thus soon confronted with a set of issues concerning the definition and status of Buddhist monks and the proper relationship between the Japanese state and Japanese Buddhism. Dōji's impact on these issues can be seen in the following events, all of which can be attributed in great part to his efforts:

1. The introduction of a large number of Buddhist sutras from T'ang China in 718. Several of these texts dealt with issues of Buddhist kingship and offered protection to Buddhist rulers and their states.
2. The transfer of Daianji, the largest temple in the Japanese islands at the time of its completion, to the capital.
3. The construction of a state temple network at which Daianji was the head.
4. The dispatch of envoys to China in 735 to search for a *vinaya* teacher to perform state-regulated ordinations of Japanese clergy.
5. Renewed construction at Hōryūji.
6. The establishment of Shōtoku as a guardian deity for the Fujiwara and the royal line.

These events, when taken together, suggest that Dōji was a principal architect of the institutional and intellectual frameworks of royal policy vis-à-vis Buddhist institutions during the Nara period. They also suggest that Dōji's understanding of Chinese Buddhist institutions fed directly into his vision of the figure of Shōtoku as a figure to whom the court should turn for superhuman assistance.

Throughout the remainder of his life, Dōji also worked to bring the Buddhist clergy under the sponsorship and regulation of the Japanese state. Dōji's biography in the *Shoku nihongi* indicates that he urged the adoption of Chinese practices regarding the assertion of state authority *vis-à-vis* the *sangha*.[32] In light of Dōji's general outlook, it also seems likely that he was extremely critical of the widespread practice of unregulated ordination.[33] Although the state's interest in restricting such practices is often ascribed to a desire to assert the court's religious authority or reduce the number of exemptions for *corvée* labor, the issue of ordination was of crucial importance for several other reasons as well. Among the most important of these were concerns that improperly ordained monks would not observe the monastic precepts and were therefore less likely to generate merit for the Japanese state. A properly ordained *sangha* was needed to obtain the protection of such figures as the Four Heavenly Kings for Japanese rulers.[34] Also, ordination was itself a transmission of the Buddha's teaching and spiritual charisma. Buddhist teachings could not flourish without a properly ordained clergy. Finally, the issue of the definition of the Buddhist monk was inseparable from the definition of the sage Buddhist ruler, or Dharma King. Such a figure would serve as both patron of the *sangha*, or monastic order, and guarantor of the *sangha*'s religious authenticity.[35]

These convictions were translated into two concrete actions on the part of the Nara court that were to have lasting impact on the development of Japanese religion. First, in 735 the court sent two monks to China to seek precept masters. Dōsen, the first Chinese monk to arrive, took up residence in Daianji and appears to have been an ally of Dōji's for the remainder of the two men's lives.[36] A second group of *vinaya* specialists, led by the Chinese monk Chienchen (J: Ganjin), arrived in 753.[37] This group, which also maintained close ties with Daianji, gave shape to a new understanding of the relationship between the Chinese and Japanese Buddhist traditions by promoting the legend that Shōtoku was an incarnation of the Chinese Buddhist patriarch Hui-ssu.

In 741, each province in the Japanese islands was also commanded to build one monastery and one nunnery for the protection of the state. This project was almost certainly influenced by the formation of such a network begun by Empress Wu in China in 690. Hsi-ming ssu, the temple at which Dōji stayed during his years in China, housed several of the most prominent monks during Empress Wu's reign. All of this suggests that Dōji was influenced in his understanding of the workings of Chinese Buddhism by his connection with this group.[38]

Probably one of the most important examples of such influences can be seen in the court's adoption of the *Golden Light Excellent King Sutra* as one of its principal scriptures. Dōji appears to have attached great importance to this work, which, as I noted earlier, was translated in 703 by the Chinese monk Yi-ching at the very temple where Dōji resided during his fifteen years in China. This text soon became one of the cornerstones of the emerging Japanese state Buddhist tradition. In 733, during Dōji's tenure as *risshi*, or *vinaya* master, for the Japanese state, the study of either the *Golden Light Excellent King Sutra* or *Lotus Sutra* was made a requirement for ordination. Both sutras were also chanted regularly at every temple in the court-sponsored temple network that was established between 737 and 741, again while Dōji served as *risshi*. As I noted in chapter 1, several quotations from this text are interspersed within the *Nihon shoki* in several passages related to Shōtoku and the establishment of the Japanese Buddhist tradition, including the *Nihon shoki's* depiction of Shōtoku during the battle between the Soga and Mononobe. Lest the reader fail to get the point, an editorial note was inserted into Kamitsumiya's biographical sketch that states that he was a Dharma King.[39] Dōji thus appears to have transformed the figure of Shōtoku into a precedent justifying Dōji's own innovations; in the *Nihon shoki*, Shōtoku served as a paradigm of sacred kingship grounded in the texts and principles that Dōji had introduced to the Japanese court. Henceforth Japanese rulers were to serve not only as sponsors but also as regulators of the Buddhist clergy.[40]

Dōji, Hōryūji, and the Fujiwara

Shortly after the death of Prince Nagaya in 729, Dōji's efforts were greatly facilitated by a series of disasters that befell the royal house and the Fujiwara. Repeated earthquakes and famines appear to have rattled the Fujiwara, and royal edicts confessing lack of virtue were issued repeatedly. In 733, these disasters started to strike close to home, as the mother of Queen Consort Kōmyō died. By 737, the heads of all four branches of the Fujiwara had succumbed to the plague, leaving Kōmyō alone as standard bearer for the Fujiwara.[41]

In search of divine help, Kōmyō appears to have turned to the spirit of Shōtoku. Shortly after the death of her mother in 733, Kōmyō, who was herself ill for an extended period of time, responded by making offerings exclusively to Hōryūji. After recovering, Kōmyō sent further gifts in 734. In 735, Gyōshin, the abbot of Hōryūji, persuaded Kōmyō to hold a Lotus service at Hōryūji. The following year, Dōji was asked to lead 300 monks in yet another Lotus service at Hōryūji, the merit from which was offered to the spirit of Shōtoku. At the ceremony, Kōmyō and the Fujiwara asked for the protection of "Shōtoku, whose august spirit still overlooks the Court."[42] Thus did the figure of Shōtoku the Dharma King assume the role not only of benefactor for the Nara state, but also as personal guardian of the Fujiwara and the royal house.

Dōji and Gyōshin were quick to exploit this opportunity. The following year, Dōji requested and received substantial contributions from Kōmyō for a sutra-reading ceremony at Daianji for the purpose of preventing disasters.[43] Gyōshin, for his part, presented Kōmyō with relics associated with Kamitsumiya. Shortly thereafter, work began on Hōryūji's Eastern complex with support from Kōmyō.[44]

Kōmyō's liturgical efforts, however, failed to relieve pressure on the Fujiwara. Following the death of Kōmyō's brother Muchimaro in 737, Muchimaro's rival Tachibana no Moroe was asked to head the government. Also heading the government was Moroe's close ally, Prince Suzuka, who was none other than Nagaya's younger brother. Moroe and the Nagaya faction at court then moved quickly to consolidate their power and settle old scores. Within a month, Shōmu *tennō* had raised the ranks of all of Nagaya's surviving children. A few months later, the accuser of Prince Nagaya was murdered.[45] Even more ominously for the Fujiwara, Moroe convinced Shōmu to move the capital away from Nara, where the Fujiwara were entrenched, to Moroe's base in the Kuni district of Yamashiro. Moroe also sought to have Prince Asaka, the son of a non-Fujiwara consort, named crown prince.[46]

Yet Kōmyō and the Fujiwara struck back. In 738, Shōmu, over the objections of most of the court, named Kōmyō's daughter Princess Abe as crown princess.[47] Plans to move the capital soon bogged down, and in 744 Prince Asaka suddenly died, quite possibly the victim of Fujiwara intrigue.[48] By 745, objections from courtiers and Buddhist institutions led Shōmu to abandon plans to build a new capital. The Fujiwara were back in control.[49]

During this period, the Fujiwara completed work on the Eastern complex at Hōryūji. Among the principal buildings was the famed Yumedono, which appears to have functioned as a mausoleum that housed the spirit of Shōtoku.[50] When work was completed on the Yumedono, a statue of Kuse Kannon—built once again "to the Prince's size"—was enshrined.[51]

Kōmyō, in the position of Queen Mother, was to remain one of the most powerful figures at court and the leading patron of Japanese Buddhism for the rest of her life.[52] She also apparently remained a fervent believer in Shōtoku, worshiping the statue of Shōtoku cum Kuse Kannon as a guardian deity. For centuries to come, the spirit of Shōtoku retained this position as the fountainhead of Japanese Buddhism, promising corporate and individual salvation as Dharma King and personal savior.[53]

Hui-ssu, Shōtoku, and the Transition to Heian Buddhism

Although Dōji died in 744, the connections between Daianji and the Shōtoku cult persisted. One of the most important developments of the Shōtoku cult in the Nara period—the legend that Shōtoku was the incarnation of the Chinese Patriarch Hui-ssu (515–577)—built upon the groundwork laid by Dōji and Dōsen at Daianji.[54] As Shōtoku himself came to be represented as a sage from across the sea, figures such as Ganjin and Saichō sought to redefine the Japanese Buddhist heritage in relation to people and events far away from the "Land of the Eight Islands."

The first reference that we have to the legend comes in a poem by one Ōmi no Mahito Mifune in 767. Mifune, who was one of the leading intellectuals of his day, spent several years as a monk and disciple of the Chinese monk Dōsen at Daianji before returning to lay life. Mifune also worked closely with several disciples of the Chinese *vinaya* master Ganjin.[55] Mifune also referred to the legend in his biography of Ganjin, the *Tō daiwajō tōseiden (Account of the Great T'ang Priest's Eastern Expedition)*, which was completed in 779. In this work, the following dialogue between Ganjin and envoys from the Japanese court is recorded:

"When the Buddhist teaching spread to the East and arrived in
the land of Japan, there was only the teaching without a teacher. Of
old in our country Shōtoku Taishi said: 'After two hundred years the

sacred teaching will flourish in Japan.' Now we seek a teacher to
fulfill this fate and make the teaching flourish." The Master replied:
"I have heard long ago, that after the Master Hui-ssu of Nan-yüeh
passed away, it was predicted that he would be reborn as a prince
in the land of Japan and that he would make the Buddhist Law
flourish and aid all sentient beings in passing over to the other shore.
I have also heard that Prince Nagaya of Japan greatly revered the
Buddhist Law and had a thousand robes made, which he offered to
virtuous monks of this land."[56]

This passage has been the subject of much discussion among Japanese
scholars who have focused on the issue of whether the Chinese actually knew
of Shōtoku prior to Ganjin's arrival in 753. Most see the passage as a fabrication on the part of Ganjin's disciples in order to win support from the Nara
court. Others have suggested that Ganjin may have heard of Shōtoku from the
Japanese monks who came to recruit him.[57]

I am inclined to believe that the legend of Hui-ssu's incarnation as
Shōtoku pre-dated the arrival of Ganjin in the Japanese islands. Ganjin is
seldom mentioned in Japanese sources in connection with Hui-ssu/Shōtoku,
and the legend was propagated by several figures with little connection to Ganjin. It is also difficult to see why the text would have Ganjin refer to Prince
Nagaya, the Fujiwara's former enemy, if the account were simply a fabrication
designed to win support from the court. This, coupled with the fact that the
propaganda value of Ganjin's claim to connection with Shōtoku would have
been minimal if the court had not already accepted Shōtoku's status as the incarnation of Hui-ssu, suggests a formulation of the legend that pre-dates Ganjin's arrival in the Japanese islands.

Regardless of whether the legend was fabricated by Ganjin's disciples or
simply used by them, however, much of the legend's appeal was clearly related
to its skillful use of the indigenous theme of the sage from across the sea who
comes to hail a Japanese ruler as sage. Here Ganjin the great *vinaya* master is
presented as having come to the Japanese islands in order to carry on the work
of the great sage Shōtoku. By presenting Shōtoku himself as a sage from across the sea, however, the legend marked a watershed moment in the development of the Shōtoku cult. With this claim, the figure of Shōtoku came to be
understood against a mythic/historical backdrop that transcended Japan itself.
Henceforth Shōtoku's life narrative would be told in terms of centuries,
stretching beyond Japan to China and even India at the time of the Buddha.

In spite of this, surprisingly little research has been done on the connections between the legend cycles of the Chinese patriarch and the Japanese
prince.[58] One possible reason for this may be a sectarian tendency to view
Hui-ssu primarily as the teacher of Chih-i, one of the preeminent Buddhist
scholars in history. Yet during his lifetime Hui-ssu was already famous for his
meditative practice at Nan-yüeh, the mountain where he apparently sought to
combine his study of the *Lotus Sutra* with practices aimed at acquiring superhuman powers and immortality.[59] Ultimately, it was Hui-ssu's association

with both the *Lotus sutra* and superhuman powers that made possible the radical expansion of the Shōtoku legend corpus.

Hui-ssu's quest for longevity and his association with the Taoist mountain Nan-yüeh later gave rise to legends that Hui-ssu could control his reincarnations and that he had knowledge of his past lives. These legends tended to emphasize both his connection with Mount Nan-yüeh in previous lives and his desire to be reborn in a land without Buddhism in his next incarnation. Hui-ssu's biography in the *Hsü kao-seng chuan* (*Further Biographies of Eminent Monks*), a text composed by the Chinese exegete and monk Tao-hsüan in 645, records several such legends:

> Hui-ssu went with over forty monks to Nan-yüeh on the 12th day of the 6th month of the 20th year Kuang-ta reign year of the Ch'en dynasty. When they arrived he said to them 'I will live here for exactly ten [more] years. After this [life] I must go far away.' [Then] Hui-ssu said: 'There is an ancient temple here. Long ago I lived in it.' According to his words, they began to dig and they uncovered the foundations of a hall and the remains of the plates and utensils that he had used. Again he went beneath a boulder: 'As I sat in meditation here, a brigand decapitated me and I died. The corpse is still here.' When they searched for it they then found a full torso of dried out bones. When they looked further down they discovered the skull. Hui-ssu took it, [reverently] and raised it to his forehead. They built a magnificent stupa for it in light of its former karma.[60]

This passage illustrates three elements that run through the Hui-ssu legend corpus. First, not only is Hui-ssu shown to have knowledge of his former lives but also proof is offered by digging up items associated with him during his previous incarnations on Mount Nan-yüeh. Second, these items are then treated as religious relics that are venerated almost as if Hui-ssu himself were a Buddha. Third, the issue of Hui-ssu's past lives is inevitably tied to the question of his next incarnation. Here as elsewhere, Hui-ssu gives notice that he wishes to spread the Buddhist teaching in a distant land.

Silla Immigrant Groups and the Elaboration of the Legend

These motifs also formed the core of the legend of Hui-ssu's reincarnation in the Japanese islands as Prince Shōtoku. The first work to expound upon the legend in detail, the *Shichidaiki* (*Records of Seven Generations*), is thought to have been written by a monk from Tōdaiji named Myōichi in 772.[61] Although the first portion of Myōichi's work is no longer extant, the text seems to have been designed to give an account of Shōtoku's life followed by an exposition of his previous incarnations on Mount Nan-yüeh as Hui-ssu. The text also includes the following legend:

> In the 7th month of the 15th year of [the reign of Suiko], Ono no Imoko was sent as an ambassador to the Great T'ang. The crown

prince [Shōtoku] then commanded him, saying: 'There is an immortal in a meditation center on Mount Heng [Nan-yüeh] in the land of the Great T'ang. He always carries with him the *Lotus Sutra*. Go to this place and ask him to return it.' Ono received this command and traveled across the ocean to the great T'ang. As he had been commanded, he went to the meditation center on Mount Heng and made inquiries. An old master came out and asked 'Who are you?' [Ono] replied, 'I am an ambassador from Japan.' And then he made obeisance and said, 'In my country there is a sage king who has commanded me to come to the Great T'ang and personally visit the meditation center on Mount Heng. I ask that you bring out the *Lotus Sutra*.' At this the old master said 'I have for a long time not transmigrated, always waiting for you. Now that you have arrived, there is nothing more for me to wait for. He then told the ambassador 'Take this sutra immediately and return quickly to your country.'... He led one hundred and twelve people back to Japan. At that time the joy of the *tennō* and the crown prince was without bounds. They had the scripture stored in the document hall at Ikaruga.[62]

This legend retains several themes common throughout the Hui-ssu legend corpus. Here as elsewhere, Hui-ssu's connection with Mount Nan-yüeh is stressed. Hui-ssu is also shown as having transmigrated to a distant land without the Buddhist Law. Once again, the legend centers on the retrieval of a relic from Hui-ssu's past life, which is then reverently received and preserved. Perhaps most importantly, however, here again we find that such motifs have been adapted to fit the common Japanese hagiographic structure wherein a sage from overseas hails a Japanese ruler as a sage king.[63]

During the early Heian period, the legend appears to have undergone rapid development in the hands of immigrant lineages associated with the early Shōtoku cult. One important text dating from the early to mid-Heian period, the *Jōgū Shōtoku Taishiden hoketsuki*, explicitly states that it was based upon sources from Shitennōji as well as sources obtained from the Kashiwade and Tsuki no Omi kinship groups. Temple records indicate that the Tsuki no Omi, an immigrant kinship group from Kazuraki, had a longstanding connection with Daianji.[64] Thus the *Hoketsuki* account of the legend offers us several important clues concerning the role of kinship groups associated with Shitennōji and Daianji in the development of the legend. The *Hoketsuki* version also shows several important developments in the legend. The text is as follows:

The prince said to the Dharma Master Hyeja: "There is a character missing in [this] phrase of the *Lotus Sutra*. How have the ones [scriptures] that you have seen been?" The Dharma Master [Hyeja] replied: "None of the *Lotus Sutras* of other nations have character either." On the 15th day of the ninth month of the Prince's 35th year

[Shōtoku] closed the doors of his palace and for seven days and seven nights received no officials and fasted. No one from his wives on down was allowed to approach him. At the time, the people wondered at this. [Hyeja] Hōshi said: The prince has entered *samadhi*—do not disturb him. On the morning of the eighth day there was a copy of the *Lotus Sutra* on the [Prince's] table. [All were] profoundly surprised and in awe [of the Prince]. After emerging from meditation [Shōtoku] often said: "How wonderful! The monks from the Great Sui were such good spiritual brethren!"[65]

Several markers in this text indicate the handiwork of the immigrant groups associated with Shitennōji. The appearance of the Koguryô monk Hyeja, for instance, echoes other legends concerning Shōtoku's rebirth in *tenjukoku* and the Pure Land. Such familiar tropes such as the immigrant sage who arrives from across the sea, the two sages who each mysteriously understand the wisdom of the other, and the familiar motif of "the people" hailing both figures as sages, all resonate with legends of such figures as Ame no Hiboko, Tsunuga no Arashito, the Kataoka beggar, and others.

The *Hoketsuki* account of the legend is perhaps most notable, however, for its focus on the miraculous copy of the *Lotus Sutra* obtained by Shōtoku. Among the most important pre-suppositions upon which the legend was constructed are the following:

1. Shōtoku/Hui-ssu had the ability to see his past lives, control his reincarnation, and enter meditative trances that allowed him to send his spirit across the sea.
2. Shōtoku was impelled to return to China to rectify the defect of a missing character in the *Lotus Sutras* in the Japanese islands.
3. Hui-ssu had left a rare and marvelous scripture on Mount Nan-yüeh.

Although the first of these premises—Hui-ssu's ability to control his reincarnation, and his mastery of Taoist meditative techniques—would have been known to anyone familiar with the Chinese Buddhist tradition, a close look at the final two presuppositions suggests that the Silla immigrant kinship groups associated with Shitennōji and Daianji played a major role in the legend's development.

This is particularly true in the case of the assertion that Shōtoku was motivated by the desire to find the character missing from copies of the text in "all other lands" as well. This motif appears to have been drawn from a legend found in the *Hung-tsan fa-hua chuan* (*Accounts Spreading the Praise of the Lotus*), a seventh-century Chinese text. In the *Hung-tsan fa-hua chuan* account of the legend, a *Lotus Sutra* chanter from Silla is plagued by a continued inability to remember one character from the *Lotus* while reciting. In a dream, he discovers that in a previous life he also was a *Lotus* chanter but that he allowed his copy of the *Lotus* to be damaged, with the result that one character had been made illegible. When the monk eventually tracks down the sutra from his past life and repairs it, he discovers that his ability to chant the entire sutra has been restored.[66]

The fact that even Chinese sources for this legend state that the protagonist is from Silla helps explain the subsequent appropriation of the legend by the kinship groups associated with Shitennōji and the early Shōtoku cult. A variation of the legend appears in the *Nihon ryōiki* as follows:

> In Kazuraki upper district, Yamato Province there was once a devotee of the *Lotus Sutra*. He came from the Tajihi family, and even before he was eight years old, he could recite the *Lotus Sutra* with the exception of one character that always escaped his memory and continued to escape it even when he was in his twenties.
>
> Once he prayed to Kannon, confessing his offenses, and had a dream. A man said to him, "In your previous existence you were the child of Kusakabe no Saru in Wake district, Iyo Province. At that time, while reciting the scripture you burned one character with a lamp so that you could no longer read it. Now go and see . . .
>
> Setting off on his quest, he reached Saru's home at last and knocked at the door. . . . [When] the mistress went to the door to see the guest, [she found] him the very image of her deceased son. . . . Saru invited him into the house, and, staring at him as he sat in the seat of honor, said, "Aren't you the spirit of my deceased son?" Their guest told them in detail about his dream and announced that the old couple were his parents. Saru, after some reminiscing, motioned to him, saying, "My late son, so and so, lived in this hall, read this scripture, and used this pitcher." The son entered the hall, opened the scripture, and found that the character which he could never remember was missing, for it had been burned with a lamp. When the young man repented of his offense and repaired the text, he could recite it correctly. Parents and son were amazed and delighted, and the son never lost the parent–child relationship and his sense of filial piety.[67]

Among the most notable features of this version of the legend, in addition to its obvious similarities with the legend of Hui-ssu's incarnation as Shōtoku, are the setting and main characters. Iyo, as we saw in chapter 2, was an early center of the Shōtoku cult. Shōtoku and his teacher Hyeja figure prominently not only in the *Hoketsuki* account of Shōtoku's miraculous sutra, but also in the *Iyo kuni fudoki*, where the two are said to have visited a hot spring and composed an inscription for a stele referring to *kotobuki no kuni*, or the land of long life.[68] Perhaps most important for our purposes, however, is the identification of the protagonist as a member of the Kusakabe kinship group. The Kusakabe were of course a kinship group closely affiliated with Shitennōji, the Abe, and the early Shōtoku cult.[69]

Hui-ssu's Buried Sutra and Vow

The third premise of the legend—that Hui-ssu left a miraculous copy of the *Lotus Sutra* on Mount Nan-yüeh—has been largely neglected by commentators. In the *Hoketsuki* account of the legend, however, the sutra is not simply an excuse to demonstrate Shōtoku's status as the incarnation of Hui-ssu. Rather, it is presented as being of the utmost importance in its own right. What the sutra could have meant can be seen from the end of the *Nan-yüeh Ssu ta ch'an-shih li-shih yuan-wen* (*Dedicatory Inscription of a Vow Taken by the Great Meditation Master Hui-ssu of Nan-yüeh*), a vow that was purportedly written by Hui-ssu in the mid-sixth century on the occasion of his copying and then burying a sutra at or near his residence on Mount Nan-yüeh:

> Through the power of this vow, may no demons or any of the myriad disasters harm this *Greater Sutra on the Perfection of Wisdom*, done in gold lettering, and this case, made with seven treasures. At the time when the world honored Maitreya appears in the world for the benefit of all the innumerable sentient beings [of the world], may he preach this *Greater Sutra on the Perfection of Wisdom*. At that time, by the power of my vow and this gold-lettered sutra, may a six-fold earthquake shake Maitreya's august world. The assembly will then lower their heads in wonder and ask the Buddha: "From what karmic cause did this earthquake occur? Oh World-Honored One, please expound upon this!"
>
> At that time Maitreya will answer his disciples, saying: "Let all with one mind join their palms together, listen well and believe. In the past there was a Buddha named Shakyamuni who appeared in the world and preached the *Greater Sutra on the Perfection of Wisdom*, and helped myriad sentient beings cross over [to enlightenment]. After this world-honored Buddha passed out of existence, the Age of the True Dharma and the Age of the Counterfeit Dharma all passed and the remaining Dharma was left in the Final Age...
>
> At that time a [copy of the] *Greater Sutra on the Perfection of Wisdom* appeared in the world. At that time there was a *bhiku* named Hui-ssu who made this copy with gold lettering and placed it in a box of lapus lazuli. He then made the following vow: 'I will help the innumerable sentient beings [of the world] cross over. In future *kalpas* when Maitreya appears in the world, this *Greater Sutra on the Perfection of Wisdom* will be preached.' You should all know that this earthquake was due to the power of this *bhiku*'s vow, and that the gold-lettered sutra and lapus lazuli case have now appeared in the world."
>
> Then the assembly will say to the Buddha, "World-honored One, with your superhuman powers, please show us this gold-lettered sutra and case!"

[Maitreya will reply] "You should all with one mind make obeisance to the past Buddha Shakyamuni. And you should with one mind bring to mind the *Greater Sutra on the Perfection of Wisdom*.

When the World-honored One has thus spoken, the Earth will again shake six-fold and a great ray of light will shoot forth and illuminate the ten limitless worlds. A marvelous fragrance will arise.... When the assembly smells this fragrance they will produce the *bodhi* mind.... At that time those in the assembly will dance with joy and together say to the Buddha:

"Then World-honored One, allow us to see the script of the sutra!"

[Then he will answer] "He who wrote this sutra made a great vow. You should all with one mind think of him and call his name. Then you will be able to see [the script]."

When he has spoken thus, then the entire assembly will call my name and say "*Namu Hui-ssu!*"[70]

This remarkable vow holds the key for unlocking the meaning of the legend of Hui-ssu's incarnation as Shōtoku. Here Hui-ssu in effect declares that he will replace Maitreya as the preacher who will save the world. The instrument of this salvation will be the copy of the *Greater Sutra on the Perfection of Wisdom* that Hui-ssu buries on Mount Nan-yüeh. I would suggest that the legend of Shōtoku's recovery of a sutra of Hui-ssu's from Mount Nan-yüeh was directly linked to Hui-ssu's vow and burial of a sutra on that mountain. This supposition is reinforced by the text of *Shichidaiki*, which quotes Chinese sources that depict Hui-ssu at Hannya Peak showing his copy of the *Lotus Sutra* to his disciples just prior to his prediction of his death and subsequent transmigration to the Japanese islands:

Now, when Master Hui-ssu saw that his life was ending he raised up his *Lotus Sutra*, his begging bowl and staff at a stone enclosure on the Hannya plateau and said to his disciples: "After I have passed away, I will go to a land without the Buddhist Law, receive a body and help transform all sentient beings.[71]

All of this suggests that whoever composed the legend built upon Hui-ssu's vow by substituting the *Lotus Sutra*, with which Hui-ssu and Shōtoku were also associated, for the *Greater Sutra on the Perfection of Wisdom*.

These motifs are further amplified in the *Shichidaiki*, which sets the Japanese portion of the story in the Yumedono at Hōryūji. As I noted earlier, since at least the time of the writing of the *Nihon shoki*, the founding of Hōryūji was attributed to Shōtoku's preaching of the *Lotus Sutra*. We have also seen that from 739 the Yumedono served as a cultic center where Kōmyō and the court prayed to Shōtoku for protection. The salvific nature of this spirit was manifested physically in an icon of Kuse Kannon, or "Kannon, the World Saver."

Thus, the legend of Shōtoku as the incarnation of Hui-ssu was far more than a simple illustration of Shōtoku's superhuman powers. Rather, the legend built upon a long tradition of hagiography concerning Hui-ssu in order to create an image of Shōtoku as a millennial savior. Shōtoku's previous lives were now shown to be those of a monk who had declared both that he would transmigrate to a land without the Buddhist law and that with the advent of Maitreya at the end of the Latter Days he, and not Maitreya, would save all sentient beings with a scripture buried on Mount Nan-yüeh. Kinship groups affiliated with Shitennōji and Daianji then merged this legend cycle with a legend from Silla of a Lotus chanter who retrieves a scripture from a former life. The result was a legend in which Shōtoku the World Savior was shown in possession of Hui-ssu's sutra, ready to assist all sentient beings in search of salvation.

Saichō, Hui-ssu, and the Sources of the Japanese Tradition

During the Heian period, the legend of Hui-ssu's incarnation as Shōtoku continued to grow in importance as monks such as the Tendai patriarch Saichō reshaped the legend in terms consistent with their personal convictions. As we saw in chapter 6, Saichō's belief in Shōtoku, which was an essential part of his personal vocation, most likely reflected the influence of his teacher Gyōhyō, a monk who trained at Daianji at the same time that Myōichi was composing the *Shichidaiki* at that temple.[72]

The importance of Shōtoku for Saichō's understanding of his own mission can be seen in the following poem, which Saichō composed at Shitennōji in 816:

> Seeking karmic strength and connection within the seas,
> I take refuge at the Palace of Shōtoku.
> I now will spread the rare doctrine taught by the teacher and leave it
> neglected no longer ...
> I ask but to make [this] the teaching of the nation,
> To protect it and help it flourish.[73]

Saichō's declaration that he "takes refuge" in his "teacher" Shōtoku strongly suggests a sense of deep personal bonding with Shōtoku's spirit. Yet the poem also makes clear that for Saichō, Shōtoku also remained the paradigmatic Dharma King of the Japanese islands. As Saichō sought to make Shōtoku's Buddhism the teaching of the nation, "To protect it and make it flourish," his individual quest was thus transformed into a quest for the corporate salvation of the Japanese state.

For Saichō, Shōtoku's status as the incarnation of a T'ien-tai patriarch confirmed his belief that the T'ien-t'ai tradition deserved a privileged place in Japanese Buddhism. Saichō believed that he was not introducing a new tradition to the Japanese islands, but rather continuing the Buddhism of Shōtoku himself. Throughout his life, Saichō thus apparently believed that Shōtoku was at once the founding figure of both the Japanese and Tendai Buddhist traditions.[74]

Perhaps most importantly, however, Saichō's reinterpretation of the legend of Hui-ssu's incarnation as Shōtoku also entailed a new understanding of the role of Japan within the Buddhist tradition. Thus the *Denjutsu isshin kaimon* (*Concerning the Essay on the One-Mind Precepts*), a biography of Saichō composed sometime around 833, refers to Shōtoku as having been at the first assembly at Vulture Peak where the *Lotus Sutra* was said to have been preached.[75] Iida argues that this belief must have been based upon the *Sui t'ien-t'ai chih-che ta-shih pie-chuan* (*Alternate Biography of the Great Teacher T'ien-tai Chih-che of the Sui*), an early biography of Hui-ssu's disciple Chih-i in which the young Chih-i first encounters his teacher Hui-ssu:[76]

> When [Chih-i] first made his obeisance, Hui-ssu said: "Of old we listened to the *Lotus Sutra* together on Vulture Peak. That karmic connection has followed us and manifested itself in the present."[77]

Because Saichō believed that Shōtoku was a reincarnation of Hui-ssu, the reference in this passage to Vulture Peak (the site where the Buddha preached the *Lotus Sutra*) helped define for Saichō the place of Japan in the Buddhist tradition. For Saichō, Shōtoku's life narrative extended all the way back to the time of the Buddha and in effect encapsulated the development of the entire Buddhist tradition. The Buddhism that had been planted in the Japanese islands by Shōtoku (and was being revived by Saichō) represented for Saichō a direct, unmediated link to the Buddha himself. As such, it also represented the apex of the Buddhist tradition.

Thus, for Saichō, the figure of Shōtoku epitomized the Japanese Buddhist tradition even as it transcended it. In Tendai texts such as the *Denjutsu isshin kaimon*, the teachings of Chinese patriarchs such as Hui-ssu and Chih-i are presented as the quintessential Buddhism of Japan, far truer to the spirit of Shōtoku than the Buddhist establishment in Nara.[78] No longer simply a guardian figure to watch over the court and nation, Shōtoku now also served as the focal point of a new narrative that situated Japanese Buddhist institutions within the broad sweep of the Buddhist tradition dating back to Shakyamuni himself. Shōtoku thus came to be a core element not only in Saichō's personal vocation but also in the self-definition of the Tendai tradition itself. In the decades and centuries that followed, as Tendai institutions and doctrines began to rival and then eclipse their counterparts on the Nara plain, the figure of Shōtoku thus came to serve as a key foundational point for the construction of the Buddhist–state paradigms of the Heian period.

Conclusion

As the Nara court was rocked by famine and internal struggles in the decades following the composition of the *Nihon shoki*, Japanese rulers increasingly sought both to support and regulate Buddhist institutions across the Japanese islands. One of the chief architects of Buddhist-state relations during the period was the eminent monk Dōji, the leading intellectual of his day and a strong devotee of the Shōtoku cult. Thanks in large part to Dōji's efforts, the court established a set of officially sponsored monasteries (*kokubunji*) across the Japanese islands that were closely overseen by members of the court's official bureaucracy. This project envisioned the establishment of a new framework for Buddhist-state relations based upon Chinese models in which the ruler served as both the chief benefactor of the *sangha* and its main regulator.

An integral part of this effort was the figure of Shōtoku, whom Dōji depicted in the *Nihon shoki* using terminology associated with the Four Heavenly Kings and the liturgical program of the *kokubunji* system. One key moment in this process came in 739 when, with Dōji's encouragement, the court sponsored the reconstruction of several buildings at Hōryūji, including one that served as Shōtoku's mausoleum. This institution served as an important spiritual bulwark for Shōmu and his chief consort Kōmyō as they sought supernatural protection from the spirits that they believed threatened both themselves and the nation. As a result, Shōtoku came to serve as a guardian deity for the increasingly troubled Fujiwara and the court.

A second key moment in the establishment of a *modus vivendi* between the court and Buddhist institutions came after Dōji helped persuade Shōmu to send envoys to China in order to, in effect, re-introduce the monastic tradition to the Japanese islands. When the noted *vinaya* master Ganjin eventually arrived at the Nara court, he asserted that his decision to come had been motivated in large part by the belief that Shōtoku was none other than the incarnation of the Chinese T'ien-t'ai Buddhist patriarch Hui-ssu. By broadening the time frame for Shōtoku's biography to include previous lives, this legend served to further elevate the status of Shōtoku even as it established a new narrative structure for understanding both the prince and the origins of the Japanese Buddhist tradition. This new narrative built upon the common trope of the sage from across the sea even as it allowed for the construction of potentially limitless linkages between the prince and Buddhist movements on the continent.

These possibilities were in turn soon exploited by the first Japanese Tendai patriarch, Saichō, who argued that Shōtoku's Buddhism was none other than that of the T'ien-t'ai tradition. Japanese Tendai thus represented itself both as an introduction of elevated Chinese Buddhist doctrine and as a return to the primary "native" Buddhism espoused by the Prince. As a result, the figure of Shōtoku came to serve as a cornerstone for the self-definition of perhaps the most influential school of the Heian period.

Perhaps most importantly, however, this narrative structure represented a new synthesis of such fundamental polarities as monk and layman, native icon and Chinese sage, Buddhist patron, ancestral deity, and warrior prince. As a result, even during Saichō's lifetime the figure of Shōtoku transcended any single ideological position or faction at court. Throughout the Heian period and beyond, the figure of Shōtoku was thus a touchstone for a wide variety of political and religious movements as Kūkai, Shinran, Nichiren, and many others were represented by their followers as the spiritual heirs—or even incarnations—of the paradigmatic prince and layman. As this synthesis was woven ever more deeply into the fabric of religious discourse during the period, the figure of Shōtoku thus served to anchor an array of disparate movements within a common constellation of symbols and concepts associated with the native sage prince from across the sea.

Conclusion

In the preceding chapters, I have argued that the roots of the early Shōtoku cult are best sought not in the career of the historical Prince Kamitsumiya but rather with the architects of the cultural/religious icon that was Prince Shōtoku. By abandoning the quest to recover the great man's thoughts and deeds, we have been able to sketch the central features of one of the foundational paradigms of Nara Japan. In so doing, we have shown how this project had its roots in the tropes of violence, genealogy, and legend that constituted the period's rapidly shifting horizons of reception. We have also seen how a small cluster of kinship groups exerted astonishingly broad and deep influence on several of the most basic structures of early Japanese culture.

Much of this project has been concerned with locating the figure of Shōtoku within the context of a sweeping project of political and cultural imagination that transformed life in the Japanese islands for centuries. Because the Shōtoku cult emerged in conjunction with such far-reaching changes across a wide spectrum of religious, political, and material culture, it has afforded a point of entry into what Nelson Goodman would term a process of world making. The story of how this world was imagined and created suggests that a potent brew of international tension and vengeful ancestors combined with continental systems of writing, ritual, and governance to produce the icons and institutions of Nara Japan.

This world was thus in many ways the product of an enormous social transformation that led to increasingly powerful mechanisms of social control. In its most obvious form, this meant not only the rise of bureaucratic structures centered upon posts, titles, and edicts but also the creation of tax registers, estates, roads, and canals.

Each of these developments was rooted in a desire on the parts of rulers and local paramounts to extend their power farther and deeper across the Japanese islands.

Yet these figures had little control over the conceptual apparatus underlying the new order. During this period, the very means by which rulers represented and exercised power was defined in terms of literary and cultic tropes controlled to a surprising degree by immigrant lineages such as the Hata and Miyake. As a result, a unique set of notions that centered on the vagaries of continental history, cosmology, silkworms, and sage rulers helped transform virtually every aspect of life at court. Driving this process was the life-and-death urgency generated by a logic of violence and propitiation that ensured that ancestors and vengeful deities dominated political as well as cultic discourse for centuries.

It was within this context that the figure of Shōtoku burst upon the cultural landscape shortly after the death of Prince Kamitsumiya. This prince of legend was a profoundly literary creation, constructed in terms of the tropes and legends of continental texts that had become paramount sources of political and cultural authority. At an even more basic level, the diffusion of writing and literacy themselves created new sources of hermeneutic authority for the immigrant lineages most at home with the textual traditions of China and the Korean Peninsula. The resulting images of Shōtoku that emerged from this process helped define Shōtoku as a royal ancestor at the foundation of the political and religious transformations that were sweeping over the Japanese islands.

These images had many facets and parts, many of which were sewn together by newly constructed histories that gave the new world a past from which it could derive a trajectory and then project a future. Historical texts such as the *Nihon shoki* and the *Kojiki* thus not only served to legitimate the contemporaneous status quo but also allowed the court to remember a time that never was, and, even more importantly, forget so much of the violence inherent in the birth of the new order.

Such processes were at work not only for the court but also for the fledgling Japanese Buddhist tradition. The establishment of this tradition as a tradition also required the creation of a foundational narrative in terms of which founders could be defined and from which an arc of development could be delineated. By creating the image of Shōtoku as a paradigmatic lay Buddhist prince, ancestor, and sage scholar, the immigrant lineages at the forefront of the early Shōtoku cult thus played a major role in establishing the parameters of Buddhist discourse in Japan. These parameters were created using the myths and legends of the Silla state temple network and established the paradigm of a Buddhist sage whose ascendancy was steeped in the blood of his enemies.

One by-product of these processes was a pattern of repeated layering within Japanese religion. At its most basic level, this meant that Shōtoku came to be located in legend at sites first occupied by the ancestors of the immigrant lineages at the forefront of his cult. On a slightly deeper level, such legends also indicated a deeper conceptual layering as the notion of first *tenjukoku* and then Buddhist pure lands were rooted in millennial legends of immigrant deities such as Sukuna Bikona no Mikoto. Because even these legends were ultimately rooted in Chinese sericulture cults, they also illustrate the degree to which changes in material culture could stimulate changes in cultic practices and even conceptions of the afterlife.

Such layering was also in many ways a by-product of the focus on the narratives of ancestry and lineage that constituted one of the dominant tropes in the religious imagination of Nara Japan. Throughout the period, social and political identities were predicated upon lineal claims. Genealogies thus served as a major field of ideological contestation in which the interests of the court and the resistance of local paramounts, immigrant kinship groups, and their ancestral deities were expressed. Seen in this light, the construction of the Shōtoku cult thus appears as one negotiated element within a massive effort to imagine and narrate a series of ancestors for rulers and courtiers in need of history.

One area where this was particularly evident was in northern Kyūshū, a region believed to be filled with vengeful deities capable of bullying and even killing rulers that displeased them. The cycle of conquest and retribution was heightened by large discrepancies between the military power of the *tennō* and the cultic power of the vengeful ancestors and deities of the defeated. As this volatile mix of fear and conquest fueled the creation of a series of royal ancestors such as Jingū and Ōjin, immigrant lineages dramatically influenced the character of the newly constructed royal heritage in terms of the founding legends of the Korean kingdoms.

This process was also apparent in the legend of Shōtoku's encounter with the beggar on the road to Kataoka. Here the logic of violence and propitiation led to the appropriation of a number of cultic elements from lineages defeated by the Soga and Kamitsumiya. As the figure of Shōtoku became identified with terrain that was formerly inhabited by his enemies, the Shōtoku cult absorbed the practices and beliefs of the vanquished and their disgruntled ancestors. As the expanding roadways and canal networks brought ever-increasing numbers of dangerous spirits ever closer to the court, rites of spirit pacification at crossroads soon became a major cultic concern both at court and in the countryside.

Such rites also helped shape—and were in turn shaped by—the emerging Buddhist tradition. Along with the adoption of new objects of worship and new conceptions of the afterlife, the introduction of Buddhist icons, texts, and narrative tropes into the Japanese islands also spurred material and social changes related to the construction of temples, icons, and so on. As expanded road and water networks facilitated travel both for Buddhist monks and hostile spirits, devotees of the itinerant monk Gyōki appropriated the Kataoka legend as they constructed a massive popular movement centered upon rites of begging and blessing. By the early Heian period, the legendary Gyōki was thus being paired with Shōtoku in narratives that focused both on material gains and on the attainment of life after death.

All of this suggests that the figure of Shōtoku served as an important bridge by means of which pre-Buddhist or non-Buddhist beliefs concerning life after death, millennialism, purification, and spirit pacification were given new expression in Buddhist vocabulary. It also suggests the remarkable degree to which immigrant ancestral cults and legends were the very stuff of which so many "native" dreams were made. As the Hata, Miyake, and others utilized their own ancestral legends, rites of spirit pacification, and immortality cults to construct the single most influential paradigm of lay Buddhism during the period, they also to a surprising degree helped lay the foundation for the state Buddhist institutions of the Nara period. This process reached an apex in the early Heian period as Saichō made Shōtoku a fundamental element in the self-definition of his own Tendai sect and, to a large degree, the template for Buddhist-state relations that endured throughout the Heian period and beyond.

The Heian Period and Beyond

Two important questions that follow from the preceding discussion concern how the figure of Shōtoku helped shape the political and religious paradigms of the Heian period and how the Shōtoku cult was in turn transformed by these paradigms. Certainly, within the Buddhist tradition, the figure of Shōtoku continued to grow in importance as successive Buddhist movements followed the lead of Dōji, Ganjin, Gyōki, and Saichō in claiming Shōtoku as a founder or spiritual ancestor. Proponents of Pure Land practices celebrated Shōtoku's status as the first Japanese figure to attain rebirth in a Pure Land. By the Kamakura period, Shinran, the founder of the Jōdo Shinshū sect of Pure Land Buddhism, was writing hymns to Shōtoku that equated him with Kannon and hailed him as both father and mother.[1] Kūkai's followers in the Shingon sect and Nichiren's Lotus movement were equally fervent in proclaiming the closeness of their connection with the prince. The fact that so many disparate religious figures could claim connection to Shōtoku is a testament to the sheer pervasiveness of the Shōtoku cult's influence on the development of Japanese conceptions of sagehood, millennialism, spirit pacification, the afterlife, and even begging. For centuries, to be a Japanese Buddhist would entail acknowledging a special bond and debt to Shōtoku.

Yet if the preceding chapters have shown anything, they have shown that the impact of the Shōtoku cult extended well beyond the bounds of the Japanese Buddhist tradition. There are several reasons for believing that many of the same kinship groups that helped build the Nara world were also principal architects in the construction of broader political and religious paradigms that emerged in the late Nara and early Heian periods. With the construction of the Heian capital in the Hata stronghold of Kadono in 793, the influence of the Hata and related kinship groups over the development of the royal cult only increased.

Much of this influence can be attributed to the inevitable cultic layering attendant upon the inscription of a new capital upon terrain inhabited by Hata gods. Throughout the early Heian period, new cults and legends were repeatedly built upon sites formerly occupied by immigrant deities and ancestors. This principle of geographic layering sheds light on one of the central theses of Abe Ryūichi's work on the famed Shingon monk Kūkai. Abe suggests that although Kūkai is often presented as a revolutionary figure who established a new sect in opposition to the Buddhist schools of Nara, Kūkai's work is best read as an attempt to create a Buddhist hermeneutic and theory of language that could bring to completion the doctrinal work of the Nara schools. Abe thus argues that Kūkai can only be understood in the context of persistent continuities between Nara and early Heian Buddhism.[2]

Ironically, the reason most frequently given for positing a rupture between Nara and Heian period Buddhism—the movement of the capital from Nara to Yamashiro—may be one of the best reasons for explaining such continuities. Firmly ensconced in Hata territory, Japanese rulers would for the next thousand years turn in moments of need to the Hata deities and shrines that literally surrounded the court. This in turn meant that the religious movements founded by figures such as Saichō, Kūkai, and others in the early Heian period developed against a horizon of reception that was, if anything, even more strongly influenced by Hata-affiliated shrines, courtiers, and deities.

One of the best illustrations of how this horizon of reception was constituted can be found in the so-called Kusuko incident of 810. In that year, the recently retired Heizei *tennō*, along with his chief consort, Fujiwara no Kusuko, and her brother, the former chancellor Fujiwara no Nakanari, sought to force the court to return to Nara. In response, Heizei's brother Saga, who had assumed the throne only months earlier, sought the assistance of the deities at the Lower Kamo shrine, the largest shrine in the capital and a Hata cultic center. Saga promised that should he prove victorious the shrine would be granted the first rank, equal even to that of the shrine of Ise. He also promised that thereafter each *tennō* would send one princess to serve as the shrine's chief officiant. Saga's subsequent victory thus entailed the creation of a new religious institution that would serve as the main ritual center for rulers in the capital for centuries.[3]

As dramatic as the Kusuko incident may have been, it was also emblematic of a broader pattern of reliance by all members of the court upon the immigrant deities that surrounded the capital. With Hata deities ensconced at such major cultic centers as the Kamo, Matsuno'o, Hiyoshi, and Kehi shrines, the court's dependence upon the Hata and other immigrant lineages only increased during the period. As a result, the cultic practices of immigrant kinship groups at the forefront of the early Shōtoku cult resonated throughout the capital, countryside, and even in the deepest mountain recesses of Japan for centuries to come.

Hata influence at prominent shrines across the region was matched by similar prominence at court and within the Buddhist ecclesial hierarchy. Because at the start of the Heian period successive heads of the Fujiwara called Hata women mother and grandmother, synergies of lineage, cult, and rank all served to elevate the position of Hata courtiers, monks, and shrines. Thus, monks such as Gomyō and Gonsō, who played such a major role in hindering the career of Saichō and aiding the career of Kūkai, were both members of the Hata. The degree of Hata influence in the ecclesial hierarchy was most spectacularly illustrated in 829, when Gomyō replaced Gonsō in the post of Sōjō, the highest post in the ecclesial hierarchy.

Yet the very success of the Hata and other immigrant lineages also helped spur the formation of nativist resistance. Such resistance is noted in the *Kogoshūi*, a compendium of ritual and mythic matters composed in 807. The text's author, Imbe no Hironari, notes the importance of immigrant kinship groups for the development of the royal cult even as he bemoans the poor treatment accorded to such groups:

> During the reign of the *tennō* at Toyoakira Palace in Karushima [Ōjin], the King of Paekche sent as tribute to the royal court a learned man named Wani, who founded the Fumi Family of Obito rank dwelling in Kawachi. Utsuki, ancestor of the Hata Family of Kimi rank, was also naturalized in Japan, with a number of people under him who were living in his one hundred and twenty estates in Korea.... These immigrants who arrived from Chin, Aya and Paekche, became naturalized in this country. Each of these groups of people were numbered by tens of thousands; nevertheless, it is most deeply to be regretted that their services to Japan have, so far, not been publicly recognized; and, still further, that the homage to the divine spirits of their respective ancestors is not yet paid with due religious ceremonies under the auspices of the court.[4]

Hironari's statement suggests that even hundreds of years after their ancestors had immigrated to the Japanese islands, immigrant lineages such as the Hata were being singled out for special treatment by members at court carrying a nativist banner. Perhaps even more revealing, however, is the fact that Hironari discusses the cultic importance of such kinship groups not for their introduction of the "foreign" Buddhist tradition but rather for the enormity of their contributions to the royal cult. Such contributions, it is clear, were only grudgingly acknowledged in the early Heian period. Later generations would erase them completely as the notion that the "foreign" kinship groups could have played a major role in shaping the pillars of the royal system became more and more problematic.

This motif of erasure, coupled with the dramatic degree to which Hata monks and Hata gods pervaded cultic life at the capital, suggests that ethnic tensions and the logic of violence and propitiation remained vital forces in cultic life across the Japanese islands. As a result, for centuries the figure of Shōtoku remained a vibrant paradigm of kingship, spirit quelling, and Buddhist practice as successive eras struggled with the tropes and tensions that first gave birth to Japan's perennial prince of legend.

Appendix: Primary Sources for the Study of the Early Shōtoku Cult

The following is a brief survey of some of the most important Nara and early Heian period sources for the study of the Shōtoku cult. For a more comprehensive discussion of general source documents from the Nara period, see Joan Piggott's *The Emergence of Japanese Kingship*.[1] For a discussion of epigraphical and textual sources that have been attributed to the reign of Suiko *tennō*, I can do no better than refer the reader to David Lurie's outstanding dissertation *The Origins of Writing in Early Japan: From the 1st to the 8th Century C.E.*[2]

GENERAL DOCUMENTS

Fudoki. These texts were gazetteers composed in response to a decree by the court in 713 that each province should submit an account of the resources, geography, and legends of the townships and districts within its borders. Throughout this book, I have used these texts not only to supplement the corpus of myths and legends contained in the sources produced at court but also as a treasure trove of information concerning the activities and location of lineages across the Japanese islands. Aoki Michiko has ably translated the surviving portions from the gazetteers of Harima, Hitachi, Hizen, Bungo and Izumo provinces.[3]

Kojiki. This text contains only one reference to Shōtoku in the genealogy section, as the text stops with the court of Suiko. Throughout this book, however, I have repeatedly turned to the *Kojiki* as a source of myths and legends related to lineages and deities associated with the early Shōtoku cult.

Nihon ryōiki. Composed sometime before 822 by the monk Kyōkai, this Buddhist tale collection is a treasure trove of information concerning everything from more popular Buddhist beliefs and practices during the period to the daily life of the non-elite segment of the population. It contains a series of legends related to the prince, including an account of the encounter with the beggar at Kataoka, that show significant differences with that found in the *Nihon shoki*. The prince also appears in a legend concerning the near death experience of one of Shōtoku's retainers. This legend is notable both for its pairing of Shōtoku with the monk Gyōki and for its depiction of the prince as possessing an elixir of immortality. The *Nihon ryōiki* also features several legends that concern members of the Hata, Kishi, Kusakabe, and other lineages related to the early Shōtoku cult.

Nihon shoki. In general I have used this text as a document that illustrates the historical imagination of the Nara court at the time of its completion in 720. Although its historical accuracy is greatly open to question, it is probable that entries for later periods were less amenable to embroidery than earlier entries. Whatever its shortcomings as a historical source, however, the text is invaluable for its wealth of genealogical information as well as for geographic detail that can be used to situate lineages and events within both the geographic and cultic landscapes of the period.

Unlike the *Kojiki*, the text does not speak with a single unified voice but rather often presents a variety of accounts of early myths and even later events. I have thus throughout this book treated the *Nihon shoki* as a site of ideological contestation in which competing lineages sought to offer their own versions of events and legends related to their ancestors and their lineal claims. I have also treated it as a major cultural and historical artifact, the construction of which reveals invaluable insight into the cultural and religious imagination of the age.

Specific references within the *Nihon shoki* to Kamitsumiya/Shōtoku reflect a diversity of views and agendas. Several passages, of course, present the prince as a paradigmatic lay Buddhist. Among the most important passages in this regard are the legend of the establishment of Buddhism in the Japanese islands, in which Shōtoku's prayers result in the victory of the pro-Buddhist forces of the Soga over the Mononobe. Other important references in this regard include the monk Hyeja's declaration upon the death of Shōtoku that the prince had been reborn in a Buddhist Pure Land, and an editorial comment within the text that Shōtoku was a Dharma King. In addition, the text recounts three temple-founding legends associated with the prince: the first states that Shōtoku built Shitennōji in fulfillment of his vow to the Four Heavenly Kings of Buddhism during the battle between the Soga and the Mononobe. The second states that the prince built Hōryūji after receiving a gift of lands in Harima Province following lectures that he gave upon the *Lotus* and *Queen Śrīmālā* sutras. Finally, the text also states that Shōtoku gave a Buddhist statue from Silla to Hata no Kawakatsu after receiving assurances that Kawakatsu would build a temple to house the image.

Equally important, however, is the information provided by the text that is not distinctively Buddhist. Most obviously, Shōtoku is presented as a member of the royal line. We are also given his genealogical background, which states that he was the son of the Yamato ruler Yōmei and his consort Anahobe no Hashihito, and we are told that Kamitsumiya served in the role of crown prince, attending to all matters of state with super-human acumen. Shōtoku is also said to have composed the first history of the Japanese islands and instituted the first continental-style system of ranks at court. More mundanely, we are told of the different names by which the prince was referred and we are assured that the prince had mastered both Buddhist and non-Buddhist forms of continental learning at a young age.

The text also hints in several places that the prince was a sage who possessed special powers over life and death. We are told, for instance, that he entered the world miraculously as his mother gave birth to him painlessly in front of a horse stable. The death narrative of the prince is designed to show both the tremendous devotion he engendered among his subjects and his death-transcending bond with the sage monk Hyeja. Finally, the prince is shown to have super-human powers of perception in his encounter with the sage-immortal who posed as a beggar at Kataoka.

These intimations of the superhuman status of the royal ancestor are reinforced in later passages related to the prince's son, Yamashiro no Ōe. The text clearly asserts that Kamitsumiya's heir had a rightful claim to the throne, that he sacrificed himself for the common good, and that Heaven and Earth manifested multiple omens foretelling the doom of Kamitsumiya's line. As with so much of the *Nihon shoki*, the picture that emerges is thus richly ambiguous, drawing upon multiple sources and serving multiple interests.

Manyōshū. This Nara-period poetic anthology contains but one poem related to the prince, purportedly composed upon meeting a beggar not at Kataoka but near Mount Tatsuta. It nonetheless contains a treasure trove of information concerning the cultic geography and religious imagination of courtiers and literate figures across the Japanese islands during the early Nara period.

Sanbōe kotoba. Composed in 984 by Minamoto Tamenori, this text is a compendium of Buddhist hagiography that was intended to illustrate the meaning and historical development of the Buddhist tradition from India to Japan. Not surprisingly, the figure of Shōtoku is featured prominently as the fountainhead of the Japanese Buddhist tradition. When read in conjunction with such works as the *Jōgū Shōtoku taishiden hoketsuki* and the *Shōtoku Taishi denryaku*, the text helps illustrate the trajectory of the development of the Shōtoku legend corpus throughout the Heian period and beyond.[4]

Shinsen shōjiroku. This genealogical compendium, which was composed sometime around 815, is important both for its role in standardizing genealogical claims during the period and for its accounts of several ancestral legends and lineages not found in other sources. Also of note is the text's format, which explicitly separates lineages that claimed descent from figures from overseas with lineages of royal descent.

Shoku nihongi. This successor volume to the *Nihon shoki*, in addition to its obvious value as a source on developments at court during the Nara period, is also useful in recording genealogical and rank claims of numerous lineages associated with the Shōtoku cult.

TEMPLE RECORDS

Daianji garan engi narabi ni ruki shizaichō. This text, which was completed sometime around 747, traces the origins of Daianji back to Prince Kamitsumiya. Daianji, in addition to serving as one of the main state temples of the Nara period, was for many years the home temple of Dōji, the most learned monk of the early eighth century and possibly an editor of the *Nihon shoki*. Because few scholars accept the *Daianji engi*'s account of the temple's origins, this portion of the text has frequently been ignored. The passage is nonetheless extremely important for understanding the development of the cult of Prince Shōtoku; the site where Kamitsumiya is said to have originally founded the temple, for instance, corresponds closely with the site of Dōji's kinship group temple. Thus, it appears that Dōji sought to associate both Daianji and Shōtoku with his ancestral home. Dōji's role in the promotion of the Shōtoku cult is discussed at some length in chapter 7.[5]

Gangōji garan engi narabi ni ruki shizaichō. Although the current form of this text is thought to date from the mid-eighth century, it is generally believed that it was based upon earlier texts that predated the *Nihon shoki*. Because the text differs at points from the *Nihon shoki* account of the introduction of Buddhism to Japan and the role of the royal house in the suppression of Buddhism, it is considered to be an especially valuable resource by scholars of early Japanese history and religion. Because Gangōji—formerly known as Asukadera—was the Soga kinship group temple, it is generally believed that the the *Gangōji garan engi* reflects the perspective of the Soga and several affiliated immigrant lineages on the introduction of Buddhism in Japan.[6] The text has been translated into English by Miwa Stevenson.[7]

Hōryūji garan engi narabi ni ruki shizaichō. In addition to a brief rehearsal of legend materials concerning Shōtoku, this text, which was completed sometime around 747, contains important entries concerning the temple's assets that suggest that Kamitumiya's lineage may have had exceptionally large land holdings. These also seem to overlap frequently with areas formerly controlled by the Mononobe, lending credence to the *Nihon shoki*'s statement that half of the Mononobe's land and slaves were given to Prince Kamitsumiya after the destruction of the Mononobe in 587. Records of other gifts, such as statues and scriptures, from members of the court have also helped scholars reconstruct the temple's development through the early Nara period.[8]

Hōryūji tōin engi. This document in its current form appears to be a Heian period account of matters related to the famed Yumedono and Eastern Complex at Hōryūji. Although material appears to have been added at several points in the text's rather complicated textual history and must be used with great care, most scholars believe that it contains materials gathered in 761.[9] The text highlights the role of the Fujiwara Queen Consort Kōmyō in the building of the complex and in the furtherance of the Shōtoku cult. I discuss Kōmyō's role influence on the Shōtoku cult in chapters 6 and 7.

WORKS ATTRIBUTED TO THE PRINCE

Sankyō gisho. These are commentaries of the *Queen Śrīmālā*, *Vimilakirti*, and *Lotus* sutras that have historically been attributed to Prince Kamitsumiya. Although they are known to have circulated in Yamato by the middle of the eighth century at the latest, these commentaries are no longer believed to have been the original compositions of the prince. As Lurie points out, there is simply no evidence that these texts were produced during Prince Kamitsumiya's lifetime, nor is there any evidence that they were produced by Kamitsumiya.[10] Discoveries of texts in Tun-huang and elsewhere in China have made it clear that the commentaries were more transcriptions than original compositions.[11] Regardless of their ultimate provenance, the commentaries nonetheless did play an important role in the development of the Shōtoku cult. During the Heian period, Yamato monks and diplomats repeatedly brought copies of the *Lotus Sutra* commentary to T'ang China as proof of the enlightened Buddhism that flourished in the land.[12]

Seventeen Article Constitution. This text is a statement of political philosophy that most likely dates from the seventh century.[13] It is comprised of seventeen admonitions concerning the proper roles of ministers and rulers. No single philosophical viewpoint dominates the text, which at various points reflects Confucian, Buddhist, and Taoist influences. Of special interest are the repeated references to the concept of the sage king (*hijiri no kimi*). This aspect of the text is treated in detail in chapter 4. Here again there is no evidence that the text was produced by Kamitsumiya or even during his lifetime. I therefore prefer to bracket the issue of authorship, treating the work as most likely a reflection of the views of the immigrant kinship groups at the forefront of the early Shōtoku cult.

EPIGRAPHICAL SOURCES RELATED TO THE PRINCE

Several pieces of epigraphy related to the prince have been the subject of long-standing scholarly debates. Unfortunately, none of the following sources can be assumed to have existed at the time of their purported construction.

Hōryūji kondō Shaka sanzō. The inscription on the aureole at the back of this statue of Shakyamuni Buddha at Hōryūji states that it was commissioned by those close to Kamitsumiya in hopes that the karmic merit generated by the act would bring about recovery from his final illness. The inscription also states that the statue was built to Kamitsumiya's size, suggesting that Kamitsumiya may have been seen as a Buddha even in the period immediately following his death.[14] Several questions remain, however, concerning the reliability of the inscription as a historical document. One particularly vexing issue involves a problematic reign year at the start of the inscription. The date of Kamitsumiya's death also differs from that given in the *Nihon shoki.*[15] Lurie notes, however, that the inscription was apparently cast along with the statue rather than simply carved into the finished work. Because most art historians agree that the statue itself closely resembles other works from the period, Lurie concludes that the text of the statue may in fact date from the Suiko era.[16] If this is indeed the case, it would suggest that a nascent cult to the prince may have begun almost immediately after his death.

Hōryūji kondō Yakushi sanzō. The inscription on the aureole at the back of this statue states that it was produced as a result of a vow by Kamitsumiya and the future ruler Suiko in the hopes that the karmic merit generated by this act would allow Kamitsumiya's father, Yōmei, to recover from illness. The inscription continues that the statue was completed only after Yōmei had died. If the inscription is to be believed, this would make it one of the earliest pieces of writing in Yamato. There are widespread doubts about the inscription's historical authenticity, however, mainly because of the apparently anachronistic use of the term *"tennō"* in reference to Suiko as well as the use of the term "sage king" (*hijiri no kimi*) in reference to what would have been a very youthful Kamitsumiya.[17]

The *Iyo kuni fudoki/Dōgo* inscription. Although only two fragments of the original *Iyo kuni fudoki* survive, one fragment contains a transcription of a stele purporting to commemorate an almost certainly fictional visit by Shōtoku and his mentor, the Koguryô monk Hyeja, to the Dōgo hot springs in Shikoku. As I argue in chapter 2, this text provides invaluable evidence that the Shōtoku cult had already spread to a comparatively remote region prior to the writing of the *Nihon shoki.* Because the text makes reference to a land of eternal life (*kotobuki no kuni* or *jukoku*), it also provides a rare glimpse into early conceptions of the afterlife during the period.[18]

Tenjukoku shūchō mei. This inscription was woven into a tapestry that was purportedly produced almost immediately following the death of Prince Kamitsumiya. Although only fragments of the tapestry exist, reconstruction of the full text has been made possible by its inclusion in the *Jōgu Shōtoku hōō teisetsu.* The inscription contains a detailed list of Kamitsumiya's wives and children, thereby offering an important glimpse into the marital and familial alliances into which Kamitsumiya entered during his lifetime. The tapestry also gives an account of the reaction of the Yamato court and Shōtoku's immediate family to his death, including a statement of their belief that he had been reborn in *tenjukoku*, a land beyond death that is not mentioned in any Buddhist sources. I discuss the meaning of this term and the worldview upon which it is based in chapter 2.[19]

SHŌTOKU HAGIOGRAPHICAL COLLECTIONS

Jōgū Shōtoku hōō teisetsu. Although scholars date the current form of this text to the eleventh century, parts of it are thought to predate the *Nihon shoki* and *Kojiki* and are thus extremely valuable. Especially important are the inclusion of the entire text of the *Tenjukoku shūchō* and an extended genealogy of Prince Kamitsumiya's lineage.[20]

Jōgū kōtaishi bosatsuden. This text, which was composed by Ganjin's disciple Ssu-t'uo between 784 and 794, also sets out in detail the legend that Shōtoku was the reincarnation of the Chinese T'ien-t'ai Buddhist patriarch Hui-ssu. This legend, which is not found in the *Nihon shoki*, is generally believed to have been the creation of Ganjin's disciples.[21] I discuss the formation of this legend at length in chapter 7.

Jōgū Shōtoku taishiden hoketsuki. This text is thought to have been composed at Shitennōji sometime during the early to mid-Heian period. It is important both for its elaboration of Shōtoku legend materials and for the view it provides of the beliefs of immigrant kinship groups associated with Shitennōji.[22] The text contains a fair amount of material also found in the *Nihon shoki*. Reference is made to the prince's role in government and in establishing the cap rank system. The prince's miraculous birth and reasons for his multiple names are also briefly mentioned, as is his role in the battle for the establishment of Buddhism in the Japanese islands.

More interesting, however, are the text's divergences with the *Nihon shoki*. In addition to providing an account of the prince's genealogy, the text emphasizes Shōtoku's close relationship with his teacher, the Koguryô monk Hyeja. Shōtoku is also said to have written numerous sutra commentaries and is explicitly associated with the *Lotus*, *Vimilakirti* and *Queen Śrīmālā* sutras. A mysterious gold-colored figure is said to have regularly appeared to the prince in his dreams to teach him about Buddhist doctrine. Shōtoku is also said to have built seven temples during his lifetime, and his death, and that of his father, are recounted with reference to the Yakushi and Shakyamuni statuary discussed earlier. The text concludes with brief references to the death of Kamitsumiya's Kashiwade wife as well as the construction of the *Tenjukoku* tapestry. The author of the text thus appears to have been drawing upon numerous sources of Shōtoku hagiography. The text has been partially translated into English by William Deal, and Shinkawa Tokio has produced an exceptional monograph on the work in Japanese.[23]

Shichidaiki. This text was composed in 772 by a monk from Tōdaiji named Myōichi. This is the first extant document that we have that sets out in detail the legend that Shōtoku was the incarnation of the Chinese T'ien-t'ai patriarch Hui-ssu. The text is also extremely important for its numerous citations of now-lost texts from the legend corpus of the Chinese monk Hui-ssu. I discuss the text and Hui-ssu in detail in chapter 7.[24]

Shōtoku Taishi denryaku. This very large work, sometimes referred to as the "*Heishi den*," contains an abundance of legends concerning the life of the prince and events related to his cult following his death.[25] As such, it is therefore an invaluable resource for understanding any number of aspects of Buddhist belief and practice during the Heian period. Although tradition ascribes the authorship of the work to a member of the Taira lineage, however, there is no agreement as to who the author might be. Because the text is quoted in the *Sanbōe kotoba*, which was completed in 984, there is general agreement that the text was most likely composed sometime during the 10th century. Within the text there are some indications that the author was closely aligned with the Shōtoku cult at Shitennōji. One important argument for viewing the *Hoketsuki* as an early Heian period document, for instance, is rooted in the fact that the *Hoketsuki* is cited in the *Denryaku*. Unfortunately, too little is known about the text to draw many further inferences from the text concerning the Shōtoku cult of the Nara period.

Tō daiwajō tōseiden. This work was completed in 779 by Ōmi no Mahito no Mifune, one of the leading intellectuals of his day and a former monk and student of the Chinese monk Dōsen of Daianji.[26] The text is an extended biography of the Chinese *vinaya* master Chien-chen (J: Ganjin) that focuses mainly on the Chinese master's travails in reaching the Japanese islands. The text is important for the study of the Shōtoku cult because it asserts that Chien-chen was motivated to come to Yamato by the legend that the Chinese monk Hui-ssu had transmigrated to Yamato in order to spread the Buddhist teaching there. I discuss this passage in chapter 7.

CHINESE AND KOREAN SOURCES

Samguk sagi. Completed in 1145, this text provides essential information concerning political events on the Korean Peninsula as well as nation-founding legends and myths of the kingdoms of Koguryô, Paekche, Silla and the Kara confederation of states. Several passages appear to record legends that might have influenced Yamato mythology, particularly myths associated with the descent of the Heavenly Grandchild as well as the Jingū/Ōjin legend cycle. Also notable in this regard is an account from the *Chronicles of Silla* (*Silla pongi*) that records an encounter between a virtuous king and a beggar on a roadside.

Samguk yusa. Although the myths and legends included in this text, which was completed in 1284, cannot be used as evidence for historical events of previous ages, they do provide an invaluable glimpse into the mythic world of 13th century Koryo. One legend of particular note is the text's account of the founding of Sachŏnwangsa, the main temple of the Silla state temple network. For more on this legend and its relation to the founding legend of Japanese Buddhism, see chapter 1.

Sui shu. Completed in 656, this official Chinese court history contains accounts of missions from the Sui to the Suiko court and provides a rare glimpse of life in the Japanese islands at the time of the Suiko court that is unfiltered by the editors of the *Nihon shoki.* The text also famously records a letter sent from the court of Suiko to the Sui ruler Yang-ti in which Yamato is referred to as "the land of the rising sun," whereas Sui China is referred to as "the land of the setting sun."

Glossary

Abe	One of the most influential kinship groups of the Asuka and Nara periods, the Abe were based originally in the Sakurai district of Yamato Province. Several branches of the Abe, however, were also based in Naniwa. Within the Kōtoku chapter of the *Nihon shoki* one Abe no Uchimaro is shown dedicating Buddhist images at Shitennōji, a temple purportedly built by Shōtoku following the victory of the pro-Buddhist Soga forces over the Mononobe in 587. Members of the Abe also appear prominently in several *Nihon shoki* accounts of military campaigns undertaken by the court in the Koshi region of Northeastern Japan. By the Nara period, several immigrant lineages at the forefront of the early Shōtoku cult are also known to have claimed common descent with the Abe.
Akaru Hime	Within the *Nihon shoki* and *Kojiki*, this deity is said to have been the wife of both Ame no Hiboko and Tsunuga Arashito. Although she was said to reside in the Himegoso shrines in Naniwa and Buzen Province, she is also depicted variously within the literature of the period as a daughter of the Sumiyoshi deities and as a vengeful goddess who demands propitiation in exchange for ceasing to kill travelers on the roadsides.
Ama no Ho no Akari no Mikoto	This fire deity was claimed as a founding ancestor by a large number of lineages, including the Wani, the Kusakabe, and the Mononobe. He appears to have been viewed as a wrathful deity—in one legend in the *Harima fudoki* he is said to have killed his own father, and he may have been associated with the death of Prince Yamato Takeru.
Ame no Hiboko	The advent of this Silla prince to the Japanese islands is recounted on multiple occasions in the *Nihon shoki* and in the

Kojiki. The cult of this prince is especially remarkable in light of the fact that these texts also state that he was the founding ancestor of both Jingū's distaff lineage and the Miyake Muraji, an immigrant kinship group at the forefront of the early Shōtoku cult. He is also said to have been the husband of Akaru Hime, a sometimes vengeful deity who resided at the Himegoso shrines in Naniwa and in Buzen Province in Kyūshū. The Izushi shrine, the largest center of the Ame no Hiboko cult, was located in Tajima Province, on the coast of the Japan/Eastern Sea. From an early point, legends associated with this deity also appear to have merged with those of Tsunuga Arashito, yet another immigrant deity from the Korean Peninsula whose cult was centered upon the coast of the Japan/Eastern Sea.

Asukadera
The kinship group temple of the Soga, this temple was one of the oldest and largest Buddhist institutions in the Japanese islands. Purportedly built by the Soga leader Soga no Umako following the victory of the pro-Buddhist forces over their Nakatomi and Mononobe rivals, the *Nihon shoki* records the construction of an extremely large icon at the temple made with metal that was said to have been donated by the Korean kingdom of Koguryô. The temple housed many immigrant monks from the Korean Peninsula, and it appears throughout the pre-Nara and Nara periods as an important institution performing rituals for the benefit of the ruler and the court. The origins and history of the temple, which was later known as Gangōji, are recounted in the *Gangōji garan engi narabi ni ruki shizaichō*.

Chimata
Crossroads or intersections of major roadways, *chimata* were of tremendous importance for the military, economic, and political systems of the Japanese islands. They were also frequently the site of rites of propitiation and pacification of dangerous spirits that were thought to travel the roadways of the Japanese islands. As such, they represent an important point of intersection between religious practice and political/material developments during the period.

Chisakobe
One of several lineages to claim descent from Kamu Yaimimi no Mikoto, the Chisakobe appear in several legends related to sericulture and the propitiation of thunder deities. The *Shinsen shōjiroku*, an early ninth-century genealogical compendium, also states that the Chisakobe were responsible for gathering up members of the Hata after that kinship group had been dispersed across the Japanese islands.

Daianji
The largest temple in the Japanese islands until the completion of Tōdaiji in 752, this temple served as the center for the state ecclesial hierarchy during the early Nara period. Dōji, the abbot of the temple, was among the foremost intellectuals of his day and a principal architect of state policy toward Buddhist institutions during the period. Dōji is also thought to have played a major role in promoting the Shōtoku cult and the reconstruction of Hōryūji, Kamitsumiya's kinship group temple.

Dōji
One of the leading intellectuals of his day, Dōji spent over fifteen years studying in T'ang China before returning to the Nara capital in 718. As the pre-eminent authority on continental culture at court, Dōji enjoyed enormous prestige and influence for the remainder of his career. He is thought to have played an important role in shaping

Buddhist–state relations during the period both through the breadth of his doctrinal knowledge and through his political skills. He is also believed to have been a strong proponent of the Shōtoku cult, presenting Queen Consort Kōmyō with Shōtoku relics and overseeing the reconstruction of much of Hōryūji, Prince Kamitsumiya's kinship group temple.

Ganjin (Chien-chen)

This Chinese precepts master was invited to the Japanese islands by envoys from Shōmu *tennō*, who hoped to re-ordain the clergy of the Japanese islands in accordance with the prescriptions of the Buddhist cannon. Although Ganjin arrived believing that he would be able to institute new standards for ordaining and regulating clergy throughout the realm, he encountered a great deal of resistance from within the ranks of the clergy. Ganjin's followers appear to have played an important role, however, in the formation of the Shōtoku legend corpus. Ganjin's disciples asserted that their master had come to the Japanese islands in the belief that he would be following in the footsteps of the Chinese monk Hui-ssu, whom Ganjin claimed as part of his Buddhist lineage.

Gyōki

A mendicant monk who is said to have preached Buddhism to the populace in contravention of the strictures of the early law codes, Gyōki has for centuries captured the imagination of scholars of Japanese religion seeking a popular Buddhist hero from the period. Although little is known for certain about Gyōki, within the *Shoku nihongi* he is at one point condemned as a "small monk" whose followers deceive the masses. Elsewhere within the same text, however, he is referred to as a bodhisattva who at the end of his life attained the highest position in the ecclesial hierarchy. Later hagiographical sources credit him with raising the funds necessary for the construction of the Great Buddha at Tōdaiji and with building numerous rest stations, bridges, roadways, and temples across the Japanese islands. The relationship between Gyōki's movement and that of the Shōtoku cult is discussed in detail in chapter 6.

Hakuji

This white pheasant was said to have been presented to the court by a member of the Kusakabe kinship group during the reign of the Yamato ruler Kōtoku as an auspicious omen. According to the *Nihon shoki*, Kōtoku and the court were so impressed by the appearance of this omen that they instituted the first era name to commemorate the event.

Hata

The Hata were an extremely large immigrant lineage that are generally thought to have originated in the Korean kingdom of Silla, although they claimed to be descended from the famed ruler Ch'in Shih-huang-ti of China. Among the most important Hata for the development of the early Shōtoku cult were those located in the Kadono district of Yamashiro Province. Within the *Nihon shoki* and the *Jōgū Shōtoku taishiden hoketsuki*, Hata figures such as Hata no Kawakatsu are shown working closely with Shōtoku. The Hata kinship group temple Kōryūji, likewise, is listed in the *Hoketsuki* as one of the seven temples founded by Shōtoku. The Hata are also cited in numerous sources from the period in conjunction with metalworking and weaving technologies. They were also said to be instrumental in several major construction projects, including the Manta canal in Kawachi and Yamashiro Provinces and, later, the Shigaraki and Heian capitals.

Hata no Kawakatsu
Purportedly the head of the Hata in the Kadono district of Yamashiro Province, Kawakatsu appears in three important episodes related to Shōtoku. In the first, he is listed as fighting on the side of the prince in the battle for the establishment of Buddhism in the Japanese islands; in the second, he is shown receiving an icon from the prince as a reward for his faithful service; and in the third, he is shown killing Ōfube no Ōshi in response to the growth of the latter's cult of the *tokoyo* deity. Given the roughly sixty-year span between the first and last of these incidents as they are narrated in the *Nihon shoki*, it is doubtful that all of these events transpired as recorded in the text.

Hibasu Hime
This legendary consort of Yamato ruler Suinin is presented in the *Nihon shoki* and *Kojiki* as the daughter of Tamba no Michinushi and granddaughter of Hiko Imasu no Mikoto, putative founding ancestor of the Kusakabe kinship group. The death of Hibasu Hime is depicted in these texts as the occasion when clay figurines known as *haniwa* came to be used in the Japanese islands. Hibasu Hime is also said to be the mother of Yamato ruler Keikō. Intriguingly, the *Kojiki* also states that the Miyake ancestor and immortal Tajima Mori made an offering of the fruits of immortality at Hibasu Hime's tomb in the Tsutsuki region of Yamashiro Province.

Himegoso shrines
Two shrines, one in Naniwa and one in Buzen Province, that housed the female immigrant deity Akaru Hime.

Hitomaro
One of the most influential poets in the courts of Temmu and Jitō, Hitomaro is credited with a major role in developing the vocabulary of divine kingship within his poetic works. A member of the Kakinomoto—a sub-group of the Wani kinship group—Hitomaro also drew heavily upon the Wani ancestral legend corpus for themes within his poetry.

Hōryūji
Prince Kamitsumiya's kinship group temple, Hōryūji has long been a central focus of scholarship on the early Shōtoku cult. In light of the temple's treasure trove of artifacts, statuary, and architecture, it is hardly surprising that it has received an enormous amount of attention from academics, monks, and lay people alike. Particularly noteworthy in this regard are several pieces of statuary purportedly built during or shortly after Kamitsumiya's lifetime, several of which bear inscriptions concerning the prince. Unfortunately, with the possible exception of one statue of Shakyamuni Buddha that is said to have been built "to the prince's size," there are compelling reasons for rejecting the traditional dating for all of these inscriptions (see appendix).

Following the death of Kamitsumiya's son Prince Yamashiro no Ōe and the main line of Kamitsumiya's lineage, the historical sources are remarkably quiet on the temple's subsequent history during the next several decades. As the *Nihon shoki* states that the temple burned to the ground during the reign of Temmu *tennō*, there is also good reason to doubt whether the temple served as the main cultic center of the early Shōtoku cult. Temple records do suggest, however, that it received moderate support from the court in the early Nara period. The temple's fortunes seem to have improved remarkably during the

Tempyō era (729–749), when the monk Dōji presented Queen Consort Kōmyō with numerous artifacts associated with the prince for inspection. Following a plague that killed four of her brothers, Kōmyō appears to have actively sought divine assistance from Shōtoku. During this period the court supported substantial building efforts at the temple, including the famed Yumedono, where an image of Kuse Kannon was installed that was also purportedly built "to the prince's size."

Hui-ssu This northern Chinese monk was famous for his meditative practice upon Mount Nan-yüeh in Southern China and for his advocacy of the *Lotus Sutra*. As the teacher of the famed exegete Chih-i, Hui-ssu also came to be regarded as a patriarch of the T'ien-t'ai (J: *Tendai*) Buddhist tradition. He was also claimed as a teacher of several monks who were later incorporated into Ch'an Buddhist lineages. Although numerous legends exist concerning his life and reincarnations, little is known of his doctrinal views. One possible source of insight into his beliefs can be seen in the *Nan-yüeh Ssu ta ch'an-shih li-shih yuan-wen*, which details a long vow that Hui-ssu purportedly took in the belief that the world had entered the final age of the dharma (Ch: *mo-fa*; J: *mappō*). Hui-ssu featured prominently in Nara and Heian Shōtoku hagiography as the belief that Shōtoku was an incarnation of Hui-ssu gained widespread currency.

Hyeja This Koguryô monk is depicted in the *Nihon shoki* as Shōtoku's teacher and spiritual companion. Within the *Nihon shoki* he proclaims Shōtoku as a sage, and he is the first figure to declare the prince had attained rebirth in a Buddhist Pure Land. Hyeja also appears in other Shōtoku legends, including the legend of Shōtoku's visit to the Dōgo hot springs as well as Shōtoku's recovery of the copy of the *Lotus Sutra* that he used in previous incarnations on Mount Nan-yüeh in China.

Inabe The Inabe, apparently an immigrant lineage from the Korean kingdom of Silla, appear at several points in the *Nihon shoki* and *Kojiki* with members of the Hata and Mononobe kinship groups. The Inabe are thought to have been based in Settsu Province, and they appear to have been closely associated with ship-building. They also appear to have had some connection with Kamitsumiya's fourth wife, Inabe Tachibana no Iratsume.

Inabe Tachibana no Iratsume Although she is not mentioned in the *Nihon shoki*, Inabe Tachibana no Iratsume is spoken of in the *Jōgū Shōtoku hōō teisetsu* as the fourth wife of Prince Kamitsumiya. She is said to have been granted permission by the Yamato ruler Suiko to commission a tapestry to depict the prince's advent in *tenjukoku*, a land beyond death. Tachibana no Iratsume is also said to have been a granddaughter of the Yamato ruler Bidatsu. The family name "Inabe" here most likely indicates that she was raised with the support of the Inabe kinship group.

Jimmu This legendary ruler is depicted in the *Nihon shoki* and *Kojiki* as the first member of the royal line to be born in the Japanese islands. Because both chronicles discuss at length the advance of Jimmu's army from Kyūshū all the way to Central Japan, this account has long fascinated scholars intent upon piecing together clues about the origins of Japanese national consciousness. Others have suggested that the account suggests lingering memories of an invasion of the Japanese islands from the Korean Peninsula. Given the obvious historical anachronisms that pervade the chronicles, however, it is probably better to view it as the product of the political and intellectual structures that began to take root in the Japanese islands probably no earlier than the fifth century.

Jingū   Also known as Okinaga Tarashihime, the origins of the Jingū legend cycle most likely lie at least in part with the Okinaga, a metalworking kinship group based in Ōmi Province and the coast of the Japan/Eastern Sea. Purportedly the mother of Ōjin and chief consort of Chūai, Jingū is depicted in the chronicles as taking up the charge given to Chūai by the Sumiyoshi deities and conquering the Korean kingdom of Silla. Intriguingly, the chronicles also state that the founding ancestor of Jingū's distaff lineage was none other than Ame no Hiboko, a Silla prince who was later worshiped as a god at a number of shrines in Kyūshū and along the coast of the Japan/Eastern Sea.

Jomei   Jomei was successor to the Yamato ruler Suiko, and the Jomei chapter of the *Nihon shoki* is notable for the conflict and maneuvering that it depicts prior to Jomei's ascension to the throne. Because Jomei was not the son of any ruler, his position may have been relatively weak. One possible response to this may have been a fostering of the cult of Okinaga Tarashihime, better known today as the Yamato ruler Jingū. Because Jomei appears to have been descended from the Okinaga, emphasizing the achievements of Okinaga Tarashihime may have been one strategy for augmenting the authority of Jomei's line. Because Jomei's descendents controlled the throne thereafter, this was to have profound consequences for the development of the royal cult in general and the cult of Jomei's most famous ancestor Jingū in particular.

Although very little can be said with any confidence about Jomei's court, the *Nihon shoki* does suggest that one of his rivals for the throne was none other than Kamitsumiya's son Prince Yamashiro no Ōe. Ironically, later texts such as the *Daianji garan engi narabi ni ruki zaichō* also suggest that Daianji temple was originally bequeathed to the young Jomei prior to his ascension to the throne by none other than Shōtoku himself.

Kamu   Listed in the *Nihon shoki* as the eldest son of the Yamato ruler Jimmu,
Yaimimi   Kamu Yaimimi no Mikoto was claimed as a founding ancestor by a
no Mikoto   number of lineages such as the Sakaibe and Chisakobe that appear to have been closely associated with rites of spirit pacification and sericulture.

Kashiwade   This lineage is of immediate note for the formation of the Shōtoku cult because both Prince Kamitsumiya and his brother, Prince Kume took Kashiwade women as their chief consorts. The establishment of Kamitsumiya's residence and kinship group temple in the Ikaruga region of Yamato is also thought to be directly related to the fact that the region was also a Kashiwade base. Further evidence suggesting Kashiwade involvement in the early Shōtoku cult can be seen in the *Jōgū Shōtoku taishiden hoketsuki*, which explicitly states that it was composed using Kashiwade sources.

Kataoka	Kataoka was an important *chimata*, or crossroads, on the Great Lateral Highway connecting the Naniwa region with the Asuka region which housed many of the courts of the seventh century. Kataoka is also in close proximity to Ikaruga, the site of Kamitsumiya's residence and kinship group temple. Shōtoku is said to have met here a figure who, though in appearance a beggar, is revealed to be a sage.
Kehi shrine	An important cultic center in the port of Tsunuga in Koshi Province on the coast of the Japan/Eastern Sea, this shrine housed the deity Tsunuga Arashito.
Kishi	An immigrant lineage from the Korean kingdom of Silla, this lineage is depicted in the *Nihon shoki* as playing an active role in diplomatic missions throughout the sixth and seventh centuries. Along with members of the Abe, Miyake Muraji, and others, they are said to have regularly performed the "Kishi dance" for the court at Shintennōji. As was often the case with immigrant lineages, the Kishi appear to have had a strong presence in ports of entry into the Japanese islands along the Japan/Eastern Sea, in Kyūshū, and in Naniwa.
Kōmyō	A daughter of Fujiwara no Fuhito and chief consort of Shōmu *tennō*, Kōmyō was also the mother of Shōmu's successor Kōken, who ascended the throne in 749. An ardent Buddhist, Kōmyō was *de facto* leader of the Fujiwara following the death of four of her brothers during the small pox epidemic of 737. During this period, she appears to have become, with the encouragement of monks such as Dōji, an ardent devotee of the Shōtoku cult.
Kōryūji	The kinship group temple of the Hata, this temple in the Kadono district of Yamashiro Province was purportedly built by Hata no Kawakatsu to house a statue given to him by Shōtoku.
Kōtoku	As depicted in the *Nihon shoki*, Kōtoku ascended to the throne in 645 in the aftermath of a successful coup by Fujiwara no Kamatari and the future ruler Tenji against the Soga leadership. Although he is credited within the *Nihon shoki* as reigning over the era of "Great Transformation" (*Taika*), the historicity of virtually all of this section of the text has been widely questioned by contemporary scholars. If the *Nihon shoki* may be believed, however, Kōtoku appears to have allied himself with his brother-in-law Abe no Uchimaro and other lineages from Naniwa against the power of Prince Naka no Ōe, the son of Saimei and Jomei known to later generations as the ruler Tenji.
Kunado	This roadside deity is said to have been created from the staff of the god Izanagi as he closed off the roadway between the land of the living and the land of the dead. Kunado was worshiped at crossroads across the Japanese islands, where he was asked to stop hostile spirits on the roadways of the Japanese islands from entering into areas of human habitation.
Kusakabe	This extremely important lineage is said in the *Nihon shoki* to have been descended from one Hiko Imasu no Mikoto, the grandfather of Hibasu Hime and a descendant of the fire deity Ama no Ho no Akari no Mikoto. The Kusakabe were prominent in Naniwa as well as in several coastal areas in Kyūshū and along the coast of the Japan/Eastern Sea. They are known to have been closely allied with several immigrant lineages, including the Kishi and the Miyake Muraji, with

whom they performed the Kishi dance at Shitennōji in Naniwa. The Kusakabe, along with the Kishi and others, are also believed to have played an important role in sponsoring Crown Prince Kusakabe, the son of Temmu *tennō* and Jitō *tennō*, at court. As a result they appear prominently throughout such court-sponsored texts as the *Nihon shoki* and the *Kojiki*. Evidence for Kusakabe involvement in the diffusion of continental culture across the Japanese islands can be seen in the fact that some sub-branches of the Kusakabe in Tamba Province also claimed the immortal Uranoshimako as an ancestor. Elsewhere in the *Nihon shoki*, a member of the Kusakabe is also said to have presented a white pheasant to the court of Kōtoku as an auspicious omen indicating Heaven's favor with Kōtoku's sagely reign.

Kusakabe, Prince	As the son of Temmu and Jitō, Kusakabe was designated as heir-apparent to the throne. Although he died before ascending to the throne, his children and grandchildren occupied the throne for virtually the entire Nara period. Kusakabe is also noteworthy because of his apparent connection with the Kusakabe-Kishi, a sub-branch of the Naniwa Kishi, an immigrant kinship group at the forefront of the early Shōtoku cult.
Kwallŭk	A priest from the Korean kingdom of Paekche who is said to have introduced calendrical and divinatory texts to the Japanese islands during the reign of Suiko.
Manta Waterway	Constructed near the border between Yamashiro and Kawachi Provinces, this waterway was an important node of transport for goods traveling between the Asuka region of Yamato and Kawachi. Although the *Kojiki* states that the waterway at Manta was built by the Hata during the reign of the semi-legendary ruler Nintoku, it is doubtful that any such project was undertaken before the reign of Suiko. The importance of Manta for the early Shōtoku cult is suggested by several passages in the *Nihon shoki* citing omens from the Manta pond that apparently were thought to foretell the downfall of Kamitsumiya's son Yamashiro no Ōe.
Miyake Muraji	An immigrant lineage that claimed descent from Tajima Mori, a figure who was said to have traveled to the land of the immortals in order to bring back the fruit of eternal life to the dying ruler Suinin. The Miyake Muraji were apparently charged with the administration of several royal estates (*miyake*), including estates in Naniwa and in Chikuzen Province in northern Kyūshū. The Miyake Muraji are also known to have intermarried with members of the Kishi and Kusakabe kinship groups.
Monk Min	According to the *Nihon shoki*, Min was sent by the Yamato ruler Jomei to China in 630 to study Buddhism. Within the *Nihon shoki*, he also appears as the final arbiter in determining the significance of omens such as the Hakuji that were presented to the court of Kōtoku. Later texts such as the *Tōshi kaden* state that Min was also tutor to the future ruler Tenji and Tenji's chief counselor, Fujiwara no Kamatari.
Mononobe	One of the largest and most powerful kinship groups of the sixth century, the Mononobe appear in the founding legend of Japanese Buddhism as leaders of the forces opposed to acceptance of the new religion. Following the defeat of the Mononobe at the hands of the

Soga, the *Nihon shoki* states that half of their lands were given to Prince Kamitsumiya, who purportedly used them to promote the diffusion of the Buddhist tradition. The importance of this lineage for the court is illustrated within the *Nihon shoki* by the text's account of the Mononobe ancestor Nigihayahi's descent to the Japanese islands independent of the royal line. Most likely as a result of the destruction of the main line of the Mononobe in 587, however, the Mononobe later claimed as their founding ancestor the fire deity Ama no Ho no Akari no Mikoto.

Although they are presented in the *Nihon shoki* as a somewhat xenophobic military lineage, the Mononobe were also among the most important liturgical lineages of the Asuka and Nara periods. The Isonokami shrine, the main shrine for the Mononobe, was among the most important in early Japan. Mononobe influence on the royal cult is also suggested in such texts as the *Sendai kuji hongi*, a Mononobe text from the early Heian period that makes reference to rites of resurrection and spirit pacification at the Isonokami shrine.

Munakata deities
These three deities are said to have been created from the sword of the god Susanoo no Mikoto. Shrines to the Munakata deities were located in the Usa district of Chikuzen Province in Kyūshū and on Okinoshima, a small island between Kyūshū and the Korean Peninsula. There is a good deal of evidence suggesting that these deities were seen as guardians of the sea passage between Kyūshū and the Korean Peninsula. In 701, one of the Munakata deities was transferred to the Matsuno'o shrine, a Hata cultic center in Yamashiro Province. This connection between the Hata and the Munakata cult most likely reflects the heavy concentration of the Hata and other immigrant lineages both in Yamashiro and in Usa.

Nagaya, Prince
One of the most influential courtiers of his day, this prince was the son of Prince Takechi, a hero of the Jinshin War and himself a son of Temmu *tennō* and a Munakata consort. Nagaya is known to have been an intellectual with a keen interest in continental learning and culture, and he is thought to have been a driving force behind the composition of the *Nihon shoki*. Nagaya's downfall came, however, when he opposed the elevation of the non-royal Fujiwara consort Kōmyō to the title of Queen Consort. In 729, he was accused of treason and using black magic to harm his rivals, and was forced to commit suicide.

Naniwa
Located on the Inland Sea, the port of Naniwa was a key point of entry for continental culture into the Japanese islands. At several points, the region served as home to the court. Naniwa was also a major base for the Abe, one of the most prominent lineages at court throughout the period, as well as a cluster of lineages from Silla, including the Kishi, Miyake Muraji, and Hata. Naniwa also housed Shitennōji, a temple purportedly built by Shōtoku in fulfillment of his vow to the Four Heavenly Kings at the end of the battle for the establishment of Buddhism in the Japanese islands. All of the aforementioned lineages are known to have performed rites at this temple.

Nintoku
Nintoku, purportedly the son and successor of the Yamato ruler Ōjin, is one of only a handful of rulers who are referred to in the chronicles as sage kings. As is the case with legends concerning Jingū and

	Shōtoku, who are also hailed as sage rulers, the Nintoku chapters of the *Kojiki* and *Nihon shoki* feature several legends that highlight immigrant lineages both in Yamashiro Province and in Naniwa.
Ōfube no Ōshi	Ōfube no Ōshi was the leader of a mass millennial movement, and his cult is the sole popular religious movement depicted in the *Nihon shoki*. Ōfube is said to have urged his followers to throw away their riches on the roadsides in order to store up greater riches and long life upon the imminent arrival of the *tokoyo* deity. Ōfube's movement is said to have been suppressed by Hata no Kawakatsu.
Ōjin	Ōjin was a semi-legendary ruler who was purportedly the son of the Yamato rulers Chūai and Jingū. Both the *Kojiki* and *Nihon shoki* accounts of his reign prominently highlight immigrant lineages from the Korean kingdoms of Paekche and Silla. He is also shown in both chronicles as having an extremely close cultic relationship with the deity of the Kehi shrine at Tsunuga. The chronicles also state that the Sumiyoshi deities promised dominion over the Korean Peninsula to Ōjin while he was still in the womb of his mother, Jingū. By the reign of Shōmu *tennō*, the cults of Ōjin and his mother Jingū received a level of support from the court surpassed perhaps only by that of the sun goddess Amaterasu no Ōkami.
Ōnamuchi no Mikoto	Originally a deity from the Izumo region along the coast of the Japan/Eastern Sea, Ōnamuchi was variously said to be the father of Ama no Ho no Akari no Mikoto, the husband of one of the Munakata deities, and a companion of Sukuna Bikona Mikoto. Ōnamuchi no Mikoto is also a central figure in the famed *kuni yuzuri* myth cycle, in which he is presented as the most powerful deity of Izumo before his submission to the authority of Hononinigi, the first royal ancestor to descend to earth.
Queen Mother of the West (Ch: Hsi-wang-mu)	The Queen Mother of the West, a female deity who was believed to govern the realm of immortals on Mount K'unlun in the western regions of China, is usually represented wearing as a headdress a weaving implement known as a *sheng*. She is said to possess the peaches of immortality, which at various times she is said to have offered to the much storied Chinese rulers King Mu of the Chou and Emperor Han Wu-ti. She is of particular note for the study of early Japanese religion because she is explicitly mentioned in at least one court liturgy traceable to the Nara period. In addition, Tajima Mori, an ancestor of the Miyake Muraji, is also depicted traveling to her realm in order to get the fruit of immortality for the dying ruler Suinin.
Saichō	As the founder of the Tendai school of Japanese Buddhism, Saichō's influence over the development of Heian Buddhism is incalculable. Because Saichō was also a devotee of Prince Shōtoku, he and his disciples also played a major role in the development of the Shōtoku cult during the early Heian period. Throughout the period, Tendai monks promoted and embellished pre-existing legends regarding Shōtoku's commentary on the *Lotus Sutra*. Perhaps most famously, they also actively asserted that Shōtoku was none other than a reincarnation of the Chinese monk Hui-ssu, which the Tendai tradition claimed as its second patriarch.

Saimei	Saimei, the chief consort and successor of Jomei, ascended the throne once following the death of Jomei and then a second time following the death of her brother Kōtoku, to whom she is said to have yielded the throne in 645. In addition to the sanguinary domestic politics that culminated in 645 with the assassination of the Soga leadership by Fujiwara no Kamatari and the future ruler Tenji, Saimei also reigned during a period of great turbulence on the Korean Peninsula. She is said to have died in 661 in Northern Kyūshū while preparing an invasion designed to reverse Silla's conquest of Paekche. The *Nihon shoki*'s account of her death appears to suggest that her downfall was caused by a demon that was later seen observing her funerary rites from a distance.
San-huang wu-ti (The Three Sovereigns and Five Thearchs)	These legendary rulers of ancient China were viewed both as culture givers and as paradigms of sage kingship across East Asia during the pre-modern period.
Shitennōji	Located in the port of Naniwa, this temple was purportedly built by Prince Kamitsumiya in fulfillment of his vow to the Four Heavenly Kings during the battle for the establishment of Buddhism in the Japanese islands. Within the *Nihon shoki*, Abe no Uchimaro, the head of the Abe during Kōtoku's reign, is depicted performing a rite installing Buddhist images at the temple. This temple, an early center of the Shōtoku cult, was also used by such immigrant lineages as the Miyake Muraji, Kishi, the Kusakabe, and the Hata, all of which were closely associated with the Abe.
Shōmu *tennō*	The son of Mommu *tennō* and a daughter of Fujiwara no Fuhito, Shōmu *tennō* came to the throne in 724 during a period of political turbulence as figures such as Prince Nagaya sought to resist the growth of Fujiwara influence at court. Shōmu's reign witnessed a variety of important developments in the history of Japanese Buddhism. Among the most important of these were the construction of a network of officially supported temples (*kokubunji*) that were to operate for the benefit of the Nara state, the suppression and then embrace of Gyōki's popular religious movement, the arrival of the Chinese precepts master Ganjin (Ch: Chien-chen) and his disciples from the south of China, and the construction of the Great Buddha at Tōdaiji in Nara. Shōmu's reign also saw renewed efforts toward rebuilding Hōryūji, the kinship group temple of Prince Kamitsumiya, and continued expansion of the early Shōtoku cult.
Soga	Following their defeat of the Mononobe in 587, the Soga were the most powerful single lineage in Yamato. Within the *Nihon shoki* they are shown as a force for the promotion of continental culture, working closely with figures such as Suiko and Kamitsumiya, both of whom were half Soga. A glance at the kinship groups that appear to have been most closely aligned with the Soga in the *Nihon shoki* also suggests that they worked closely with a network of immigrant lineages from the Korean kingdom of Paekche—so much so that it appears entirely

possible that the Soga themselves had roots in the Peninsula. Regardless of where they were "really" from, however, their influence upon the political and religious culture of the Japanese islands cannot be denied.

Soga influence declined dramatically, however, following the Jinshin War in 672. Because they supported Prince Ōtomo, who was crushed in the conflict by the future ruler Temmu, the Soga had little influence at court when Temmu and his successors commissioned official histories such as the *Nihon shoki* and the *Kojiki*. Because these projects were greatly shaped by Soga adversaries such as the Kusakabe, Kishi, Miyake and Hata, much of the *Nihon shoki* depicts the Soga in a decidedly unfavorable light. They are depicted as brazenly assassinating one ruler and, later, usurping the prerogatives of another. They are also blamed for the death of Kamitsumiya's son Yamashiro no Ōe and the destruction of the prince's main line of descent. Thus, although the Soga played a leading role in the diffusion of the Buddhist tradition in the Japanese islands and helped lay the groundwork for the emergence of the *tennō*-centered state, the final word on their accomplishments—as well as their relationship to Shōtoku—was written by their adversaries.

Soga no Umako
Leader of the Soga following the death of his father, Soga no Iname, Umako is credited in the *Nihon shoki* with working with Prince Kamitsumiya to establish Buddhism in the Japanese islands and to establish continental-style governmental and cultural forms. He is nonetheless also portrayed as a usurper who arranges for the assassination of the Yamato ruler Sushun.

Suiko
The daughter of the Yamato ruler Kimmei and his Soga consort, Suiko came to the throne in the aftermath of the Soga victory in the battle for the establishment of Buddhism in the Japanese islands. Although the *Nihon shoki* states that Prince Kamitsumiya oversaw governmental affairs during much of Suiko's reign, there is no way of knowing to what degree, if any, the prince exerted influence over the policies of the Suiko court. There is good reason, however, to believe that Suiko's reign was an important moment in the development of the political and religious institutions of the Japanese islands. Suiko's reign witnessed the proliferation of Buddhist temples across the Kinai region of Japan, the rise to prominence of the Soga kinship group and their affiliated immigrant lineages, the re-opening of relations with the Sui and then T'ang empires, and the arrival of numerous missions from the Korean kingdoms. These missions were of great cultural as well as diplomatic import, as scholar-monks from Yamato were taken to the continent for study while large numbers of monks from the continent also arrived in the Japanese islands to staff the burgeoning number of temples. In so doing they also helped transmit knowledge of continental culture both at court and in the countryside.

Sukuna Bikona no Mikoto
Hailed as the "*tokoyo* deity" by Jingū in the *Nihon shoki* and *Kojiki*, this deity is said to have crossed over to the Japanese islands from the Korean Peninsula. Although he does not figure prominently within the mythological sections of the *Nihon shoki* and *Kojiki*, he is nonetheless depicted as having created the world with the deity Ōnamuchi no

Mikoto, with whom he is frequently paired. As I discuss in chapter 2, there is some evidence that this god was also the object of popular worship as something of a millennial savior. He is also said to have died and been resurrected at the Isaniwa shrine in Iyo Province at the very site where Shōtoku was said to have had erected a stele commemorating his visit to the hot spring there with the Koguryô monk Hyeja.

Sumiyoshi deities — These three gods are said in the *Nihon shoki* and *Kojiki* to have killed the the Yamato ruler Chūai following Chūai's refusal to obey their command to immediately go and conquer the Korean kingdom of Silla. Following Chūai's death, the gods are shown aiding Jingū, Chūai's main consort and successor, in conqueror Silla. They also are shown pledging to give dominion over the Korean Peninsula to Jingū's as yet unborn son, the future ruler Ōjin. As a result, Ōjin is occasionally referred to as "the sovereign in the womb" within court chronicles. By the early Heian period, there is good reason to believe that the Sumiyoshi cult had merged with the cults of Jingū and Akaru Hime, the wife of Jingū's distaff ancestor, the Silla prince Ame no Hiboko.

Tachibana — A type of Japanese orange, this fruit appears in multiple contexts as a symbol of immortality. Among the most noteworthy such references are statements in the *Nihon shoki* and *Kojiki* identifying the *tachibana* as the fruit of immortality that was brought back from the world of immortals by Tajima Mori, the ancestor of the Miyake Muraji. The *tachibana* apparently also played a role in the mass millennial movement of Ōfube no Ōshi in the seventh century, as Ōfube preached that the *tokoyo* deity would appear on the *tachibana* tree as an insect that "in every way resembles the silkworm."

Takechi, Prince — The son of Temmu and a Munakata consort, this prince was a hero in the Jinshin War that brought Temmu to power. His son, Prince Nagaya, would later challenge the Fujiwara for power during the first decades of the Nara period, but he was eventually forced to commit suicide after being accused of treason and plotting to harm his rivals.

Tamba no Michinushi — The son of Hiko Imasu no Mikoto, the putative founder of the Kusakabe kinship group, the *Nihon shoki* and *Kojiki* state that Tamba no Michinushi conquered Tamba for the Yamato ruler Sujin. He is also said to be the father of Hibasu Hime.

Temmu — The son of Jomei and Saimei and brother of Tenji, Temmu came to the throne following his success in the brief Jinshin War of 672. Temmu is credited with accelerating the centralization of power begun by his brother Tenji and with laying the foundations for the Nara state. Temmu is also credited with promoting many sacerdotal innovations geared toward enhancing the prestige of the throne. Among the most important of these were the establishment of a Council of Shrine Affairs (*Jingikan*), a Bureau of *Yin-Yang* Affairs (*Ommyōryō*), the establishment of a cluster of temples that were specially designated for royal support (*Daiji*), and the transmission of scriptures and priests across the Japanese islands. During Temmu's reign the title of *tennō*, a term with powerful associations with Chinese *yin-yang* and Taoist cults, came to be regularly used with reference to the ruler. The term "manifest god" likewise appears to have come into use during Temmu's reign. Because Temmu's lineage controlled the throne until the almost the end of the Nara period, his influence, both direct and indirect, on the formation of the political and cultic institutions of the period is incalculable.

Tenji   The eldest son of Jomei and Saimei, Tenji assumed the throne in 668, although he is believed to have been effectively in power for much longer. During his ascendancy, large numbers of refugees from the Korean kingdoms of Paekche and Koguryô are believed to have immigrated to the Japanese islands. The resulting influx of continental technologies and conceptions, along with the pressures created by the insecurity of the Yamato court vis-à-vis Silla and the T'ang, are thought to have created a new impetus for the increased centralization of power in the hands of the ruler and the creation of the first set of law codes in the Japanese islands. Tenji was succeeded by his brother, who was known to later generations as Temmu tennō.

Tenjukoku   A land beyond death to which Kamitsumiya's wife Inabe Tachibana no Iratsume apparently believed the prince had gone after death. Although the nature and source of this belief has been debated centuries, the conception of tenjukoku appears to be linked to the tokoyo cults associated with immigrant deities such as Sukuna Bikona no Mikoto.

Tenjukoku   Purportedly a tapestry produced at the request of Prince Kamitsu-
Shūchō   miya's fourth wife, Inabe Tachibana no Iratsume that depicts the prince's ascent into "tenjukoku." Although fragments of what is believed to be the original tapestry remain along with an old copy, the meaning of the work's numerous images has proven elusive. Fortunately, the inscription written on the tapestry was recorded in the Jōgu Shōtoku hōō teisetsu and is therefore known to us.

Tokoyo   A heavenly world beyond death. Within the Nihon shoki and Kojiki, only two gods are specifically referred to as tokoyo deities. These are Sukuna Bikona no Mikoto, a deity that is said to have lived in the Japanese islands on the coast of the Japan/Eastern Sea, and the tokoyo worm divinity worshiped by the followers of Ōfube no Ōshi.

Tsunuga   Tsunuga Arashito was a legendary prince from the Korean Peninsula
Arashito   who is said in the Kojiki to have emigrated to the Japanese islands upon hearing of the sage virtue of the Yamato ruler Sujin. From an early point, legends of this deity appear to have merged with those of the Silla Prince Ame no Hiboko. The main cultic center for Tsunuga Arashito was the Kehi shrine in the port of Tsunuga on the coast of the Japan/Eastern Sea. Like Ame no Hiboko, Tsunuga Arashito is said to have been the husband of Akaru Hime, a sometimes vengeful deity who resided at the Himegoso shrines in Naniwa and in Buzen Province in Kyūshū. The importance of this deity for the cults of Jingū and Ōjin is dramatically illustrated in a legend in which the god and the future ruler Ōjin exchange names.

Uji, Prince   Prince Uji, purportedly the son of the Yamato ruler Ōjin and a consort from the Wani kinship group, is depicted in the Nihon shoki and Kojiki as actually returning to life in order to console his grieving younger brother, the future ruler Nintoku.

Urano-
shimako

Claimed as an ancestor by Kusakabe lineages in Tamba Province, this figure purportedly traveled to the land of the immortals under the sea, only to foolishly return and lose his chance at eternal life.

Wani
kinship
group

This kinship group, which claimed descent from the fire deity Ama no Ho no Akari no Mikoto, is believed to have been one of the most influential lineages of the fifth and sixth centuries. Evidence for this can be seen from the fact that the Wani are said in the *Nihon shoki* and *Kojiki* to have provided no fewer than nine consorts to seven rulers during this period. Among the many prominent royal ancestors to claim the Wani as their distaff lineage were Yamato Takeru and Prince Uji. Intriguingly, both of these figures are depicted in the *Kojiki* and *Nihon shoki* as virtuous princes who die before ascending the throne and are then resurrected. Sometime in the mid-sixth century, however, the Wani are believed to have divided into smaller lineages such as the Ono, the Kasuga and the Kakinomoto. This last lineage is of immediate note because the poet Kakinomoto Hitomaro utilized numerous tropes and themes from Wani legend cycles as he helped create the poetic vocabulary of sacred kingship during the reigns of Tenji and Temmu.

Yamashiro
no Ōe

Prince Kamitsumiya's son by a Soga consort, this prince is presented in the *Nihon shoki* as the rightful heir to the throne, who nonetheless chooses death rather than precipitate a war that would bring grief to the people. By the time of the completion of the *Nihon shoki* this event was already being presented in supernatural terms. There is some evidence suggesting that this prince may have been raised by the Hata in Yamashiro Province.

Yamato
no Aya

This cluster of immigrant lineages centered in Yamato Province is depicted in the *Nihon shoki* as working extremely closely with the Soga kinship group during the height of Soga power. Several members of the Yamato no Aya were also among the most famous monks from the Asuka and Nara periods. Virtually all of the first monks that were sent to the Korean kingdom of Paekche to study in the Suiko period were from these lineages. Many, upon their return, took up residence in Asukadera, the kinship group temple of the Soga. In light of the fact that Prince Kamitsumiya himself traced Soga ancestry on both his paternal and distaff sides, it is hardly surprising that members of these lineages are also believed to have been among the earliest Shōtoku devotees.

Yamato
Takeru

Purportedly the son of the Yamato ruler Keikō and a woman from the Wani kinship group, this legendary prince is credited by the *Kojiki* and *Nihon shoki* with bringing several northeastern provinces under Yamato control. Cultically, the figure of Yamato Takeru appears to have exerted substantial influence over the Yamato court—Temmu *tennō*, for instance, apparently believed his final illness was caused by the spirit of this prince's sword. The *Nihon shoki* and *Kojiki* accounts of the prince's death are also noteworthy for their depiction of the prince's death and resurrection in terms reminiscent of Chinese tales of immortals who achieve liberation from the corpse.

Notes

INTRODUCTION

1. I realize that the concept of "immigrant," like race or ethnicity, is socially constructed. In the following pages, I use the term "immigrant kinship group" to refer to any kinship group that claims as its founding ancestor a figure that was said to have come to the Japanese islands from across the sea. I similarly use the term "immigrant deity" to refer to any god that is explicitly said to have crossed over to the Japanese islands from across the sea. Similarly, in most cases I use the term "Yamato"—an early term for the Japanese islands—in place of "Japan" in order to highlight the fact that "Japan" itself was being constructed at just this time. I reserve use of the terms "Japan" and "Japanese" to refer to situations and events that are best understood in the context of national symbols and institutions that were constructed by the time of the writing of the *Nihon shoki*.

2. For an excellent discussion of the formation of notions of ethnicity and nation in the Japanese islands, see Batten, *To the Ends of Japan*, 87–100.

3. Ōyama, *Nagayaōke mokkan to kinsekibun*, 198–206.

4. I discuss the role of the Hata in the early Shōtoku cult throughout this book. Hōryūji and Shitennōji are discussed at length in chapters 1 and 7. Kamitsumiya's association with the Mononobe will be discussed in chapters 1 and 5.

5. Ienaga, "Shōtoku Taishi no Bukkyō," 64–81.

6. Inoue Mitsusada, *Nihon kodai no kokka to Bukkyō*.

7. Ōno, *Shōtoku Taishi no kenkyū*.

8. Sakamoto Tarō, *Shōtoku Taishi*.

9. Kanaji Isamu. *Shōtoku Taishi shinkō*.

10. Nakamura Hajime, *Shōtoku Taishi*.

11. Much of Tamura's best work concerning the Korean Peninsula can be found in Tamura, *Nihon Bukkyōshi 4*, Tamura, *Kodai Chōsen to Yamato*, and Tamura, *Tsukushi to Asuka: Nihon kodaishi o miru me*. Tamura also

highlighted Shōtoku's connections with the Korean Peninsula in Tamura and Kawa-gishi, *Shōtoku Taishi to Asuka Bukkyō*.

12. See Ōyama, *Shōtoku taishi no shinjitsu*, and Ōyama, *Shōtoku taishi no tanjō*.

13. For specialists in the field, this focus on Shitennōji and Kōryūji, as opposed to Kamitsumiya's kinship group temple Hōryūji, may be surprising. This decision has been dictated by the fact that the main object of this study is the legendary Shōtoku and not the historical Prince Kamitsumiya. Several decades prior to the composition of the *Nihon shoki*, Hōryūji had burned to the ground, and it was not entirely rebuilt until after the composition of the text. I therefore view the temple as in many ways an important product, not source, of the early Shōtoku cult. For similar reasons, this book does not focus on the various sub-lineages of the Soga kinship group in spite of the fact that the Soga were probably the single most important political and cultural force during Kamitsumiya's lifetime. The Soga never fully recovered, however, from the Jinshin war of 672, and it is doubtful that their influence in the period leading up to the *Nihon shoki* was as great as the immigrant lineages most closely associated with Shitennōji and Kōryūji. Within this volume, however, I do consider the influence of several immigrant lineages from the Korean kingdom of Paekche that were closely associated with the Soga.

14. I have, where possible, made reference to such sources from the Korean Peninsula as the *Samguk sagi* (*Historical Records of the Three Kingdoms*), a twelfth-century court history, and the *Samguk yusa* (*Memorabilia from the Three Kingdoms*), a thirteenth century collection of legends related to the history of Buddhist tradition in the Korean Peninsula. Unfortunately, however, the late dating of these texts means that they must be handled with extreme caution by the scholar seeking to draw con-clusions concerning cultic and ideological orientations that existed some 500 years earlier. For similar reasons, I have also refrained from use of later Shōtoku hagiog-raphy such as the *Shōtoku Taishi denryaku* (*Chronological Biography of the Crown Prince Shōtoku*).

15. For a genealogy of the term, see Eriksen, "Ethnicity, Race and Nation," 33–42.

16. George De Vos, "Ethnic Pluralism: Conflict and Accommodation," 9.

17. Batten, *Ends of Japan*, 91.

1. Nelson Goodman, *Ways of World Making*, 6.

2. Ernest Renan, *Oevres Complètes*, I: 892. The passage is quoted and discussed in Benedict Anderson, *Imagined Communities*, 199.

3. Geoffrey Bennington, "Postal Politics and the Institution of the Nation," 121.

4. In addition to Piggott's work on Japanese kingship, William Wayne Farris has made an enormous contribution to our understanding of how political and cultural developments on the Korean helped shape this process with his *Sacred Texts and Buried Treasures*. Other important English-language works on the period include Piggott, *Tōdaiji and the Nara Imperium*, 10–127; Naoki, "The Nara State," 221–268; and Sonoda, "Early Buddha Worship," 370–415.

5. These first three of these titles were officially prescribed for use in court rites in the *Yōrō ritsuryō* (*Law Codes of the Yōrō Period*), which were compiled sometime around 720. Although the original text of the law codes no longer exists, it has been reconstructed on the basis of early commentaries. For the relevant passage see Inoue Mitsusada, *Ritsuryō*, 343. One of the most influential such commentaries—the *Ryōshūge* (*Assembled Explanations of the Law*), was compiled by a member of a Hata sub-

lineage in 868. This text may be found in *SZKT* 23–24. I will discuss the concept of the sage ruler and its relation to the early Shōtoku cult in chapter 4.

6. For works specifically addressing the importance of Korean immigrants in early Japan see Ueda, *Kikajin*; Hirano, *Kikajin to kodai kokka*; Inoue Mitsuo, *Kodai no Nihonjin to toraijin*; Imai, *Kikajin to shaji*, and Mizoguchi, *Kodai shizoku no keifu*.

7. Much of my thinking on this topic has been influenced by Anderson's *Communities* and Hobsbawm's *Invention of Tradition*.

8. The translation is from Cornelius Kiley, "Surnames in Ancient Japan," 178. The original text may be found in *Shinsen shōjiroku*, preface. Saeki, 1: 145. Kiley concludes by noting that "The *Shinsen shōjiroku* reflects an attitude whereby all persons of acknowledged foreign origin, however thoroughly naturalized in the cultural sense, are equally alien (Kiley, "Surnames," 185).

9. I will discuss this phenomenon in connection with the development of the Jingū/Ōjin legend cycle in chapter 3.

10. This legend has been discussed by a large number of Japanese scholars. For a brief overview of Japanese scholarship on the legend, see Tamura, *Nihon Bukkyōshi*, 1: 68–84. See also Hiraoka, *Nihon jiinshi no kenkyū*, 22–43.

11. For an overview of the history of the Shōtoku cult, see Hayashi, *Taishi shinkō no kenkyū*; Tanaka, *Shōtoku Taishi shinkō no seiritsu*; and Ōno, *Shōtoku Taishi no kenkyū*.

12. I will discuss the roles of Dōji, Ganjin and Saichō in the early Shōtoku cult in chapter 7. For a summary of the prominent role of the figure of Shōtoku in Buddhist movements of the Kamakura period, see Kanaji, *Shōtoku Taishi shinkō*, 151–184. Over the centuries, the importance of Shōtoku as a Buddhist symbol of the Japanese state continued to increase in importance. Over time the number of temples tracing their descent to Shōtoku swelled into the hundreds as monk and layperson alike were drawn into the Shōtoku cult. Shōtoku's importance as a cultural icon continues in contemporary Japan, where he has been the subject of innumerable popular and scholarly books, articles, and symposia.

13. *NSK*, Kimmei 13.10. Kojima 2: 417–419. Aston 2: 65–67.

14. For the Soga, see Mayuzumi, *Soga shi to kodai kokka*; Hino, *Nihon kodai shizoku denshō*, 343–474; and Katō, *Soga shi to Yamato ōken*.

15. *NSK*, Kimmei 13.10. Kojima 2: 419; Aston 2: 67.

16. See, for instance, the *Gangōji garan engi narabi ni ruki shizaichō* (*Historical Account and Inventory of Holdings of Gangōji*), a document that was submitted to the court in 747 but is believed to contain material that is much older. The text may be found in Takeuchi, *Nara ibun* 2: 383–393. For an English translation of the text, see Stevenson, "The Founding of the Monastery Gangōji and a List of Its Treasures," 299–315. Further materials related to Asukadera/Gangōji have been collected in Iwaki, *Gangōji hennen shiryō*, and Mizuno Ryūtarō, *Nihon kodai no jiin no shiryō*, 21–101. For a brief comparison of the *NSK* and the *Gangōji engi*, see Sonoda, "Early Buddha Worship," 370–379.

17. Sonoda, "Early Buddha Worship," 375–376.

18. *NSK*, Sushun, period before enthronement, seventh month. Kojima 2: 513–514; Aston 2: 114.

19. *NSK*, Sushun, period before enthronement, seventh month. Kojima 2: 515; Aston 2: 115.

20. The significance of these texts for the court is discussed in Piggott, *Emergence of Japanese Kingship*, 146–147. The *Golden Light Sutra* may be found in *T* 16: 335–357 (no. 663). The *Golden Light Excellent King Sutra* may be found in *T* 16: 403–457 (no. 665). For specific examples of quotations from these scriptures within the *Nihon*

shoki, as well as a broader discussion of the reception of these sutras in Japan, see Tamura, *Nihon Bukkyōshi* 1: 68–84. For the origins and importance of scriptures concerning the Four Heavenly Kings within the greater East Asian Buddhist tradition, see Orzech, *Politics and Transcendent Wisdom.* I will discuss Dōji's role in the formation of the Shōtoku cult in detail in chapter 6.

21. de Visser, *Ancient Buddhism in Japan,* 434.

22. The official title of the State temples was in fact "Temple for the Protection of the Country by the Four Heavenly Kings of the Golden Light Sutra."

23. Inoue Kaoru, *Nihon kodai no seiji to shūkyō,* 236.

24. *NSK,* Temmu 12.3. Kojima 3: 407; Aston 2: 350. *NSK,* Jitō 5.8.13. Kojima 3: 518–519; Aston 2: 403. For a thorough discussion of source materials related to the Four Heavenly Kings Temple, see Hiraoka, *Nihon jiin shi no kenkyū,* 22–81.

25. For the Kishi, see Miura, "Kishi ni tsuite," 27–45, and Katō, *Kishi to Kawachi no Aya shi,* 9–109. For the Abe, see Katō, *Yamato seiken to kodai shizoku,* 55–92.

26. Kishi influence at court during this period seems to have been particularly strong. The Kusakabe Kishi, a sub-branch of the Kishi kinship group, are thought to have helped raise Prince Kusakabe, Temmu's son and crown prince. See Ōhashi, *Nihon kodai no ōken to shizoku,* 199–207. I will further discuss the participation of progeny in the ancestral cults of adoptive families in chapter 3.

27. *Shinsen shōjiroku,* Naniwa, Kōbetsu section. Saeki, 1: 194.

28. For the Hata, see Katō, *Hata shi to sono tami* and Hino, *Nihon kodai shizoku no denshō,* 225–359. See also Hirano, "Hatashi no kenkyū," 25–47.

29. *SNG,* Wadō 7.2.9. Aoki 1: 211.

30. *Shinsen shōjiroku,* Naniwa, Kōbetsu section. Saeki, 1: 1–94.

31. Miura, "Kishi ni tsuite," 32–37. I will refer again to this kinship group shortly.

32. *SNG,* Tempyō 6.3.15. Aoki 2: 277.

33. For the Kishi dance see Ōhashi, *Nihon kodai no ōken to shizoku,* 184–198.

34. See, for instance, *NSK,* Temmu 4.2.13. Kojima 3: 359; Aston 2: 327. Gemmei was referred to as the Princess Abe even in the Chinese histories. See Tsunoda and Goodrich, *Japan in the Chinese Histories,* 52. The use of the name Abe again most likely indicates that Gemmei was raised with Abe support.

35. Sakamoto, *Six National Histories,* 72.

36. Sakamoto believes that epigraphy from Hōryūji was ignored even on such basic points as Shōtoku's death (which the *Nihon shoki* lists as occurring in 621 when the inscription from the Hōryūji Shakyamuni triad indicates that Shōtoku died in 622). See Sakamoto, *Six National Histories,* 47–48 and 70–71. As I noted in the introduction, however, it is possible that the Hōryūji epigraphy was created after the composition of the *Nihon shoki.* Please also note that, although this temple had many incarnations and many names, for heuristic purposes I shall refer to it throughout the text as Hōryūji. For a detailed review of Hōryūji's complicated architectural history, see Kidder *The Lucky Seventh* and Ōta Hirotarō, *Nanto shichidaiji no rekishi to nenpyō,* 3: 1–77.

37. Gari Ledyard long ago made the interesting suggestion that much of the Japanese islands and the Korean could be considered as a single cultural sphere bound together not by land but by water. See Ledyard, "Galloping Along with the Horseriders: Looking for the Foundations of Japan," 217–254. Ledyard's attempt to revive Egami Namio's "horserider theory," which posits the conquest of Yamato by horse riding peoples from the mainland, however, is much more problematic. For a critique of Ledyard's position, see Edwards, "Event and Process in the Founding of Japan: The Horserider Theory in Archeological Perspective," 265–295. For an overview of Egami's

views as they have developed over the years, see Egami, *Egami Namio no Nihon ko-daishi*. For critiques of the theory by Japanese scholars, see Sahara, *Kiba minzoku wa konakatta*, and Mizuno Yū, *Nihon kodai minzoku to kokka*. For by far the best discussion of the historiography of relations between Yamato and the Korean Peninsula, see Farris, *Sacred Texts*, 55–122.

38. Inoue Mitsusada, "The Century of Reform," 173.

39. See Tamura, *Nihon Bukkyōshi* 4: 145–149. Much can also be gleaned about the role of Paekche monks in Japan from Best, *Buddhism in Paekche*, 96–141.

40. *STZ* 3: 61. For a brief overview of scholarship on the text, see Tanaka, *Shōtoku Taishi shinkō*, 42–46.

41. *NSK*, Suiko 30.7. Kojima 2: 579; Aston 2: 149–150.

42. Tamura, *Nihon Bukkyōshi* 4: 176.

43. *NSK*, Suiko 31. Kojima 2: 581; Aston 2: 150–151.

44. Inoue Mitsusada treats this period in detail in "Century of Reform," 189–193.

45. Thus the *Hoketsuki* highlights Hata no Kawakatsu's role in aiding Shōtoku during the battle against the Mononobe. See *STZ* 3: 56. For the Hata's military connections to Yamashiro no Ōe, see Yokota, "Metsubō mae ni okeru Jōgū ōka," 126–144. I will discuss Yamashiro no Ōe's connections with the Hata further in chapter 4.

46. The elimination of Emishi's branch of the Soga did not by itself did not spell the end of Soga influence. Members of other Soga sub-lineages, for instance, occupied some of the highest ranks at Tenji's court. If we accept, however, that the Soga exercised very substantial authority in the pre-Tenji period, then it seems fair to assume that the overall influence of this kinship group had eroded to a significant degree by the end of the century.

47. Tamura, *Nihon Bukkyōshi* 4: 198–200.

48. Hirano, "Hatashi no kenkyū," 34–37. Tamura, *Nihon Bukkyōshi* 4: 198.

49. For the Arima incident, see Inoue Mitsusada, "Century of Reform," 203–204.

50. See Batten, "Foreign Threat and Domestic Reform," 83–112. See also Inoue Mitsusada, "Century of Reform," 201–216.

51. Batten, "Foreign Threat and Domestic Reform," 215–216.

52. For Tenji's reign, see Piggott, *Emergence of Japanese Kingship*, 102–126.

53. For the Jinshin War, see Naoki, *Jinshin no ran*, and Farris, *Heavenly Warriors*, 41–45.

54. Naoki, *Jinshin no ran*, 204–231.

55. In the chapters that follow, I will discuss the role of these same immigrant kinship groups in the development of shrine worship.

56. For the political/religious dynamic of this period, see Piggott, *Emergence of Japanese Kingship*, 236–279. The attempt to create a Buddha-land through the construction of a network of temples had several precedents in China and Silla and may have been influential in the decision by the Yamato court in 738 to establish a network of temples across the Japanese islands. See Rhi Ki-young, "Brief Remarks on the Buddha-Land Ideology in Silla During the Seventh and Eighth Centuries," 163–181.

57. Chinese commentaries on the Shōtoku commentaries appear as early as 773 See Iida, *Shōtoku Taishiden no kenkyū*, 301. Shōtoku was believed to have written commentaries on three sutras: the *Lion's Roar of Queen Śrīmālā Sutra* (Ch: *Sheng-man shih-tzu hu i-sheng ta fang-pien fang-kuang ching*; J: *Shōman shishikō ichijyō daihōben hōkō kyō*, T 12: 217–223 (no. 353)), the *Vimilakirti Sutra* [Ch: *Wei-mo-chieh suo-shuo ching*; J: *Yuimakitsu shosetsu kyō*, T 14: 537–557 (no. 475)], and the *Lotus Sutra* [Ch: *Miao-fa*

lien-hua ching, J: *Myōhōrengekyō, T* 9: 1–62 (no. 262)]. The first of these, known as the *Shōmangyō gisho,* may be found in *T* 56: 1–19 (no. 2185). The second, known as the *Yuima gisho,* may be found in *T* 56: 20–64 (no. 2186). The third, known as the *Hokkekyō gisho,* may be found in *T* 56: 64–128 (no. 2187).

58. Iida, *Shōtoku Taishiden no kenkyū,* 263.

59. Thus the *Hōryūji garan engi narabi ni ruki shizaichō (Historical Account and Inventory of Holdings of Hōryūji)* begins it's narrative of the temple's origins with an account of how the "Dharma King Shōtoku" received donations of land in Harima province for the construction and maintenance of the temple after he preached the *Lotus Sutra* at court "with the appearance of a monk" See Takeuchi, *Nara ibun* 1: 344. In the *Gangōji garan engi,* similarly, he appears as a chief advocate of training monks and nuns with Paekche teachers in order to establish a Buddhist clergy with a proper understanding of the Buddhist precepts (Takeuchi, *Nara ibun* 1: 385–386).

60. The *Jōgū Shōtoku hōō teisetsu* in its current form can probably be traced back only as far as the eleventh century, but parts of the text are almost certainly much older. It is thought to have been composed at Hōryūji. The *Teisetsu* may be found in *STZ* 3: 9–22. The text has also been analyzed in detail in Ienaga, *Jōgū Shōtoku hōō teisetsu no kenkyū,* and Sakamori, Satō, and Yajima, *Jōgū Shōtoku hōō teisetsu no chūshaku to kenkyū.* For a partial English translation of the text, see Deal, "Hagiography and History: The Image of Prince Shōtoku," 316–333.

61. For the origins of the concept of the Dharma King, see Strong, *The Legend of Asoka,* 38–70. I will discuss the development of this concept in Yamato in chapter 7. For the inscription on the Shakyamuni statue, see Takeuchi, *Nara ibun* 3: 962. David Lurie has reviewed scholarly thought on the origins of both the statue and the inscription and concludes that both may in fact date from close to the death of the prince. See Lurie, *The Origins of Writing in Early Japan,* 418–419.

62. The *Goshuin engi* was purportedly discovered at the temple in 1007. The text may be found in *DNBZ* 85: 305–307. The *Denryaku* may be found in *STZ* 3: 71–122. Although both the authorship and date of the *Denryaku* are unknown, I treat it as a Shitennōji affiliated text in light of a statement in its preface that it was created using the *Hoketsuki* and other Shitennōji sources. In addition, the date given in the *Denryaku* for the prince's death accords with that of the *Nihon shoki* as opposed to that given in Hōryūji epigraphy and sources. For the sources for the *Denryaku,* see Abe Yasurō and Yamazaki, *Shōtoku Taishi denshū,* 325–334; Iida, *Shōtoku Taishiden no kenkyū,* 15–37; Tanaka, *Shōtoku Tashi shinkō no seiritsu,* 59–73; and Abe Ryūichi, "Muromachi izen seiritsu Shōtoku Taishiden kirui shoshi," 511–558.

63. The number of temples claiming to have been founded by Shōtoku continued to expand for centuries. The *Hōryūji garan engi,* however, lists seven temples as having been built by the prince. In addition to Hōryūji and Shitennōji, these include the Hata kinship group temple Kōryūji, Chūgūji, Tachibanadera, Hokkiji, and Katsurakidera. Although it is not clear why the number seven was chosen, it has been suggested by Guth and others that this reflected a contemporary belief that a *cakravartin* ruler had seven treasures with which to rule his state. See Guth, "Pensive Prince of Chūgūji," 209–210. It is also possible, however, that belief in Shōtoku's seven temples mirrored a Silla legend that Silla was the true Buddha-land and that the seven Buddhas of previous epochs had each built one temple in Silla.

64. The most important exception was Hōryūji, which, as I noted above, had as its main image a statue of Shakyamuni "built to the prince's size." See Guth, "Pensive Prince of Chūgūji," 208.

65. Tamura, *Nihon Bukkyōshi* 1: 177–184.

66. See Hayami, *Miroku shinkō*, 58–64.

67. See Hayami, *Miroku shinkō*, 58–64. Yamato rulers were by no means the only sovereigns who sought to use the figure of Maitreya as a means of bolstering their authority. Examples of Chinese monarchs who claimed to be incarnations of Maitreya can be found in China as early as the fifth century and continued down to the time of the Empress Wu in the early eighth century. See Nattier, "Meanings of the Maitreya Myth," 30–32.

68. Nattier, "Meanings of the Maitreya Myth," 23–51.

69. For the *hwarang*, see Mishina, *Shiragi no Karō no kenkyū*, and Lancaster, "Maitreya in Korea," 135–153.

70. Because of a scarcity of Korean sources, there is considerable debate as to the nature of the *hwarang* fraternities in seventh-century Silla. Katata has pointed out, however, that the *Nihon shoki* version of the founding legend of Yamato Buddhism presents Shōtoku as a fifteen or sixteen year old youth entering battle. He therefore suggests that this description of the Yamato prince was modeled on the *hwarang* youth. See Katata, *Nihon kodai shinkō to Bukkyō*, 177–179.

71. Miyake-Kishi Irishi's mission is recorded in *NSK*, Temmu 4.7.7. Kojima 3: 364–365; Aston, 2: 329.

72. For Yakushiji, see Ōta, *Nanto shichi daiji*, 107–143.

73. *Samguk yusa* in *T* 49: 972b (no. 2039).

CHAPTER 2

1. There are several possible readings for this name. Throughout this chapter, I will for convenience in referencing continue to follow Aston in using the reading "Ōfube." This reading was also used by Robert Ellwood, "A Cargo Cult in Seventh Century Japan," 222–238. I will discuss Katō Kenkichi's compelling argument for reading the name as "Mibu" shortly.

2. *NSK*, Kōgyoku 3.7. Kojima 2: 93–95; Aston 2: 188–189. Note that, as we saw in chapter 1, Hata no Kawakatsu also appears in the *Nihon shoki* receiving a *hanka shii*-type image of Maitreya from Shōtoku.

3. For an overview of early conceptions of *tokoyo*, see Sugano, *Kojiki setsuwa no kenkyū*, 192–229. I will review scholarship on Ōfube's cult shortly.

4. Throughout this work, I will refrain from using this term to denote a distinct religious system of the period. For an excellent summary of academic discussions concerning the category of "Shinto," see John Breen and Mark Teeuwen, "Introduction: The Shinto Past and Present," 1–12.

5. The dating of the tapestry has been a subject of intense controversy, as has the status of its inscription. Historians working mainly from the inscription are still hotly debating the subject. One powerful salvo arguing for a later dating of the text may be found in Ōyama, *Nagayaōke mokkan*, 309–324. Even Ōyama, however, accepts the likelihood that the tapestry and inscription existed in the mid-eighth century. Lurie notes that the inscription on the tapestry does not say that it was actually produced at the time of the prince's death, and that a tapestry was apparently donated to Hōryūji by Jitō *tennō* (reigned 690–697) [Lurie, *Origins of Writing in Early Japan*, 416–417]. More recent art historical scholarship focusing on the tapestry itself has tended to accept the authenticity of the text's early date. See, for example, Ōhashi, *Tenjukoku shūchō no kenkyū* and Pradel, *Fragments of the Tenjukoku Shūchō Mandara*. For the purposes of this chapter, I will treat the tapestry as a late

seventh-century artifact, although a slightly earlier or later dating would not signifi-
cantly affect my argument about the development of the Shōtoku cult.

6. An annotated rendering of the text can be found in Deguchi and Hiraoka,
Shōtoku taishi nanto Bukkyō shū, 223–229.

7. For a summary of these efforts, see Ōno, *Jōdai no jōdokyō*, 45–78.

8. See, for example, Hino, *Kodai shizoku*, 312–335.

9. Hayashi, "Tenjukoku shūchō mei," 325–337. The origins of the Yumedono
icon are unclear. The *Hōryūji tōin engi* (*Historical Record of the Eastern Complex of
Hōryūji*) cites temple records from 761 indicating Kōmyō's devotion to the statue
[*DNBZ* 85: 127–129]. The text is discussed in Hayashi, *Taishi shinkō no kenkyū*,
73–83, and Ōyama, *Nagayaōke no mokkan*, 278. I will discuss the Yumedono Kuse
Kannon in greater detail in chapters 6 and 7.

10. *NSK*, Suiko 29.2.5. Kojima 2: 577–9; Aston 2: 148–149.

11. I will discuss this theme in greater detail in chapter 4.

12. *NSK*, Suiko 13.4.1. Kojima 2: 551; Aston 2:133–134.

13. Although this body of water is routinely referred to as the "Japan Sea" in
Japan, on the Korean Peninsula, it is referred to as the "Eastern Sea." Because the
perception of colonial resonances in the term "Japan Sea" has resulted in strenuous
resistance to its use on the Korean Peninsula, I shall throughout the text refer to it as
the "Japan/Eastern Sea."

14. For relations between Yamato, Sui/T'ang China and the Korean kingdoms,
see Kaneko, "Zuitō kōdai to higashi Ajia," 15–41.

15. For relations between Koshi and early Yamato, see Hara Hidesaburō, "Ōken to
tōhō e no michi," 165–188, and Tateno, "Koshi no kuniguni to gōzokutachi," 189–209.

16. References to official guest residences appear in the *Nihon shoki* as early as
570 (*NSK*, Kimmei 31.4. Kojima 2: 457–458; Aston 2: 87–88). There is some indirect
evidence suggesting that numerous lineages associated with the early Shōtoku cult
were closely involved with these institutions. The text notes that members of the Kishi
and Kashiwade—both lineages that we have already seen were closely associated with
the early Shōtoku cult—were sent to receive foreign emissaries at these guest residences. The first reference to the settling of Koguryô immigrants within the *Nihon
shoki* also highlights the role of the Kishi, who are said to have brought Koguryô
artisans to Nukata Sato in the Yamabe district of Yamato (*NSK*, Ninken 6. Kojima 2:
261–263; Aston 1: 396–397). I will discuss the importance of this village for the eminent monk Dōji, one of the most prominent advocates of the Shōtoku cult in the Nara
period, in chapter 7.

17. Matsuo, "Nihonkai chūbu no kofun bunka," 110–112. For a more general
discussion of the role of Yamato in East Asian politics of the fifth century, see Inoue
Mitsusada, "Yūryakuchō ni okeru ōken to higashi ajia," 72–117.

18. My thinking on the role of Koguryô and Tsunuga in seventh-century Yamato
politics and culture has been greatly influenced by Kadowaki, *Nihon kaiiki no kodaishi*.

19. *Kojiki*, Nintoku chapter. *SNKBZ* 1: 287.

20. I will discuss this in greater detail later.

21. The prince's genealogy is given at the beginning of the *Jōgū Shōtoku hōō
teisetsu*. See *STZ* 3: 11–12. For Kamitsumiya's kinship alliances, see Tōyama, "Umako to
Shōtoku Taishi," 127–148.

22. This area also housed the tomb of Tajima Mori, an ancestor of the Miyake
kinship group, who will be discussed at length in this chapter and in chapter 3. The
presence of a royal estate (*miyake*), the region's links with the Hata, and the presence of
the tomb of a Miyake ancestor all suggest that the Miyake kinship group also had a

strong connection with the area. I will discuss the importance of canals and estate administration for the early Shōtoku cult in greater detail in chapter 3.

23. For a discussion of the numerous branches of the Abe, including the Abe Hiketa, see Katō, *Yamoto seiken to kodai shizoku*, 56–61.

24. Thus, the Abe Hiketa no Omi appear in *NSK*, Saimei 4.4 (Kojima 3: 219–221; Aston 2: 252), *NSK*, Saimei 5.3 (Kojima 3: 221–223; Aston 2: 260), and *NSK*, Saimei 6.3 (Kojima 3: 231; Aston 2: 263–264) as leading campaigns in the region. For the Abe's role in the Koshi campaigns, see Sekiguchi, *Emishi to kodai kokka*, 20–66.

25. The Shiragi shrine is listed as one of the court-supported shrines in the region in *Engishiki*, fascicle ten. *SZKT* 26: 264.

26. Note that because the boundaries between Koguryô, Silla, and other, smaller states on the Korean Peninsula were in constant flux, immigrant kinship groups and deities were occasionally referred to as being from one or the other country interchangeably.

27. *NSK*, Suinin 2.10. Kojima 1: 301; Aston 1: 166.

28. *NSK*, Suinin 2.10. Kojima 1: 303–305; Aston 1: 167–168.

29. I will discuss the role of immigrant deities such as Arashito in the development of the Jingū/Ōjin legend cycle in chapter 3.

30. *Kojiki*, Chūai chapter. *SNKBZ* 1: 253–254.

31. Tsukaguchi, *Jingū kōgō densetsu*, 112–122.

32. I will discuss the name "Izasa Wake" shortly.

33. *NSK*, Suinin 3.3. Kojima 1: 305; Aston 1: 169.

34. *Kojiki*, Ōjin chapter. *SNKBZ* 1: 275–278. I will discuss this legend in detail in chapter 3.

35. I will discuss both the legend and the sword in greater detail in chapter 3. The importance of the place name "Isasa" for Ame no Hiboko and other immigrant deities will be discussed shortly.

36. *Kojiki*, Ōjin chapter. *SNKBZ* 1: 277–278.

37. The ritual waving of scarves was also an important element in rites for the dead. I will treat this in detail in chapter 5.

38. For silk production in Tajima during the period, see Yoshikawa, "Kodai Tajima no sen'i seisan to ryūtsu," 9–27.

39. For a genealogical analysis of several lineages in the region, see Yoshida Akira, "Kodai Tajima no gōzoku to bumin," 1–39. See also Kadowaki, *Nihon kaiki no kodaishi*, 275–298. For the Hata's connection with Ame no Hiboko, see Ōhashi Nobuya, *Kodai gōzoku to toraijin*, 56–64.

40. *NSK*, Suinin 90.7.14. Kojima 1: 335; Aston 1: 186.

41. *NSK*, Suinin 100.3.12. Kojima 1: 336–337; Aston 1: 186–187. The legend also appears in *Kojiki*, Suinin chapter. *SNKBZ* 1: 211–212. I will discuss the *Kojiki* account in chapter 5.

42. Tajima Mori's lament also highlights a view of *tokoyo* colored by continental conceptions of immortality. Not only is his text filled with allusions to tales of Chinese immortals (*hsien-jen*) but he also explicitly declares that "*tokoyo* is where the immortals conceal themselves, and no common man can go there." The fact that Tajima Mori did in fact attain entry into *tokoyo* can thus be taken as an assertion that he was adept at continental immortality techniques. I will discuss this and other legends of otherworld journeys and resurrection in chapter 5.

43. I will discuss the phrase "weak waters" in chapter 5.

44. This is also tentatively suggested in Shinkawa, *Nihon Kodai no girei to hyōgen*, 110–111.

45. See, for instance, *Shan-hai-ching*, fourth fascicle, in *Shan-hai-ching chiao-chu*, 407. For the connections between the cults of the Queen Mother of the West and the Weaver Maiden, see Kominami, *Saiōbō to tanabata denshō*. The Queen Mother of the West is also discussed with great erudition in Loewe, *Ways to Paradise*, esp. 86–134.

46. For a dramatic illustration of the importance of weaving motifs for cult of Akaru Hime, see *Hizen fudoki*, Ki District. *SNKBZ* 5: 315–317, where this deity represents herself in the form of looms. For a broader discussion of the influence of silkworm cults and weaving deities on the formation of early tropes of kingship and courtly romance, see Como, "Silkworms and Consorts in Nara Japan," 111–131.

47. *NSK*, Age of the Gods, Book 1, section 8. Kojima 1: 106–107; Aston 1: 62–63. The motif of a small child appearing from a floating fruit or gourd is a common trope in continental literature on immortals. The wren, similarly, was a prominent symbol of Silla kingship. I will discuss Sukuna bikona no Mikoto further in chapter 3.

48. *NSK*, Age of the Gods, Book 1, section 8. Kojima 1: 103; Aston 1: 59–60.

49. *Kojiki*, Chūai chapter. *SNKBZ* 1: 255. The toasts may also be found in *NSK*, Jingu 13.2. Kojima 1: 449; Aston 1: 244–245. The translation of the toasts is from Cranston, *Waka Anthology*, 1: 26–27.

50. Mitani, "Hitachi kuni fudoki kara shūgo shisō e," 251–259.

51. *Montoku jitsuroku*, Saikō 3. *SZKT* 3: 86. The text is also discussed in Mitani, "Hitachi kuni fudoki kara shūgo shisō e," 255.

52. Mitani states that the reference to stones resembling monks surrounding the images indicates that by the mid-ninth century the deities' association with the Medicine Buddha Yakushi was already firmly established. See Mitani, "Hitachi kuni fudoki kara shūgo shisō e," 255–256.

53. The question of where Sukuna Bikona no Mikoto and Ōnamuchi no Mikoto have returned from is also answered slightly differently here than in the *Nihon shoki* passage quoted earlier. Whereas in the *Nihon shoki* and *Kojiki* Sukuna Bikona no Mikoto is always referred to as having gone to *tokoyo*, here the gods declare that they have returned from the "Eastern Sea," a common means of referring to the Korean Peninsula.

54. Hirano, "Hatashi no kenkyū," 37–40. I will discuss the role of marriage and adoption customs in Yamato religion in chapter 3.

55. Note that the Inabe were the only lineage to be directly represented in the name of Kamitsumiya's purported fourth wife. Although one of the most prominent lineages of the Nara period was named "Tachibana," this lineage was created only in 708, long after Kamitsumiya and all who knew him had passed from the scene. For a brief summary of the origins and fortunes of the Tachibana lineage, see Sakamoto and Hirano, *Nihon kodai shizoku jinmei jiten*, 413–414.

56. The characters for *jukoku* are identical to those of *tenjukoku* except for the omission of the prefix "ten" (heavenly).

57. Please note that I am not asserting here that Shōtoku actually went to Iyo, only that the *Iyo kuni fudoki* claims that he did.

58. *Iyo kuni fudoki*, Yu district. *SNKBZ* 5: 505–506.

59. One further area of concern among Japanese scholars has centered upon the interpretation of the term *jukoku*, which I have rendered "Land of Long Life." In 1959, Akimoto Kichirō, in the *Nihon koten bungaku taikei* edition of the *Fudoki*, proposed a new reading for these two characters. Rather than treating the two as a nominal compound, Akimoto suggested that the character traditionally as a read as "long life" should be read as a verb. Thus, rather than read the term as "*jukoku*," or, "Land of Long

Life," Akimoto suggested that the text should be read as *"kuni o hisashiku suru,"* meaning "gives long life to the land." In support of this, Akimoto noted that an extant manuscript of the *Shaku nihongi*, the medieval text that cites the inscription, contains a note that gives this reading (Akimoto, *NKBT* 2: *Fudoki*, 494). Akimoto's suggestion was subsequently taken up by Ōno Tatsunosuke in 1972, who argued for the reading on the basis of his belief that *tenjukoku* should refer to a Buddhist Pure Land. Since there is no reason to believe that what is being referred to here is Buddhist, he argued, the term *"jukoku"* must refer to something other than *tenjukoku* (Ōno, *Jōdai no jōdokyō*, 67).

While Akimoto's reading is certainly possible, however, it is far from clear that his reading is the most natural for these characters. To begin with, the interpretation "gives long life to the land" hardly seems appropriate to the local context, which, as we shall see shortly, is clearly concerned with helping individuals, and not the nation, attain long life. In addition, during the pre-modern period this was never the dominant interpretation of the text. As a result, most scholars who believe the characters must indicate Amida's Pure Land continue to read the characters as *"jukoku."* Thus, this reading is given in the Heibonsha edition of the text (Yoshino Yutaka, trans., *Fudoki*, 330–331), as well as the 1997 *NSKBZ* edition of the text. The traditional reading of *jukoku* is also given in Jōdai Bunken o Yomukai ed., *Fudoki itsubun chūshaku*, 518. What is perhaps most striking about the positions of both camps, however, is that ultimately their main justifications are driven not by linguistic considerations but rather by projects of retrieval. One side believes that the text should refer to a Pure Land and that therefore the characters should be read as *kotobuki no kuni*, or the "land of long life." One side has given up on relating the text to Prince Kamitsumiya and Buddhist doctrine, and therefore assumes that it should have an entirely different meaning. Once we abandon such projects of retrieval, however, there is little reason to read the text as anything other than a local legend that refers to a land of long life known as *kotobuki no kuni*.

60. This literature is summarized in Kodai Bunken o Yomukai, *Fudoki itsubun chūshaku*, 550–556. After a detailed reading of the medieval sources, the editors conclude that although there is ample room to doubt the historical accuracy of the Dōgo inscription's claim that Prince Kamitsumiya visited Shikoku, the text of the *Iyo kuni fudoki* remnant itself is very likely from the early Nara period. For the citation within the *Shaku nihongi*, see *ST Koten chūshaku hen* 5: 339–340.

61. The text may be found in Takeuchi, *Nara ibun* 2: 363.

62. For *mokkan* that demonstrate the Hata were at Tachibana sato, see Matsubara, *Kodai no chihō gōzoku*, 204. For a discussion of the nature of *mokkan* and their importance for the study of this period, see Piggott, "*Mokkan*: Wooden Documents from the Nara Period," 449–470. See also Farris, *Sacred Texts and Buried Treasures*, 201–232.

63. Relations between the Iyo Hata and the Abe were so close, in fact, that the Iyo Hata successfully petitioned the court in 766 to change their name to Abe. *SNG*, Tempyō Jingo 2.3; Aoki 3: 113. The background for this incident is also discussed in Katō, *Yamato seiken*, 59.

64. *Iyo kuni fudoki*, Yu district. *SNKBZ* 5: 505–506.

65. The hot spring in Ōkita appears to have been a shrine center for Akaru Hime, yet another Silla immigrant deity and the wife of the Miyake ancestor Ame no Hiboko. I will discuss the Akaru Hime cult further in chapter 3 The role of Silla immigrant kinship groups in cults of resurrection and immortality will be discussed in chapter 5.

66. *NSK*, Kōgyoku 3.7. 2. Kojima 3: 93–95; Aston 2: 188–189. The translation of the song is from Cranston, *Waka Anthology*, 120.

67. Shimode, *Nihon no jingi to Dōkyō*, 188–199; Hino, *Kodai shizoku*, 312–335.

68. Ellwood, "Cargo Cult," 222–238.

69. Hirano, "Hatashi no kenkyū," 37–40.

70. Katō, *Yamoto seiken*, 196–205.

71. The Ōfube's connection with other Silla immigrant groups has been thoroughly discussed in Hirano, "Hatashi no kenkyū," 37–40.

72. Hirano, "Hatashi no kenkyū," 38–39. Note that the characters read "Ōikube" in the shrine name are identical to the characters read "Ōfube."

CHAPTER 3

1. Because Saimei twice assumed the throne, she was posthumously given the titles of both Kōgyoku and Saimei. For convenience, I will refer to her as Saimei throughout this chapter.

2. The lone exception that I have found is Naoki Kōjirō, who suggested that Saimei's death in Northern Kyūshū may have been the basis for the legend that the ruler Chūai died there centuries earlier. See Naoki, *Nihon kodai shizoku to tennō*, 163–164. I will discuss the Chūai legend shortly.

3. *NSK*, Saimei 7.5.9, 7.7.24, and 7.8.1. Kojima 3: 242–244; Aston 2: 271.

4. *NSK*, Shuchō 1.6.10. Kojima 3: 461; Aston 2: 377. The sword was believed to have originally belonged to Yamato Takeru, a prince and royal ancestor who will be discussed at length in chapter 5. The cultic ramifications of both the sword and Temmu's death will also be discussed shortly.

5. *NSK*, Chūai 9.2. Kojima 1: 417; Aston 1: 222. *Kojiki*, Chūai chapter. *SNKBZ* 1: 243.

6. In accordance with contemporary academic usage, in this chapter I will use modern readings for several shrines and deities. Thus I will refer to Sumiyoshi and not Sumie, Hachiman and not Yahata, and so forth.

7. The meaning of this term is obscure. I assume that it means the road to the underworld.

8. *Kojiki*, Chūai, part 2. *SNKBZ* 1: 243–245.

9. *NSK*, Chūai, 8.9.5. Kojima 1: 410–411; Aston 1: 221.

10. In chapter 2 we discussed Akaru Hime in the context of her role as wife of Ame no Hiboko and Tsunuga Arashito. Akaru Hime is listed as a child of the Sumiyoshi deities in the *Sumiyoshi taisha jindaiki* (*Records of the Age of the Gods from the Great Sumiyoshi shrine*), a mid-Nara to early Heian period text. The text has been edited and annotated by Tanaka in his *Sumiyoshi taisha jindaiki no kenkyū*. The Sumiyoshi cult and Akaru Hime are also discussed in Mayumi, *Nihon kodai saishi no kenkyū*, 194–219.

11. *NSK*, Suinin 88.7.10. Kojima 1: 332–334; Aston 1: 185–186. This sword was also discussed briefly in chapter 2.

12. He was also the father of the sage Tajima Mori, with whom I dealt in chapter 2 and to whom I will refer below.

13. Although the Jingū/Ōjin cult has been the subject of extensive research, I have greatly benefited from the following works: Mishina, *Nissen shinwa densetsu no kenkyū*; Tsukaguchi, *Jingū kōgō densetsu*; and Naoki, *Nihon kodai shizoku to tennō*, 153–201. In what follows, I will draw from the considerable contributions of all of these scholars. Whereas these scholars have tended to treat the legend's development from the per-

spective of the royal house, however, my interpretation will emphasize the connections of immigrant kinship groups such as the Miyake and Hata with the fearsome deities of northern Kyūshū and the Yamato court's need for their sanction and protection.

14. This section of the *Nihon shoki* is notoriously unreliable and many questions remain as to the history of this period. For an attempt to recreate the circumstances leading up to and following the Iwai rebellion, see Oda, "Iwai no hanran," 159–175 and Yamao, *Tsukushikimi Iwai no sensō*, 105–149. Iwai's descendants, it should be noted, appear to have played a significant role in Yamato society. I will treat the figure of Nichira, the legendary teacher of Shōtoku and a member of Iwai's kinship group, in chapter 5.

15. See Inoue Hideo, "Chiku, Toyo, Hi no gōzoku to Yamato chōtei," 138–158.

16. Naoki, *Naniwa miya to Naniwatsu no kenkyū*, 32–53.

17. The role of each of these kinship groups in estate administration is alluded to in Miura, "Kishi ni tsuite," 27–46. Naoki Kōjirō discusses the involvement of the Miyake, Hata, Kishi and Kusakabe in estate administration in Naoki, *Naniwamiya to Naniwatsu no kenkyū*, 43–49 and 60–70. See also Hirano, "Hatashi no kenkyū," 42–47.

18. The Natsu royal estate is generally believed to have been the forerunner of the Dazaifu administrative complex. For a discussion of the role of the Miyake in the estate's administration as well as an overview of the development of the area as a Yamato administrative center, see Itakusu Kazuko, "Rango no Kyūshū to Yamato seiken," 219–242.

19. For an extended discussion of the role of such majestification and the construction of cultural and religious monuments in the "poetics of power" of the period, see Piggott, *Todaiji and the Nara Imperium*, 10–127.

20. Yokota, *Asuka no kamigami*, 184–193.

21. *Kojiki*, Ōjin chapter. *SNKBZ* 1: 257. Okinaga genealogies are discussed at length in Yokota *Asuka no kamigami*, 184–197.

22. *Kojiki*. Ōjin chapter. *SNKBZ* 1: 277.

23. Ame no Hiboko's route is given in *NSK*, Suinin 3.3. Kojima 1: 305; Aston 1: 169–170. The purported tomb of the Miyake ancestor Tajima Mori, likewise, is located in the Tsutsuki district of Yamashiro in the same tomb range as that of Jingū. I will discuss shortly several instances where legends and cultic centers of the Jingū/ Ōjin cult in Kyūshū were located in areas populated by adherents of the cults of Ame no Hiboko and his estranged wife, Akaru Hime.

24. *Kojiki*, Nintoku chapter. *SNKBZ* 1: 287. In chapter 2 I argued that this estate was also closely connected with Shōtoku's lineage. Please note that I am only claiming that the *Kojiki* links the canal and the Hata with Nintoku—not that the canal was actually built during Nintoku's reign.

25. Naoki, *Naniwa miya to Naniwatsu no kenkyū*, 67–70.

26. This ritual linkage was no doubt related to the Naniwa Sumiyoshi shrine's proximity to Akaru Hime shrines in Manta and the island of Himejima—two areas dominated by the Miyake, Hata, Kishi, and Kusakabe kinship groups. It also reflects the Naniwa Sumiyoshi shrine's proximity to the Naniwa royal estate and the Kyūshū Sumiyoshi shrine's proximity to the Natsu royal estate; both of these estates, in addition to being major administrative centers, were administered by the Miyake kinship group. For more on Akaru Hime in Naniwa and Manta, see Mayumi, *Nihon kodai saishi*, 194–206.

27. Mayumi, *Nihon kodai saishi*, 197–201. I will discuss purification rites for foreign dignitaries in chapter 5.

28. This is discussed in Mayumi, *Nihon kodai saishi*, 201.

29. Naoki Kōjirō's thesis, in fact, was that virtually the entire legend cycle was rooted in events that took place during the reign of Jomei's chief consort and successor, Saimei. See Naoki, *Nihon kodai no shizoku*, 153–172. I have in this section also benefited enormously from the work of Tsukaguchi, *Jingū kōgō*, 11–107, Yokota, *Asuka no kamigami*, 193–197, and Ōhashi, *Nihon kodai no ōken to shizoku*, 211–234.

30. Naoki has pointed out that Saimei's posthumous name also included the term "Tarashihime" and that Chūai's genealogy as it appears in the *Nihon shoki* contains figures with names that closely resemble Jomei's immediate ancestors. See Naoki, *Nihon kodai shizoku*, 163–169. Jomei's relations with the Okinaga are also discussed in Yokota, *Asuka no kamigami*, 193–197.

31. For the Abe and Sakurai, see Yokota, *Asuka no kamigami*, 226–238. For the Okinaga and Jomei's lineage, see Tsukaguchi, *Jingū kōgō*, 98–102. Ironically, Jomei was chosen over Shōtoku's son Yamashiro no Ōe.

32. For an excellent discussion of the intra-lineal politics of the Jomei/Saimei line during the Nara period, see Ronald Toby, "Why Leave Nara?" 331–347.

33. This issue is discussed thoroughly in Tsukaguchi, *Jingū kōgō*, 87–107.

34. Naoki, *Nihon kodai shizoku*, 154–155.

35. *SNG*, Tempyō 9.4. Aoki 2: 313.

36. Offerings were also made to the Ise and Miwa shrines, which housed the highest deities of Heaven and Earth, respectively. Although these shrines cannot be considered as Jingū/Ōjin shrines, the Miwa and Ise divinities are nonetheless depicted in both the *Nihon shoki* and the *Kojiki* as assisting Jingū. This issue is discussed thoroughly in Tsukaguchi, *Jingū kōgō*, 87–107.

37. Because I treated the relationship between the Kehi shrine and the Jingū/Ōjin cult in great detail in chapter 2, I will make only passing reference to it in this chapter.

38. For a discussion of how such preparations for invasion helped spur the creation of the Ritsuryō state, see Batten, "Foreign Threat and Domestic Reform: The Emergence of the Ritsuryō State," 83–112.

39. Ueda, *Kodai no Dōkyō to Chōsen*, 54. The characters for "Ōama" are sometimes read as "*watatsuumi*" when applied to this kinship group. In order to clarify this group's connection with the prince, I will retain the reading "Ōama" throughout this chapter.

40. The Ōama are generally thought to have been centered in the Ōama district of Bungo province in close proximity to the Usa district, where the Munakata officiated at the Hachiman shrine. Villages and shrines bearing the name "Ōama" are also known to have existed in the Munakata districts of Chikuzen and Buzen provinces. Note also that the Atsuta shrine in Owari province was also located adjacent to a district named "Ama."

41. For the cultic activities of the Munakata, see Shinkawa Tokio, "Munakata to Usa," 357–380.

42. Takeuchi, *Nara ibun* 1: 113. This is discussed in Oda Fujio, "Kikajin bunka to dazaifu," 265–271.

43. Temmu's posthumous name is discussed in Ueda, *Kodai no Dōkyō to Chōsen*, 51–57.

44. The importance of the Munakata deities on the island of Oki no Shima is vast and beyond the scope of this chapter. See Oda, *Okinoshima* for several articles on the topic.

45. Wada, "Okinoshima," 184–197.

46. Susanoo's arrival in the Japanese islands from Silla is described in *NSK*, Age of the Gods, Book 1, section 8. Kojima 1: 99; Aston 1: 57. See Yokota, *Asuka no kamigami*, 30–47, for a brief discussion of the Munakata birth narrative in the context of the politics of the Temmu era.

47. Taketani, *Kodai shizoku*, 350–361.

48. *NSK*, Richū 5.3.1, 5.9.19, 5.10.11, 6.1.6. Kojima 2: 90–92; Aston 1: 307–308. This legend has also been treated briefly in Taketani, *Kodai shizoku*, 351–354.

49. I will discuss Kusakabe cultic activities in both Kyūshū and Owari Province in chapter 4.

50. For Prince Kusakabe and the Kusakabe Kishi, see Ōhashi, *Nihon kodai no ōken to shizoku*, 193–195. I will discuss in detail the role of the Kusakabe in the cult of Yamato Takeru and cults of exorcism and resurrection in chapter 5.

51. This sword also played a prominent role in the legend cycle of Prince Yamato Takeru, a royal ancestor who purportedly effected his own resurrection shortly after his burial. I will discuss the importance of Yamato Takeru and other legends of resurrection and immortality for the early Shōtoku cult in chapter 5.

52. Yokota, *Asuka no kamigami*, 50–51.

53. Ueda discusses the genealogical and cultic connections between Temmu, the Ōama and the Atsuta shrine in Ueda, *Kodai no Dōkyō to Chōsen bunka*, 54–57.

54. Because Kōken reigned twice, she was given the titles of both Kōken and Shōtoku.

55. I will discuss Prince Nagaya in detail in chapter 6.

56. These ties were apparently enduring: Prince Takechi's descendents remained the chief officiants at the Munakata shrine in Yamato for centuries. On this point, see Yokota, *Asuka no kamigami*, 35–39.

57. *Chikuzen fudoki*, Ito district. *SNKBZ* 5: 541.

58. I will discuss this trope in relation to the formation of the concept of the sage king in chapter 4.

59. *Kojiki*, Ōjin chapter. *SNKBZ* 1: 275–278.

60. For the identification of Ōjin and Hachiman during the Nara and early Heian periods, see Nakano, *Hachiman shinkō*, 84–99. The connections between the Himegoso shrine, the Hachiman shrine and the Ōjin cult are discussed in Mishina, *Nissen shinwa*, 96–98.

61. I have based my translation on Inoue Hideo, *Sankoku shiki* 1: 15–16. The passage is from the first fascicle of the *Silla Pongi*. Mishina has analyzed this legend extensively in Mishina, *Nissen shinwa*, 263–305.

62. For a discussion of the roots and meaning of Ōjin's birth narrative, see Mishina, *Nissen shinwa*, 68–76. See also Tanigawa Ken'ichi, "Ōjintei to dansei shinwa," 203–229.

63. *Chikuzen fudoki*, Ito district. *SNKBZ* 5: 542–543.

64. Chūai is identified as the Kehi deity in a remnant from the *Echizen fudoki* (*Records of the Customs and Lands of Echizen*) concerning the Kehi shrine. See *SNKBZ* 5: 580. Although the dating of this text is problematic, Chūai is also listed in several medieval sources as one of seven gods at the shrine, which were apparently already in place by the time of composition of the *Engishiki* in 927.

65. The legend also shows striking similarities with the legend of the advent of the "rock-standing" Sukuna Bikona no Mikoto to the Japanese islands. As we saw in chapter 2, the *tokoyo* deity Sukuna Bikona no Mikoto was worshipped in the form of miraculous stones on the coast of Noto province following his arrival from the

Korean Peninsula. In much the same way, here we find stones being worshipped as markers of Ōjin's birth following his mother's arrival from the Korean Peninsula.

CHAPTER 4

An earlier version of this chapter first appeared under the title "Ethnicity, Sagehood and the Politics of Literacy in Asuka Japan" in *Japanese Journal of Religious Studies* 30 (Spring 2003): 61–84. I am grateful to the editors for their permission to include this material in this volume.

1. *NSK*, Keitai 7.6. Kojima 2: 301; Aston 2: 9.

2. Although starting from an extremely low base, the diffusion of literacy in Yamato was surprisingly rapid. Piggott notes that archeological discoveries indicate that literacy and Chinese learning had spread to even comparatively remote regions by the end of the seventh century. See Piggott, *Emergence of Japanese Kingship*, 152–155. For by far the best discussion in English of the origins of Japanese writing and literacy, see Lurie, *The Origins of Writing in Early Japan*, 176–245.

3. The *Nihon shoki* does contain an almost certainly spurious entry stating that one Prince Uji studied the Five Classics under the Paekche scholar Wani during Ōjin's reign (*NSK*, Ōjin 16.2. Kojima 1: 484, Aston 1: 262). I will discuss Prince Uji in greater detail in chapter 5.

4. *NSK*, Suiko 1.4.10. Kojima 2: 531; Aston 2: 122.

5. *NSK*, Suiko 29.2.5. Kojima 2: 577–579; Aston 2: 148–149. This text was also discussed in chapter 2.

6. The relationship between truth and power is, of course, a theme that in one way or another pervades virtually all of Foucault's work. For one of Foucault's more succinct explanations of his views, see Foucault, *Power/Knowledge*, 109–133.

7. For an English-language account of the development of governmental structures in the Temmu era, see Piggott, *Emergence of Japanese Kingship*, 127–167. Piggott also argues that provincial governors functioned primarily as ritualists sent out by the court to extend the literate culture of the capital to provincial elites (*ibid.*, 152–155).

8. *NSK*, Suiko 10.10. Kojima 2: 539; Aston 2: 126.

9. *NSK*, Suiko 31.4.17. Kojima 2: 586; Aston 2: 153.

10. The translation is from Tsunoda and Goodrich, *Japan in the Chinese Dynastic Histories*, 37. The original text may be found in Zhonghua Shuju, *Sui shu* 6: 1827.

11. See *Manyōshū*, Book 1, no. 29. Kojima, Tōno, and Kinoshita 1: 42–43. The term is used in a poem from Temmu's reign attributed to Kakinomoto Hitomaro. I will discuss Hitomaro's role in the formation of the concept of the sage king in chapter 5. Hitomaro's contribution to the development of the *tennō* as a manifest deity is discussed in Piggott, *Emergence of Japanese Kingship*, 158–160.

12. Thus we have in the *Nihon shoki* legends of rulers such as Kōgyoku and Yūryaku receiving auspicious responses to their petitions to Heaven to the accompaniment of cries of "A ruler of great virtue!" from the people. See *NSK*, Yūryaku 4.2. Kojima 2: 160; Aston 1: 342, and *NSK*, Kōgyoku 1.8.1. Kojima 3: 65; Aston 2: 175.

13. Thus sage kingship was not sacred kingship. The emergence of notions of the *tennō*'s divinity is discussed in Piggott, *Emergence of Japanese Kingship*, 155–161.

14. Thus, shortly before the death of Kamitsumiya's son Prince Yamashiro no Ōe, the *Nihon shoki* records numerous omens at the Manta Canal, an area with which, as we saw in chapter 2, the prince's lineage appears to have been intimately connected.

See *NSK*, Kōgyoku 2.7, Kojima 3:75; Aston 2: 180; *NSK*, Kōgyoku 2.8.15, Kojima 3:75; Aston 2: 180; *NSK*, Kōgyoku 2.9. Kojima 3: 77; Aston 2: 180; and *NSK*, Kōgyoku 2.10. Kojima 3:79; Aston 2: 181.

15. Tamura Enchō, *Nihon Bukkyōshi* 4: 419–441.

16. Tamura, *Nihon Bukkyōshi* 4: 419–441.

17. For a list of such omens, see Tamura, *Nihon Bukkyōshi*, 4: 420–422.

18. Wechsler, *Offerings of Jade and Silk*, 13–14.

19. These events are discussed in Wright, *The Sui Dynasty*, 159 and 134–136, respectively.

20. Wechsler, *Offerings of Jade and Silk*, 55–78.

21. This incident is discussed in Kaneko, "Zuitō Kōdai to Higashi Ajia," 28–33. I will refer to this incident again shortly.

22. *NSK*, Hakuji 1.2.1. Kojima 3: 181; Aston 2: 237. This section of the *Nihon shoki* is famously controversial among Japanese historians who have noted numerous anachronisms and inconsistencies. Yet while the text may be a flawed vehicle for helping us to understand the Japanese islands of the mid-seventh century, in many ways the very constructed nature of the text makes it even more valuable for the scholar seeking to understand the religious and intellectual climate at the time of the composition of the *Nihon shoki*.

23. *NSK*, Taika 4.2.8. Kojima 3: 169; Aston 2: 230–231. This event was also discussed in chapter 1.

24. The Abe were never able to challenge Prince Naka no Ōe (later the ruler Tenji) for complete control at court. Nonetheless, the importance of the move to Naniwa for the Abe and Kōtoku is suggested by the fact that in 653 Tenji left Naniwa for the Asuka area of Yamato, taking most of the court with him in the process. That Tenji felt he needed to take such an unusual step indicates that Naniwa was not a conducive base for him.

25. *NSK*, Hakuji 1.2.9. Kojima 3: 182–183; Aston 2: 237.

26. *NSK*, Hakuji 1.2.15. Kojima 3: 184–185; Aston 2: 237.

27. *NSK*, Hakuji 1.2.15. Kojima 3: 182–183; Aston 2: 238–239.

28. For a masterful study of the origins and nature of this paradigm, see Lewis, *Writing and Authority in Early China*, 195–241.

29. For the role of the Dharma King during the Age of the Decline of the Dharma, see Nattier, *Once Upon a Future Time*, 119–132.

30. The emergence of historical accounts of sage figures is treated in detail in Lewis, *Writing and Authority in Early China*, 53–97.

31. For Chinese sources related to the *San-huang wu-ti*, see Nakajima, ed. *San-kōgotei Ka, U, sen Shin shiryō shūsei*, and Naitō, *Naitō Konan zenshū*, 10: 22–31.

32. The classic work on the introduction of Chinese texts into the Japanese islands remains Kojima, *Jōdai Nihon bungaku to Chūgoku bungaku*.

33. *Shih-chi, Wu-ti pen-chi*. Takigawa, *Shiki kaichū kōshō*, 19–35.

34. Naitō, *Naitō Konan zenshū*, 10: 22–31.

35. Mark Edward Lewis notes the close connection between divination, writing, and the Duke of Chou, the paradigmatic adviser to the Chou ruler King Wu. See Lewis, *Writing and Authority in Early China*, 209–218. Henceforth I will refer to all sage advisors, counselors, etc., as *sakashihito*.

36. This process, and its implications for the later development of the Taoist tradition in China, are discussed in Anna Seidel, "Image of the Perfect Ruler in Early Taoism," 216–247.

37. Although the habit of translating the Japanese term *kenpō* here as "Constitution" is by now so ingrained that there is probably no hope of changing the terminology, the sense of the text is much closer to seventeen admonishments.

38. Ōno, *Shōtoku taishi no kenkyū*, 206–207. For a critical edition of the *Kuan-tzu*, see T'ang Hsiao-chun, *Hsin-yi Kuan-tzu tu-pen*.

39. *NSK*, Suiko, 12.4.3. Kojima 2: 545–546; Aston: 2: 130.

40. *NSK*, Suiko 12.4.3. Kojima 2: 549; Aston 2: 132.

41. *NSK*, Suiko 12.4.3. Kojima 2: 549; Aston 2: 132.

42. *NSK*, Kimmei, period prior to enthronement. Kojima 2: 359; Aston 2: 36. The text is a paraphrase from the *Chou pen-chi* chapter of the *Shih-chi*, where the sage king Chou Wen-wang is praised in almost exactly the same terms. See Takigawa, *Shiki kaichū*, 60, and Kojima 2: 359, n.9.

43. *NSK*, Kimmei, period prior to enthronement. Kojima 2: 357. Aston 2: 36.

44. *Shih-chi*, T'ai-kung shih-chia, second fascicle. Takigawa, *Shiki kaichū*, 535.

45. *Shih-chi*, Chou-pen chi, fourth fascicle. Takigawa, *Shiki kaichū*, 60.

46. This supposition is also supported by the fact that Chiang T'ai-kung appears to have been a particularly venerated figure among the Yamato elite. In addition to being one of the most famous sage counselors, he was also the reputed author of the *Liu t'ao* (*Six Quivers*), a text on military and political strategy that apparently had been transmitted to Yamato prior to Tenji's reign. An annotated edition of the text may be found in Wu Hsi-fei, ed., *Hsin-yi liu-t'ao tu-pen*. The esteem in which the *Liu t'ao* was held can be seen from a passage in the *Tōshi kaden* (*Biographies of the Fujiwara Family*), which states that the future ruler Tenji and Fujiwara Kamatari studied the text with the monk Min shortly before seizing power. The *Kaden* also asserts that Tenji and Kamatari based their strategy for the elimination of the Soga based upon Chiang T'ai-kung's teachings. See Takeuchi, *Nara ibun* 3: 875.

47. *NSK*, Kimmei, period prior to enthronement. Kojima 2: 357–358; Aston: 36–37.

48. I will discuss cultic layering at Fukakusa and other cultic centers associated with the early Shōtoku cult in greater detail in chapter 6.

49. This is discussed briefly in *SNBKZ* 2: 571 n.7. For the original quote, see Lu Pi, *San-kuo-chih chi-chieh*, 564.

50. *NSK*, Suiko 21.11.2. Kojima 2: 571; Aston 2: 145.

51. In compiling this list, I have restricted myself to instances where the terms *hijiri no kimi* and *hijiri no mikado* are actually used. I have also counted all such references in the Constitution as one instance. Note that the term *hijiri* did not take on a connotation of mountain asceticism until much later. See Kleine, "Hermits and Ascetics in Ancient Japan," 1–47.

52. W. G. Aston takes this to be a reference to Suiko. See Aston, 2: 163. The editors of the Nihon Koten Bungaku Taikei edition of the *Nihon shoki* make clear, however, that the intended referent is Shōtoku. See *NKBT* 68: 225, n.15 and n.17.

53. Shōtoku is also referred to by the term "sage king" in Hōryūji sources such as the inscription from the Yakushi triad. I have not included these instances due to difficulties in confirming their dates. In chapter 6 I will examine instances where Shōtoku is hailed not as a sage king but as a sage.

54. Ōhashi, *Kodai kokka no seiritsu to Okinagashi*, 87–107.

55. It seems extremely likely that a Kishi document was the source for this report; records from another Kishi ambassador are explicitly referred to in *NSK*, Saimei 5.7.3. Kojima 3: 227; Aston 2: 263.

56. Kano, "Miketsu kuni to Kashiwadeshi," 275–282.

CHAPTER 5

1. With the exception of the second term on this list, all terms can be read as *hijiri*. I will discuss the significance of the phrase "no ordinary man" below.

2. *NSK*, Yūryaku 22.7. Kojima 2:207; Aston 1: 368.

3. A list of Uranoshimako shrines can be found in Shimode, *Kodai shinsen shisō no kenkyū*, 189. The popularity of the Uranoshimaka cult along the Tamba coast during this period is also emphasized in Takioto, "Uranshimako denshō no seiritsu kiban." 40–53.

4. *Tango fudoki*, Yosa district. *SNKBZ* 5: 472–480. The legend may also be found in *Manyōshū*, Book 9, nos. 1740 and 1741. Kojima, Tōno, and Kinoshita 2: 414–417. Shimode discusses both texts in Shimode, *Kodai shinsen shisō no kenkyū*, 178–186.

5. *Shinsen shōjiroku*, Yamashiro Kuni Kobetsu, Kusakabe Sukune. Saeki, 1: 187.

6. *NSK*, Kōgen 7.2. Kojima 1: 260–261; Aston 1: 148.

7. Suinin's Tamba consorts are listed in *NSK*, Suinin 15.8. Kojima 1: 315; Aston 1: 174 and *Kojiki*, Suinin chapter. *SNKBZ* 1: 210. Tamba no Chinushi is credited in the *Nihon shoki* with subduing the Tamba region for the royal house (*NSK*, Sujin 10.9.9. Kojima 1: 277; Aston 1: 155). The prominence given to this Kusakabe ancestor in the court chronicles doubtless reflects the fact that the Kusakabe were the dominant kinship group in the Tamba region in the Asuka and early Nara periods. It also helps to explain the large number of Uranoshimako shrines in the Tamba region.

8. *NSK*, Suinin 32.7.6. Kojima 1: 325–327; Aston 1: 180–181.

9. Hirabayashi, *Tanabata to sumō no kodaishi*, 14. *NSK*, Suinin 7.7.7. Kojima 1: 313–314; Aston 1: 173–174.

10. Hirabayashi, *Tanabata to sumō no kodaishi*, 22–49. Hibasu hime's connection with the Kusakabe also helps to explain the fact that Nomi no sukune, the group's founding ancestor and the hero of this story, was himself purportedly buried in an area of Harima prefecture known as "Kusakabe Mura." Thus, the Kusakabe appear in legends showing: (1) the origins of ritual figurines placed within and around tombs; (2) the establishment of the Haji and Ishizukuri, two kinship groups charged with handling royal death rituals; and (3) Uranoshimako's journey to and from *tokoyo*. The seventh day of the seventh month is also, of course, the festival of the Weaver Maiden and Cowherd, to which I referred in chapter 2 in conjunction with the formation of the concept of *tenjukoku*. In chapter 6 we shall also see that such rites were an important influence upon the formation of the monk Gyōki's religious movement.

11. *Kojiki*, Suinin chapter. *SNKBZ* 1: 211–212. According to the *NKBZ* editors, the distinction between the two types of implement was that the first (*kage*) retained tree leaves while the other (*hoko*) did not (*ibid.*, 212, n.6). I have already discussed the *Nihon shoki* version of this legend in chapter 2.

12. Shimode briefly discusses several lineages that claimed descent from female immortals in Shimode, *Kodai shinsen shisō no kenkyū*, 137–140.

13. The institution of the office of crown prince was of course a much later development. For a brief discussion of the term's meaning during Shōtoku's day, see Piggott, *Emergence of Japanese Kingship*, 82.

14. *NSK*, Nintoku prologue to reign. Kojima 2: 27–29; Aston 1: 276–277.

15. *NSK*, Sujin 10.9. Kojima 281–282; Aston 1: 157–158.

16. Piggott, *Emergence of Japanese Kingship*, 158–161.

17. See Yoshimura, *Kakinomoto Hitomaro*, 52–102.

18. *Manyōshū*, Book 2, no. 207. Kojima, Tōno, and Kinoshita 1: 138–140. The translation is from Ebersole, *Ritual Poetry and the Politics of Death in Early Japan*, 192–194.

19. During Kamitsumiya's lifetime, this crossroad was also the site where Soga no Katashi Hime, the first Soga woman to serve as consort to a Yamato ruler, was reburied with much fanfare along with her husband Kimmei. *NSK*, Suiko 20.2. Kojima 2: 567; Aston 2: 143. The incident is referred to briefly in the context of *chimata* rites in Maeda, *Nihon kodai no michi*, 20–21.

20. Maeda, *Nihon kodai no michi*, 209–210.

21. *Harima fudoki* (*Records of the Customs and Land of Harima*), Kago district, Hire no Oka. *SNKBZ* 5: 23. For an excellent translation of *Fudoki* from Hitachi, Izumo, Harima, Bungo, and Hizen provinces, see Aoki Michiko, *Records of Wind and Earth*.

22. Yoshimura, *Kakinomoto Hitomaro*, 90–92. As I argued in chapter 2, this motif of *kushi* as an elixir of life can also be found in the cult of the *tokoyo* deity Sukuna Bikona no Mikoto. See, for example, *NSK*, Jingū 13.2.17, Kojima 1: 449; Aston 1: 244–245, where Sukuna Bikona no Mikoto is hailed as a "Prince of Liquors" (*kushi no kami*). Note that, much as we saw in chapter 3, this legend centering upon Yamato Takeru's mother Waki no Iratsume again underscores the importance of distaff ancestry in early Japan.

23. *Tango fudoki*, Yosa district. *SNKBZ* 5: 473–479.

24. This legend contains several parallels with the Shōtoku legend corpus—not only are Yamato Takeru and Shōtoku both sage princes who never ascend to the throne, but they both figure prominently in legends of resurrection and have wives named "Tachibana," the fruit of immortality.

25. *Kojiki*, Keikō chapter, *SNKBZ* 1: 227. The translation is from Cranston, *Waka Anthology*, 20. Sugano Masao notes that the motif of spreading rugs before entering the sea mirrors the Luck of the Sea legend, where the fire god Ho no Susori no Mikoto spreads rugs on the waves before journeying to *tokoyo* beneath the sea. See Sugano, *Kojiki setsuwa no kenkyū*, 221.

26. *Engishiki*, section ten. *SZKT* 26: 312.

27. *NSK*, Keikō 40. Kojima 1: 386–387; Aston 1: 210–211.

28. For more on this aspect of the Yamato Takeru legend cycle, see Como, "Silkworms and Consorts in Nara Japan," 111–131. The motif of the immortal who leaves behind an article of clothing after achieving "liberation from the corpse" is of course an important element in a number of legends of Chinese immortals. Robert Ford Campany has recently suggested that this belief was originally related to funerary rites involving figures that impersonate the deceased. See Campany, *To Live as Long as Heaven and Earth*, 52–60.

29. *NSK*, Suiko 21.11 and 21.11.2. Kojima 2: 569–571; Aston 2: 144–145. This legend appears in somewhat altered forms in later texts such as the *Hoketsuki* and the *Nihon ryōiki*. I will deal with these versions in chapter 6.

30. *NSK*, Suinin 100.3.12. Kojima 1: 336–337; Aston 1: 186–187. I discussed this legend in chapter 2.

31. *NSK*, Suiko 29.2.5. Kojima 2: 577–579; Aston 2: 148–149.

32. Ama no Ho no Akari no Mikoto's status as the founding ancestor of the Ibuki kinship group is discussed in detail in Mayumi, *Nihon kodai saishi*, 304–309.

33. *NSK*, Keikō 51.8. Kojima 1: 388–389; Aston 1: 211. This sword was discussed in chapter 3 in conjunction with the death of Temmu *tennō*.

34. I have included Izanami in this list because even in *ne no kuni* she is said to be "still as she was when alive." I will discuss this legend shortly.

35. In addition to the *Nihon shoki* legend of Ōnamuchi no Mikoto's death from fire, the *Harima fudoki* contains a legend that states that he was killed by his son, who

was none other than Ama no Ho no Akari no Mikoto. See *Harima fudoki*, Shikama-gun, Iwa no sato. *SNKBZ* 5: 31–32.

36. *NSK*, Age of the Gods, Book 1, section 5. Kojima 1: 43; Aston 1: 22–23.

37. This legend is discussed at length in Taketani, *Kodai shizoku denshō*, 130–175. Note also that, following the elimination of the main Mononobe line by the Soga, the remaining Mononobe lineages reverted to claiming Ama no Ho no Akari no Mikoto as their founding ancestor. For more on the relationship between the Soga and Mononobe, see Mayuzumi, *Mononobe, Sogashi to kodai ōken*.

38. Kishi, "Kodō no rekishi," 106–107. Kishi notes that the Mononobe apparently controlled much of the highway connecting Yamato and Kawachi provinces at the height of the power, while the Soga controlled much of the area to the southern Great Lateral Highway. The Mononobe also controlled such important travel nodes as Kataoka, and the Heguri mountain range as well as the important port of Naniwa on the coast of the Inland Sea as well. For archeology concerning the northern Great Lateral Highway, see Senda, "Kinai," 30–34.

39. *Sendai kuji hongi*. Tennō hongi, Jimmu 1.11. *ST Koten hen* 8: 124. The text reads:

> The heavenly deity instructed that if there were an area [of the body] in pain, [one should] use these ten regalia, saying "One, two, three, four, five, six, seven, eight, nine, ten *furu be, yura yura to furube*." Done in this way, the dead will come back to life. This is the original spirit shaking spell. The origins of the *Mitama shizume matsuri* are to be found here.

40. Matsumae discusses the relationship between court rites of spirit pacification and the Isonokami shrine in Matsumae, *Kodai denshō to kyūtei saishi*, 115–127. I will discuss the importance of ritual speech-acts (*kotohoki*) at *chimata* for the cults of Shōtoku and Gyōki in chapter 6.

41. *Shinsen shōjiroku*, Yamashiro Shinban. Saeki, 1: 307. Katō also discusses the Sakaibe's involvement in *chimata* rites as well as their connections with the Abe and foreign embassies in Katō Kenkichi, *Yamato seiken to kodai shizoku*, 94–105.

42. For a good discussion of Hata cooperation with the Chisakobe and Sakaibe in cultic matters, see Katō Kenkichi, *Hatashi to sono tami*, 45–54.

43. *NSK*, Bidatsu 12.10. Kojima 2: 485; Aston 1: 100.

44. The name "Arashito" appears to have been an ancient Korean term of respect; other than in the cases of Tsunuga no Arashito and Nichira's father, the term is used in the *Nihon shoki* only in the case of the king of Mimana. Note that Nichira here also fulfills the pattern we saw in previous chapters of the sage who arrives from across the sea in order to enter the service of the king of Yamato.

45. The *Harima fudoki*, for instance, records a legend that a member of the Hi no Kimi came to a Silla immigrant center in the Shikama district and married a young woman whom he had brought back from the dead. See *Harima fudoki*, Shikama District, Mino Township. *SNKBZ* 5: 42–43.

46. During the sixth century, the Hi no Kimi apparently were also with the local Iwai and Silla in Iwai's rebellion. These links with Silla probably explain the fact that in the following legend Nichira comes back to life for the sole purpose of asserting the innocence of Silla envoys who might have been blamed for his murder.

47. The Hi no Kimi were not the only lineage from Kyūshū to be so affected. The *Nihon shoki* lists the Tsukushi no Kuni no Miyatsuko, a major lineage from Kyūshū, as a sublineage of the Abe (*NSK*, Kōgen 7.2. Kojima 1: 261; Aston 1: 148). Oda Fujio notes in this regard the existence of yet another lineage in the region known

as the Tsukushi Hi no Kimi. He suggests that the Hi no Kimi and Tsukushi no Kuni no Miyatsuko must therefore have frequently intermarried. See Oda, "Iwai no hanran," 165.

48. Wada Atsumu has argued that these rites were linked from an extremely early date and that their object was the god Kunado. Kunado, of course, was the deity who stands watch at the gateway to *Ne no kuni*, the land to which both ritual impurities and the spirits of the dead must go at the end of the year. See Wada, *Nihon kodai no girei, saishi to shinkō*, 2: 335–354. These rites are also discussed in Maeda, *Nihon kodai no michi*, 2–14. The *Michiae no matsuri* invocation (*norito*) from the Heian period may be found in *NKBT* 1: 431–433. For the *Hoshizume no matsuri* invocation, see *NKBT* 1: 428–430. For the *Yasojima no matsuri*, see Takigawa, *Ritsuryō to daijōsai*, 221–328; and Uwai, *Nihon kodai no shizoku to saishi*, 62–82.

49. Takigawa, *Ritsuryō to daijōsai*, 253.

50. For a brief description of these rites as well as several important archeological finds, see Kaneko Hiroyuki, "Bukkyō, Dōkyō to banjin suhai," 167–191.

51. The importance of foreign embassies for the development of the Great Lateral Highway is emphasized in Kishi Toshio, "Kōdō no rekishi," 93–107. The Taishi Michi is thought to have been built for Kamitsumiya after his move to the Ikaruga region of Yamato near Kataoka. See Senda Minoru, "Kinai," 38.

52. For a list of this and other such sites, see *NKBT* 67: 614–615, n.19. *Chimata* rites for foreign envoys are also discussed briefly by Maeda, *Nihon kodai no michi*, 212–221, and Mayumi, *Nihon kodai saishi*, 199–203.

53. Toyama Mitsuo discusses Soga kinship alliances and their geopolitical implications in Toyama, "Umako to Shōtoku Taishi," in *Sogashi to kodai kokka*, 127–168. See especially p. 143, where he argues that after the fall of the Mononobe the Soga used such alliances to dominate the Great Lateral Highway from Asuka to Naniwa, thereby ensuring control over communication with the continent.

54. Numerous lineages claiming descent from Kamu Yaimimi no Mikoto are listed in *Kojiki*, Jimmu chapter. *SNKBZ* 1: 162.

55. *NSK*, Suizei, period prior to accession. Kojima 1: 243–245; Aston 1: 140.

56. *NSK*, Sushun, period prior to accession, Kojima 2: 515; Aston 2: 115.

57. For Umehara's major work on the subject, see Umehara, *Kakusareta jūjika*. For a more concise summary of Umehara's position, see Umehara, "Shōtoku Taishi," 107–138.

CHAPTER 6

1. *Chimata* rites are discussed at length in Maeda, *Nihon kodai no michi to chimata*. For the development of early Japanese road networks, see Kinoshita, *Kodai dōrō*.

2. For the text of the *Gyōki nenpu*, see Inoue Kaoru, *Gyōki jiten*, 255–275. See also Inoue Mitsusada, *Nihon kodai shisōshi no kenkyū*, 355–411. For the *Gyōki bosatsuden*, see *ZGR* 8: 439–441. For an English translation of the *Bosatsuden*, see Augustine, *Buddhist Hagiography*, 134–138.

3. For the views of each of these scholars, see Inoue Mitsusada, *Nihon kodai shisōshi*; Nakai, *Gyōki to kodai Bukkyō*; Nemoto, *Nara Bukkyō to Gyōki denshō*; and Yoshida Yasuo, *Gyōki to ritsuryō kokka*.

4. For a discussion of the practices of the *ubasoku*, see Nakai, *Gyōki to kodai Bukkyō*, 3–82. See also Sakuma, *Nihon kodai sōden*, 35–47. The female equivalent of the term *ubasoku* was *ubai*.

5. Nakai, *Gyōki to kodai Bukkyō*, 49–82.

6. The *Daisōjō sharibyōki* is Gyōki's epitaph as carved on his gravestone. The text may be found in Inoue Kaoru, ed., *Gyōkisan o kangaeru*, 28. For a translation and brief discussion of the text, see Augustine, *Buddhist Hagiography*, 16.

7. Japanese secondary and primary sources related to Gyōki are discussed in Augustine, *Buddhist Hagiography*, 32–46.

8. Gyōki's biography is given in the *SNG*, Tempyō Shōhō 1.2.2. Aoki 2: 61–63. The image of Gyōki in the *Nihon ryōiki* is discussed in Yoshida Yasuo, *Gyōki to ritsuryō*, 127–152.

9. Thus the *Daisōjō sharibyōki*, for instance, refers neither to the court's early attempts to proscribe Gyōki's movement nor, more surprisingly, to the activities that Gyōki purportedly undertook on behalf of the court during the latter part of his life.

10. For Gyōki's kinship affiliations, see Yoshida Yasuo, *Gyōki to ritsuryō*, 1–24. For the cultic affiliations of Wani's descendents, see Inoue Mitsusada, *Nihon kodai shisōshi*, 412–468.

11. For Dōshō, see Sakuma, *Nihon kodai sōden*, 48–76.

12. Sakuma, *Nihon kodai sōden*, 26–30. Sakuma also discusses Dōshō at length in *Nihon kodai sōden*, 48–76.

13. Sakuma, *Nihon kodai sōden*, 30.

14. This is discussed briefly in Augustine, *Buddhist Hagiography*, 17.

15. Yoshida Yasuo, *Gyōki to ritsuryō*, 25–83; Nemoto, *Nara Bukkyō to Gyōki denshō*, 25–82.

16. Takamiyadera also served as the ordination temple of Gyōhyō, who was not only a member of the Tsuki no Omi but also the teacher of the famed Tendai patriarch Saichō. Saichō, who was an avid Shōtoku devotee, in turn credited Gyōhyō with introducing him to Shōtoku worship. For Takamiyadera and the Shōtoku cult, see Iida, *Shōtoku taishiden*, 339–341.

17. *Nihon ryōiki* 1.4. *SNKBT* 30: 12–13. See also Kyoko Motomachi Nakamura, trans., *Miraculous Stories from the Japanese Buddhist Tradition*, 110.

18. Yoshida Yasuo, *Gyōki to ritsuryō*, 31–34.

19. See Iida, *Shōtoku taishiden*, 340.

20. *SNG*, Yōrō 1.04, Aoki 2: 67.

21. See, for example, *SNG*, Yōrō 6.7. Aoki 2: 121–123. This is discussed briefly in Augustine, *Buddhist Hagiography*, 24.

22. These events are discussed briefly in Yoshida Yasuo, *Nihon kodai no bosatsu to minshū*, 263–266. Note that *"ubai"* is the female equivalent of *"ubasoku."*

23. Katō Kenkichi, *Hatashi to sono tami*, 190.

24. For the inscription, see Takeuchi, *Nara ibun* 2: 612. For temples purportedly built by Gyōki during this period, see Augustine, *Buddhist Hagiography*, 40.

25. Inoue Kaoru, "Gyōki no shōgai." 17–18 Yoshida has drawn up a list of temples attributed to Gyōki in the *Gyōki nenpu* in his *Gyōki to ritsuryō*, 318–320. Augustine provides a list of 49 temples purportedly built by Gyōki in Augustine, *Buddhist Hagiography*, 40–44. For a discussion of the location of the Gyōki's 49 temples, see Senda Minoru, "Shijūku-in wa dokoka," 229–239.

26. *SNG*, Tempyō 3.8.7. Aoki 2: 247–248. This event is discussed by Yoshida in *Gyōki to ritsuryō*, 216–218. For the names of the Settsu training halls, see Augustine, *Buddhist Hagiography*, 40–41.

27. Yoshida Yasuo, *Gyōki to ritsuryō*, 208–209. This point is also made in Hōjō, "Gyōki to gijutsusha shūdan," 108.

28. This tapestry was discussed at length in chapter 2. Gyōki's probable connection with Inabe artisans is also posited in Hōjō, "Gyōki to gijutsusha shūdan," 108–125.

29. *Kojiki*, Nintoku chapter. *SNKBZ* 1: 287.

30. *Gyōki nenpu*, in Inoue, *Gyōki jiten*, 261. For Shimamaro, see Nakamura Shūya, *Hatashi to Kamoshi*, 168–186.

31. *SNG*, Tempyō 13.10.16. Aoki 3: 399–401.

32. Augustine, *Buddhist Hagiography*, 41–44.

33. This and other areas of Hata participation in Gyōki's movement are discussed in Hōjō, "Gyōki to gijutsusha shūdan," 117–124.

34. *Nihon ryōiki* 1.5. *SNKBT* 30: 13–17. See also Kyoko Motomachi Nakamura, *Miraculous Stories*, 113–115.

35. The biographies of Shōtoku and Gyōki as well as further legends of the afterlife may be found at the beginning of both of the *Nihon ōjō gokurakuki* and the *Dainihonkoku hokekyōkenki*. See *NST* 7: 11–19 and *NST* 7: 47–54. Legends of Shōtoku and Gyōki also appear at the beginning of the second section of the *Sanbōe kotoba*. See *SNKBT* 31: 77–88 and 92–96. See also Kamens, *The Three Jewels*, 174–190 and 197–206.

36. This legend is discussed briefly in conjunction with the Jingū/Ōjin cult in Yokota Ken'ichi, *Asuka no kamigami*, 197–209.

37. *Nihon ryōiki* 2.12. *SNKBT* 30: 79–80. See also Kyoko Motomachi Nakamura, *Miraculous Stories*, 176–177.

38. Both "Fukaosa" and "Fukakusa" appear in different editions of the text. I will conform to the usage of the *Gyōki nenpu*, which refers to the site as Fukakusa.

39. This derivation is suggested in Yokota, *Asuka no kamigami*, 200, as well as Hirabayashi, *Tanabata to sumō no kodaishi*, 170–171. For a broader discussion of the role of weaving in early Japanese religion, see in addition Como, "Silkworms and Consorts in Nara Japan," 111–131. We shall see shortly that the use of looms as ritual offerings in rites of spirit propitiation is well-attested in both the archeological record and in textual sources from the period.

40. Katata, *Nihon kodai shinkō to Bukkyō*, 142–144.

41. Other *hokai* that we have seen in previous chapters include the *Furu hokai* used by the Mononobe in rites of spirit pacification/resurrection at the Isonokami shrine as well as Jingū's toast to her son Ōjin following his return from the Kehi shrine in Tsunuga. For an example of *hokai* referring to crabs, see *Kojiki*, Ōjin chapter. *SNKBZ* 1: 262–263, where Ōjin composes a wedding toast for his Wani consort. I shall discuss a well-known funerary ode for a crab from the *Manyōshū* shortly.

42. *Hizen fudoki*, Ki no Kōri, Himegoso Sato. *SNKBZ* 5: 317–318.

43. To give but one example, see *Nihon ryōiki*, 1.3, where a spirit from the crossroads terrorizes Gangōji temple. See *SNBKT* 30: 8–11, and Kyoko Motomachi Nakamura, *Miraculous Stories*, 105–108.

44. *Kojiki*, Ōjin chapter. *SNKBZ* 1: 277.

45. The translation is from Philippi, *Norito*, 42. The original text may be found in *NKBT* 1: 416–420.

46. The translation is from Philippi, *Norito*, 56. The original text may be found in *NKBT* 1: 436–437.

47. The translation is from Philippi, *Norito*, 54. The original may be found in *NKBT* 1: 432–433.

48. *NSK*, Suiko 21.12. Kojima 2: 569–571; Aston 2: 144–145. The translation is from Cranston, *Waka Anthology*, 113.

49. *Manyōshū*, Book 16, no. 3886. Kojima, Tōno, and Kinoshita 4: 139–141. Cranston, *Waka Anthology*, 761.

50. Nishimura, "The Prince and the Pauper," 302.

51. *Nihon ryōiki*, 1.4. *SNBKT* 30: 12–13. See also Kyoko Motomachi Nakamura, *Miraculous Stories*, 108–109.

52. On this point, see Katata, *Nihon kodai shinkō*, 142.

53. For a summary of the political events of this period, see Piggott, *Emergence of Japanese Kingship*, 245–247. I will discuss these events in greater detail in chapter 7.

54. Ōyama, *Nagayaōke mokkan to kinsekibun*, 276–281.

55. See Yoshikawa, "Gyōki jiin bodain to sono terada," 371–390.

56. Yoshikawa, "Gyōki jiin bodain to sono terada," 388–390.

57. This does not, of course, mean that they were *not* Buddhist—indeed, the legend of Shōtoku and the beggar at Kataoka was later explained as a meeting of the Chinese monks Hui-ssu and Bodhidharma. Yet even this gloss demonstrates the ease with which boundaries between Buddhist and local cultic traditions could be crossed and recrossed in pre-modern Japan.

CHAPTER 7

1. The best discussion of Hōryūji's records is in Mizuno, *Nihon kodai no jiin to rekishi*, 227–272. See also Tanaka, *Shōtoku Taishi shinkō no seiritsu*, 255–275; and Ōyama, *Nagayaōke mokkan to kinsekibun*, 203–205.

2. *NSK*, Tenji 9.4.30. Kojima 3: 285–286; Aston 2: 293.

3. This debate has been complicated by the fact that Hōryūji records make no reference to this event. The reconstruction of Hōryūji is discussed in detail in Edward Kidder, *The Lucky Seventh: Early Hōryūji and Its Time*, 275–316.

4. I will discuss the rebuilding of the Yumedono shortly.

5. Takeuchi, *Nara ibun* 2: 366–367; Mizuno, *Nihon kodai no jiin to rekishi*, 190–194.

6. Mizuno, *Nihon kodai no jiin*, 190–193.

7. Takeuchi, *Nara ibun* 2: 367. This is discussed in Mizuno, *Nihon kodai no jiin*, 195–200.

8. Inoue Hideo, "Nukatabe to Yamato ōken," 106.

9. Mizuno, *Nihon kodai no jiin*, 191–194.

10. There is some evidence, however, to support the text's assertion that Kamitsumiya had constructed a chapel at a palace in Akunami. Fragments from a banner from Hōryūji now stored in the Shōsōin refer to the Akunami Kori mentioned in the text. Because this area is extremely close to Ikaruga, the site of Kamitsumiya's main residence, as well as Hōryūji, Shimizu Masaji has argued that Kamitsumiya could very well have had a smaller residence in the area with a small chapel attached. This would go a long way towards explaining the close links between the two temples. To date, however, there is no archeological evidence to support Shimizu's hypothesis. See Shimizu, "Asuka to Ikaruga," 162–163.

11. *Harima kuni fudoki*, Iibo district. *SNKBZ* 5: 57.

12. See, for example, Hishida, "Harima no kofun to jiin," 50–51.

13. Takeuchi, *Nara ibun* 1: 344; Mizuno, *Nihon kodai no jiin*, 230.

14. *NSK*, Suiko 14.7. Kojima 2:554; Aston 2: 135. For a translation and discussion of the historical importance of the *Shōmangyō*, see Wayman and Wayman, *The Lion's Roar of Queen Śrīmālā*.

15. Mizuno, *Nihon kodai no jiin*, 245–255.

16. This seems likely even if we accept the *Nihon shoki*'s assertion that the lands were a gift from Suiko. Suiko herself was known as the Princess Nukata prior to her

enthronement. Suiko's links with the Nukatabe suggest that the gift of lands from the Iibo district may have been related to the presence of the Nukatabe in that area.

17. There is also some reason to believe that the same cluster of kinship groups connected with the Harima estates of Hōryūji may also be connected with Kumakori dera, the temple in Nukata sato that Shōtoku is said to have bestowed upon Jomei. One intriguing entry from the Ninken chapter of the *Nihon shoki* depicts a member of the Kishi kinship group settling refugees from Koguryô in just this township (*NSK*, Ninken 6. Kojima 2: 263; Aston 1: 396–397).

18. Inoue Kaoru, *Nihon kodai no seiji*, 233–258. In addition to the work of Inoue and Ōyama already cited, my thinking on Dōji has been greatly influenced by Sakuma, *Nihon kodai sōden*, 205–225.

19. Dōji's biography may be found in *SNG*, Tempyō 16.10. Aoki 2: 447–448.

20. Inoue Kaoru, *Nihon kodai no seiji*, 233–241. For Tao-hsüan and Dōji, see Ōyama, *Nagayaōke mokkan to kinseki*, 85–93.

21. Prior to her elevation to the position of Queen Consort, Kōmyō was known as Asukahime. For convenience I will refer to her throughout this chapter as Kōmyō.

22. Nagaya's downfall is described in the *Shoku nihongi* in a series of entries beginning in 729. See *SNG*, Tempyō 1.2. Aoki 2: 205. These events are recounted in Piggott, *Emergence of Japanese Kingship*, 245–247.

23. The *Greater Sutra on the Perfection of Wisdom* may be found in *T* 5–7 (no. 220). The full text of the vow may be found in Takeuchi, *Nara ibun* 2: 610–611. The vow has been analyzed in detail in Shinkawa, "Nara jidai no Dōkyō to Bukkyō," 284. See also Ōyama, *Nagayaōke mokkan*, 93–98.

24. Shinkawa, "Nara jidai no Dōkyō to Bukkyō," 291–293. Along with Dōji's name, the names of five members of Nagaya's staff are also appended to the vow. Intriguingly, four bear names that indicate that they were from Silla immigrant kinship group families such as the Hata and Miyake.

25. See Shinkawa, "Nara jidai no Dōkyō to Bukkyō," 297–301. These connections are also apparent from Dōji's involvement in the editing of the founding legend of Japanese Buddhism, which, as I argued in chapter 1, was based upon a temple legend from the Silla State temple network.

26. See Wada, *Kodai no girei to saishi* 2: 181–215.

27. For Prince Takechi's cultic associations, see Yokota, *Asuka no kamigami*, 30–46.

28. Yokota, *Asuka no kamigami*, 39.

29. Kaneko, "Tojō to saishi," 198–226. See also Matsumoto, "Munakata, Okinoshima annai," 258–282.

30. The ability of the Munakata deities to intimidate rulers was discussed in chapter 3.

31. Inoue Kaoru, *Nihon kodai no seiji to shūkyō*, 254–258.

32. *SNG*, Tempyō 16.10. Aoki 2: 447–448.

33. Inoue Kaoru, *Nihon kodai no seiji to shūkyō*, 254–258. Sakuma has also argued that Nagaya's outlook was closely in line with Dōji's on these matters. See Sakuma, *Nihon kodai sōden*, 208–218.

34. Strictly speaking, improperly ordained monks were not monks at all. After the arrival of Ganjin in 753, the court urged all members of the clergy to undergo reordination.

35. For an assessment of the understanding of the precepts in the Japanese islands prior to the arrival of Ganjin, see Ishida, *Ganjin—sono kairitsu shisō*, 17–42.

36. The Chinese reading of this monk's name is "Tao-hsüan." In order to avoid confusion with the exegete Tao-hsüan referred to earlier, however, I shall use the Japanese reading for this monk's name.

37. Due to the widespread use of the Japanese reading of Chien-chen's name, I will refer to him throughout the text as Ganjin. For Ganjin's life as well as a lengthy discussion of the text, see Andō, *Ganjin*. See also Ishida, *Ganjin—sono kairitsu shisō*, 269–326.

38. For the political and ideological role of Buddhist institutions in China during this period, see Forte, *Political Propaganda and Ideology in China*. See also Weinstein, *Buddhism Under the Tang*, 1–51.

39. *NSK*, Yōmei 1.1. Kojima 2: 500; Aston 2: 107.

40. I discussed this legend's connections with Shitennōji and Silla temple legends in chapter 1. Yoshida Kazuhiko has argued that several entries from the *Nihon shoki* pertaining to Shōtoku also contain distinctive characteristics found in other works attributed to Dōji. See Yoshida, "Dōji no bunshō" in *Shōtoku Taishi no shinjitsu*, 273–313.

41. Piggott, *Emergence of Japanese Kingship*, 251–255. For the classic analysis of the importance of disease within not only court politics but virtually every element of life in the Japanese islands during the Nara period and beyond, see Farris, *Population, Disease, and Land in Early Japan* 645–900, esp. 18–73.

42. The court's petition of Shōtoku's spirit is recorded in the *Hōryūji tōin engi* (*Historical Record of the Eastern Complex at Hōryūji*), *DNBZ* 85: 127. This event is also discussed in Hayashi, *Taishi shinkō no kenkyū*, 73–83 and Ōyama, *Nagayaōke mokkan*, 278. For an extended discussion of the *Hōryūji tōin engi*, see Tōno, "Shoki no Taishi shinkō to Jōgūōin," 453–466.

43. *SNG*, Tempyō 9.4.8. Aoki 2: 315; Inoue, *Nihon kodai no seiji*, 252–254.

44. Ōyama, *Nagayaōke mokkan*, 278–279. Kōmyō's decision to rely so heavily on Hōryūji for help is all the more remarkable in light of the normal custom of spreading royal support among a wide range of shrines and temples in times of crisis.

45. Ōyama, *Nagayaōke mokkan*, 282–283.

46. Piggott, *Emergence of Japanese Kingship*, 252.

47. She later assumed the throne and is known today as Kōken.

48. Piggott, *Emergence of Japanese Kingship*, 260.

49. Piggott, *Emergence of Japanese Kingship*, 261–262.

50. Ōyama has noted similarities between the Yumedono's octagonal architectural configuration and the octagonal mausoleum for Fujiwara Muchimaro, which was also built at this time. See Ōyama, *Nagayaōke mokkan*, 278–284. For a discussion of rites that were performed on the purported anniversary of Shōtoku's death, see Hayashi, *Taishi shinkō no kenkyū*, 25–44

51. For this icon, see Ōyama, *Nagayaōke mokkan*, 306–309. See also Hayashi, *Taishi shinkō no kenkyū*, 71. Note that Hōryūji housed an image of Shakyamuni Buddha that was also said to be built to the prince's size.

52. Piggott has argued that the Queen-consort's Household Agency functioned as an extralegal bureaucracy that allowed the Fujiwara to bypass the Council of State for much of the period. See Piggott, *Emergence of Japanese Kingship*, 268–269.

53. Ōyama, *Nagayaōke mokkan*, 307. The identification of Shōtoku as an incarnation of Kuse Kannon is discussed in Fujii, "Kuse Kannon no seiritsu," 317–338.

54. Ironically, at the time of Hui-ssu's death in 577, Kamitsumiya was apparently already three years old.

55. Both the dating of the poem and Mifune's relationship with Ganjin are discussed in Tanaka, *Shōtoku Taishi shinkō*, 31.

56. Takeuchi, *Nara ibun* 3: 896.

57. These arguments are rehearsed in Wang, *Shōtoku Taishi jikū chōetsu*, 126–139.

58. Important exceptions are Wang, *Shōtoku Taishi*, 140–158; and Nakao, "Shōtoku Taishi Nangaku Eishi," 16–33.

59. My understanding of Hui-ssu has been greatly shaped by Magnin, *La vie et ouevre de Huisi [515–577]*, Kawakatsu Yoshio, "Chūgokuteki shin Bukkyō keisei e no enerugi," 501–537, and Nakao, "Shōtoku Taishi Nangaku Eishi," 16–33.

60. *Hsü kao-seng chuan. T* 50: 563b (no. 2060). Similar legends apparently also circulated in several now-lost texts from the first decades of the eighth century. Many of these are cited in the *Shichidaiki*, a Japanese text dated to 772, which I will discuss shortly. For an extremely important discussion of Chinese sources for the Hui-ssu legend cycle preserved in the *Shichidaiki* and other early Japanese texts, see Nakao, "Shōtoku Taishi Nangaku Eishi," 22–28.

61. The full text may be found in Takeuchi, *Nara ibun* 3: 890–894. See also Hayashi, *Taishi shinkō*, 149–188; and Tanaka, *Shōtoku Taishi shinkō*, 26–40.

62. Takeuchi, *Nara ibun* 3: 891–892.

63. One final work from the Nara period, the *Jōgū Taishi bosatsuden* (*Biography of the Bodhisattva Crown Prince above the Palace*), also set forth the legend. This text was apparently composed by Ganjin's disciple Ssu-t'uo in 788. As Ssu-t'uo's work relies heavily upon the *Shichidaiki* for Japanese sources, I will not discuss it in detail here. The text may be found in *STZ* 3: 49–51. It is discussed briefly in Tanaka, *Shōtoku Taishi shinkō*, 41–42 and 158. See also Iida, *Shōtoku Taishiden*, 73–109.

64. For the Tsuki no Omi's relationship to this legend, see Iida, *Shōtoku Taishiden*, 338–341. Since, as I noted in the introduction, both Kamitsumiya and his brother took consorts from the Kashiwade kinship group, the Kashiwade had an obvious interest in promoting the Shōtoku cult. The Kashiwade also claimed common descent with the Abe and appear to have overseen such Silla immigrant kinship groups as the Miyake at several places in the Japanese islands.

65. The text may be found in *STZ* 3: 56–57.

66. *Hung-tsan fa-hua chuan. T* 51: 41c (no. 2067).

67. *Nihon ryōiki*, 1: 18. *SNKBT* 30: 31–32. See also Kyoko Motomochi Nakamura, *Miraculous Stories*, 129–130.

68. *Iyo kuni fudoki*, Yu district. *SNKBZ* 5: 505–506.

69. As I noted in chapter 2, the Hata were also important in this region. The Iyo Hata, like the Kusakabe, also enjoyed close relations with the Abe, so much so that they officially changed their name to Abe in the late Nara period. See *SNG*, Tempyō Jingo 2.3. Aoki 4: 123.

70. *Nan-yüeh Ssu ta ch'an-shih li-shih yuan-wen. T* 46: 787c-788b (no. 1933).

71. *Shichidaiki*. Takeuchi, *Nara ibun* 3: 894.

72. Iida, *Shōtoku Taishiden no kenkyū*, 337–342.The classic analysis of Saichō's career is Groner, *Saichō*. For the post-Saichō Tendai movement, see Groner, *Ryōgen and Mount Hiei*. Gyōhyō's kinship group was the Tsuki no Omi, which, as we saw earlier, is known to have contributed sources for the composition of the *Hoketsuki*. Gyōhyō thus represents an important link between Saichō, Shitennōji/Daianji, and the Naniwa kinship groups at the forefront of the early Shōtoku cult.

73. *Denjutsu isshin kaimon. T* 74: 647c (no. 2379). The *Denjutsu isshin kaimon* is a work by Saichō's disciple Kōjō that was completed in 834. The text is discussed variously in Hayashi, *Taishi shinkō*, 195; Wang, *Shōtoku Taishi*, 380–393; and Tanaka, *Shōtoku Taishi shinkō*, 161–164.

74. Saichō's successors continued this theme for centuries to come. For the introduction of Shōtoku legends to China, see Wang, *Shōtoku Taishi*, 233–324.

75. *Denjutsu isshin kaimon. T* 74: 654c (no. 2379).

76. Iida, *Shōtoku Taishiden*, 311.

77. *Sui t'ien-t'ai chih-che ta-shih pie-chuan (Alternate Biography of the Great Teacher T'ien-tai Chih-che of the Sui). T* 50: 191c (no. 2050).

78. Thus the third fascicle of the *Denjutsu isshin kaimon* recounts the history of the Buddhist tradition from Shakyamuni down to the transmission of Buddhism in Japan in terms of the legend of Shōtoku and the beggar on the road to Kataoka and the legend of Shōtoku as an incarnation of Hui-ssu. The text may be found in *T* 74: 651c–658a (no. 2379).

CONCLUSION

1. Shinran wrote almost two hundred hymns to Shōtoku. See *Dai Nihon hōzo-kusan'ō Shōtoku Taishi hōsan (Hymns in Praise of the Crown Prince Shōtoku, King of Great Japan, the Land of Scattered Millet)*, STZ 5: 37–60, and *Kōtaishi Shōtoku hōsan (Hymns in Praise of the Royal Crown Prince Shōtoku)*, STZ 5: 19–35. He also wrote one hagiographical work, *Jōgū Taishi goki (August Records of the Crown Prince of the Upper Palace)*, SSS 1:493–498. For the importance of Shōtoku for the formation of Shinran's vocation, see Lee, *Shinran's Dream*.

2. Abe summarizes his views in the introduction and "Prolegemon" to Abe Ryūichi, *Weaving of Mantra*, 1–66.

3. This incident is discussed briefly in Adolphson, *Gates of Power*, 32.

4. The translation, slightly amended, is from Katō and Hoshino, *Kogoshūi or Gleanings from Ancient Stories*, 38. The original text may be found in *ST koten hen* 5: *Kogoshūi*, 35.

APPENDIX

1. Piggott, *Emergence of Japanese Kingship*.

2. David Lurie, *The Origins of Writing in Early Japan*, 399–422.

3. Aoki Michiko, *Records of Wind and Earth*. Extant texts, remnants and citations of now-lost *Fudoki* have been collected in *SNKBZ* 5.

4. Passages related to Shōtoku may be found in *SNKBT* 31: 77–88. For an extremely able English translation, see Kamens, *The Three Jewels*, 174–190.

5. The text may be found in Takeuchi, *Nara ibun* 1: 366–382. See also Ōyama, *Nagayaōke mokkan*, 270–341.

6. The text may be found in Takeuchi, *Nara ibun* 1: 383–393. For relevant Asu-kadera/Gangōji related materials, see Iwaki, *Gangōji hennen shiryō* 1. For a brief comparison of the *NSK* and the *Gangōji engi*, see Sonoda, "Early Buddha Worship," 370–379. See also Mizuno, *Nihon kodai no jiin to rekishi*, 21–101.

7. Stevenson, "The Founding of the Monastery Gangōji and a List of Its Treasures," 299–315.

8. The text may be found in Takeuchi, *Nara ibun* 1: 344–365. See also Mizuno, *Nihon kodai no jiin*, 227–271. I discuss this in greater detail in chapter 6.

9. The text may be found in *DNBZ* 85: 127–129. The text is discussed in Hayashi, *Taishi shinkō no kenkyū*, 73–83. See also Tōno, "Shoki no Taishi shinkō to Jōgūōin," 453–466.

10. Lurie, *Origins of Writing in Early Japan*, 427–429. The commentary on the Queen *Śrīmālā* may be found in *T* 56: 1–19 (no. 2185). The commentary on the *Vimilakirti Sutra* may be found in *T* 56: 20–64 (no. 2186). The commentary on the *Lotus Sutra* may be found in *T* 56: 64–128 (no. 2187).

11. Ōno, *Shōtoku taishi no kenkyū*, 91–138. See also Inoue Mitsusada, *Nihon kodai shisōshi*, 161–226.

12. For the transmission of the Shōtoku legend cycle to China, see Wang, *Shōtoku taishi jiku chōetsu*, esp. 250–266 and 367–380.

13. For the Constitution, see Ōno, *Shōtoku Taishi*, 171–211.

14. The text of the inscription may be found in *STZ* 3: 472–473.

15. For a critical assessment of the text, see Ōno, *Shōtoku Taishi*, 210–213.

16. Lurie, *Origins of Writing*, 435.

17. The text of the inscription may be found in *STZ* 3: 471. For a cogent assessment of the inscription's historical validity, see Ōyama, *Nagayaōke mokkan*, 208–210.

18. This text can be found in *SNKBZ* 5: 505–506. I discuss this text in detail in chapter 2.

19. For an annotated version of the text, see Deguchi and Hiraoka, *Shōtoku taishi nanto Bukkyō shū*, 223–229. Secondary literature on both the tapestry and the inscription is extensive. For a representative sample of scholarly positions, see Ōyama, *Nagayaōke mokkan*, 309–324; Ōhashi, *Tenjukoku shūchō no kenkyū*; Pradel, *Fragments of the Tenjukoku Shūchō Mandara*, and Ōno, *Shōtoku Taishi*, 45–91.

20. Piggott has given a concise summary of the text as well as a brief account of its importance for historians of the period. See Piggott, *Emergence of Japanese Kingship*, 295–296. For the full text and analysis, see Ienaga, *Jōgu Shōtoku hōō teisetsu no kenkyū* and Sakamori, Satō, and Yajima, *Jōgu Shōtoku hōō teisetsu no chūshaku to kenkyū*. The text may also be found in *DNBZ* 71: 119–121, and *STZ* 3: 9–22.

21. The text may be found in *STZ* 3: 46–50. For Ganjin and Shōtoku, see Wang, *Shōtoku taishi jiku chōetsu*, 126–139.

22. The text may be found in *STZ* 3: 53–62. Shinkawa Tokio has analyzed the text with special attention to the role of the immigrant kinship groups affiliated with Shitennōji in its formation. See Shinkawa, *Jōgū Shōtoku Taishiden hoketsuki no kenkyū*.

23. Deal, "Hagiography and History," 316–333.

24. The full text may be found in Takeuchi, *Nara ibun* 3: 890–894. The text is also discussed in detail in Hayashi, *Taishi shinkō no kenkyū*, 149–188.

25. The text may be found in *STZ* 3: 71–122.

26. The full text may be found in Takeuchi, *Nara ibun* 3: 895–908. For Ganjin's life as well as a lengthy discussion of the text, see Andō Kōsei, *Ganjin*. See also Ishida, *Ganjin—sono kairitsu shisō*, esp. 269–326.

Works Cited

REFERENCE WORKS

Dai Nihon Bukkyō zensho. Suzuki Gakujutsu Zaidan, ed. 100 vols. Tokyo: Kōdansha, 1970–1973.
Nara ibun. Takeuchi Rizō, ed. 3 vols. Tokyo: Tokyōdō Shuppan, 1962.
Nihon koten bungaku taikei. 100 vols. Tokyo: Iwanami Shoten, 1958–1968.
Nihon shisō taikei. 67 vols. Tokyo: Iwanami Shoten, 1970–.
Shin Nihon koten bungaku taikei, Satake Akihirō, et. al., ed. 100 vols. Tokyo: Iwanami Shoten, 1989–2005.
Shinpen Nihon koten bungaku zenshū. 88 vols. Tokyo: Shōgakkan, 1994–2002.
Shinshū shiryō shūsei. Chiba Jōryū and Ishida Mitsuyuki, eds. 13 vols. Kyoto: Tōhōsha Shuppan, 1983.
Shintei zōhō kokushi taikei. Kuroita Katsumi, ed. 60 volumes. Tokyo: Yoshikawa Kōbunkan, 1972.
Shintō taikei. 52 vols. Tokyo: Seikōsha, 1998–2001.
Shōtoku taishi zenshū. Fujiwara Yūsetsu, ed. 5 vols. Tokyo: Ryūkōsha, 1944.
Taishō shinshū daizōkyō. Takakusu Junjirō and Watanabe Kaigyoku, eds. 85 vols. Tokyo: Daizō Shuppan Kabushiki Kaisha, 1932.
Zoku gunsho ruijū. Hanawa Hokonoichi, ed. 37 vols. Tokyo: Taiheiyō Daigo Kōjō, 1957–1959.

PRIMARY SOURCES

Chin-kuang-ming ching (Skt: *Suvarna-prabhāsattama-rāja sūtra,* J: *Konkōmyōkyō*). Dharmaksema, trans. In *T* 16: 335–357 (no. 663).
Chin-kuang-ming tsui-sheng-wang ching (Skt: *Suvarna-prabhāsattama-rāja sūtra,* J: *Konkōmyō saishōōkyō*). Yi-ching, trans. In *T* 16: 403–457 (no. 665).
Daianji garan engi narabi ni ruki shizaichō. In *Nara ibun* 2: 366–382. 3 vols. Tokyo: Tokyōdō Shuppan, 1962.
Dai Nihon hōzokusan'ō Shōtoku Taishi hōsan. By Shinran. In *STZ* 5: 37–60.

Dai Nihonkoku hokekyōkenki. By Chingen. In *NST* 7: *Ōjōden, Hokekenki*, ed. Ienaga Saburō and Ōsone Shōsuke, 43–219. Tokyo: Iwanami Shoten, 1974.

Dai Nihon ōjō gokurakuki. By Yoshishige no Yasutane. In *NST* 7: *Ōjōden, Hokekenki*, ed. Ienaga Saburō and Ōsone Shōsuke, 9–42. Tokyo: Iwanami Shoten, 1974.

Daisōjō sharibyōki. In *Gyōkisan o kangaeru*, ed. Inoue Kaoru, 28. Osaka: Sakai Gyōki no Kai, 1998.

Denjutsu isshin kaimon. By Kōjō. In *T* 74: 634–659 (no. 2379).

Engishiki. In *SZKT* 26: *Kōtaishiki, Kōninshiki, Engishiki*, ed. Kuroita Katsumi. Tokyo: Yoshikawa Kōbunkan, 1972.

Fudoki. In *SNKBZ* 5: *Fudoki*, ed. Uegaki Setsuya. Tokyo: Shōgakkan, 1997.

Gangōji garan engi narabi ni ruki shizaichō. In *Nara ibun* 2: 383–393.

Gyōki bosatsuden. In *ZGR* 8: 439–441.

Gyōki nenpu. In *Gyōki jiten*, ed. Inoue Kaoru, 255–275. Tokyo: Kokusho Kangyōkai, 1997.

Hokekyō gisho. In *T* 56: 64–129 (no. 2187).

Hōryūji garan engi narabi ni ruki shizaichō. In *Nara ibun* 2: 344–365.

Hōryūji tōin engi. In *DNBZ* 85: 127–129.

Hsü kao-seng chuan. By Tao-hsüan. In *T* 50: 425–708 (no. 2060).

Hung-tsan fa-hua chuan. By Hui-hsiang. In *T* 51: 12–47 (no. 2067).

Jōgū kōtaishi bosatsu den. By Ssu-t'uo. In *STZ* 3: 49–51.

Jōgū Shōtoku hōō teisetsu. In *STZ* 3: 9–22.

Jōgū Shōtoku taishiden hoketsuki. In *STZ* 3: 53–62.

Jōgū Taishi goki. By Shinran. In *SSS* 1:493–498.

Kogoshūi. By Imbe Hironari. In *ST koten hen* 5: *Kogoshūi*, ed. Iida Mizuho. Tokyo: Shintō Taikei Hensankai, 1986.

Kojiki. In *SNKBZ* 1: *Kojiki*, ed. Yamaguchi Yoshinori and Kōnoshi Takamitsu. Tokyo: Shōgakkan, 1997.

Kōtaishi Shōtoku hōsan. By Shinran. In *STZ* 5: 19–35.

Kuan-tzu. In *Shin-yi Kuan-tzu tu-pen*, ed. T'ang Hsiao-chun. Taipei: San-min Shu-chu, 1996.

Liu-t'ao. In *Hsin-yi liu-t'ao tu-pen*, ed. Wu Hsi-fei. Taipei: San-min Shu-chu, 1996.

Manyōshū. In *SNKBZ* 6–9: *Manyōshū*, ed. Kojima Noriyuki, Tōno Haruyuki, and Kinoshita Masatoshi. Tokyo: Shōgakkan, 1971.

Miao-fa lien-hua ching (Skt: *Saddharma-puṇḍarīka sūtra*, J: *Myōhōrengekyō*). Kumārajīva, trans. In *T* 9:1–62 (no. 262).

Nan-yüeh Ssu ta ch'an-shih li-shih yuan-wen. By Hui-ssu. In *T* 46: 787–788 (no. 1933).

Nihon Montoku tennō jitsuroku. In *SZKT* 3: *Nihon kōki, Shoku Nihon kōki, Nihon Montoku tennō jitsuroku*, ed. Kuroita Katsumi. Tokyo: Yoshikawa Kōbunkan, 2000.

Nihon ryōiki. By Kyōkai. In *SNKBT* 30: *Nihon ryōiki*, ed. Izumoji Osamu. Tokyo: Iwanami Shoten, 1996.

Nihon shoki. In *SNKBZ* 2–4: *Nihon shoki*, ed. Kojima Noriyuki, Naoki Kōjirō, Kuranaka Susumu, Mōri Masamori and Nishimiya Kazutami. 3 vols. Tokyo: Shōgakkan, 1994.

Ryōshūge. In *SZKT* 23–24: *Ryōshūge*, ed. Kuroita Katsumi. Tokyo: Yoshikawa Kōbunkan, 2000.

Samguk sagi. By Kim Pu-sik. In Inoue Hideo, trans., *Sankoku shiki*. Tokyo: Heibonsha, 1980.

Samguk yusa. By Iryŏn. In *T* 49: 953–1019 (no. 2039).

Sanbōe kotoba. By Minamoto Tamenori. In *SKBTK* 31: *Sanbōe kotoba chūkōsen*, ed. Mabuchi Kazuo, Koizumi Hiroshi, and Konno Tōru. Tokyo: Iwanami Shoten, 1997.

Sendai kuji hongi. In *ST, koten hen* 8: *Sendai kuji hongi,* ed. Kamata Jun'ichi. Tokyo: Shintō Taikei Hensankai, 1980.

Shaku nihongi. By Urabe Kanekata. In *ST, koten chūshaku hen* 5: *Shaku nihongi,* ed. Onoda Mitsuo. Tokyo: Shintō Taikei Hensankai, 1986.

Shan-hai-ching. In *Shan-hai-ching chiao-chu,* ed. Yüan K'o. Taipei: Lejin Books, 1995.

Sheng-man shih-tzu hu i-sheng ta fang-pien fang-kuang ching. (Skt: *Śrīmālādevīsimhanāda sūtra,* J: *Shōman shishiko ichijyō daihōben hōkō kyō*). Gunabhadra, trans. In *T* 12: 217–223 (no. 353).

Shichidaiki. In *Nara ibun* 3: 890–894.

Shih-chi. In *Shiki kaichū kōshō,* ed. Takigawa Kametarō. Tokyo: Tōhō Bunka Gakuin Tōkyō Kenkyūjo, 1934.

Shinsen shōjiroku. In Saeki Arikyo, *Shinsen shōjiroku no kenkyū.* 6 vols. Tokyo: Yoshikawa Kōbunkan, 1962.

Shitennōji goshuin engi. In *DNBZ* 85: 305–307.

Shoku nihongi. In *SNKBT* 12–16: *Shoku nihongi,* ed. Aoki Kazuo, Inaoka Kōji, Sasayama Haruo, and Shirafuji Noriyuki. Tokyo: Iwanami Shoten, 1989–1998.

Shōmangyō gisho. In *T* 56: 1–19 (no. 2185).

Shōtoku Taishi denryaku. In *STZ* 3: 71–122.

Sui shu. 6 vols. Beijing: Zhonghua Shuju, 1973.

Sui T'ien-t'ai Chih-che ta-shih pieh-chuan. By Kuan Ting. In *T* 50: 191–197 (no. 2050).

Sumiyoshi taisha jindaiki. In Tanaka Tsuguhito, *Sumiyoshi taisha jindaiki no kenkyū.* Tokyo: Kokusho Kankōkai, 1985.

Ta po-jo po-luo mi-tuo ching (Skt: *Mahāprajñāpāramitā sūtra,* J: *Dai hannya haramita kyō*). Hsüan-tsang, trans. In *T* 5–7 (no. 220).

Tō daiwajō tōseiden. By Ōmi no Mahito Mifune. In *Nara ibun* 3: 895–908.

Tōshi kaden. In *Nara ibun* 3: 875–886. 3 vols.

Wei-mo-chieh suo-shuo ching (Skt: *Vimalakīrtinirdeśa sūtra,* J: *Yuimakitsu shosetsu kyō*). Kumārajīva, trans. In *T* 14: 537–557 (no. 475).

Wei shu. In *San-kuo-chih chi-chieh,* ed. Lu Pi, 1–686. Beijing: Chung-hua Shu-chu, 1982.

Yuima gisho. In *T* 56: 20–64 (no. 2186).

SECONDARY SOURCES

Abe, Ryūichi. *The Weaving of Mantra.* New York: Columbia University Press, 1999.

Abe Ryūichi. "Muromachi izen seiritsu Shōtoku Taishi denkirui shoshi." In *Shōtoku Taishi ronshū,* ed. Shōtoku Taishi Kenkyūkai, 511–558. Kyoto: Heirakuji Shoten, 1971.

Abe Yasurō and Yamazaki Makoto. *Shōtoku Taishi denshū.* Kyoto: Rinsen Shoten, 2006.

Adolphson, Mikael. *Gates of Power.* Honolulu: University of Hawaii Press, 2000.

Akimoto Kichirō, *Nihon koten bungaku taikei 2: Fudoki.* Tokyo: Iwanami Shoten, 1987.

Anderson, Benedict. *Imagined Communities.* London: Verso, 1983.

Andō Kōsei. *Ganjin.* Tokyo: Yoshikawa Kōbunkan, 1967.

Aoki Michiko. *Records of Wind and Earth: A Translation of Fudoki with Introduction and Commentaries.* Ann Arbor: Association for Asian Studies, 1997.

Aston, W. G., trans. *Nihongi: Chronicles of Japan from the Earliest Times to A.D. 697.* 2 vols. Rutland, Vt., and Tokyo: Tuttle, 1972.

Augustine, Jonathan. *Buddhist Hagiography in Early Japan: Images of Compassion in the Gyōki Tradition.* London: Routledge Curzon, 2005.

Babha, Homi, ed. *Nation and Narration*. London: Routledge, 1993.

Batten, Bruce. "Foreign Threat and Domestic Reform: The Emergence of the Ritsuryō State." *Monumentica Nipponica* 41.2 (1986): 83–112.

———. *To the Ends of Japan*. Honolulu: University of Hawaii Press, 2003.

Bennington, Geoffrey. "Postal Politics and the Institution of the Nation." In *Nation and Narration*, ed. Homi K. Babha, 121–138. London: Routledge, 1993.

Best, Jonathan. *Buddhism in Paekche*. Ph.D. dissertation, Harvard University, 1976.

Breen, John, and Mark Teeuwen. "Introduction: The Shinto Past and Present." In *Shinto in History*, ed. John Breen and Mark Teeuwen, 1–12. Honolulu: University of Hawaii Press, 2000.

———, eds. *Shinto in History*. Honolulu: University of Hawaii Press, 2000.

Brown, Delmer, ed. *Cambridge History of Japan 1: Ancient Japan*. Cambridge: Cambridge University Press, 1993.

Campany, Robert Ford. *To Live as Long as Heaven and Earth: A Translation and Study of Ge Hong's Traditions of Divine Transcendents*. Berkeley: University of California Press, 2002.

Como, Michael. "Silkworms and Consorts in Nara Japan." *Asian Folklore Studies* 64 (2005): 111–131.

Cranston, Edwin. *Waka Anthology*. Stanford, CA: Stanford University Press, 1993.

Deal, William. "Hagiography and History: The Image of Prince Shōtoku." In *Religions of Japan in Practice*, ed. George Tanabe, 316–333. Princeton: Princeton University Press, 1999.

Deguchi Jōjun and Hiraoka Jōkai, eds. *Shōtoku taishi nanto Bukkyō shū*. Machida: Tamagawa Daigaku Shuppanbu, 1972.

De Vos, George. "Ethnic Pluralism: Conflict and Accommodation." In *Ethnic Identity*, ed. George De Vos and Lola Romanucchi-Ross. Palo Alto: Mayfield Publishing Company, 1975.

De Vos, George, and Lola Romanucchi-Ross, eds. *Ethnic Identity*. Palo Alto: Mayfield Publishing Company, 1975.

Ebersole, Gary. *Ritual Poetry and the Politics of Death in Early Japan*. Princeton: Princeton University Press, 1989.

Edwards, Walter. "Event and Process in the Founding of Japan: The Horserider Theory in Archeological Perspective." *Journal of Japanese Studies* 9 (Summer 1983): 265–295.

Egami Namio. *Egami Namio no Nihon kodaishi: kiba minzoku setsu yonjūgonen*. Tokyo: Daikōsha, 1992.

Ellwood, Robert. "A Cargo Cult in Seventh Century Japan." *History of Religion* 23.3 (1984): 222–238.

Eriksen, Thomas Hylland. "Ethnicity, Race and Nation." In *The Ethnicity Reader*, ed. Montserrat Guibernau and John Rex, 33–42. Cambridge: Polity Press, 1997.

Farris, William Wayne. *Heavenly Warriors: the Evolution of Japan's Military, 500–1300*. Cambridge, Mass: Council on East Asian Studies, Harvard University, 1992.

———. 1985. *Population, Disease, and Land in Early Japan. 645–900*. Cambridge, Mass.: Harvard University Press.

———. *Sacred Texts and Buried Treasures*. Honolulu: University of Hawaii Press, 1998.

Forte, Antonino. *Political Propaganda and Ideology in China at the End of the Seventh Century*. Napoli: Istituto Universario Orientale, 1976.

———, ed. *Tang China and Beyond*. Kyoto: Istituto Italiano di Studi sull'Asia Orientale, 1983.

Foucault, Michel. *Power/Knowledge: Selected Interviews and Other Writings, 1972–1977* New York: Pantheon Books, 1980.

Fujii Yukiko. "Kuse Kannon no Seiritsu." In *Shōtoku taishi no shinjitsu*, ed. Ōyama Seiichi, 317–338. Tokyo: Heibonsha, 2003.

Fujisawa Norihiko. "Shisa no matsuri." In *Nihon no shinkō iseki*, ed. Kaneko Hiroyuki, 281–307. Tokyo: Yūzankaku, 1998.

Goodman, Nelson. *Ways of World Making*. Indianapolis: Hackett, 1985.

Groner, Paul. *Ryōgen and Mount Hiei*. Honolulu: University of Hawaii Press, 2002.

———. *Saichō*. Honolulu: University of Hawaii Press, 2000.

Guibernau, Montserrat, and John Rex, eds. *The Ethnicity Reader*. Cambridge: Polity Press, 1997.

Guth, Christine. "The Pensive Prince of Chūgūji." In *Maitreya, the Future Buddha*, ed. Helen Hardacre, 191–214. New York: Cambridge University Press, 1988.

Hara Hidesaburō. "Ōken to tōhō e no michi." In *Shinpan kodai no Nihon 7: chūbu*, ed. Kobayashi, Tatsuo and Hara Hidesaburō, 165–188. Tokyo: Kadokawa Shoten, 1993.

Hardacre, Helen, ed. *Maitreya, the Future Buddha*. New York: Cambridge University Press, 1988.

Hatai Hiromu. *Tennō to kajio no denshō*. Tokyo: Gendai Shichōsha, 1982.

Hayami Tasuku. *Miroku shinkō—mō hitotsu no jōdo shinkō*. Tokyo: Hyoronsha, 1973.

———, ed. *Ronshū Nihon Bukkyōshi*. Tokyo: Yūzankaku, 1986.

Hayashi Mikiya. *Taishi shinkō no kenkyū*. Tokyo: Yoshikawa Kōbunkan, 1980.

———. "Tenjukoku shūchō mei." In *Shōtoku taishi sankō*, ed. Shitennōji Kangakuin, 325–337. Osaka: Sōhonzan Shitennōji, 1979.

Heibonsha Chihō Shiryō Center, ed., *Nihon rekishi chimei taikei 27: Kyōto-fu*.

Hino Akira. *Nihon kodai shizoku denshō no kenkyū, zoku hen*. Kyoto: Nagata Bunshōdō, 1982.

Hirabayashi Akihito. *Tanabata to sumō no kodaishi*. Tokyo: Hakusuisha, 1998.

Hirano Kunio. "Hatashi no kenkyū." *Shigaku zasshi* 70.3 (1961): 25–47.

———. *Kikajin to kodai kokka*. Tokyo: Yoshikawa Kōbunkan, 1993.

Hiraoka Jōkai. *Nihon jiin shi no kenkyū*. Tokyo: Yoshikawa Kōbunkan, 1981.

Hishida Tetsuo. "Harima no kofun to jiin." In *Kikan kōkogaku 60: Tokushū: toraikei shizoku no kofun to jiin*, 48–51. Tokyo: Yūzankaku, 1997.

Hitsumoto Seiichi, ed. *Fudoki no kōkogaku 2: Harima fudoki no maki*. Tokyo: Dōseisha, 1994.

Hobsbawm, Eric. *The Invention of Tradition*. Cambridge: Cambridge University Press, 1983.

Hōjō Katsutaka. "Gyōki to gijutsusha shūdan." In *Gyōki jiten*, ed. Inoue Kaoru, 108–125. Tokyo: Kokusho Kangyōkai, 1997.

Ienaga Saburō. *Jōgū Shōtoku hōō teisetsu no kenkyū*. Tokyo: Sanseidō, 1972.

———. *Nihon Bukkyōshi*. 3 vols. Kyoto: Hōzōkan, 1969.

———. "Shōtoku Taishi no Bukkyō." In *Nihon Bukkyōshi*, ed. Ienaga Saburō, 1: 64–81. 3 vols. Kyoto: Hōzōkan, 1967.

Iida Mizuho. *Shōtoku taishiden no kenkyū*. Tokyo: Yoshikawa Kōbunkan, 2000.

Ikeda On, ed. *Kodai o kangaeru: Kara to Nihon*. Tokyo: Yoshikawa Kōbunkan, 1992.

Imai Keiichi. *Kikajin to shaji* Kyoto: Sōgeisha, 1969.

Inoue Hideo. "Chiku, Toyo, Hi no gōzoku to Yamato chōtei." In *Kodai no Nihon 3: Kyūshū*, ed. Kagamiyama Takeshi and Tamura Enchō, 138–158. Tokyo: Kadokawa Shoten, 1970.

————. "Nukatabe to Yamato ōken." In *Kodai ōken to shizoku,* ed. Tsuruoka Shizuo, 105–147. Tokyo: Meichō Shuppansha, 1988.

Inoue Kaoru, ed. *Gyōki jiten.* Tokyo: Kokusho Kangyōkai, 1997.

————. "Gyōki no shōgai." In *Gyōki jiten,* ed. Inoue Kaoru, 9–22. Tokyo: Kokusho Kangyōkai, 1997.

————, ed. *Gyōkisan o kangaeru.* Osaka: Sakai Gyōki no Kai, 1998.

————. *Nihon kodai no seiji to shūkyō.* Tokyo: Yoshikawa Kōbunkan, 1961.

Inoue Mitsuo. *Kodai no Nihonjin to toraijin: kodaishi ni miru kokusai kankei.* Tokyo: Akashi Shoten, 1999.

Inoue Mitsusada. "The Century of Reform." In *Cambridge History of Japan 1: Ancient Japan,* ed. Delmer Brown, 1: 163–221. Cambridge: Cambridge University Press, 1993.

————. *Nihon kodai no kokka to Bukkyō.* Tokyo: Iwanami Shoten, 1971.

————. *Nihon kodai shisōshi no kenkyū.* Tokyo: Iwanami Shoten, 1970.

————, ed. *NST 3: Ritsuryō.* Tokyo: Iwanami Shoten, 1976.

————. "Yūryakuchō ni okeru ōken to higashi ajia." In *Chōsen sangoku to Wagoku,* ed. Inoue Mitsusada, 72–117. Tokyo: Gakuseisha, 1980.

Ishida Hisatoyo, ed. *Shōtoku Taishi jiten.* Tokyo: Kashiwa Shobō, 1997.

Ishida Mizumaro. *Ganjin—sono kairitsu shisō.* Tokyo: Daizō Shuppan, 1974.

Itakusu Kazuko. "Rango no Kyūshū to Yamato seiken." In *Iwai no ran,* ed. Oda Fujio, 219–242. Tokyo: Yoshikawa Kōbunkan, 1991.

Itō Seiji, ed. *Nihon shinwa kenkyū 3: Izumo shinwa, Hyūga shinwa.* 3 vols. Tokyo: Gakuseisha, 1977.

Iwaki Takatoshi. *Gangōji hennen shiryō.* 3 vols. Tokyo: Yoshikawa Kōbunkan, 1983.

Jōdai Bunken o Yomukai, ed. *Fudoki itsubun chūshaku.* Tokyo: Kanrin Shobō, 2001.

Kadowaki Teiji. *Nihon kaiiki no kodaishi.* Tokyo: Tokyo Daigaku Shuppankai, 1986.

Kagamiyama Takeshi and Tamura Enchō, eds. *Kodai no Nihon 3: Kyūshū.* Tokyo: Kadokawa Shoten, 1970.

Kamens, Edward. *The Three Jewels.* Ann Arbor: Center for Japanese Studies, University of Michigan, 1988.

Kanaji Isamu. *Shōtoku taishi shinkō.* Tokyo: Shunjūsha, 1979.

Kaneko Hiroyuki. "Bukkyō, Dōkyō to banjin suhai." In *Kodaishi 5: Kami to matsuri,* ed. Kanasaki Hiroshi and Sahara Makoto, 167–191. Tokyo: Shōgakkan, 1999.

————. "Tojō to saishi." In *Okinoshima to kodai saishi,* ed. Oda Fujio, 198–226. Tokyo: Yoshikawa Kōbunkan, 1998.

Kaneko Shūichi. "Zuitō kōdai to higashi ajia." In *Kodai o kangeru: Kara to Nihon,* ed. Ikeda On, 15–41. Tokyo: Yoshikawa Kōbunkan, 1992.

Kano Hisashi. "Miketsu kuni to Kashiwadeshi." In *Kodai no Nihon 5: Kinki,* ed. Tsuboi Kiyotari and Kishi Toshio, 263–282. Tokyo: Kadokawa Shoten, 1970.

Katata Osamu. *Nihon kodai shinkō to Bukkyō.* Kyoto: Hōzōkan, 1991.

Katō Genchi and Hoshino Hikoshiro, trans. *Kogoshūi or Gleanings from Ancient Stories.* Tokyo: Zaidan Hojin Meiji Seitoku Kinen Gakkai, 1924.

Katō Kenkichi. *Hatashi to sono tami.* Tokyo: Hakusuisha, 1998.

————. *Kishi to Kawachi no Aya-shi.* Tokyo: Hakusuisha, 2001.

————. *Sogashi to Yamato ōken.* Tokyo: Yoshikawa Kōbunkan, 1983.

————. *Yamoto seiken to kodai shizoku.* Tokyo: Yoshikawa Kōbunkan, 1991.

Kawakatsu Yoshio. "Chūgokuteki shin Bukkyō keisei e no enerugi." In *Chūgoku chūsei no shūkyō to bunka,* ed. Fukunaga Mitsuji, 501–537. Kyoto: Kyoto Daigaku Jinbun Kagaku Kenkyūjo, 1972.

Kidder, Edward. *The Lucky Seventh: Early Hōryūji and Its Time*. Tokyo: International Christian University, 1999.

Kiley, Cornelius. "Surnames in Ancient Japan." *Harvard Journal of Asian Studies* 29 (1969): 177–189.

Kinoshita Ryō. *Kodai dōro*. Tokyo: Yoshikawa Kōbunkan, 1996.

Kishi Toshio. "Kodō no rekishi." In *Kodai no Nihon 5: Kinki*, ed. Tsuboi Kiyotari and Kishi Toshio, 93–108. Tokyo: Kadokawa Shoten, 1970.

Klein, Christoff. "Hermits and Ascetics in Ancient Japan: The Concept of *Hijiri* Reconsidered." In *Japanese Religions* 22.2 (1997): 1–47.

Kobayashi Tatsuo, and Hara Hidesaburō, eds. *Shinpan kodai no nihon, 7: chūbu*. Tokyo: Kadokawa Shoten, 1993.

Kojima Noriyuki. *Jōdai Nihon bungaku to Chūgoku bungaku*. 3 vols. Tokyo: Hanawa Shobō, 1962–1965.

Kominami Ichirō. *Saiōbō to tanabata denshō*. Tokyo: Heibonsha, 1991.

Kurano Kenji, ed. *NKBT 1: Kojiki, Norito*. Tokyo: Iwanami Shoten, 1963.

Lancaster, Lew. "Maitreya in Korea." In *Maitreya, the Future Buddha*, ed. Helen Hardacre, 135–153. New York: Cambridge University Press, 1988.

Ledyard, Gary. "Galloping Along with the Horseriders: Looking for the Foundations of Japan." *Journal of Japanese Studies* 1 (Summer 1975): 217–254.

Lee, Kenneth. *Shinran's Dream: The Importance of Shōtoku Worship in Shinran's Amida Buddhism*. Ph.D. Dissertation, Columbia University, 2001.

Lewis, Mark Edward. *Writing and Authority in Early China*. New York: State University of New York Press, 1999.

Loewe, Michael. *Ways to Paradise*. London: George Allen and Unwin, 1979.

Lurie, David Barnett. *The Origins of Writing in Early Japan: From the 1st to the 8th Century C.E.* Ph.D. dissertation, Columbia University, 2001.

Maeda Haruto. *Nihon kodai no michi to chimata*. Tokyo: Yoshikawa Kōbunkan, 1996.

Magnin, Paul. *La vie et ouevre de Huisi [515–577], les origines de la Secte Buddhique Chinoise du Tiantai*. Paris: Ecole Francais d'Extreme Orient, 1979.

Matsubara Hironobu. *Kodai no chihō gōzoku*. Tokyo: Yoshikawa Kōbunkan, 1988.

Matsumae Takeshi. *Kodai denshō to kyūtei saishi*. Tokyo: Hanawa Shobō, 1990.

Matsumoto Hajime. "Munakata, Okinoshima annai." In *Okinoshima to kodaisaishi*, ed. Oda Fujio, 258–282. Tokyo: Yoshikawa Kōbunkan, 1998.

Matsuo Akihiko. "Nihonkai Chūbu no Kofun Bunka." In *Shinpan kodai no Nihon 7*, eds. Tsuboi Kiyoshi and Hirano Kunio, 99–118. Tokyo: Kadokawa Shoten, 1994.

Mayumi Tsunetada. *Nihon kodai saishi no kenkyū*. Tokyo: Gakuseisha, 1978.

Mayuzumi Hiromichi, ed. *Kodai kokka no rekishi to denshō*. Tokyo: Yoshikawa Kōbunkan, 1992.

———. "Kodai kokka to Sogashi." In *Sogashi to kodai kokka*, ed. Mayuzumi Hiromichi, 1–12. Tokyo: Yoshikawa Kōbunkan, 1991.

———. *Mononobe, Sogashi to kodai ōken*. Tokyo: Yoshikawa Kōbunkan, 1995.

———, ed. *Sogashi to kodai kokka*. Tokyo: Yoshikawa Kōbunkan, 1991.

Mishina Shōei. *Nissen shinwa densetsu no kenkyū*. Tokyo: Heibonsha, 1972.

———. *Shiragi no Karō no kenkyū*. Tokyo: Heibonsha, 1976.

Mitani Ei'ichi. "Hitachi kuni fudoki kara shūgō shisō e." In *Nihon shinwa*, ed. Nihon Bungaku Kenkyū Shiryō Kankōkai, 1: 251–259. 2 vols. Tokyo: Yūseidō, 1989.

Miura Keiichi. "Kishi ni tsuite." *Nihonshi kenkyū* 34 (1957): 27–45.

Mizoguchi Mutsuko. *Kodai shizoku no keifu*. Tokyo: Yoshikawa Kōbunkan, 1987.

Mizuguchi Tomio. "Harima fudoki seiritsu jidai no jiin to shūraku." In *Fudoki no kōkogaku 2: Harima fudoki no maki*, ed. Hitsumoto Seiichi, 267–289. Tokyo: Dōseisha, 1994.

Mizuno Ryūtarō. 1993. *Nihon kodai no jiin to shiryō*. Tokyo: Yoshikawa Kōbunkan.

Mizuno Yū. *Nihon kodai no minzoku to kokka*. Tokyo: Daiwa Shobō, 1975.

Naitō Konan. *Naitō Konan zenshū*. 10 vols. Tokyo: Chikuma Shoten, 1970.

Nakai Shinkō. *Gyōki to kodai Bukkyō*. Kyoto: Nagata Bunshodo, 1991.

Nakajima Toshio, ed. *Sankōgotei Ka, U, sen Shin shiryō shūsei* Tokyo: Kyūko Shoin, 2001.

Nakamura, Kyoko Motomochi, trans. *Miraculous Stories from the Japanese Buddhist Tradition*. Cambridge: Harvard University Press, 1973.

Nakamura Hajime. *Shōtoku Taishi*. Tokyo: Tōkyō Shōseki, 1990.

Nakamura Shūya. *Hatashi to Kamoshi*. Kyoto: Rinsen Shoten, 1984.

Nakano Hatayoshi. *Hachiman shinkō*. Tokyo: Hanawa Shoten, 1985.

———. *Hachiman shinkō to shugendō*. Tokyo: Yoshikawa Kōbunkan, 1998.

Nakao Ryōshin. "Shōtoku Taishi Nangaku Eishi goshin setsu no hensen." *Hanazono kenkyū kiyō* 21 (1990): 16–33.

Naoki Kōjirō. *Jinshin no ran*. Tokyo: Hanawa Shobō, 1973.

———. *Naniwamiya to Naniwatsu no kenkyū*. Tokyo: Yoshikawa Kōbunkan, 1994.

———. "The Nara State." In *Cambridge History of Japan 1: Ancient Japan*, ed. Delmer Brown, 1: 221–268. Cambridge: Cambridge University Press, 1993.

———. *Nihon kodai shizoku to tennō*. Tokyo: Hanawa Shobō 1964.

Nattier, Jan. "Meanings of the Maitreya Myth." In *Maitreya, the Future Buddha*, ed. Helen Hardacre, 23–51. New York: Cambridge, University Press, 1988.

———. *Once upon a Future Time*. Berkeley: Asian Humanities Press, 1991.

Nemoto Seiji. *Nara Bukkyō to Gyōki denshō no tenkai*. Tokyo: Yūzankaku, 1992.

Nihon bungaku kenkyū shiryō sōsho. *Nihon shinwa*. 2 vols. Tokyo: Yūseidō, 1989.

Nishimura Sey. "The Prince and the Pauper." *Monumenta Nipponica*, 40.3 (1985): 299–310.

Oda Fujio. "Iwai no hanran." In *Kodai no Nihon 3: Kyūshū*, ed. Kagamiyama Takeshi, 159–175. Tokyo: Kadokawa Shoten, 1970.

———, ed. *Iwai no ran*. Tokyo: Yoshikawa Kōbunkan, 1991.

———. "Kikajin bunka to dazaifu." In *Kodai no Nihon 3: Kyūshū*, ed. Kagamiyama Takeshi, 265–271. Tokyo: Kadokawa Shoten.

———, ed. *Okinoshima to kodai saishi*. Tokyo: Yoshikawa Kōbunkan, 1988.

Ōhashi Katsuaki. *Tenjukoku shūchō no kenkyū*. Tokyo: Yoshikawa Kōbunkan, 1995.

Ōhashi Nobuya. *Kodai gōzoku to toraijin*. Tokyo: Yoshikawa Kōbunkan, 2004.

———. *Kodai kokka no seiritsu to Okinagashi*. Tokyo: Yoshikawa Kōbunkan, 1984.

———. *Nihon kodai no ōken to shizoku*. Tokyo: Yoshikawa Kōbunkan, 1996.

Okada Seishi, ed. *Daijōsai to niiname*. Tokyo: Gakuseisha, 1979.

Okada Yoshirō. "Sogashi to Jōgū ōka." In *Kodai ōken to shizoku*, ed. Tsuruoka Shizuo, 205–232. Tokyo: Meichō Shuppansha, 1988.

Ōno Tatsunosuke. *Jōdai no jōdokyō*. Tokyo: Yoshikawa Kōbunkan, 1972.

———. *Shōtoku taishi no kenkyū*. Tokyo: Yoshikawa Kōbunkan, 1970.

Orzech, Charles. *Politics and Transcendent Wisdom: the Scripture for Humane Kings in the Creation of Chinese Buddhism*. University Park, Pa: Pennsylvania State University Press, 1998.

Ōta Hirotarō. *Nanto shichi daiji no rekishi to nenpyō*. 3 vols. Tokyo: Iwanami Shoten, 1979.

Ōyama Seiichi. *Nagayaōke mokkan to kinsekibun*. Tokyo: Yoshikawa Kōbunkan, 1998.

————, ed. *Shōtoku taishi no shinjitsu*. Tokyo: Heibonsha, 2003.

————. *Shōtoku taishi no tanjō*. Tokyo: Yoshikawa Kōbunkan, 1999.

Piggott, Joan. *The Emergence of Japanese Kingship*. Stanford: Stanford University Press, 1997.

————. "*Mokkan*: Wooden Documents from the Nara Period." *Monumenta Nipponica* 44.1 (1990): 449–470.

————. *Tōdaiji and Nara Imperium*. Ph.D. dissertation, Stanford University, 1987.

Philippi, Donald. *Norito*. Princeton: Princeton University Press, 1990.

Pradel, Maria del Rosario. *Fragments of the Tenjukoku Shūchō Mandara: Reconstruction of the Iconography and the Historical Contexts*. Ph.D. dissertation, UCLA, 1997.

Renan, Ernest. *Ouevres Complètes*. 10 vols. Paris: Calman-Lévy, 1947–1961.

Rhi Ki-young. "Brief Remarks on the Buddha-Land Ideology in Silla during the Seventh and Eighth Centuries." In *Tang China and Beyond*, ed. Antonio Forte, 163–181. Kyōto: Istituto Italiano di Studi sull'Asia Orientale, 1983.

Saeki Arikyo. *Shinsen shōjiroku no kenkyū*. 6 vols. Tokyo: Yoshikawa Kōbunkan, 1962.

Sakamori Takuya, Satō Makoto and Yajima Izumi, eds. 2005. *Jōgū Shōtoku hōō teisetsu no chūshaku to kenkyū*. Tokyo: Yoshikawa Kōbunkan.

Sakamoto Tarō. *Shōtoku Taishi*. Tokyo: Yoshikawa Kōbunkan, 1979.

————. *Six National Histories*. Vancouver: UBC Press, 1991.

Sakamoto Tarō and Hirano Kunio. *Nihon kodai shizoku jinmei jiten*. Tokyo: Yoshikawa Kōbunkan, 1990.

Sakamoto Tarō, Ienaga Saburō, Inoue Mitsusada and Ōno Susumu, eds. *NKBT: Nihon shoki*, 67–68. Tokyo: Iwanami Shoten, 1988.

Sakamoto Tarō Hakase Koki Kinenkai, ed. *Nihon kodaishi ronshū*. Tokyo: Yoshikawa, 1974.

Sakuma Ryū. *Nihon kodai sōden no kenkyū*. Tokyo: Yoshikawa Kōbunkan, 1983.

Seidel, Anna. "Image of the Perfect Ruler in Early Taoism," *History of Religion* 9.2–3 (1969–1970): 216–247.

Sekiguchi Akira. *Emishi to kodai kokka*. Tokyo: Yoshikawa Kōbunkan, 1992.

Senda Minoru. "Kinai." In *Kodai dōro*, ed. Kinoshita Ryō, 27–58. Tokyo: Yoshikawa Kōbunkan, 1996.

————. "Shijūku-in wa dokoka." In *Gyōki jiten*, ed. Inoue Kaoru, 229–239. Tokyo: Kokusho Kangyōkai, 1997.

Shimizu Masaji. "Asuka to Ikaruga." In *Sogashi to kodai kokka*, ed. Mayuzumi Hiromichi, 148–168. Tokyo: Yoshikawa Kōbunkan, 1991.

Shimode Sekiyo. *Kodai shinsen shisō no kenkyū*. Tokyo: Yoshikawa Kōbunkan, 1986.

Shinkawa Tokio. *Jōgū Shōtoku taishiden hoketsuki no kenkyū*. Tokyo: Yoshikawa Kōbunkan, 1979.

————. "Munakata to Usa." In *Kodai Nihon 3: Kyūshū, Okinawa*, ed. Shimojō Nobuyuki and Hirano Kunio, 357–380. Tokyo: Kadokawa Shoten, 1991.

————. "Nara Jidai no Dōkyō to Bukkyō." In *Ronshū Nihon Bukkyōshi*, ed. Hayami Tasuku, 277–308. Tokyo: Yūzankaku, 1986.

Shitennōji Kangakuin, ed. *Shōtoku taishi sankō*. Osaka: Sōhonzan Shitennōji, 1979.

Shōtoku Taishi Kenkyūkai, ed. *Shōtoku Taishi ronshū*. Kyoto: Heirakuji Shoten, 1971.

Sonoda Kōyū. "Early Buddha Worship" In *Cambridge History of Japan: Ancient Japan*, ed. Delmer Brown, 360–415. Cambridge: Cambridge University Press, 1993.

Stevenson, Miwa. "The Founding of the Monastery Gangōji and a List of Its Treasures." In *Religions of Japan in Practice*, ed. George Tanabe, 299–315. Princeton: Princeton University Press, 1999.

Strong, John. *The Legend of Asoka*. Princeton: Princeton University Press, 1983.

Sugano Masao. *Kojiki shinwa no kenkyū*. Tokyo: Ōfūsha, 1973.

Taketani Hisao. *Kodai shizoku denshō no kenkyū*. Tokyo: Kasama Shoin, 1971.

Takeuchi Rizō, ed. *Nara ibun*. 3 vols. Tokyo: Tokyōdō Shuppan, 1962.

Takigawa Masajirō. *Ritsuryō to daijōsai*. Tokyo: Kokushokan Kyōkai, 1988.

Takioto Yoshiyuki. "Uranshimako denshō no seiritsu kihan." In *Kodai kokka no rekishi to denshō*, ed. Mayuzumi Hiromichi, 40–53. Tokyo: Yoshikawa Kōbunkan, 1992.

Tamura Enchō. *Kodai Chōsen to Yamato*. Tokyo: Kōdansha Gakujutsu Bunko, 1985.

———. *Nihon Bukkyōshi*. 6 vols. Kyoto: Hōzōkan, 1982–1983.

Tamura Enchō and Kawagishi Kōkyō, eds. *Shōtoku taishi to Asuka Bukkyō*. Tokyo: Yoshikawa Kōbunkan, 1985.

———. *Tsukushi to Asuka: Nihon kodaishi o miru me*. Tokyo: Rokkō Shuppan, 1990.

Tanabe, George, ed. *Religions of Japan in Practice*. Princeton: Princeton University Press, 1999.

Tanaka Tsuguhito. *Shōtoku taishi shinkō no seiritsu*. Tokyo: Yoshikawa Kōbunkan, 1983.

———. *Sumiyoshi taisha jindaiki no kenkyū*. Tokyo: Kokusho Kankōkai, 1985.

Tanigawa Ken'ichi. "Ōjintei to dansei shinwa." In *Nihon shinwa kenkyū: Izumo shinwa, Hyūga shinwa*, ed. Itō Seiji, 3: 203–229. 3 vols. Tokyo: Gakuseisha, 1977.

Tateno Kazumi. "Koshi no kuniguni to gōzokutachi." In *Shinpan kodai no Nihon 7: chūbu*, ed. Kobayashi Tatsuo and Hara Hidesaburō, 189–209. Tokyo: Kadokawa Shoten, 1993.

Terakawa Machio. "Kakinomoto Hitomaro." In *Yamanobe no michi*, ed. Wada Atsumu, 191–220. Tokyo: Yoshikawa Kōbunkan, 1999.

Toby, Ronald. "Why Leave Nara?" *Monumenta Nipponica*, 40.3 (1985): 331–347.

Tōno Masayuki. "Shoki no Taishi shinkō to Jōgūōin." In *Shōtoku Taishi jiten*, ed. Ishida Hisatoyo, 453–466. Tokyo: Kashiwa Shobō, 1997.

Tōyama Mitsuo. "Umako to Shōtoku Taishi." In *Sogashi to kodai kokka*, ed. Mayuzumi Hiromichi, 127–148. Tokyo: Iwanami, 1991.

Tsuboi Kiyoashi and Hirano Kunio, eds., *Shinpan kodai no Nihon 7: Chūbu*. Tokyo: Kadokawa Shoten, 1994.

Tsuboi Kiyotari and Kishi Toshio, eds. *Kodai no Nihon 5: Kinki*. Tokyo: Kadokawa Shoten, 1970.

Tsukaguchi Yoshinobu. *Jingū kōgō densetsu no kenkyū*. Osaka: Sōgensha, 1980.

Tsunoda Ryusaku and L. Carrington Goodrich. *Japan in the Chinese Histories*. Pasadena: P. D. and Ione Perkins, 1951.

Ueda Masaaki. *Kikajin*. Tokyo: Chūō Koronsha, 1965.

———. *Kodai no Dōkyō to Chōsen*. Kyoto: Jinbun Shoin, 1989.

Umehara Takeshi. *Kakusareta jūjika*. Tokyo: Shūeisha, 1982.

———. "Shōtoku Taishi." In *Shōtoku Taishi sankō*, ed. Shitennōji Kangakuin, 107–138. Osaka: Chugai Nipposha, 1979.

Uwai Hisayoshi. *Nihon kodai no shizoku to saishi*. Tokyo: Jinbun Shoin, 1990.

de Visser, M. W. *Ancient Buddhism in Japan*. Leiden: E. J. Brill, 1935.

Wada Atsumu. *Kodai no girei to saishi*. 3 vols. Tokyo: Hanawa Shobō, 1995.

———. "Okinoshima to Yamato ōken." In *Okinoshima to kodai saishi*, ed. Oda Fujio, 164–198. Tokyo: Yoshikawa Kōbunkan, 1998.

———, ed. *Yamanobe no michi*. Tokyo: Yoshikawa Kōbunkan, 1999.

Wang Yung. *Shōtoku taishi jiku chōetsu: rekishi o ugokashita eshi kōshin setsu*. Tokyo: Taishūkan Shoten, 1994.

Wayman, Alex and Hideko Wayman, trans., *The Lion's Roar of Queen Śrīmālā*. New York: Columbia University Press, 1974.

Wechsler, Howard. *Offerings of Jade and Silk*. New Haven: Yale University Press, 1985.

Weinstein, Stanley. *Buddhism Under the T'ang*. Cambridge: Cambridge University Press, 1987.

Wright, Arthur. *The Sui Dynasty*. New York: Alfred A. Knopf, 1978.

Yagi Atsuru. "Harima no Miyake." In *Kodai no Nihon 5: Kinki*, eds. Tsuboi Kiyotari and Kishi Toshio, 178–195. Tokyo: Kadokawa shoten, 1970.

Yamachika Kumiko. "Michi to matsuri." In *Nihon no shinkō iseki*, ed. Kaneko Hiroyuki, 211–236. Tokyo: Yūzankaku, 1998.

Yamao Yukihisa. *Tsukushikimi Iwai no sensō*. Tokyo: Shin Nihon Shuppansha, 2001.

Yokota Ken'ichi. *Asuka no kamigami*. Tokyo: Yoshikawa Kōbunkan, 1992.

———. "Metsubō mae ni okeru Jōgū ōka no seiriki ni tsuite." In *Shōtoku taishi to Asuka Bukkyō*, ed. Tamura Enchō and Kawagishi Kōkyō, 126–144. Tokyo: Yoshikawa Kōbunkan, 1985.

Yoshida Akira. "Kodai Tajima no gōzoku to bumin" *Tajimashi kenkyū* 25.1 (2002): 1–39.

Yoshida Kazuhiko. "Dōji no bunshō." In *Shōtoku taishi no shinjitsu*, Ōyama Seiichi, ed., 273–313. Tokyo: Heibonsha, 2003.

Yoshida Takehiko. "Kyūshū ōchō to Yamato seiken." In *Kodai ōken to shizoku*, ed. Tsuruoka Shizuo, 65–104. Tokyo: Meichō Shuppansha, 1988.

Yoshida Yasuo. *Gyōki to ritsuryō kokka*. Tokyo: Yoshikawa Kōbunkan, 1987.

———. *Nihon kodai no bosatsu to minshū*. Tokyo: Yoshikawa Kōbunkan, 1988.

Yoshikawa Shinji. "Gyōki jiin bodain to sono terada." In *Nihon kodai shakai no shiteki tenkai*, ed. Sonoda Kōyū, 371–390. Tokyo: Hanawa Shobō, 1999.

———. "Kodai Tajima no sen'i seisan to ryūtsu." *Tajimashi kenkyū* 23.3 (2000): 9–27.

Yoshimura Teiji. *Kakinomoto Hitomaro*. Tokyo: Risōsha, 1984.

Yoshino Yutaka, trans. *Fudoki*. Tokyo: Heibonsha, 1969.

Index

Abe kinship group, 193*n*23, 201*n*24
  Hata kinship group and, 212*n*69
  Shitennōji and, 20, 38
  Shōtoku cult and, 106–107
  sources on, 198*n*31
Abe no Uchimaro, 24, 25
Abe, Princess, 142, 188*n*34
Abe Ryūichi, 159
Akaru Hime, 59, 61, 63, 71–73, 125,
  194*n*46, 196*n*10, 197*n*26
Ama no Ho no Akari no Mikoto, 95,
  103, 108, 204*n*32
Ame no Hiboko, 197*n*23
  cultic centers of, 53
  Hata kinship group and, 124
  Hui-ssu/Shōtoku legend and,
    145, 146
  Jingū/Ōjin and, 71
  in *Kojiki*, 41–42
  legend of, 69–73
  Miyake Muraji and, 62
  in *Nihon shoki*, 41
  Ōfube's cult and, 53
  Okinaga Tarashihime and, 62
  other deities and, 44
  Silla lineage and, 41, 71
  Suinin and, 58–59
  travels of, 63
  Tsunuga no Arashito and, 41–42
  wrath of, 61

Aoki Michiko, 161
Arima, Prince, 25
Asoka, 27, 80
astrology/magic, Chinese, 78–79
Asukadera temple, 22, 27

Batten, Bruce, 9, 26
beggars/begging, 111, 112, 115, 124,
  128–130, 131. *See also* Kataoka
  beggar
Bidatsu, 18, 36–37
blessings. *See* hokai
Bodhidharma, Hui-ssu and, 209*n*57
Bodhisattva, as royal title, 80, 81,
  85–86
Buddha
  Lotus Sutra of, 151
  Shōtoku life narrative and, 150
Buddha-land, 189*n*56
Buddhism
  chimata rites and, 117
  Chinese state, 137, 139–140, 152
  Confucianism and, 76, 80
  establishment of, 5, 15, 111, 112, 133
  as "foreign" religion, 34–35
  history and, 133, 213*n*78
  Hui-ssu's spreading of, 145
  Japanese state, 18, 137–138, 139,
    140–141, 152

Buddhism (continued)
  Kamakura period, 187n12
  Nihon shoki and, 11, 17–18
  Paekche, 22–23, 25
  popular legends of, 122
  priest/ tutors of, 77
  sage king and, 76
  Shinto v., 7, 34
  spirit pacification and, 138
  tales of, 113
  Temmu and, 25
  Tendai, 3, 17, 150, 151
  Yamato court and, 15, 31
Buddhist hermeneutics, 159
burial service groups, 96

canals, 37, 60, 62–63, 64, 111, 112, 119,
    132, 199n14
Chang Liang, 85
Chiang T'ai-kung, 85, 202n46
Chih-i, 143, 151
Ch'i Huan-kung, 85
Chikuzen area, 60, 61–63, 69, 70, 71
Chikuzen cults, 69
Chikuzen fudoki (Records of the Customs
    and Lands of Chikuzen), 69, 72
chimata rites/deities, 11–12, 107–108, 111,
    117, 127, 138–139, 204n19, 205n41,
    206n1, 206n52
Chinese royal titles, adoption of, 14
Chinese state Buddhism, 137, 139–140, 152
Chinese textual tradition
  despots constrained by, 83–84
  governance and, 77–83
  immigrant kinship groups and,
    76–77, 80
  introduction of, 91
  Kojiki and, 14
  Nihon shoki and, 14
  regulation of, 84
  sage king in, 79, 84, 85
  Shōtoku and, 75–76
  significance of, 77
Ch'in Shih-huang-ti, Emperor, 83–84
Chisakobe kinship group, 105, 106,
    107–108
Chisakobe shrine, deity of, 135
Chou Wen-wang, 85
Chūai, 57–58, 199n64

clergy, ordination of, 118, 139, 140, 210n34
Confucianism, 76, 80, 82–83, 85
court liturgies, 125–127, 131
crossroads. See chimata rites/deities

Daianji garan engi narabi ni ruki shizaichō
    (Historical Account and Inventory of
    Holdings of Daianji), 134–135, 163
Daianji temple, 134–137, 139, 145
Dainihonkoku hokekyō kenki (Miraculous
    Tales of the Lotus Sutra in the Great
    Land of Japan), 122, 208n35
Daisōjō sharibyōki (Gravestone Memorial
    of the Senior Primary Prelate), 113,
    115, 207n6
deities. See chimata rites/deities; fire cult/
    gods; immigrant deities; Silla,
    kingdom of; spirit pacification;
    Sumiyoshi deities; vengeful deities
Denjutsu isshin kaimon (Concerning the
    Essay on the One-Mind Precepts), 151,
    213n78
despotism, divination and, 83–84
De Vos, George, 9
Dharma King, 201n29
  Kamitsumiya as, 141
  ordination and, 140
  origins of, 190n61
  as orthodoxy guardian, 84
  sage king and, 80
  Shōtoku as, 12, 27–28, 133
divination, 11, 79–84, 117
Dōgo inscription, 48–49, 51
Dōji, 25, 33, 210nn24
  Chinese kingship and, 138
  Chinese state Buddhism and, 137,
    139–140
  Daianji temple and, 134, 136
  Fujiwara kinship group and, 137,
    141–142
  Golden Light Excellent King Sutra and,
    19, 20
  Hōryūji temple and, 133, 134, 139,
    141–142, 152
  Japanese state Buddhism and,
    137–138, 139
  monk status and, 139
  Nagaya and, 137–139
  Nihon Shoki and, 133

preeminence of, 137, 152
role of, 12, 17
in *Shoku nihongi*, 139
Shōtoku cult and, 133, 139, 152
Shōtoku transformed by, 141
sources on, 210*nn*18–20
Dōsen, 140, 142
Dōshō, 115–116, 207*nn*11–12

edict of 717, 117, 118
Eison, 17
Ellwood, Robert, 52
Enchō, Tamura, 28
Ensei, the Venerable, 116
epigraphical sources, 165
estates, royal, 60–61, 197*n*17
ethnicity, 4, 8–9, 10, 22–24, 31, 76, 88, 185*n*2

fire cult/gods, 95, 103–105, 104*t*, 106, 107, 108, 204*n*32
Five Classics, 84
Five Thearchs, 84
Foucault, Michel, 77, 200*n*6
Four Heavenly Kings, 19, 29, 30, 140, 152, 188*n*20
Four Heavenly Kings temple, 19, 20, 24, 25, 29, 30, 188*nn*22
Fudoki (gazetteers), 161
Fujiwara kinship group, 130, 137, 138, 139, 141–142, 152
funerary rites, 193*n*37
    development of, 97–102
    of Hibasu Hime no Mikoto, 95–96
    Kusakabe, 95, 203*n*10
    kushi (comb) motif in, 100–101
    of Mononobe kinship group, 105
    personal effects in, 99–101, 101*t*
    of Wani kinship group, 98–101
    woven items in, 99–100
Futsunushi no Mikoto, 104

Gangaku, 116, 128
Gangōji garan engi narabi ni ruki shizaichō (Historical Account and Inventory of Holdings of Gangoji), 163–164, 187*n*16

Gangōji temple, 112, 115, 117
Ganjin, 12, 17, 140, 142–143, 210*nn*34–35, 211*n*37
Gemmei, 20, 21, 69, 188*n*34
genealogies. *See* lineage(s)
Golden Light Excellent King Sutra, 19–20, 30, 137, 140–141
Goodman, Nelson, 30, 155
Greater Sutra on the Perfection of Wisdom, 138, 148, 149, 210*n*23
Great Kudara temple, 135
Great Lateral Highway, 107, 108, 109, 206*n*51, 206*n*53
Gyōhyō, 207*n*16
Gyōki, 12
    birth/ancestry of, 115
    building works of, 118, 119, 120, 131–132, 207*n*25
    Dōshō and, 115–116
    edict criticizing, 117, 118
    epitaph of, 207*n*6
    at Gangōji, 117
    gentry's support of, 118, 119, 120, 131, 208*n*33
    Hata kinship group and, 119, 120, 131, 208*n*33
    Ina waterway and, 119
    influence of, 112–113
    in Izumi, 118
    Kataoka legend and, 157
    Kusakabe kinship group and, 118
    life of, 112
    man v. legend, 114
    in *Nihon ryōiki*, 112, 113–114, 115, 116–117, 119, 122–123
    resurrection legends and, 122
    scholarship, 113–114
    in *Shoku nihigoni*, 112, 113, 118, 122
    Shōtoku and, 111–132
    sources for, 113–114, 207*nn*7–10
    at Takamiyadera temple, 116–117, 120
    temples built by, 118
Gyōki bosatsuden (Biography of the Bodhisattva Gyōki), 112, 113, 115, 116, 117, 119
Gyōki movement
    court reaction to, 117
    expansion of, 118
    geography of, 117–119

Gyōki movement (*continued*)
  importance of, 112
  non-Buddhist elements of, 114–115, 131
  ordination in, 118
  spirit pacification and, 115, 121–125, 130
Gyōki nenpu (*Gyōki Chronology*), 112, 113,
  114, 115, 117, 118, 119, 123
Gyōshin, 141

Hachiman shrine, 71
Hajime, Nakamura, 6
hakuji (white pheasant), 81–83, 95
Harima kuni fudoki, 136, 205n45
Hata Horikawa no Kimitari, 120
Hata kinship group
  Abe kinship group and, 212n69
  Ame no Hiboko and, 124
  canal expansion and, 63, 64
  Chisakobe kinship group and, 105–106
  cults of, 74, 122–123, 205n42
  ecclesial hierarchy and, 159–160
  Gyōki and, 119, 120, 131, 208n33
  immigrant deities and, 50, 159
  lineage of, 34
  Munakata group and, 67
  Ōfube's cult and, 53
  Otokuni shrine and, 117
  royal estates and, 60, 197n17
  sage counselor and, 87–88
  Shōtoku cult and, 20, 21, 42, 50, 56,
    185n4
  temple of, 23
  tokoyo cult and, 37
  Tsunuga no Arashito and, 124
  waterways and, 119
Hata no Miyatsuko no Kawakatsu, 33, 52,
  189n45, 191n2
Hata no Ōtsuchi, 87–88
Hata no Shimamaro, 119
the heavenly sovereign, 4
Heishi den. See *Shōtoku Taishi denryaku*
Hibasu Hime no Mikoto, 95–96, 97,
  203n10
hijiri (sage). *See* sage counselors;
  sagehood; sage king
hijiri no kimi. *See* sage king
Hiko no Imasu Mikoto, 95
Himegoso shrine, 71
Hino Akira, 52

Hi no Kimi kinship group, 106–108,
  205nn45–47
Hirabayashi Akihito, 96
Hirano Kunio, 48, 52, 65
hitogata (substitute bodies), 138, 139
Hitomaro, 107
Hizen fudoki (*Records of the Customs of the
  Land of Hizen*), 124–125
hokai (blessings), 208n41
  begging and, 124
  court liturgies and, 125–127, 131
  importance of, 115
  Kataoka beggar and, 128–129
  religious discourse and, 132
  role of, 111
  in Shōtoku hagiography, 128–130
  spirit pacification and, 124, 125
  in Yamato ritual, 126–127
*Hōryūji garan engi narabi ni ruki shizaichō
  (Historical Account of the Inventory of
  Holdings of Horyuji*), 136, 164,
  190n59
Hōryūji kondō Shaka sanzō (inscription),
  165
Hōryūji kondō Yakushi sanzō
  (inscription), 165
Hōryūji temple
  Daianji temple and, 134–137
  Doji and, 133, 134, 139, 141–142, 152
  epigraphy from, 188n36
  estates of, 136–137, 210n17
  founding of, 149
  Kamitsumiya and, 5, 22, 134, 186n13
  Kōmyō and, 141
  in *Nihon shoki*, 21, 134, 136–137
  rebuilding of, 133, 134, 139, 142, 152
  in *Shoku nihongi*, 134
  Shōtoku cult and, 27, 134, 138,
    190nn63–64
  statuary in, 35
Hōryūji tōin engi, content of, 164
Hsü kao-seng chuan (*Further Biographies
  of Eminent Monks*), 144
Hui-ssu/Shōtoku legend, 12, 140,
  142–151, 152, 212n54
  Ame no Hiboko and, 145, 146
  Bodhidharma and, 209n57
  buried sutra/vow in, 148–150
  Chih-i and, 151
  Daianji and, 145

Hyeja and, 145, 146, 147
Kataoka beggar and, 146
Lotus Sutra in, 143–150
Saichō and, 150–151
Shitennōji and, 145, 147
Silla immigrant groups and, 144–147
sources on, 212nn59–60
Tsunaga no Arashito and, 146
*Hung-tsan fa-hua chuan (Accounts
     Spreading the Praise of the Lotus)*, 146
hwarang fraternities, 28, 191n70
Hyeja
    death narrative of, 103
    in Hui-ssu legend, 145, 146, 147
    as sage, 41, 90
    on sage kings, 89, 90
    Shōtoku and, 49, 76–77

Ienaga Saburō, 10
immigrant deities, 16, 38–48, 193n26.
        See also Akaru Hime; Ame no
        Hiboko
    Hata kinship group and, 50, 159
    millennial movements and, 11
    Ōfube's cult and, 53
    in Pure Land belief, 39, 51
    royal cult and, 55
    sage king and, 41
    Shōtoku cult and, 35, 38–39, 73
    Silla immigrants and, 48, 70–71
    Sukuna Bikona no Mikoto, 44–51
    thematic affinities of, 44, 48
    Tsunuga no Arashito, 38–42, 50
    Yamato rulers' reliance on, 56
immigrant kinship groups
    ancestral traditions of, 10
    Chinese texts and, 76–77, 80
    concept of, 185n1
    conflicts between, 10, 22–30
    cultic/political activities of, 55
    cultural change and, 14
    divination texts of, 11
    ideology and, 31
    lineage and, 9
    literary/cultic control by, 156
    misconceptions regarding, 7
    naming of, 16
    power balance between, 24
    power/literacy of, 77

resistance to, 160
rivalry among, 24–27
role of, 8
royal estates and, 60, 197n17
royal legends and, 11
sage counselors and, 87, 90
sage king and, 87–88
technologies imported by, 5, 14, 38
temples/shrines of, 13–14
tenjukoku and, 48–51
works on, 187n6
Yamato authority and, 10–11, 60–74, 77
immigrant priests, Pure Land belief
        and, 36
immortality, early conceptions of, 94–102
Inabe kinship group, 48, 120, 194n55,
        207n28
Inabe Tachibana no Iratsume, 48, 118
Ina waterway, 119
Inoue Kaoru, 118
Inoue Mitsusada, 112
Ippen, 17
Isamu, Kanjai, 6
Isasa, port of, 44–45
Isasa, sword of, 41, 44
Iwai rebellion, 60, 61, 197n14
*Iyo kuni fudoki (Records of the Customs
        and Lands of Iyo)*, 48–49, 147,
        194n57
Iyo kuni Fudoki/Dōgo inscription, 165
Izanami, 104, 104t, 204n34
Izushi, port of, 53
Izushi shrine, 42

Japanese cultural identity, 9, 31
Japanese kingship, 186n4
Japanese national discourse, 5–7
Japanese state Buddhism, 18, 137–138,
        139, 140–141, 152
Jimmu, 105
Jingū, 3, 11
    ancestor cult of, 56
    banquet toasts of, 45–48
    legend of, 10
    Silla conquered by, 58
    Sukuna Bikona no Mikoto and, 46
Jingū/Ōjin
    Ame no Hiboko and, 71
    as state guardians, 65–66

Jingū/Ōjin cult, 198n36
  centers of, 66
  development of, 59, 64
  dominance of, 74
  in Kyūshū, 69–73
  Okinaga kinship group and, 62
  Shōtoku cult and, 73
  Silla deities and, 70–71
  sources of, 73
  sources on, 196n13, 208n36
Jinshin War, 26, 189n53
Jitō tennō, 20, 69
Jōgū kōtaishi bosatsuden, 166
Jōgū Shōtoku hōō teisetsu, 166, 190n60
Jōgū Shōtoku taishiden hoketsuki
  (Supplemental Record to the
  Biography of Crown Prince Shōtoku of
  the Upper Palace), 22, 24, 27, 28,
  145, 163, 166
Jōgū Taishi bosatsuden (Biography of the
  Bodhisattva Crown Prince above the
  Palace), 212n63
Jomei, 64, 79, 80, 135–136, 198n31
jukoku (Land of Long Life), 194n59

Kakinomoto no Hitomaro, poetry of,
  98–99
Kamitsumiya, Prince, 4, 7–8
  chapel of, 209n10
  Constitution and, 86
  Daianji and, 135
  dates of, 5
  death of, 13, 36, 76
  as Dharma King, 141
  estate of, 137
  as executioner, 109
  Great Lateral Highway and, 109
  heirs to, 37
  Hōryūji temple and, 5, 22, 134, 186n13
  Jomei v., 135–136
  Kashiwade kinship group and, 212n64
  lineage of, 37–38
  Manta area and, 37–38
  power/literacy and, 77
  rituals coopted by, 109
  sagehood of, 93, 94
  Shitennōji and, 5
  Shōtoku v., 4–5, 6, 12, 33, 155
  Soga kinship group and, 5

  sources on, 5
  tapestry honoring, 34
  works attributed to, 164
Kamu Yaimimi no Mikoto, 105–109, 135,
  206n54
Kanimanji legend, 122–123, 124
Karu crossroads, spirit pacification at, 99
Kashiwade kinship group, 212n64
Kataoka beggar, 104t
  Abe/Hi no Kimi interactions and,
    106–107
  fire cults and, 105
  as ghost of vanquished, 109
  Gyōki and, 157
  hokai and, 128–129
  Hui-ssu/Shōtoku legend and, 146
  Mononobe kinship group and, 104, 105
  ode of, 129–130
  resurrection of, 102, 105
  sagehood of, 94
  Shōtoku and, 102–105, 108, 117,
    128–130
  Takamiyadera tale and, 117
  violence and, 157
  Wani ancestral legends and, 101–102,
    103, 104
Kataoka, chimata rites in, 107–108
Katō Kenkichi, 52–53, 105, 117
Kawachi no Aya kinship group, 115
Kehi shrine, 38–41, 44–45
Kimmei, 18, 36–37, 86–87
kingship, conceptions of, 10, 14, 15, 111,
  133, 138
Ki no Asomi Kiyohito, 20
Kishi dance, 20–21, 188n33
Kishi kinship group, 20, 60, 188n26,
  192n16, 197n17
Koguryô, kingdom of, 36–37, 38, 65,
  192n16, 192n18
Kōgyuko, abdication of, 24
Kojiki, 4
  Ame no Hiboko in, 41–42
  Chinese textual tradition and, 14
  deities, vengeful, in, 56–59
  Shōtoku in, 161
  Silla State in, 58
  Sukuna Bikona no Mikoto in, 45–48
  Tajima Mori in, 96–97
  Tsunuga no Arashito in, 39
  Yamato Takeru in, 103

Kōken *tennō*, 69
Kōmyō, Queen Consort, 138, 141, 142, 210n21, 211n44
Korean kingdoms. *See* Koguryô, kingdom of; Paekche, kingdom of; Silla, kingdom of
Korean peninsula
  national legends of, 72
  Ōjin's dominion over, 71
  religious discourses of, 14
  sources on, 185n11
  technologies imported from, 5, 14, 38
  tutors from, 75–76, 77
  Yamato ambitions in, 58
Kōryūji temple, 8, 23, 117, 186n13
Koshi no Ubai, 117
Koshi region, 36–39
kotobuki no kuni (land of long life), 147
Kōtoku, 24, 81–82, 83, 95
Kuan-tzu, 85, 86, 202n38
Kūkai, 159
Kunado no Kami, 104, 206n48
Kusakabe kinship group
  death rituals of, 95, 203n10
  Gyōki and, 118
  hakuji and, 95
  lineage of, 42, 69, 95
  in *Lotus Sutra* legend, 147
  sagehood/resurrection and, 97
  in *Shinsen shōjiroku* (genealogical compendium), 95
  Shitennōji and, 81, 118
  Shōtoku cult and, 68, 81
  Suinin and, 95
Kusakabe Muraji Shikibu, 81
Kusakabe no Obito Maro, 118
Kusakabe, Prince, 21, 68, 69, 199n50
Kusanagi sword, 68
Kuse Kannon, 54, 130, 142, 149, 211n53
kushi (comb) motif, 100–101
Kusuko incident, 159
Kwallŭk, 78, 79, 80
Kyōkai, 116–117
Kyūshū
  deities of, 70–71
  Jingū/Ōjin legend in, 69–73
  revolt in, 119
  vengeful deities of, 157
  Yamato authority in, 60–74
  Yamato court and, 59

learning, violence and, 93
lineage(s)
  chronicles and, 10
  construction of, 16, 17, 38, 61–63, 73
  Hata, 34
  immigrant kinship group, 9
  Kamitsumiya, 37–38
  kingship and, 10
  Kusakabe, 42, 69, 95
  Miyake, 34
  Nichira, 106
  reincarnation and, 152
  Shōtoku, 192n21
  Silla, 41, 71
  violence against, 93
literacy
  authority and, 156
  diffusion of, 9–10, 200n2
  Korean tutors of, 75
looms, 124–125
Lotus Sutra, 143–144
  Buddha's preaching of, 151
  Greater Sutra of the Perfect Wisdom and, 149
  in Hui-ssu/Shōtoku legend, 143–150
  in *Nihon ryōiki*, 147
  Shōtoku's commentaries on, 164, 166
  Shōtoku's devotion to, 27, 151

Maitreya, 28, 149, 150, 191n67
Manjuśri, 121–122
Manta area, Kamitsumiya and, 37–38
Manta canal, 119, 199n14
Manyōshū (Anthology of Ten Thousand Leaves), 95, 163
Matsumae Takeshi, 105
millennial cults, 11, 33–35, 51, 150
Minamoto Tamenori, 163
Min, omen interpretation by, 82
Mishina Shōei, 72
Mitama shizume matsuri rite, 105
Mitsusada, Inoue, 6
Miyake kinship group, 20, 21
  canal expansion and, 63, 64
  cultic success of, 74
  lineage of, 34
  royal estates and, 60, 197n17
  Tajima Mori and, 42
Miyake Muraji, 62

Miyake no Omi Fujimaro, 20
Mizuno Ryūtarō, 135, 136
Mommo *tennō*, 69
monks
  censure of, 117
  resurrection of, 116
  status of, 133, 139
Mononobe kinship group
  ascendancy of, 104
  destruction of, 5, 22, 93, 107, 109
  rituals, 105
  Kataoka beggar and, 104, 105
  Soga v., 18, 109, 141, 205nn37–38
Mount Nan-yüeh, 144
Munakata cult, 41, 44, 67–69, 139,
  198nn39
Munakata kinship group, 66–67
Myōe, 17
Myōichi, 144
Myŏngnang, 30

Nagaya, Prince, 69, 130, 137–139,
  141–142, 210n22
Nakai Shinkō, 112
Nakatomi kinship group, 18
Naniwa kinship groups, 20–21, 26,
  28, 81
Naoki Kōjirō, 60, 64
Nationalism, Japanese, 5–7
Nemoto Seiji, 112, 116
Nichira, 106, 107
Nichiren, 17
Nihon Montoku tennō jitsuroku (*Veritable
  Records of Montoku Tennō*), 47–48
Nihon ōjō gokurakuki (*Japanese Records
  of Birth in the Pure Land*), 122,
  208n35
Nihon ryōiki
  begging/blessing in, 128, 129–131
  content of, 161–162
  Gyōki in, 112, 113–114, 115, 116–117, 119,
    122–123
  Lotus Sutra in, 147
  Ōtomo no Yasunoko in, 121
  spirit pacification in, 129
Nihon shoki, 4, 8
  Ame no Hiboko in, 41
  Buddhism and, 11, 17–18
  Chinese textual tradition and, 14

completion of, 13, 133, 134
composition of, 14, 77, 86
content of, 162–163
Dōji and, 133
editing of, 30
ethnic conflicts in, 22–24
flaws of, 201n22
genealogical tropes in, 16
hakuji in, 81–83
Hōryūji temple in, 21, 134, 136–137
Kamu Yaimimi no Mikoto in, 108
Korean tutors in, 75
lineage/power and, 61
Mononobe defeat in, 109
Munakata deities in, 67
Naniwa kinship groups and, 20–21
narrative of, 18–20
Nichira in, 106
Ōfube's cult in, 33–34, 52
omens in, 79, 81–82
Pure Land in, 35–36
resurrection legends in, 103–104, 104t
sagehood in, 76, 86, 89t, 94t
Silla state in, 29–30, 58
Sukuna Bikona no Mikoto in, 45–48
Tajima Mori in, 42–44
Tsunuga no Arashito in, 39–40
Uranoshimako in, 94–95
vengeful deities in, 56–59
Yamato Takeru in, 103
Nomi no Sukune, 96
Nukatabe kinship group, 136, 210n16
Nukata, Princess, 209n16

Ōama kinship group, 198nn39–40
Ōama, Prince, 26, 66, 67
Ōdono no hokai (*Blessing of the Great
  Palace*), 125
Ōfube kinship group, 196n71
Ōfube no Ōshi, cult of, 33–35, 43, 51–54,
  191n1
Ōjin. *See also* Jingū/Ōjin
  ancestor cult of, 56
  birth of, 58, 72
  in Chikuzen, 71
  at Kehi shrine, 44–45
  Korean Peninsula dominion of, 71
  legend of, 10
  Silla kinship groups and, 71

sources on, 62, 199nn60
Sukuna Bikona no Mikoto and, 46
Tsunuga no Arashito and, 40–41
Okinaga kinship group, 62
Okinaga Tarashihime, 62, 63, 64–65
omens. *See* divination
Ōmi no Mahito Mifune, 142
Ōnamuchi no Mikoto, 47, 51, 104, 104*t*,
    204n35
Ōno Tatsunosuke, 6, 86
Otokuni shrine, 117, 122
Ōtomo no Yasunoko, 121–122
Ōtomo, Prince, 26
Owari Muraji, 68–69
Owari shrine, 68–69
Ōyama Seiichi, 4–5, 6, 7

Paekche Buddhism, 22–23, 25
Paekche, kingdom of
    deities of, 21
    immigrants from, 15
    Yamato contact with, 18
Paekche kinship groups
    dominance of, 22
    Emperor Tenji and, 26
    Shōtoku cult and, 21
Paekche/Silla rivalry, 24–27
power, knowledge and, 77, 79
Pure Land, 11
    first Japanese reference to, 34
    immigrant deities and, 51
    in *Nihon shoki*, 35–36
    Shōtoku in, 5, 49
Pure Land belief
    immigrant deities in, 39, 51
    immigrant priests and, 36
    Inabe Tachibana no Iratsume and, 48
    Shōtoku cult and, 33, 35–44
    tenjukoku tapestry and, 35, 48
    tokoyo cults and, 35

Queen Mother of the West cult, 43–44,
    53, 194n45

reincarnation, 144–147, 149, 150, 152
resurrection
    fire cult/gods and, 103–105, 104*t*

of Gangaku, 116, 128
Gyōki and, 122
of Kataoka beggar, 102, 105
Kusakabe kinship group and, 97
local cults of, 108
of monks, 116
of Nichira, 106
in *Nihon shoki*, 103–104, 104*t*
of Ōtomo no Yasunoko, 121–122
of Prince Uji, 97, 103
rites of, 108
Shōtoku and, 94, 122
sources of, 95
spell of, 105
of Yamato Takeru, 103
royal cult
    immigrant deities and, 55
    local cults v., 61
    Munakata and, 67–69
    Shōtoku and, 55

Sach'ŏnwangsa temple, 29, 30
sacred stones, 47
sage counselors, 76, 86–89, 90
sagehood, 202n51, 203n1
    classifications of, 84–86
    conceptions of, 11, 94–102
    ethnicity and, 76, 88
    etymology of, 78
    fire/death rituals and, 95
    Great Lateral Highway and, 109
    of Hyeja, 41, 90
    of Kamitsumiya, 93, 94
    of Kataoka beggar, 94
    Kusakabe kinship group and, 97
    in *Nihon shoki*, 76, 86, 89t, 94t
    of Prince Uji, 94
    in Shōtoku cult, 88, 89, 94, 143
    Tajima Mori and, 94
    of Uranoshimako, 94
    violence and, 93, 103
sage king, 200n13
    Buddhist elements of, 76
    in Chinese textual tradition, 79, 84, 85
    concept of, 3, 11
    in Confucianism, 76, 82–83, 85
    Dharma King and, 80
    Hyeja on, 89, 90
    immigrant deity cults and, 41

sage king (continued)
  immigrant kinship groups and, 87–88
  as immortal, 85
  Kōtoku as, 81–82
  local cults and, 88
  in Nara period, 14
  omens and, 79, 81
  origin of, 84
  ruler's legitimacy and, 85
  in Seventeen-Article Constitution, 86
  in Shih-chi (Records of the Historian), 84
  Shōtoku cult and, 88, 89, 94, 143
  as Son of Heaven, 79
  in Taoism, 85
  term, use of, 89–90
  types of, 84
  Yamato use of, 88, 89–90
Saichō, 12, 17
  biography of, 151
  Chinese Buddhism and, 152
  death of, 3
  Gyōhyō and, 207n16
  Hui-ssu/Shōtoku legend and, 150–151
  sources on, 212n72, 213nn73–74
  vocation of, 150
Saikabe ritualists, 108
Saimei, 56–57, 64, 65, 66, 135, 196nn1–2,
    198n30
Sakaibe kinship group, 105, 205n41
Sakamoto Tarō, 6, 188n36
sakashihito. See sage counselors
Sakuma Ryū, 115, 116
Samguk sagi (Historical Records of the
    Three Kingdoms), 167, 186n14
Samguk yusa (Memorabilia from the Three
    Kingdoms), 29, 167, 186n14
Sanbōe kotoba (Illustrated Words on the
    Three Jewels), 122, 163
Sankyō gisho (commentaries), 164
Sendai kuji hongi (Records of Old Matters
    from Previous Ages), 105
Seventeen-Article Constitution, 7–8, 86,
    102–103, 164, 202n37
Shaku nihongi, 195n59
Shakyamuni, Shōtoku and, 27–28
Shichidaiki (hagiography), 166
Shichidaiki (Records of Seven Generations),
    144, 149, 150
Shih-chi (Records of the Historian), 84
Shimode Sekiyo, 52

Shinkawa Tokio, 138
Shinran, 17, 213n1
Shinsen shōjiroku (Newly Compiled
    Records of Kinship Groups), 15–16,
    61–62, 95, 105, 163, 187n8
Shintō, Buddhism v., 7, 34
Shiragi Jinja (Silla shrine), 38
Shitennōji goshuin engi (Account of the
    Origins of Shitennōji with the Regental
    Handprint), 28, 190n62
Shitennōji temple, 186n13
  Abe kinship group and, 20, 38
  building of, 109
  as cult center, 25
  founding of, 20, 22
  Hui-ssu/Shōtoku legend and, 145, 147
  Kamitsumiya and, 5
  Kusakabe kinship group and, 81, 118
  legends of, 211n40
  Shōtoku cult and, 147, 190n63
  Shōtoku images at, 27
  Silla implements at, 23
  as Temple of Four Heavenly Kings,
    19, 30
  texts affiliated with, 28
Shoku nihongi, 114
  content of, 163
  Dōji in, 139
  Dōshō in, 115
  Gyōki in, 112, 113, 118, 122
  Hōryūji temple in, 134
  monks censured in, 117
Shōmu tennō, 69, 134, 142, 152
Shōtoku. See also Hui-ssu/Shōtoku legend
  accomplishments of, 17
  Asoka and, 27
  attributes of, 5
  authority of, 136
  in battle, 18–19
  Buddha and, 150
  Chinese knowledge of, 143
  Chinese textual tradition and, 75–76
  contemporary interest in, 187n12
  continental culture and, 15
  court debates and, 133
  as cultural translator, 158
  dates of, 3
  death of, 23, 76, 103
  as Dharma King, 12, 27–28, 133
  as disputed symbol, 21–22

as divine king paradigm, 141
Doji's transformation of, 141
as Fujiwara guardian, 141
Ganjin and, 140
genealogy of, 192n21
as guardian, 12, 28, 138, 139, 141, 152
Gyōki and, 111–132
hagiography of, 128–130, 166–167
Heian period shaped by, 158
as high priest, 27
Hyeja and, 49, 76–77
immigrant images of, 27–29
incarnations of, 152–153
Kamitsumiya v., 4–5, 6, 12, 33, 155
Kataoka beggar and, 102–105, 108, 117,
    128–130
in Kojiki, 161
Korean tutors and, 75–76
as Kuse Kannon, 54, 142, 211n53
lineage of, 192n21
as literary creation, 156
Lotus Sutra and, 27, 143–150, 151,
    164, 166
Maitreya and, 28, 150
as millennial savior, 150
names of, 4
Naniwa kinship groups and, 28
Nukatabe kinship group and, 136
ode to beggar of, 128–129
Ōtomo no Yasunoko and, 121–122
as priest-king, 31
as protective deity, 133
in Pure Land, 5, 49
resurrection legends and, 94, 122
royal cult and, 55
as sage king, 89
Saichō and, 151
as savior/patriarch, 19, 54, 142
Shakyamuni and, 27–28
Soga leadership v., 18
sources on, 8
sutra commentaries by, 164, 166
in Temmu's reign, 27
temples founded by, 190n63
in Tendai Buddhism, 151
as warrior king, 28
works attributed to, 164
Shōtoku cult
    Abe/Hi no Kimi and, 106
    Abe kinship group and, 106–107

afterlife and, 33
bifurcation of, 21, 23
building works of, 121
centers of, 122–123
deities/ancestors of, 35
divination by, 83
Doji and, 133, 139, 152
ethnic identity and, 31
geography of, 117
hakuji and, 81–83
Hata kinship group and, 20, 21, 42, 50,
    56, 185n4
Hōryūji and, 27, 134, 138, 190nn63–64
immigrant deities and, 35, 38–39, 73
immigrant kinship groups and, 3–4
Jingū/Ōjin cult and, 73
Kusakabe kinship group and, 68, 81
millennial cults and, 11
Pure Land belief and, 33, 35–44
royal authority and, 17, 77
sagehood and, 88, 89, 94, 143
Shitennōji and, 27, 147, 190n63
Silla immigrant groups and, 41, 55, 136
sources on, 161–167
spirit fear and, 130
spirit pacification and, 111, 121–125
Sukuna Bikona no Mikoto and, 51
Takamiyadera temple and, 116–117
tenjukoku and, 50–51
violence and, 14, 93, 109, 135–136
Wani legend influence on, 102
Shōtoku legend, transmission of, 214n12
Shōtoku studies, 5–7
Shōtoku Taishi denryaku (Chronological
    Biography of the Crown Prince
    Shōtoku), 28, 163, 166, 186n14,
    190n62
silkworm shrine, 123, 124
Silla implements, at Shitennōji, 23
Silla, kingdom of, 4
    conquest of, 64–65
    deities from, 21, 54, 63
    Four Heavenly Kings and, 29
    Jingū/Ōjin and, 70–71
    Jingū's conquest of, 58
    king cult figures of, 56
    in Kojiki, 58
    Maitreya worship in, 28
    Munakata cult and, 67
    in Nihon shoki, 29–30, 58

Silla, kingdom of (*continued*)
  Sumiyoshi deities and, 58
  T'ang Empire and, 25–26, 29–30
  Temmu and, 29
  temple network in, 11
Silla kinship groups
  Ame no Hiboko and, 41, 71
  Hui-ssu legend and, 144–147
  immigrant deities and, 48, 70–71
  influence of, 26
  lineages of, 41, 71
  Ōfube's cult and, 53
  Ōjin legend cycle and, 71
  Shōtoku cult and, 41, 55, 136
  Sukuna Bikona no Mikoto and, 48
  technologies and, 38
Silla mythology, Yamato adoptions of, 63
Silla/Paekche rivalry, 24–27
Silla shrine, 38
Soga kinship groups
  alliances of, 206n53
  decline of, 24, 26
  divinatory power of, 79
  Emperor Tenji and, 25
  influence of, 189n46
  Kamitsumiya and, 5
  Koshi region and, 38
  millennialism and, 34–35
  Mononobe v., 18, 109, 141, 205nn37–38
  Shōtoku v., 18
  victory of, 22
Soga no Emishi, 24
Soga no Iname, 18
Soga no Katashi Hime, 204n19
Sonoda Kōyū, 18
spirit pacification
  Buddhist development and, 138
  in court ritual calendar, 108, 125–126
  cult dissemination and, 115
  Fujiwara and, 130
  on Great Lateral Highway, 108
  Gyōki movement and, 115, 121–125, 130
  Hi no Kimi kinship group and, 106
  hokai and, 124, 125
  importance of, 11, 115
  increased concern over, 133
  Jimmu and, 105
  at Karu crossroads, 99
  looms in, 124–125
  in *Nihon ryōiki*, 129

Saimei and, 135
Shōtoku cult and, 111, 121–125
spread of, 121
sumō and, 96
Temmu and, 135
violence and, 93, 94
Wani kinship group and, 99
in Yamato ritual, 108, 126–127
Sui dynasty, 37, 78, 81, 111
Suiko, as Princess Nakuta, 209n16
Suiko court, 35, 111, 161
Suinin, 42, 58–59, 95, 96, 203n7
Sui shu (The Sui History), 78, 167
*Sui t'ien-tai chih-che ta-shih pie-chuan
  (Alternate Biography of the Great
  Teacher T'ien-Tai Chih-che of the
  Sui)*, 151
Sui Yang-ti, 81, 86
Sukuna Bikona no Mikoto, 44–51, 53, 73,
  157, 194n53, 199n65, 204n22
Sumiyoshi Daijin, 59, 61
Sumiyoshi deities, 57–59, 61, 63
Sumiyoshi shrine, 63, 71
Susanoo no Mikoto, 67, 199n46
sutra commentaries, 164, 166, 189n57
Suzuka, Prince, 141

Tachibana no Moroe, 141
Tachibana no Ōiratsume. *See* Inabe
  Tachibana no Iratsume
tachibana (orange) symbol, 35, 42
tachibana worm cult, 53
Tajima Mori, 192n22
  cultic centers of, 53
  Hibasu Hime and, 97
  in *Kojiki*, 96–97
  lament of, 193n42
  legend of, 42–44, 102–103
  Miyake kinship group and, 42
  in *Nihon shoki*, 42–44
  sagehood and, 94
  Suinin and, 96
  tomb of, 197n23
Takamiyadera tale, 117
Takamiyadera temple, 116–117, 120
Takechi, Prince, 67, 199n56, 210n27
Takeuchi no Sukune no Mikoto, 45–46
Tamura Enchō, 7
Tamura, Prince, 134–135

T'ang China, 25–26, 29–30, 81, 139
Tango kuni fudoki (Records of the Customs and Land of Tango), 95
Tao-hsüan, 137, 144
Taoism, 85
T'arhae, legend of, 71–73
Tatsuta Highway, 107
technologies, importation of, 5, 14, 38
Temmu, Emperor
  as Buddhist patron, 25
  bureaucracy under, 77
  Naniwa kinship groups and, 26
  posthumous name of, 198n43
  reforms of, 26–27
  reign of, 20, 67, 68
  Shōtoku and, 27
  Silla and, 29
  sources on, 199n53
  spirit pacification and, 135
  T'ang Empire and, 29
  vengeful spirits and, 135
Temple for the Protection of the Country by the Four Heavenly Kings of the Golden Light Sutra, 188n22
Temple of the Four Heavenly Kings. See Four Heavenly Kings Temple
Tendai Buddhism, 3, 17, 150, 151
Tenji, Emperor, 25, 26
tenjujoku (heavenly land of long life), 34, 43, 48–51, 157
Tenjukoku shūchō mei (inscription), 165
tenjukoku tapestry, 34–35, 43, 48–51, 118, 191n5, 214n19
Three Sovereigns, 84
Tō daiwajō tōseiden (Account of the Great T'ang Priest's Eastern Expedition), 142, 167
tokoyo cults
  bacchanalian, 46–47
  continuities between, 53
  Hata kinship group and, 37
  Ōfube no Ōshi and, 33–35, 51–54
  Pure Land belief and, 35
  Queen Mother cult and, 43–44
  sources on, 191n3
  Sukuna Bikona no Mikoto and, 44
  Uranoshimako and, 100
  Wani kinship group and, 98–102
tokoyo insect, 52, 53
Tsukaguchi Yoshinobu, 41

Tsuki no Omi immigrant kinship group, 145, 212n64
Tsukishine no Hime, 38
Tsukushi no Kuni no Miyatsuko Iwai, rebellion of, 60, 61, 197n14
Tsunuga no Arashito, 38–42, 44, 50, 53, 124, 146, 205n43

Ueda Masaaki, 68
Uji, Prince, 94, 97–98, 103, 200n3
Umashimaji no Mikoto, 105
Umayado, Prince (Shōtoku), 4, 134–135
Umehara Takeshi, 109
Uranoshimako cult, 94–95, 100, 203n3
Usa Hachiman shrine, 74

vengeful deities, 11, 56–59, 61, 139, 157
vengeful spirits. See spirit pacification
violence
  Kataoka beggar and, 157
  logic of, 93, 94, 105, 135–136
  sagehood and, 93, 103
  Shōtoku cult and, 14, 93, 109, 135–136
  spirit pacification and, 93, 94
  Yamato authority and, 93

Wani kinship group, 95
  funerary rites of, 98–101
  Kataoka beggar and, 101–102, 103, 104
  legends of, 98–102, 103, 104
  Prince Uji and, 97–98
  Shōtoku cult and, 102
  spirit pacification and, 99
  tokoyo and, 98–102
Weaver Maiden cult, 44, 123, 124, 194n45
weaving, cultic significance of, 42, 43, 44, 53, 99–100, 124–125, 194n46, 208n39
Wu, Empress, 140

Yakushi Buddha, 47, 117
Yakushiji temple, 29
Yamashiro no Ōe, Prince, 24, 37, 52, 119
Yamato authority
  Buddhism and, 15
  in Chikuzen region, 61–63

Yamato authority (*continued*)
  continental influence on, 111
  genealogy construction and, 61–63, 73
  immigrant kinship groups and, 10–11,
    60–74, 77
  in Kyūshū, 60–74
  marriage and, 66
  royal estates and, 60–61, 197*n*17
  sage king and, 88, 89–90
  Silla mythology and, 63
  violence and, 93
Yamato counselors, 86–89
Yamato court
  astrology/magic at, 78
  Buddhism and, 15, 31
  Chinese texts at, 75, 77
  cult resistance to, 56
  immigrant kinship groups and, 10–11
  immigrant literacy and, 77
  isolation of, 26
  Koguryô and, 36–37
  Korean scholars at, 75
  Kyūshū and, 59
  Paekche contact with, 18
  ranks in, 8
  Shōtoku's death and, 78
  spirit pacification rites and, 108,
    125–126

Sui China and, 81
  weakness of, 31
  writing and, 14
Yamato ritual, 126–127
Yamato rulers, 3, 6, 7
  ancestral legend cycles and, 55
  deities feared by, 56–59, 61
  genealogical tropes and, 17
  immigrant ancestors and, 11
  immigrant deities and, 56
  Korean ambitions of, 58
  power of, 55
  Sumiyoshi deities and, 57–59, 61
  sun kinship of, 78
  Tsunuga Arashito and, 39, 40
Yamato Takeru, 28, 101–102, 103, 196*n*4,
    199*n*51, 204*nn*23
Yi-ching, 137, 140
Yōrō ritsuryō (Law Codes of the Yōrō
    Period), 186*n*5
Yoshida Yasuo, 112, 113, 115, 116, 117
Yoshikawa Shinji, 130, 131
Yumedono icon, 192*n*9
Yumedono temple, 134, 142, 149,
    211*n*50

Zudain temple, 131